JUNGIAN PERSPECTIVES ON REBIRTH AND RENEWAL

This book brings together an international selection of contributors on the themes of rebirth and renewal. With their emphasis on evolutionary ancestral memories, creation myths, and dreams, the chapters in this collection explore the indigenous and primordial bases of these concepts.

Presented in eight parts, the book elucidates the importance of indirect, associative, mythological thinking within Jungian psychology and the efficacy of working with images as symbols to access unconscious creative processes. Part I begins with a comparative study of the significance of the phoenix as symbol, including its image as Jung's family crest. Part II focuses on Native American indigenous beliefs about the transformative power of nature. Part III examines synchronistic symbols as liminal place/space, where the relationship between the psyche and place enables a co-evolution of the psyche of the land. Part IV presents Jung's travels in India and the spiritual influence of Indian indigenous beliefs on his work. Part V expands on the rebirth of the feminine as a dynamic, independent force. Part VI analyzes ancestral memories evoked by the phoenix image, exploring archetypal narratives of infancy. Part VII focuses on eco-psychological, synchronistic carriers of death, rebirth, and renewal through mythic characterizations. Finally, Part VIII explores the mythopoetic, visionary dimensions of rebirth and renewal that give literary expression to indigenous people/primordial psyche re-navigated through popular literature. The chapters both mirror and synchronize a rebirth of Jungian and non-Jungian academic interest in indigenous peoples, creation myths, oral traditions, and narrative dialogue as the "primordial psyche" worldwide, and the book includes one chapter supplemented by an online video.

This collection will be inspiring reading for academics and students of analytical psychology, Jungian, and post-Jungian studies and mythology, as well as analytical psychologists, Jungian analysts, and Jungian psychotherapists.

Elizabeth Brodersen is a Jungian analyst in private practice in Frankfurt, Germany and an accredited training analyst at the C.G. Jung Institute in Zürich. She completed her doctorate in psychoanalytic studies at the University of Essex and is co-chair of the IAJS Executive Committee with Michael Glock. She is author of *Laws of Inheritance: A post-Jungian study of twins and the relationship between the first and other(s)* (Routledge).

Michael Glock is CEO of Bloom Factor Inc., creative director, digital architect, and author platform expert, and gained his doctorate in philosophy from Pacifica Graduate Institute. He has developed concepts such as Cultural Futuristics, Way Forward Engineering, Designing Destiny, and is co-chair of the IAJS Executive Committee with Elizabeth Brodersen.

To access the online video which accompanies Evangeline Rand's chapter, please request a password at http://www.evangelinerand.com/life_threads_orissa_awakenings.html

JUNGIAN PERSPECTIVES ON REBIRTH AND RENEWAL

Phoenix Rising

Edited by Elizabeth Brodersen and Michael Glock

Routledge
Taylor & Francis Group

LONDON AND NEW YORK

First published 2017
by Routledge
2 Park Square, Milton Park, Abingdon, Oxon OX14 4RN

and by Routledge
711 Third Avenue, New York, NY 10017

Routledge is an imprint of the Taylor & Francis Group, an informa business

British Library Cataloguing in Publication Data
A catalogue record for this book is available from the British Library

Library of Congress Cataloguing in Publication Data
Names: Brodersen, Elizabeth, editor. | Glock, Michael, editor.
Title: Jungian perspectives on rebirth and renewal:
phoenix rising / edited by Elizabeth Brodersen and Michael Glock.
Description: Abingdon, Oxon; New York, NY : Routledge, 2017. |
Includes bibliographical references. Identifiers: LCCN 2016025366 |
ISBN 9781138193093 (hardback: paper) |
ISBN 9781138193123 (pbk.: paper) | ISBN 9781315639550 (ebook)
Subjects: | MESH: Jungian Theory | Symbolism | Unconscious (Psychology) |
Mythology–psychology Classification: LCC BF173.J85 | NLM WM 460.5.J9 |
DDC 150.19/54–dc23 LC record available at https://lccn.loc.gov/2016025366

ISBN: 978-1-138-19309-3 (hbk)
ISBN: 978-1-138-19312-3 (pbk)
ISBN: 978-1-315-63955-0 (ebk)

Typeset in Bembo
by Out of House Publishing

This book is dedicated to the memory of Professor Donald Fredericksen

CONTENTS

NOTES ON CONTRIBUTORS

Maryann Barone-Chapman

Maryann Barone-Chapman is a Professional Member of AJA in private practice in London, completing her doctoral research on personal, cultural and collective complexes of the unconscious on delayed motherhood in the School of Social Sciences at Cardiff University. Maryann has previously run mind–body workshops with fertility challenged women at the Bridge Center London, and taught at the International School of Analytical Psychology (ISAP) in Zürich on the Word Association Experiment and Jung's Complex Theory as methodology in Psychosocial Research. Her interest in female development and procreative identity has been realized in various publications, *The Hunger To Fill An Empty Space* (Journal of Analytical Psychology, 2007), and in edited collections *Sulphur Rises Through the Blackened Body* (Routledge, 2014), and *Gender Legacies of Jung & Freud as Epistemology in Emergent Feminist Research on Late Motherhood* (Behavioral Science, 2014).

John Beebe

Born in 1939, John Beebe graduated from Harvard University and the University of Chicago Medical School. He trained in psychiatry at Stanford University Medical Center and in Jungian analysis at the C.G. Jung Institute of San Francisco. The founding editor of the *San Francisco Jung Institute Library Journal* (now published as *Jung Journal: Culture and Psyche*), he was also the first American co-editor of the London-based *Journal of Analytical Psychology*. In his writings and lectures throughout the world, he has offered additions and extensions to Jung's theories of archetypes, psychological types, dreams, conscience and moral character, and sexuality and gender. Through his workshops, reviews, and theoretical essays about movies over four decades, he has made himself a pioneer in the Jungian interpretation of film as a quintessentially psychological art. He is the editor of C.G. Jung's *Aspects of the Masculine* (1989), the author of *Integrity in Depth* (1992), and the co-author (with

Virginia Apperson) of *The Presence of the Feminine in Film* (2008). His book *Patterns and Energies in Psychological Type: The Reservoir of Consciousness* will be published by Routledge in 2016. He is in private practice of psychotherapy in San Francisco.

Jerome S. Bernstein

Jerome S. Bernstein, M.A.P.C., NCPsyA., is a Jungian analyst in private practice in Santa Fe, New Mexico and a senior analyst on the teaching faculty of the C.G. Jung Institute of Santa Fe. He is the author of *Power and Politics, the Psychology of Soviet-American Partnership* (Shambhala 1989); *Living in the Borderland: The Evolution of Consciousness and the Challenge of Healing Trauma* (Routledge 2005); co-editor, along with Philip Deloria, *C.G. Jung and the Sioux Traditions* by Vine Deloria, Jr. (Spring Books: 2009); "Healing Our Split: Participation Mystique and C.G. Jung," *Shared Realities* (Fisher King Press 2014), numerous articles on international conflict, personal and collective trauma, as well as on various analytical topics. He lectures and teaches internationally. The current focus of his work is the construction of a meta-language to facilitate dialogue between the Dominion Psyche and the Reciprocity Psyche utilizing Jungian theory and Quantum theory as a conceptual bridge.

Elizabeth Brodersen

Elizabeth Brodersen, Ph.D., born in South Wales, UK, is an IAAP Jungian analyst currently in private practice in Frankfurt, Germany. She is also an accredited training analyst at the C.G. Jung Institute in Zürich. She received her doctorate in 2014 from the Centre of Psychoanalytic Studies at the University of Essex, UK. Her book *Laws of Inheritance: A Post-Jungian Study of Twins and the Relationship Between the First and Other(s)* was published by Routledge in 2015. She is currently Co-Chair of the International Association for Jungian Studies executive committee with Michael Glock.

John Demenkoff

John Demenkoff, born 1949, was educated at Harvard Medical School and qualified as an M.D. in 1974. He received his Ph.D. from Pacifica Institute in 2014 and is board certified in Internal and Pulmonary Medicine as well as in Senior Consultant Mayo Clinic, Phoenix, Arizona. His Jungian odyssey began in Ithaca circa 1989 when he met Don Fredericksen who introduced him to Jung's *Memories, Dreams, and Reflections*. After moving to Phoenix in 2001 the geographic proximity to coastal California enabled him to attend Pacifica Graduate Institute in Santa Barbara. In 2014 he completed his doctorate in Mythological Studies with a dissertation titled *Evolution and Emergence of the Masculinities: Epiphanies and Epiphenomena of the Male Athlete and Dancer*.

Daphne Dodson

Daphne Dodson, Ph.D., is a global qualitative researcher primarily conducting studies in the fields of infectious and auto-immune diseases. Her specific areas of interest include cultural psychology, the imagination, and memory.

Matthew A. Fike

Matthew A. Fike, Ph.D., is a Professor of English at Winthrop University in Rock Hill, South Carolina, where he teaches courses in the human experience, critical thinking, Shakespeare, and Renaissance literature. His most recent monograph is *The One Mind: C.G. Jung and the Future of Literary Criticism* (Routledge 2014).

Michael Glock

Michael Glock, Ph.D., is CEO of Bloom Factor, Inc. as its creative director and managed marketing/business automation expert. He received his PhD in philosophy from Pacifica Graduate Institute and has developed such concepts as Cultural Futuristics and Way Forward Engineering. His special interest lies in understanding hidden psychological dimensions and cultural complexes and the way they expose teleological thrusts and directions. He is co-chair of the IAJS Executive Committee with Elizabeth Brodersen.

Jeanne A. Lacourt

Jeanne A. Lacourt, Ph.D., (MS)LPC, NCC, is a Professor of American Indian Studies at St. Cloud State University in Minnesota, a Professional Counselor, and an Analyst-in-training with the Inter Regional Society of Jungian Analysts. Her current writings explore the intersections of Indigenous and Jungian Studies.

Kiley Q. Laughlin

Kiley Laughlin is a doctoral candidate at Pacifica Graduate Institute in Santa Barbara, California. He is currently completing his dissertation on the final image in C.G. Jung's Red Book. He has published several scholarly articles on Jungian thought to include *The Individuation Project* (2013), *The Archetypal Leader* (2014), *Towards a Science of Gnosis* (2015), and *Spectrum of Consciousness: Color Symbolism in the Typology of C.G. Jung*. He is deeply interested in analytical psychology and the new physics, as well as archetypal symbolism in contemporary film and literature. Kiley is currently writing a paper on the comparisons between Jungian epistemology and the participatory paradigm of the new physics. Kiley is also a US Army Reservist who drills in Northern California. He has been in the US Army for over 20 years and has served in Iraq and the Balkans.

Konoyu Nakamura

Konoyu Nakamura, Ph.D., is Professor of Clinical Psychology at Otemon Gakuin University in Osaka, Japan. She is involved in clinical work at her private practice in Kyoto as a Jungian-oriented psychotherapist. She obtained her Ph.D. from Konan University in 1997 for her dissertation, "Clinical Psychology for Eating Disorders." She contributed several book chapters, for example, "The Image emerging: the therapist's vision at a critical point of therapy," in L. Huskinson (ed.), *Dreaming the Myth Onwards: New Directions in Jungian Therapy and Thought*. New York: Routledge (2008); "No-Self, initiating the transcendent: the image of Mahavairocana-tathagata emerging from the therapist at a crucial point in therapy," in D. Mathers et al. (eds.), *Self and No-Self: Continuing the Dialogue Between Buddhism and Psychotherapy*,

Routledge (2009). She is a member of the Executive Committee of the International Association for Jungian Studies.

Eileen Nemeth

Eileen Nemeth is a practicing analytical Psychologist with a private practice in Zürich, Switzerland. Her work as an analytical Psychologist and psychotherapist combines her training as a Jungian analyst, dance therapist, and former dancer, teacher, and choreographer. She is a guest teacher at the Jung Institute in Zürich and ISAP Zürich. She was an active member of ISAP and a training analyst there until 2012. Circling all of her work is a strong focus on creativity and the integration of body in analytical and psychotherapeutic work.

Sarah D. Norton

Sarah D. Norton received her Master's Degree from Pacifica Graduate Institute in the field of Depth Psychology with an Emphasis in Jungian and Archetypal Studies. Sarah currently lives in Spotsylvania, Virginia where she is writing her dissertation for Pacifica in the same field. Sarah's working dissertation title: *Arctic Mediums: An Imaginal Exploration of Ice Through Text, Nature, and the Arts*, is a depth psychological exploration of climate change focused on the melting of the polar icecaps. Sarah is also a certified dream group facilitator through the Haden Institute in Flat Rock, North Carolina and the editor of the bi-annual publication *The Rose in the World* which is dedicated to bringing Wisdom into its readers' lives and sacred spaces through dreams, Jungian Psychology, and spirituality.

Evangeline A. Rand

Evangeline Rand, Ph.D., a former teacher, has been a practicing Psychologist (Canada) since 1982 during which time she started the Child Sexual Abuse Treatment Program in Edmonton. She was adjunct faculty with the Doctor of Ministry program of St. Stephens Theological College for 22 years and is currently an adjunct faculty member for the Art Therapy Program at Adler University, Vancouver. Her books include *Recovering from Incest: Imagination and the Healing Process* (1989), *Recovering Feminine Spirituality* (1994/2015) and more recently, *A Jasmine Journey: Carl Jung's Travel to India and Ceylon 1937 and 1938 and Jung's Vision During Illness – "Something New" emerging from Orissa 1944* (2012). During the past 12 years Dr. Rand has explored the recognition and support of human resilience journeying through trauma, and studies and teaches fundamental discoveries and creations of Geometry and primary number inspired by the work of Professor Emeritus Keith Critchlow. Dr. Rand is an embroidering textile artisan with current interest in the ancient and ongoing interface of Indian handmade, simple, and fabulous textiles with global trade, cultures, and politics.

Susan Rowland

Susan Rowland, Ph.D., is Chair of MA Engaged Humanities and the Creative Life at Pacifica Graduate Institute, California, and formerly Professor of English and

Jungian Studies at the University of Greenwich, UK. She is author of a number of books on literary theory, gender and Jung including *Jung as a Writer* (2005); *Jung: A Feminist Revision* (2002); *C. G. Jung in the Humanities* (2010) and *The Ecocritical Psyche: Literature, Evolutionary Complexity and Jung* (2012). She also researches detective fiction with a book, *From Agatha Christie to Ruth Rendell* (2001) and, *The Sleuth and the Goddess in Women's Detective Fiction* (2015). Her new book on transdisciplinary *Jung, Remembering Dionysus*, will be available in 2016.

Susan E. Schwartz

Susan E. Schwartz, Ph.D., Jungian analyst and clinical Psychologist is a member of the New Mexico Association of Jungian Analysts, the International Association of Analytical Psychology and American Psychological Association. She has taught for Jungian Developing Groups in Poland and South Africa and participated in various conferences, workshops, and lectures in her community, state, and in and out of the country. Susan has several articles in the online journals *Plath Profiles* and *Depth Insights*; a chapter in the text *Counseling and Psychotherapy* and a chapter in *Perpetual Adolescence: Jungian Analyses of American Pop Culture*. She has a private practice in Jungian Psychology in Paradise Valley, Arizona.

Sulagna Sengupta

Sulagna Sengupta is a Jungian scholar based in India. She is the author of "Jung in India," Spring Journal Books, 2013. Her areas of research are psychology, history, culture, and mythology. She is a postgraduate in English with certification in Depth Psychology from The India Jung Center, Bangalore. Sulagna specializes in archival research and has worked in several archival repositories in India and abroad. She is currently engaged in researching her next full-length work. Sulagna is also a consultant on Diversity & Inclusion and offers strategic human process solutions to business organizations in India.

Thomas Singer

Thomas Singer, M.D., is a psychiatrist and Jungian psychoanalyst practicing in the San Francisco Bay Area. He has written and edited many books, including a series on the notion of the cultural complex as it appears in Australia (*Placing Psyche*), Latin America (*Listening to Latin America*) and Europe (*Europe's Many Souls*). He co-edited *The Cultural Complex*. In addition, he and Virginia Beane Rutter have organized conferences in Santorini, Greece that have resulted in two volumes about *Ancient Greece, Modern Psyche*. Dr. Singer also has a long-term interest in ARAS (The Archives for Research into Archetypal Symbolism), a non-profit foundation that explores the relationships between symbolic image and psyche in cultures around the world through publications and ARAS.org., an online site.

Vanya Stier-Van Essen

Vanya Stier-Van Essen, B.S.N., R.N., M.A., was born in Brazil and is currently working on her Ph.D. in Depth Psychology with an Emphasis in Jungian and Archetypal

Studies at Pacifica Graduate Institute. Her research is focused on the mythic image of Eve's transgression and on the psychological significance of feminine transgression in myth. In addition to working on her research, writing, and teaching, Vanya offers community programs and events (including circles, workshops, educational seminars, and retreats) with the intention of creating space and opportunity for soul-making and deep engagement with the creative imagination.

Jeff Strnad

Jeff Strnad, Ph.D., is the Charles A. Beardsley Professor of Law at Stanford University. Professor Strnad is an economist, a lawyer, and a licensed and practicing psychotherapist. Professor Strnad's published research spans a wide range of disciplines, including law, statistics, psychology, finance, and economics. He currently teaches mental health law and two courses aimed at the psychological and life development of law students at Stanford Law School. His education includes a Ph.D. in Economics from Yale University, a J.D. from Yale University, and an M.A. in Counseling Psychology from Pacifica Graduate Institute where he developed an interest in Depth Psychology and Jungian studies.

ACKNOWLEDGMENTS

This vivid and emotive collection of chapters stem from the IAJS conference on Rebirth and Renewal in Phoenix, Arizona, 2014. We are deeply indebted to all the contributors included in this collection who wrote their chapters following on from the conference and to those conference participants who could not have their work published at this time. The process of selecting and editing these eighteen chapters has been a rich, sustaining, and enjoyable experience. We particularly wish to thank Dr. Stephani Stephens, Co-Chair of the Phoenix conference, for the initial idea of publishing these conference chapters with Routledge and for her enthusiastic support throughout the planning of this publication. We also want to thank Dr. Marybeth Carter for her active help on the Phoenix conference programme and planning committees without which the conference would have been less vibrant and meaningful.

We give special thanks to our inspiring Routledge editor, Susannah Frearson, who not only attended the Phoenix conference, but who has unwaveringly accompanied us throughout the publishing process with her deft support and patience. We are indebted to the Routledge production team on their excellent proof editing skills, indexing, and general support.

All references from Jung's *Collected Works* listed in this collection are translated by R.F.C. Hull and edited by H. Read, M. Fordham, G. Adler, and William McGuire and published in the UK by Routledge, London, and in America by Princeton University Press, Bollingen Series XX, 1953–1992. These references are listed to paragraph number. Page numbers are cited for Jung's *Memories Dreams and Reflections, C.G. Jung's Letters* and *Visions: Notes of the Seminar Given in 1930–1934* in two volumes.

In all cases where client material has been used, the confidentiality and anonymity of client identity has been protected.

We gratefully acknowledge copyright permission to publish the following images and texts:

Images

For Kiley Laughlin's chapter: the copper engraving of Michael Maier at the age of 48, from the *Atlanta fugiens*, 1617 by Matthäus Merian; The Mountain of the Adept, *Cabala*, 1654, by Stephen Michelspacher; The sequence of stages in the alchemical process, *Alchymia*, 1606, by Andreas Libravius. Permission has been granted for all by Routledge and Kegan Paul and Princeton.

For Jerome Bernstein's chapter: "The Eye of Africa" is permitted by courtesy of NASA. gov.

For Thomas Singer's chapter: Figures 4.1, 4.2, and 4.3, Dr. Henderson's drawings (whole, dream 1, dream 2) are reproduced with permission from Dr. Henderson.

Figure 4.4, Snake drawing, reproduced with permission of the artist, Thomas Singer.

Figure 4.6, Rod Moss: "The Interpretation of Dreams" is reproduced here with permission of the artist.

Image 4.7 from the Jungarai Wanu story is included by permission of Japaljarri Spencer and Dr. Craig San Roque.

For John Demenkoff's chapter: Figure 15.2 was originally published in Falkowski, *Tracing Oxygen's Imprint on the Earth's Metabolic Evolution*, Science 24, March 2006 pp. 1724–1725 and is reprinted here by permission. Image credit: P. Huey/Science.

For Sulagna Sengupta's chapter: "Paramapada Sopanam" permission to include this image has been given courtesy of Jung Family Archive and Andreas Jung.

Text

For Thomas Singer's chapter "The Burden of Modernity: Three Takes on the Snake and Recombinant Visionary Mythology," permission has been granted by Routledge to use these previous works: In Part I, material has been adapted from the chapter, "In the Footsteps: The Story of an Initiatory Drawing by Dr. Joseph Henderson," in *Initiation: The Living Reality of an Archetype*, edited by Thomas Kirsch, Virginia Beane Rutter, and Thomas Singer (Routledge, 2007). In Part II, the material has been adapted from a chapter "The Circus Snake: A Numinous, Initiatory Calling from Below," in *Being Called: Scientific, Secular and Sacred Perspectives*, edited by David Bryce Yaden, Theo D. McCall, and J. Harold Ellens (Singer, Praeger, 2015). Finally, in Part III, with his permission, the author quotes from Craig San Roque's "Living People, Living Language, Living Symbol," *ARAS Connections* 4 (2014): http://aras.org/sites/default/files/docs/00075SanRoque.pdf. The authors also refer to his chapter "The Kore Story: Persephone's Dog," in *Ancient Greece, Modern Psyche: Archetypes Evolving*, edited by Virginia Beane Rutter and Thomas Singer (Routledge, 2015).

For Daphne Dodson's chapter "Rebirthing Biblical Myth: *The Poisonwood Bible* as Visionary Art" permission has been granted by HarperCollins and the Frances Goldin Literary Agency to quote from *The Poisonwood Bible*. Copyright © 1998.

Material for John Beebe's chapter "Responses to a Film about Integrity" has been permitted from *The Presence of the Feminine in Film* (2008) by Cambridge Scholars publishers.

EDITORS' INTRODUCTION

Phoenix Rising: Jungian Perspectives on Rebirth and Renewal

Elizabeth Brodersen and Michael Glock

This collection of chapters is inspired by the idea of how "light in nature" (Jung, 1954a, paras. 388–391) builds imaginal shapes that spark a "rebirth and renewal" phenomenology in the individual and collective psyche. As natural *scintillae* or fiery, seminal numen, Jung speculates that such phenomena spark the world soul into existence by acting as "seeds of light broadcast in the chaos" (para. 388). As Jung explains, "this light is the *lumen naturae* which illuminates consciousness and the *scintillae* are the germinal luminosities shining forth from the darkness of the unconscious" (para. 389). Through a renewed, experiential contact with this creative, *affective* inner light, whether through a specific image of nature, such as the fiery phoenix bird, or as a mythic liminal space/place in the natural world, through dreams or other creative expression, the psyche is regenerated. Jung (1954b, paras. 321–322) argues that the collective unconscious is the *ancestral heritage* of all representation and that it should be theoretically possible to peel back each layer, until we reach the psychology of even the worm or amoeba. With their emphasis on evolutionary ancestral memories, creation myths, and dreams, these chapters explore the *indigenous/primordial* roots of "rebirth and renewal."

Phoenix Image as Symbol

The phoenix image as a symbol, itself, of "rebirth and renewal" underlines the significance that Jung and post-Jungians (Walker, 2002, pp. 3–24; Adams, 2001, pp. 334–371) attach to images which drew the IAJS Jungian conference planning committee to its location in 2014, to Phoenix, Arizona. Jung, however, differentiates an image from a symbol (1961a, para. 589). He explains that "when there is only an image, it is merely a word-picture, like a corpuscle with no electric charge." A symbol, on the other hand, is pregnant and alive with a multiplicity of meaning which accounts for its *numinosity*. Jung (1961a, para. 578) further distinguishes between *natural* and *cultural* symbols. The former are derived from unconscious contents and can be traced back to their archaic roots. Jung (1951a, para. 152; 1943, paras. 151, 184) emphasizes the importance of *primordial, natural* symbols, such as the phoenix, because they unite disparities within the psyche between conscious/unconscious, mind/body, subjective/objective *affective* components more effectively than intellectual understanding through cultural symbols or language alone. Jung's interest in *natural* symbols lay in their creative ability to redirect and transform blocked, unconscious, instinctual energy into more meaningful life pathways (1948, paras. 92–94) where cultural symbols have failed in this task.

Jung (1954c, para. 281) associates the imaginary phoenix bird as a fiery manifestation which combines the four alchemical colors of black (*prima materia*), white (*purification*), gold (*illumination*), and red (*sacrifice and resurrection*) as a *mysterium coniunctionis* imbued within its plumage. The phoenix thus becomes a living *theriomorphic* symbol of the Self (*the worm and the bird*). Jung (1951b, para. 315) differentiates conscious aspects of the ego from non-ego aspects of the Self which are unconscious and suppressed: these take the form of *theriomorphic* symbols because such symbols can embody a wider spectrum of instinctual, ambivalent content than human form. The phoenix is a well-known allegory of the resurrection of Christ and the dead (Jung, 1954c, para. 285); as a symbol of *transformation and rebirth* (Jung, 1911–1912/1952a, para. 165), the phoenix embodies the *burning* renunciation of desire. Jung connects the phoenix symbol to a definition of individuation, differentiating it from a soft "new age" experience that does not dialogue creatively with the reality of hot, painful, unconscious, complex emotions, nor the withdrawal and assimilation of difficult "shadow" projections within a closed, analytical container. Jung (1954b, para. 283) describes this process as "reserved for hell" with the "death" of the ego as the personality moves to take its central position between consciousness and the unconscious (Jung, 1929, para. 67).

The first complete account of the imaginary androgynous phoenix bird by Lactantius (c AD 260–340) applauds the phoenix's numinosity and its thousand year longevity as the parent of nature itself living in the grove of the sun. Lactantius describes the beauty of its plumage as "sky ripe pomegranates" and "wild poppies" with a glittering tail variegated with yellow and whose spots redden to a purple hue. Fitted with a crown of golden sun rays on its head, its white beak is dashed with emerald green (Lactantius, trans. Duff & Duff, 1961, pp. 651–655).

Fabricius (1976, pp. 207–209) emphasizes the introverted, self-fertilizing properties of the phoenix bird which recreates itself without a partner, analogous to the individuation process as distinct from the maturation process, which needs an outer sexual partner to propagate. When the phoenix bird anticipates its own death, it makes a nest of wood and resins, which it exposes to the full force of the sun's rays. As the nest catches fire, the phoenix is burnt to ashes, yet out of the ashes forms a larva (worm/caterpillar) which grows into a chick and then into another phoenix, the bird's projected and immortal *doppelgänger*.

The phoenix also appears at the Temple of the Sun in Heliopolis, Egypt (Nigg, 1999, p. 383), thus associating itself with the Egyptian *Benu* bird and the passage of the Egyptian sun god Osiris/Ra who undergoes death and dismemberment (night-time) to arise as Horus/Ra (day-time) resulting in a revitalization of the ego as the emergent Self (Jung, 1911–1912/1952b, paras. 351–354). As *Rauch Elohim* (Jung, 1954d, para. 50) the phoenix spark embodies "the spirit, breath, wind and blowing…"

The Importance of Location as Psyche and Symbol

The phoenix image as location reconnects us to our indigenous/primordial past using Singer's (2010) proposition that every modern metropolis, allegorically acts as a soul's guide. Jung (1911–1912/1952c, para. 223) argues that "the suggestive power of the environment is itself a consequence of the *numinosity* of the image and intensifies it in turn." The city was named Phoenix in the late nineteenth century because it "rose up" like the phoenix, out of the ashes, using as its foundation the disused irrigation canal system of the previous 2000-year-old Hohokam indigenous culture and was rebuilt. One could argue that the Phoenix city as symbol acts as a guide to the modern psyche (the conscious ego) with its once indigenous/primordial foundations (the unconscious) hidden and often dried up through lack of contact. Its cross-roads location in the arid, hot, desert valley of the sun, of Maricopa County, Arizona, *and* Salt River, reconnects the city in several ways to the transforming, irrigating function of nature: new growth out of primordial water canals using salt, fire, sand, and ashes as its alchemical ingredients.

Hillman (1994, pp. 145–179) amplifies the importance of salt, its purification and fixing properties which when given the correct dissolved dosage as tears, participates in the healing alchemical process. The phoenix bird itself sheds tears giving symbolic access to the dissolving, cleansing, and healing of wounds. As an image of fire, (Jung, 1911–1912/1952a, paras. 171–175) the phoenix image embodies this passion, its painful sacrifice, and its reversal into the renewal of life after such renunciation. Elsewhere, Jung (2009, pp. 235–237) compares his own soul to a hot, burnt-out desert (such as that found around Phoenix); he suggests that the quiet solitude found in such bereft terrain heals too much extroversion.

Rebirth and Renewal of the Ascendant Matrilineal Function

The phoenix as a bird reconnects us to evolutionary, prelapsarian, imaginative Palaeolithic/Neolithic rebirth images of women, in the form of women-bird hybrids, as depictions of bird goddesses displaying beaks, claws and bird feet (Gimbutas, 1989, pp. 3–41). Such women goddesses as birds expressed the ascendant freedom and power to "soar" in their minds, later banned, branded, and burnt as witches or harpies under patrilineal primogeniture. The phoenix image of burning itself in the act of creative destruction also expresses the fear, ambivalence, and the actual pain of childbirth, the fiery, sharp (the beak) clawing pain (bird's feet) of contractions which simultaneously opens into new life. The phoenix's connection to the fertility trickster, Kokopelli, underscores the risk that creation can kill as well as create new life. Chapters in this collection, particularly by Dodson, Rowland, Stier-Van Essen, Beebe, Sengupta, Barone-Chapman, and Nakamura, constellate a "rebirth and renewal" of the feminine matrilineal principle through the trickster archetype embedded in unconscious complexes, resurrecting the independent, ascendant, creative function of the archaic goddess, earlier depicted as the winged sky mother serpent (cf. Florescano, 1999, pp. 198–199; Brodersen, 2015, p. 30). The freedom to find the missing clues in the process of facilitating independent thinking banned since the Middle East Genesis Myth (Bible, 1989 edition, *OT* Genesis 3:8) is reborn.

The Importance to Jung of Archaic, Imaginative, Associative, Indirect Thinking

This collection legitimizes the use of associative, imaginative, *indirect* thinking (cf. Adams, 2004, pp. 2–19) within academic discourse. The phoenix as an imaginative symbol emphasizes the importance of mythological, archaic images found in Jung's definitions of two kinds of thinking, *direct* and *indirect* (1911–1912/1952d, paras. 4–48). These definitions are not new (cf. Schiller, 1795, pp. 64–72; James, 1890, Vol. 2, pp. 44–75) but Jung and post-Jungians such as Adams (2001, p. 121 and 2004, pp. 2–19) allocate a specific *directed* and *active* value to *indirect, horizontal, associative* thinking found in dreams and myth because they allow *affective* subjectivity through unconscious images to enter, hitherto repressed under *directed, hierarchical* thinking. Including affect has the capacity to heal the mind–body split (Jung, 1954a, para. 400) which enhances cognition, not hinders it (Congram, 2008, pp. 160–177).

Recent archeological and anthropological research (Donald, 1991, pp. 162–268; Renfrew & Morley, 2009; Lewis-Williams & Pearce, 2005; Lewis-Williams & Challis, 2011) all stress a symbolic, innovative, cognitive *continuum* found in Palaeolithic–Neolithic cultural expressions of cave art, drama, music, and dance that widens the definition of an evolutionary educative human intelligence before the onset of hierarchical primogeniture ca. 3000 BCE rationalized by the *OT* Genesis myth. Such findings also contest the allocation of fixed binary gender roles (Joyce, 2008) as well as legitimizing *indirect* associative thinking as innovative.

An Overemphasis on German Aestheticism by Stressing Other Ethnologies

These chapters serve to redress the recent psychoanalytical academic interest which places the birth of the modern psyche, for example, McGrath (2012), Ffytche (2012) and Bishop (2008, 2011) and the genesis of unconscious processes within the context of classical German mysticism, theosophy, and aestheticism of Eckhart (c 1260–1327), Böhme (1575–1624), Goethe (1749–1832), Schiller (1750–1805), and Schelling (1775–1854). German-speaking cities such as Berlin, Frankfurt, Munich, Vienna, Basel, and Zürich are central locations that reflect the spirit of this historical and linguistic middle-European discourse. This *genius loci* (cf. Kozljanic, 2012), however, tends to ignore Jung's clinical work on the etiology of neurosis and psychosis where he places more emphasis on assimilating individual subjectivity through older, *indirect*, horizontal, nomadic, shamanic discourse, particularly through dreams, to allow disassociated, unacceptable, "treacherous," dissenting impulses, first in the form of threatening animals as non-ego forms to enter into dialogue (cf. Smith, 1997; Adams, 2008, pp. 231–242; Merchant, 2012; Jung, 1961a, paras. 578–606; Brodersen, 2015, pp. 163–187).

The recent emphasis on German aestheticism has significantly underplayed Jung's indebtedness to indigenous peoples he met on his world travels to America, North Africa, Kenya, Uganda, India, and Ceylon, which had a profound effect on the evolution of his clinical theories attached to "nature" and *natural* symbols as the experiential generators of "rebirth and renewal" (see Eliade, 1964; Jung, 1961b, pp. 288–313).Through such contact, Jung experienced a new emotional immediacy to life (ibid., p. 270) which he likened to a deep unconscious engagement with the primordial "shadow" ethnic other (p. 273).

Chapters in this collection by Singer, Stier-Van Essen, and Sengupta depict the snake/serpent as one *theriomorphic* image to stress the unconscious, creative, animalistic aspects of "rebirth and renewal" subordinated and disinherited in the creationist, patrilineal *OT* Genesis myth. Other chapters reflect on the role the *OT* Genesis myth played historically in fixing gender roles to the detriment of both sexes and excluding animals by offering multifaceted, evolutionary interpretations of "rebirth and renewal" through nature (see chapters by Lacourt, Dodson, Singer, and Sengupta for images of trees, eagles, bears, beavers, ants, and snakes/serpents, respectively).

A proliferation of scholarly works has already been published on Jung's encounters with indigenous peoples: Burleson (2005) on Africa; Collins & Molchanov (2013), Sengupta (2013), and Rand (2013) on India; Deloria, Jr. (2009), Lacourt (2010, 2012), and Bernstein (2005, 2012) on Native America. This collection expands on the work of Rand, Lacourt, Bernstein, and Sengupta, while introducing new authors working with primordial symbols.

Jung's Interest in the "Fourth" Psychological Function

The collection begins with Laughlin's chapter which charts Jung's (1954c, paras. 276–293) fascination with sixteenth-century Count Michael Maier's quest to find a feather of the ubiquitous phoenix, with his own world travels in pursuit of a sighting of the bird. Unlike Maier, Jung gives this pursuit a conscious psychological underpinning as the individuation process in search of wholeness (Tilton, 2003, pp. 12, 255). For Jung, the phoenix bird attempts to retrieve the missing "fourth" function, the evolutionary animal ancestor soul buried in the unconscious alongside feminine creativity. As the ubiquitous phoenix image is constellated in multiple "hot" locations from America, Egypt, Africa, Asia to Arab countries, it embodies an all-encompassing, evolutionary meaning of "rebirth and renewal" rather than a creationist, Middle-Eastern *NT* symbol of Christ's crucifixion and resurrection (Jung, 1954c, para. 286).

Each part offers a *multiplication* of synchronistic chapters as "offspring" of the phoenix image (cf. Abraham, 1998, p. 152; Jung, 1954a, paras. 393–394) with its four cardinal points linking them to Jung's own journeys in search of the phoenix: USA (West); Europe (Central) Africa; India (South) and expanding them to include Japan (East) and the Polar Axes as *anima mundi* expressions of the individuation process linking the personal and objective psyche as eco-critical, psychological, co-evolutions of the world soul (Hillman, 1983, p. 26; Singer & Kimbles, 2004; Singer, 2010; Bernstein, 2005; Dodds, 2011; Rowland, 2012). Each chapter explores "rebirth and renewal" phenomenology as *lumen naturae* (cf. Jung, 1954a, para. 389) whether through dreams, imagination, myth, or literature.

Part I begins with Laughlin's comparative study of the significance of the *Phoenix as symbol,* including its image as Jung's family crest, followed by Part II on chapters by Jerome Bernstein and Jeanne Lacourt that focus on *Native American* indigenous beliefs about the transformative power of nature. Bernstein uses the term "indigenous psyche" as the "psyche-left-behind" since the expulsion of Adam and Eve in *OT Genesis* from the Garden of Eden where we lost a direct, immediate contact with nature as "itself." Lacourt celebrates natural human origins in the form of trees and animal ancestors, such as the bear, and beaver. In such origins there is no split between the human and animal psyche. Part III offers two chapters that focus on synchronistic symbols as *liminal place/space*. Singer (cf. Singer, 2010, *Psyche and the City*) asks whether myths are a synchronistic source of renewal for modernity. He explores the snake symbol as a response to the ordeal of modernity and reaffirms its place as a transforming creative matrix, evoking the ancient Greek healer, Asclepius, in his medicinal use of snake properties in death, rebirth, and renewal processes (Ronnberg & Martin, 2010, pp. 194–197). The relationship between the psyche and place enables a co-evolution of the psyche of the land in a process of "rebirth and renewal." Dodson explores eco-psychological readings of the Genesis myth in Africa as a *sacred* indigenous space/place freed-up from *OT* patrilineal interpretation. She interprets Kingsolver's novel *The Poisonwood Bible* (1998) as a cultural "rebirth and renewal" with oneself, primordial nature, and the earth's ecosystem.

Part IV emphasizes Jung's travels in India and the spiritual influence *Indian indigenous* beliefs played in his psychological understanding of "rebirth and renewal." The rich colored textures (Rand) plus the close contact of humans to animals as gods *and* goddesses (Sengupta; Beebe) restores an integrity which is in sharp contrast to the orderly, static, hierarchical mid-European Christian monotheism. Part V expands on the *rebirth of the feminine* through the phoenix symbol of "rebirth and renewal." Stier-Van Essen returns to the *OT* Genesis myth reinterpreting the moment of Eve's transgression as a necessary act of rebellion and dissent using the snake as an analogue of "rebirth." Rowland concentrates on modern mystery detective fiction written by women (Fairstein, Grafton) as manifestations of the trickster goddess reborn and energized by symbols that reproduce ancient patterns in modern culture.

Part VI presents chapters on familial constellations of *ancestral memories* evoked by the creative ubiquitous phoenix image. Strnad explores an archetypal biblical account of infancy embedded as "rebirth," relating this dynamic to Melanie Klein's narrative of infancy. Nemeth takes creation myths of "rebirth and renewal" that constellate "being welcome in the world" by comparing client dream material to myth, showing that similar symbols are generated through both myth and dreams. Barone-Chapman examines intergenerational memories through Jung's work with unconscious complexes (WAE). She explains the vicissitudes of childhood trauma and gender sacrifice through the case study of one research participant's complex of inferiority, which revealed her ambivalent relationship to becoming a mother, including changing her sexual identity in order to create what she had missed from early life: a family.

Part VII focuses on three chapters which deal with *eco-psychological,* synchronistic carriers of death, rebirth, and renewal through diverse *anime* symbols of the world psyche embedded in mythic characterizations. Nakamura suggests that the wrecked World War II Japanese naval battleship, *Yamato,* transformed symbolically into the heroic comic book *Space Battleship Yamato* designed to ameliorate the future threat of nuclear destruction. Demenkoff uses the myth of Prometheus to analyze human dependency on oxygen and regenerative processes through endosymbiosis, while Norton movingly examines polar ice "calving" in a cracking-open/groaning "rebirth and renewal" process. Part VIII explores *mytho-poetic, visionary* dimensions of "rebirth and renewal" through chapters that give literary expression to the indigenous people/primordial psyche, stemming from Africa and Native America in Haggard's *She* (Fike) and Miss Frank Miller's Fantasies in Jung's *Collected Works*, Vol. 5 (Schwartz). Both stress "rites of passage" as *psycho-visionary* death–rebirth processes embedded as *anima* and *animus* projections re-experienced within the deep structures of popular narrative and ontologically re-navigated.

References

Abraham, L. (1998). *The Dictionary of Alchemical Imagery.* Cambridge and New York: Cambridge University Press, 2001.

Adams, M.V. (2001). *The Mythological Imagination.* Putnam, CT: Spring Publications.

Adams, M.V. (2004). *The Fantasy Principle, Psychoanalysis of the Imagination.* Hove, UK and New York: Brummer-Routledge.

Adams, M.V. (2008). "Imaginology, the Jungian Study of the Imagination," in S. Marlan (ed.), *Archetypal Psychologies, Reflections in Honour of James Hillman,* pp. 225–242. New Orleans, LA: Spring Journal.

Bernstein, J. (2005). *Living in the Borderland: The Evolution of Consciousness and the Challenge of Healing Trauma.* Hove, UK and New York: Routledge.

Bernstein, J. (2012). "Guest Editor's Introduction," in N. Cater (ed.), *Native American Culture and the Western Psyche: A Bridge Between.* New Orleans, LA: Spring Journal.

Bible, The (1989) *The Revised English Edition.* Oxford and Cambridge: Oxford University Press.

Bishop, P. (2008). *Analytical Psychology and German Classical Aesthetics, Vols. 1 and 2.* Hove and New York: Routledge.

Bishop, P. (2011). *Reading Goethe at Midlife, Ancient Wisdom, German Classicism and Jung.* New Orleans, LA: Spring Journal.

Brodersen, E. (2015). *Laws of Inheritance: A Post-Jungian Study of Twins and the Relationship Between the First and Other(s).* Hove, UK and New York: Routledge.

Burleson, B. (2005). *Jung in Africa.* London: Continuum.

Collins, A. & Molchanov, E. (eds.) (2013). *Jung and India*. New Orleans, LA: Spring Journal.

Congram, S. (2008). "Arts-informed Learning in Manager–Leader Development," in R.A. Jones, A. Clarkson, S. Congram, & N. Stratton (eds.), *Education and Imagination, Post Jungian Perspectives*. Hove, UK and New York: Routledge.

Deloria, V. Jr. (2009). *C.G. Jung and the Sioux Traditions, Dreams Visions, Nature and the Primitive*. New Orleans, LA: Spring Journal Books.

Dodds, J. (2011). *Psychoanalysis and Ecology at the Edge of Chaos*. London and New York: Routledge.

Donald, M. (1991). *Origins of the Modern Mind*. Cambridge, MA and London: Harvard University Press.

Eliade, M. (1964). *Shamanism, Archaic Techniques of Ecstasy*. Princeton, NJ: Princeton University Press, 1974.

Fabricius, J. (1976). *Alchemy, The Medieval Alchemists and their Royal Art*. London: Diamond Books, 1989.

Ffytche, M. (2012). *The Foundations of the Unconscious: Schelling, Freud and the Birth of the Modern Psyche*. Cambridge: Cambridge University Press.

Florescano, E. (1999). *The Myth of Quetzalcoatl*, L. Hochroth (trans.). Baltimore, MD and London: The Johns Hopkins University Press.

Gimbutas, M. (1989). *The Language of the Goddess*. New York and London: Thames and Hudson, 2006.

Haggard, H.R. (1886). *She*. London and New York: Penguin Classic, 2012.

Hillman, J. (1983). *Archetypal Psychology: A Brief Account*. Dallas, TX: Spring Publications, 1993.

Hillman, J. (1994). "Salt: A Chapter in Alchemical Psychology," in S. Marlan (ed.), *Salt and the Alchemical Soul: Ernest Jones, C.G. Jung, James Hillman*. Woodstock, CT: Spring Publications, 1995.

James, W. (1890). *The Principles of Psychology, Vol. 2*. New York: Dover Publications, 1950.

Joyce, R.A. (2008). *Ancient Bodies, Ancient Lives*. London: Thames and Hudson.

Jung, C.G. (1911–1912/1952a). "Song of the Moth," in *Collected Works*, Vol. 5, *Symbols of Transformation* (2nd edn). London: Routledge and Kegan Paul, 1995.

Jung, C.G. (1911–1912/1952b). "Symbols of the Mother and of Rebirth," in *Collected Works*, Vol. 5, *Symbols of Transformation* (2nd edn). London: Routledge and Kegan Paul, 1995.

Jung, C.G. (1911–1912/1952c). "The Transformation of Libido," in *Collected Works*, Vol. 5, *Symbols of Transformation* (2nd edn). London: Routledge and Kegan Paul, 1995.

Jung, C.G. (1911–1912/1952d). "Two Kinds of Thinking," in *Collected Works*, Vol. 5, *Symbols of Transformation* (2nd edn). London: Routledge and Kegan Paul, 1995.

Jung, C.G. (1929). "The Detachment of Consciousness from the Object. Commentary on the Secret of the Golden Flower," in *Collected Works*, Vol. 13, *Alchemical Studies* (2nd edn). London: Routledge and Kegan Paul, 1981.

Jung, C.G. (1943). "The Archetypes of the Collective Unconscious," in *Collected Works*, Vol. 7, *Two Essays in Analytical Psychology* (2nd edn). London: Routledge and Kegan Paul, 1990.

Jung, C.G. (1948). "On Psychic Energy," in *Collected Works*, Vol. 8, *The Structure and Dynamics of the Psyche* (2nd edn). London: Routledge and Kegan Paul, 1991.

Jung, C.G. (1951a). "Psychological Aspects of the Mother Archetype," in *Collected Works*, Vol. 9i, *The Archetypes of the Collective Unconscious* (2nd edn). London: Routledge and Kegan Paul, 1991.

Jung, C.G. (1951b). "The Psychological Aspects of the Kore," in *Collected Works*, Vol. 9i, *The Archetypes and the Collective Unconscious* (2nd edn). London: Routledge and Kegan Paul, 1991.

Jung, C.G. (1954a). "On the Nature of the Psyche," in *Collected Works*, Vol. 8, *The Structure and Dynamics of the Psyche* (2nd edn). London: Routledge and Kegan Paul, 1991.

Jung, C.G. (1954b). "The Structure of the Psyche," in *Collected Works*, Vol. 8, *The Structure and Dynamics of the Psyche* (2nd edn). London: Routledge and Kegan Paul, 1991.

Jung, C.G. (1954c). "The Personification of the Opposites," in *Collected Works*, Vol. 14, *Mysterium Coniunctionis* (2nd edn). London: Routledge and Kegan Paul, 1992.

Jung, C.G. (1954d). "Paradoxa," in *Collected Works*, Vol. 14, *Mysterium Coniunctionis* (2nd edn). London: Routledge and Kegan Paul, 1992.

Jung, C.G. (1961a). "Healing the Split," in *Collected Works*, Vol. 18, *The Symbolic Life* (2nd edn). London: Routledge and Kegan Paul, 1993.

Jung, C.G. (1961b). Compiled and edited by A. Jaffé. *Memories, Dreams and Reflections*. London: Fontana, 1963.

Jung, C.G. (2009). *The Red Book*, S. Shamdasani (ed.). New York and London: W.W. Norton.

Kingsolver, B. (1998). *The Poisonwood Bible*. London and New York: HarperCollins.

Kozljanic, R.J. (2012). "Genius Loci and the Numen of the Place. A Mytho-phenomenological Approach to the Archaic," in P. Bishop (ed.), *The Archaic, The Past in the Present*. Hove, UK and New York: Routledge, pp. 69–92.

Lacourt, J.A. (2010). "My Father Was a Bear: Human–Animal Transformation in Native American Teachings," in G.A. Bradshaw & N. Cater (eds.), *Minding the Animal Psyche*, Vol. 83. New Orleans, LA: Spring Journal.

Lacourt, J.A. (2012). "Coming Home, Knowing Land, Knowing Self," in N. Cater (ed.), *Native American Culture and the Western Psyche: A Bridge Between*. New Orleans, LA: Spring Journal.

Lactantius. (1961) *Phoenix from Minor Latin Poets*, J.W. Duff & A.M. Duff (trans.). Cambridge, MA: Harvard University Press.

Lewis-Williams, D. & Pearce, D. (2005). *Inside The Neolithic Mind*. London: Thames & Hudson.

Lewis-Williams, D. & Challis, S. (2011). *Deciphering Ancient Minds*. London: Thames & Hudson.

McGrath, S.J. (2012). *The Dark Ground of the Spirit, Schelling and the Unconscious*. London and New York: Routledge.

Merchant, J. (2012). *Shamans and Analysts, New Insights into the Wounded Healer*. Hove, UK and New York: Routledge.

Nigg, J. (1999). *Fabulous Beasts. A Treasury of Writings from Ancient Times to the Present*. New York: Oxford University Press.

Rand, E. (2013). *A Jasmine Journey, Carl Jung's Travel to India and Ceylon 1937/8 and Jung's Vision During Illness "Something New" Emerging from Orissa, 1944*. Living Infinity Books.

Renfrew, C. & Morley, I. (eds.) (2009). *Becoming Human: Innovations in Prehistoric Material and Spiritual Culture*. New York: Cambridge University Press.

Ronnberg, A. & Martin, K. (eds.) (2010). *The Book of Symbols, Reflections on Archetypal Images*. Köln, Germany: Taschen Verlag.

Rowland, S. (2012). *The Ecocritical Psyche*. Hove, UK: Routledge.

Schiller, F. (1795). *On the Aesthetic Education of Man in a Series of Letters*. R. Snell (trans. and Introduction). London and New York: Dover Publishers, 2004.

Sengupta, S. (2013). *Jung in India*. New Orleans, LA: Spring Journal Books.

Singer, T. (ed.) (2010). *Psyche and the City: A Soul's Guide to the Modern Metropolis*. New Orleans, LA: Spring Journal Books.

Singer, T. & Kimbles, S. (eds.) (2004). *The Cultural Complex. Contemporary Jungian Perspectives on Psyche and Society*. Hove, UK and New York: Brunner Routledge.

Smith, C.M. (1997). *Jung and Shamanism in Dialogue*. New York and Mahwah, NJ: Paulis Press.

Tilton, H. (2003). *Quest of the Phoenix: Spiritual Alchemy and Rosicruciamism in the World of Count Michael Maier*. Berlin: De Gruyter.

Walker, S.F. (2002). *Jung and Jungians on Myth*. London and New York: Routledge.

PART I

The Phoenix as Symbol

1

PHOENIX RISING

A Comparative Study of the Phoenix Symbol as a Goal of Alchemical Work and the Individuation Process

Kiley Q. Laughlin

Introduction

This chapter explores the archetypal symbolism in the final chapter of Michael Maier's (1617) seminal work *Symbols of the Golden Table of the Twelve Nations*, which Maier presents as a dessert to the main course, a recapitulation of the foregoing work. The chapter is entitled "A Subtle Allegory" and describes the journey of a pilgrim, presumably Maier himself, who embarks on a quest in search of the mystical phoenix. Maier called this quest a "peregrination" (para. 1). That Jung viewed the peregrination as "an odyssey in search of wholeness" (1944a, para. 302, fig. 97) suggests that he put it on a par with his principle of individuation, the personality's tendency to move toward wholeness and self-realization. Jung further suggested that Maier's phoenix symbolizes the archetype of the self, the center and totality of the psyche, and the origin and goal of the individuation process. Thus, this chapter contends that Maier's "A Subtle Allegory" prefigures a number of Jungian ideas that include the ideas of the self and individuation.

Beyond Jung's (1955–1956a) initial investigation and some supplementary commentary by Edward Edinger's (1995) psychological study of "A Subtle Allegory" is scarce and deserves further inquiry. Outlining the basic premise of Maier's (1617) allegorical work, I explore the similarities between Jung's individuation process and Maier's peregrination, drawing parallels between the archetype of the self in analytical psychology and the phoenix symbol in Western alchemy. Because "A Subtle Allegory" is replete with a plethora of religious and philosophical symbols, a single chapter would not suffice to adequately exhaust its full scope. Thus, I have limited myself to the core ideas that parallel the basic postulates of Jungian psychology, providing a brief sketch of what I consider the central themes of the allegory punctuated by my commentary and suppositions.

Before proceeding, the reader could benefit from a few introductory remarks on *Symbols of the Golden Table of the Twelve Nations* (Maier, 1617). Maier's book consists of over 600 pages of mythological, historical, and alchemical allusions. Thus, any extensive survey of the entire work is beyond the scope of this comparative study. Rather, this chapter focuses on developing a better understanding of "A Subtle Allegory" in regards to its depth psychological significance. Jung's (1955–1956a) *Mysterium Coniunctionis*, Tilton's (2003) *The Quest for the Phoenix*, and "A Subtle Allegory" serve as the three primary sources used while researching this chapter. Lastly, due to the citing of multiple sources, the names Mercurius, Mercury, and Hermes all appear in this chapter. They all describe the same mythologem portrayed in Greek, Roman, and the alchemical tradition, and therefore are used interchangeably.

C.G. Jung and the Phoenix Symbol

The phoenix symbol apparently had special significance for Jung. In fact, the original coat of arms of the Jung family depicted a phoenix. Jung indicated that the bird was an appropriate symbol for the family name, which suggests "young," "youth," and "rejuvenation" (1961, p. 232). Jung studied the phoenix symbol as early as 1911, having researched the myth of the phoenix during his preparatory reading for his 1912 publication of *Psychology of the Unconscious*, in which he compared the phoenix symbol with such divine figures as Osiris, Christ, and Mithras (1911–1912/1952a, para. 165). The phoenix has often been associated with the symbol of the rising sun and the myth of the hero, which would have likely evoked a strong emotional reaction from Jung. As he explained:

> The bird probably signifies renewed ascent of the sun, the rebirth of the phoenix, and is at the same time one of those "helpful animals" who render supernatural aid during the birth: birds as aerial beings symbolize spirits or angels. Divine messengers frequently appear at these mythological births, as can be seen from the use we still make of *god-parents*.
>
> (1911–1912/1952b, para. 538)

Although there are nearly 100 references to the phoenix in Jung's collected works he mentions the bird only twice in his *Red Book, Liber Novus* (2009). He wrote the following on January 2, 1914: "When I comprehended my darkness, a truly magnificent night came over me and my dream plunged me into the depths of the millennia, and from it my phoenix ascended" (2009, p. 274). In another passage in *Liber Novus*, Jung (2009) made an oblique reference to the phoenix:

> I did not know what was happening to me, since simply everything powerful, beautiful, blissful, and superhuman had leaked from my maternal womb; none of the radiant gold remained. Cruelly and unthinkably the sunbird spread its wings and flew up into infinite space.
>
> (p. 287)

In the foregoing passages, Jung seems to have employed the phoenix as a metaphor to describe what he was experiencing psychologically – a rebirth or transformation – during his confrontation with the unconscious or what he frequently referred to as the spirit of the depths in *Liber Novus*. Furthermore, given Jung's apparent affinity for the phoenix it is not surprising that in *Mysterium Coniunctionis* he dedicated 24 pages of in-depth analysis to Maier's "A Subtle Allegory" in which the phoenix symbol plays a prominent role.

Count Michael Maier

Count Michael Maier (1568–1622) (Figure 1.1) was an alchemist, physician, and counselor to Emperor Rudolf II (1552–1612). According to J.B. Craven (2003), Maier's association with Rudolf II directly contributed to his fame and his prolific outpouring of works. Maier also spent time in England where he counseled King James I and befriended the alchemist Robert Fludd. Both Fludd and Maier were affiliated with the Order of the Rosy Cross, a secret society also known as the Rosicrucians. Jung suggested that Maier was one of the founders of the group (Jung, 1961, p. 232; 1955–1956a, para. 312). That Maier's ideas helped shape the dominant

FIGURE 1.1 Copper Engraving of Michael Maier at the age of 48, from the Atalanta fugiens. 1617, by Matthäus Merian

zeitgeist of the seventeenth century is an understatement, for his ideas and literary works influenced such seminal figures as Isaac Newton. Betty Dobbs has suggested that Maier inspired Newton "to dabble with his 'chemical' interpretation of myth and hieroglyph and study the older texts of the alchemical canon" (Dobbs as cited in Tilton, 2003, p. 7). Maier dedicated his life to the pursuit of alchemical knowledge and his works are riddled with religious and mythological allusions. His work and ideas figured prominently in Jung's hermeneutic understanding of alchemy. There seems to be a serendipitous kinship between the two men spanning across three centuries of time. In fact, another Dr. Carl Jung, presumably one of Jung's ancestors, was a seventeenth-century contemporary of Maier in Mainz, Germany. However, nothing else is known about the man (Jung, 1961, p. 233).

The Grand Peregrination

With the goal of attaining a single phoenix feather, Maier, a pilgrim in his story, sets out on a horizontal journey across the four continents, Europe, America, Asia, and finally Africa (Maier, 1617). Maier viewed the phoenix feather as a universal panacea, which he considered a "remedy for anger and sorrow" (para. 1). He associated each continent with one of the four Platonic elements: earth, water, air, and fire.

> Europe stands for earth, America for water, Asia for air, and Africa for fire; and earth cannot become air except through the medium of water; nor can water become fire except through the medium of air. I determined, then, to go first to Europe, which represents the grossest, and last to Africa, which represents the most subtle element.
>
> (para. 1)

Each continent could be viewed psychologically as a function of consciousness: Europe (sensation), America (feeling), Asia (thinking), and Africa (intuition). Jung (1955–1956a, para. 287) felt Africa corresponded to Maier's inferior function, which would place it the farthest from his ego consciousness (Figure 1.2).

During Maier's journey he hears rumors that the phoenix may be found near the Erythraean Sibyl, who Jung interpreted as an anima figure (1955–1956a, para. 287). After completing his travels in Europe, America, and Asia, Maier arrives at a crossroads marked by a statue of Mercurius with a silver body and a golden head. As Maier suggests, Mercurius's hand points the way to paradise. It is only at this juncture, when he begins to go south, that his journey assumes a surreal quality. This correlates to Jung's (1940, para. 222) observation that the inferior function often has a numinous aspect and is associated with the personality's inner soul image or anima.

Having traveled for 365 days, Maier reaches the Erythraean Sea at the end of July during "the intense heat" of summer (Maier, 1617, "Africa: Fire," para. 1). The Erythraean Sea is another name for the Red Sea which is geographically situated between the Arabian Peninsula and the horn of Africa. Besides the blazing heat,

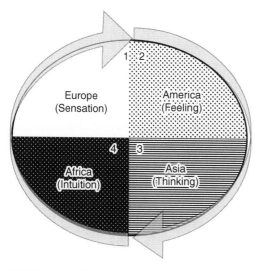

FIGURE 1.2   Typological Mandala. 2014, by Kiley Laughlin

the world begins to take on an irregular form to Maier who encounters exotic polymorphous creatures such as "satyrs, cynocephali, and semi-human beings" ("Africa: Fire," para. 1). Maier also reports that in that region of the Red Sea an animal is found with the name of *Ortus* (i.e., rising or origin). According to Jung,

> The Ortus is the alchemical "animal" which represents the living quaternity in its first synthesis. In order to become the ever-living bird of the spirit it needs the transforming fire, which is found in "Africa," that is, in the encounter with and the investigation of the fourth function and the animal soul represented by Ortus.
>
> (1955–1956a, para. 282)

Similarly, Maier (1617) believed that the legend of this creature referred to the phoenix, which was said to have originated in that region of the world. Jung (1955/1956a) viewed the Ortus as an analogue of the tetramorph mentioned in the book of Ezekiel, which combines features of the four fixed signs of the zodiac, and thus their corresponding element: Taurus (Ox/earth), Leo (Lion/fire), Scorpio (Eagle/water), and Aquarius (Angel/air) (1955–1956a, para. 285). One could say that the tetramorph is a uniting symbol par excellence that combines the four platonic elements into an amalgamated whole. Thus it seems that the phoenix, Ortus, and tetramorph all symbolize in varying degrees the Anthropos, the original man. When viewed psychologically these images suggest an individuated personality that has integrated the four psychological functions, no doubt a Herculean labor also symbolized by Christ on the four-points of the cross. In this way, the phoenix's death and rebirth seem to aptly symbolize Christ's death and subsequent return to the world, albeit in a transfigured body. To emphasize this point Jung turned to St. Ambrose who declared "Let this bird teach us by his example to believe in the resurrection" (Jung, 1955–1956a, p. 215). Elsewhere, Jung wrote "In order to understand the phoenix myth it is important to know that in Christian hermeneutics the phoenix is made an allegory of Christ, which amounts to a reinterpretation of the myth" (1955–1956b, para. 474).

Jung (1956/1963) thought that the African leg of Maier's journey represented the alchemist's arrival at the gateway to his inferior function, which as previously discussed seems to correspond to Maier's intuitive faculties.

> The fourth function has its seat in the unconscious. In mythology the unconscious is portrayed as a great anima, for instance Leviathan, or as a whale, wolf, or dragon. We know from the myth of the sun-hero that it is so hot in the belly of the whale that his hair falls out.
>
> (1955–1956a, para. 277)

Maier eventually encounters the Erythraean Sibyl, who suggests that he consult Mercurius regarding the whereabouts of the phoenix. She also provides the following instructions to Maier: "This Mercury you may expect to find somewhere near the seven mouths of the Nile; for he has no fixed habitation, but is to be found now in one of these mouths, and now in another" (Maier, 1617, "Africa: Fire," para. 1). Maier identifies the Erythraean Sybil with the same oracle that foretold the coming of Christ (cf. Jung, 1955–1956a, para. 277).

Maier resumes his journey and makes his way to Alexandria to explore the seven mouths of the Nile: the Bolbitic, Sebbenitic, Pelusian, Tanitic, Phanitic, Medesian, and the Canopic. At this point, Maier's journey shifts from a horizontal axis to a vertical one, to employ the spatial metaphor of the cross. Maier is now entering the unknown, plumbing the depths of his unconscious through contact with his anima and inferior function. The vertical motif is reminiscent of Christ's descent to Hell and eventual ascent to Heaven following his resurrection. The motif suggests a pending transformation of ego consciousness. Jung provided some helpful commentary on the vertical motif: "Ascent and descent, above and below, up and down, represent an emotional realization of the opposites, and this realization gradually leads, or should lead, to their equilibrium" (1955–1956a, para. 296).

En route to the Canopic mouth, Maier encounters an ancient Christian burial ground where each year on a certain day in May dead bodies gradually rise from their graves until they are completely visible to passers-by. The dead bodies then sink back again into their tombs (Maier, 1617). Interestingly, Maier's mention of the resurrected dead coincides with a dream that Jung described in his autobiography:

> In the dream I was coming from the city, and saw before me a similar lane with a long row of tombs. They were pedestals with stone slabs on which

the dead lay. They reminded me of old church burial vaults, where knights in armor lie out-stretched. Thus the dead lay in my dream, in their antique clothes, with hands clasped, the difference being that they were not hewn out of stone, but in a curious fashion mummified. I stood still in front of the first grave and looked at the dead in who was a person of the eighteen-thirties. I looked at his clothing with interest, whereupon he suddenly moved and came to life. He unclasped his hands; but that was only because I was look-ing at him. I had an extremely unpleasant feeling, but walked on and came to another body. He belonged to the eighteenth century. There exactly the same thing happened: when I looked at him, he came to life and moved his hands. So I went down the whole row, until I came to the twelfth century – that is, to a crusader in chain mail who lay there with clasped hands. His figure seemed carved out of wood. For a long time I looked at him and thought he was really dead. But suddenly I saw that a finger of his left hand was begin-ning to stir gently.

(1961, p. 173)

In addition to the obvious Christian allusions, the passages from both Maier and Jung suggest that there is something active in the unconscious that like a living rhizome stirs beneath the earth waiting to carry out its purpose. Jung noted, "As the 'Tabula smaragdina' shows, the purpose of the ascent and descent is to unite the powers of Above and Below" (1955–1956a, para. 288). Jung referred to this vertical process – ascending and descending – as a "transcension" or *transitus* and although he did not explicitly explain what it is, he suggests that its operative factor is none other than Mercurius (para. 288).

Ascent and Descent

Maier (1617) associated the seven mouths of the Nile to the seven planets known to the ancient world, which included the Sun and the Moon. Jung added that "The experience of the fourth quarter, the region of fire (i.e., the inferior func-tion) is described by Maier as an ascent and descent through the seven planetary spheres" (1955–1956a, para. 288). Reading this psychologically, the planetary spheres could be viewed as archetypal centers within the personality; as such the seven planets represent different archetypal qualities of the personality. This pic-ture accords with Jung's view: "The ascent through the planetary spheres meant something like a shedding of the characterological qualities indicated by the horo-scope" (para. 308).

Mercury stands out as an anomaly from the other gods in that he has "no fixed habitation" but can move freely throughout all of the spheres, or as Jung articu-lated: "Mercurius is the spiritus vegetativus, a living spirit, whose nature it is to run through all the houses of the planets, i.e., the entire Zodiac" (1955–1956a, para. 298). As Maier transits these planetary spheres, his personality ostensibly undergoes a transformation that is tantamount to an encounter with the gods within. Having opined that Maier's "exciting adventure has left us a psychological document which is a perfect example of the course and the symbolism of the individuation process" (1955–1956a, para. 297), Jung apparently believed that Maier was allegorizing his own journey toward wholeness and self-realization. Ultimately, Maier's peregrination seems to depict, in his search for the phoenix feather, a circumambulation of the self in superlative allegorical form.

While retracing his steps, Maier eventually finds Mercurius "where the people had at first appeared to know nothing about him" (1617, "Africa; Fire," para. 2). Maier does not specify at which mouth he located Mercurius, however, Tilton (2003, p. 230) suggested that it is the Tanitic mouth, corresponding to the planet Mercury. Mercurius welcomes Maier and imparts to him esoteric secrets. This hermetic knowledge is accompanied by Mercurius's disclosure of the location of the phoenix bird. Maier's apparent initiation into the arcana is an important supposition, which Jung aptly discerned: "Hermes hands over his art and wisdom to his pupil Maier and thus equips him to do something himself and to work with the aid of the magic caduceus" (1955–1956a, para. 305). The allegory takes on an anticlimactic turn when Maier learns that the phoenix is away for two weeks on another errand. Maier resolves to return home to Europe with the intention of someday returning to Egypt to discover the panacea as the remedy against anger and sorrow.

Secrets of the Phoenix and the Self

It seems strange that after having come so far Maier would abandon his quest and return to Germany without acquiring a phoenix feather. This conundrum merits further consideration. It would seem that the story's protagonist experiences a change of attitude after having realized that the true prize is the journey itself, which amounts to a sort of inner alchemical transformation. Jung implied that concealing the secret of the phoenix was a part of Maier's intent. Secrets after all imply a symbolic value. If this were not the case, there would be no point to keeping secrets and the heart of mystery would not create so much allure. Jung (1955–1956a, para. 312) provided some helpful commentary on this point:

> The essential thing is the hiding, an expressive gesture which symbolizes something unconscious and "not to be named" lying behind it; something, therefore, that is either not yet conscious or cannot or will not become conscious. It points, in a word, to the presence of an unconscious content, which exacts from consciousness a tribute of constant regard and attention. With the application of interest the continual perception and assimilation of the effects of the "secret" become possible.

Thus, the panacea of the phoenix as relief from sorrow and anger, seems synonymous with knowledge of the self, which is central to Jung's ideas of individuation and the transcendent function, the "continual process of getting to know the counterposition in the unconscious" (1955–1956a, para. 257). Jung (1955–1956a, para. 214) aptly articulated Maier's hard-won knowledge of the self:

> It is worth noting that the animal is the symbolic carrier of the self. This hint is borne out by modern individuals who have no notion of alchemy. It expresses the fact that the structure of wholeness was always present but was buried in profound unconsciousness, where it can always be found again if one is willing to risk one's skin to attain the greatest possible range of consciousness through the greatest possible self-knowledge – a "harsh and bitter drink" usually reserved for hell.

At the end of his journey, Maier realizes that the secret of the phoenix was with him all along and thus there was no need to await its return in Egypt. The secrets that Mercurius imparted to him appear to have altered his plans. Jung (1955–1956a, para. 312) discerned this possibility: "Let us assume that Maier's sudden silence is no mere accident but was intentional or even a necessity." Perhaps Mercurius helped Maier understand that the phoenix was actually not a thing but a living idea which he had possessed all along, a sort of inner desideratum. Jung (1955–1956b, para. 486) alluded to this point:

> It is characteristic of Maier's views that the idea of most importance is not Mercurius, who elsewhere appears strongly personified, but a substance brought by the phoenix, the bird of the spirit. It is this inorganic substance, and not a living being, which is used as a symbol of wholeness, or as a means towards wholeness, a desideratum apparently not fulfilled by the Christ-symbol.

The phoenix then could be viewed as a uniting symbol that can reconcile the opposites and create a sort of gnosis. Interestingly, Maier (1617) places the phoenix as the object of his journey rather than Mercurius, who fulfills his role as a psychopomp and revelator. Mercurius, as in the mythic tradition, acts as a guide to the alchemist on his peregrination. Thus, one could say that Mercurius constitutes the means of the peregrination whereas the phoenix suggests its *telos*.

There is a peculiar illustration in Jung's *Collected Works*, Vol. 12, *Psychology and Alchemy* that throws light on the symbolic relationship between Mercurius and the phoenix. The illustration is titled "The Mountain of the Adepts" (Figure 1.3) and depicts a statue of Mercurius at the apex of a mountain; the phoenix is buried within the mountain where Mercurius stands. The illustration indicates that the phoenix is buried, even hidden, within material reality and is the goal of the alchemical opus. The phoenix is shown perched atop the sun and the moon which suggests that it is produced through the Sol-Luna coniunctio, a union of opposites. In another illustration from *Psychology and Alchemy* (Figure 1.4), the phoenix image is elevated to the top of the alchemical sphere. Jung (1944b, para. 400) commented

FIGURE 1.3 The Mountain of the Adept. *Cabala*, 1654, by Stephen Michelspacher

that "The Phoenix on the sphere, cremating itself … is the sign of the multiplication and increase."

Tilton (2003, p. 231) presented a similar idea by suggesting that Maier "found the phoenix in the face of its absence." It seems that Maier purposefully wove into his allegory an obscure reference to the Egyptian hieroglyph for the phoenix depicted in *The Hieroglyphics of Horapollo*, which, according to Tilton (2003, p. 231), "indicates a traveler who returns from a long journey to his native land, again do the Egyptians draw a phoenix." In this way, Maier seems to be hinting that he himself has become a living symbol of the phoenix or, in Jungian terms, a vessel of the self. Jung (1955–1956b, para. 515) wisely observed that Maier

> found neither Mercurius nor the phoenix, but only a feather – his pen! This is a delicate hint at his realization that the great adventure had led to nothing beyond his copious literary achievements, whose merits would no doubt have gone unremembered had it depended solely on the spirit of the next three centuries.

Jung suggested that the real alchemical work takes place within the human personality, which supports the basic premise of Maier's allegory.

FIGURE 1.4 The Sequence of Stages in the Alchemical Process. Alchymia, 1606, by Andreas Libvius

Conclusion

Throughout this chapter I have sought to shed light on the similarities between some of Jung's key ideas and the major alchemical themes that are present in "A Subtle Allegory" (Maier, 1617). I have also suggested that Maier's peregrination through the four continents of the world could be viewed as a spatial metaphor of his personal psychology. In this way, one could view the four continents as figurative approximations of sensation, feeling, thinking, and intuition. Together, they not only comprise a quaternity but a three dimensional mandala projected onto the surface of the globe.

When Maier arrives at the Red Sea he begins to enter into *terra nigra* which marks the gateway to his inferior function: intuition. At this juncture of his journey, the peregrinating alchemist encounters the Erythraean Sybil who imparts special insights to him. It is important to note that without the Erythraean Sybil, Maier would not know where to look for Mercurius and would effectively be lost, which suggests that she orients him psychologically. Viewed another way, Maier's descent into Africa points toward the *nigredo* stage of the alchemical work, which is the "initial stage of the individuation process" (Jung, 1944c, para. 116). Thus, life itself could be seen as a grand peregrination wherein the individual is torn between inner and outer forces. Maier's alchemical treatise seems to allude to Jung's individuation process some 300 years before the advent of analytical psychology. If nothing else, Maier's peregrination suggests that knowledge of the total personality requires a figurative voyage through all four continents so that the ego may exercise all four functions of consciousness; and this is consistent with Jung's conclusions:

> The aim of the mystical peregrination is to understand all parts of the world, to achieve the greatest possible extension of consciousness … Not a turning away from its empirical "so-ness," but the fullest possible experience as reflected in the "ten thousand things" – that is the goal of the peregrination.
> (1955–1956a, para. 284)

Postscript

When I began researching the symbol of the phoenix there was no way I could have anticipated to what degree it would influence my own personal individuation journey. In January 2014, a representative from the California State Partnership Program contacted me to see if I was available to provide instruction to the Nigerian Navy. As a service-member in the California Army National Guard, I enthusiastically agreed to participate in the mission. The trip to Nigeria would include key leader engagements and a class on Jungian typology. Before departing, terrorism in Nigeria reached a flashpoint on April 15, 2014 when the Nigerian terrorist group Boko Haram kidnapped over 200 school girls, whose whereabouts, as of the time I am writing this chapter, are still unknown. In light of these developments, I was curious whether the trip would mean anything beyond matters of military affairs and international diplomacy.

Interestingly, the word *Nigeria* is derived from the Latin root for black, *niger*. Viewed through the lens of alchemy, one could associate Nigeria with the nigredo. Jung (1955–1956c, para. 646) pointed out that "The nigredo corresponds to the darkness of the unconscious, which contains in the first place the inferior personality, the shadow." I thought this peculiar because shadow figures in my dreams frequently appear as pitch-black native Africans, perhaps merely a way for my psyche to effectively contrast my persona and shadow.

The mission proceeded as planned and without incident in May 2014. However, on the final day of instruction, I looked up at the wall behind me and noticed the Nigerian Navy's emblem with the image of a phoenix. I was astonished by this meaningful coincidence, which seemed synchronistic. After further research I discovered that the Nigerian national symbol is a phoenix. Jung (1958, para. 660) hypothesized that "the archetypes possess the quality of 'transgressiveness'; they can sometimes manifest themselves in such a way that they seem to belong as much to society as to the individual; they are therefore numinous and contagious in their effects." I view the multiple occurrences wherein I stumbled upon the phoenix motif between January and May of 2014 as demonstrative of this phenomenon. These chance groupings of the phoenix motif, which culminated during my visit to Nigeria, seemed to run parallel to my intense study of the research topic.

Jung (1952, para. 827) noted a similar experience he had while researching the fish motif. He counted no fewer than six chance encounters with fish-related themes during one 24-hour period. Viewed this way, one could say that the synchronicity I experienced in Africa was predicated on my research of the phoenix symbol and suggests the constellation of an archetype which momentarily brought psyche and physis into a state the Chinese call *Tao*. That the archetype has both a psychic and physical aspect, or what Jung termed psychoid, suggests that consciousness has a unique function. For experience has shown that the conscious observer is not an isolated spectator but rather an active participant who unwittingly collaborates with the world at large. Consciousness seems to matter as much as matter does; in fact, the former and the latter could very well originate from the same thing, or what Jung called the *unus mundus* (1955–1956c, para. 622). In this way, the implications of the synchronicity hypothesis seem to stress a new ethic of individual responsibility and one could say that we all are pilgrims on a peregrination that moves us toward our own figurative phoenix.

References

Craven, J.B. (2003). *Count Michael Maier: His Life and Writings*. Berwick, ME: Nicolas-Hays.

Edinger, E. (1995). *The Mysterium Lectures: A Journey Through C.G. Jung's Mysterium Coniunctionis*. Toronto: Inner City Books.

Jung, C.G. (1911–1912/1952a). "The Song of the Moth," in *Collected Works*, Vol. 5, *Symbols of Transformation* (2nd edn). New York: Pantheon Book, Inc., 1956.

Jung, C.G. (1911–1912/1952b). "The Dual Mother," in *Collected Works*, Vol. 5, *Symbols of Transformation* (2nd edn). New York: Pantheon Book, Inc., 1956.

Jung, C.G. (1940). "Concerning Rebirth," in *Collected Works*, Vol. 9i, *The Archetypes and the Collective Unconscious* (2nd edn). Princeton, NJ: Princeton University Press, 1968.

Jung, C.G. (1944a). "The Symbolism of the Mandala," in *Collected Works*, Vol. 12, *Psychology and Alchemy*. New York: Pantheon Book, Inc., 1953.

Jung, C.G. (1944b). "The Work," in *Collected Works*, Vol. 12, *Psychology and Alchemy*. New York: Pantheon Book, Inc., 1953.

Jung, C.G. (1944c). "The Initial Dreams," in *Collected Works*, Vol. 12, *Psychology and Alchemy*. New York: Pantheon Book, Inc., 1953.

Jung, C.G. (1952). "Synchronicity: An Acausal Connecting Principle," in *Collected Works*, Vol. 8, *The Structure and Dynamics of the Psyche* (2nd edn). Princeton, NJ: Princeton University Press, 1969.

Jung, C.G. (1955–1956a). "The Personification of the Opposites," in *Collected Works*, Vol. 14, *Mysterium Coniunctionis* (2nd edn). Princeton, NJ: Princeton University Press, 1970.

Jung, C.G. (1955–1956b). "Rex and Regina," in *Collected Works*, Vol. 14, *Mysterium Coniunctionis* (2nd edn). Princeton, NJ: Princeton University Press, 1970.

Jung, C.G. (1955–1956c). "Adam and Eve," in *Collected Works*, Vol. 14, *Mysterium Coniunctionis* (2nd edn). Princeton, NJ: Princeton University Press, 1970.

Jung, C.G. (1958). "Flying Saucers: A Modern Myth of Things Seen in the Skies," in *Collected Works*, Vol. 10, *Civilization in Transition* (2nd edn). Princeton, NJ: Princeton University Press, 1970.

Jung, C.G. (1961). *Memories, Dreams and Reflections.* A. Jaffé (ed.), R. & C. Winston (trans.). New York: Vintage Books, 1989.

Jung, C.G. (2009). *The Red Book: Liber Novus*, S. Shamdasani (ed.), Philemon Series, Reader's edition. New York: W.W. Norton.

Maier, M. (1617). "A Subtle Allegory," in *Symbols of the Golden Table of the Twelve Nations.* Available at: www.levity.com/alchemy/maier.html (accessed August 18, 2016).

Tilton, H. (2003). *The Quest for the Phoenix: Spiritual Alchemy and Rosicrucianism in the Work of Count Michael Maier (1569–1622).* New York: Walter de Gruyter.

PART II

Native America

2

BORDER*LAND* CONSCIOUSNESS

Re-establishing Dialogue between the Western Psyche and the Psyche-Left-Behind

Jerome S. Bernstein

Introduction

From my Jungian perspective, the archetypal drama represented by the expulsion of Adam and Eve is at the heart of the Garden of Eden Story in the Hebrew Bible which is *the* foundational myth of Western civilization. I propose that the expulsion of Adam and Eve from the Garden of Eden for the "sin" of eating the fruit of the Tree of Knowledge *resulted* in the cleavage of species *Homo sapiens* from its pre-expulsion at-one-ness with Nature. What we have come to know as Western civilization and its brilliant offspring, science, and technology, was birthed at the cost of the Western psyche's forced split from Nature.

In Jung's last essay, written shortly before his death, he wrote the following:

> Nothing is holy any longer. Through scientific understanding our world has become dehumanized. [Our] immediate communication with nature is gone for ever …
>
> No wonder the western world feels uneasy, for it does not know how much … it has lost through the destruction of its numinosities … Its moral and spiritual tradition has collapsed and has left a *worldwide disorientation and dissociation*.
>
> (1961, paras. 585, 581, emphasis added)

That split from Nature ultimately has resulted in the Western psyche's overspecialization and dissociation, which in the present era threatens to take our species over the cliff of Global Climate Change toward annihilation. The symptoms of the latter are the commodification of the Earth and the resultant loss of the Western psyche's spiritual connection with itself and with all of life.

Euro-America has long projected mana onto the indigenous populations of the world, especially Native Americans, as if they had all the answers (Deloria, 1999).

Indigenous peoples do not carry the mana projected onto them. But they do have communication with Nature and can speak Nature's language. Theirs is a psyche that operates on laws and principles different from those of the Western psyche. I call this the Psyche-Left-Behind. It seems that what the Euro-American psyche is seeking is a re-connection and dialogue, a communion, with that psyche and through that, a reparative relationship with Nature in its natural sacralized, spirit-filled form (cf. Deloria, 1999).

This is a view supported by an increasing number of physicists doing research in quantum mechanics. Christophe le Mouël, a theoretical physicist, states (2014, pp. 25, 44–45)

> we report on modern studies on the quantum structure of cognition, which supports Jung's insight that there is an ineradicable level of indeterminism in the psyche, a creative place within us which places us in the vicinity of the wisdom of nature.

Dr. Le Mouël is referring to what Jung called the "psychoid dimension." His phrase, "ineradicable level of indeterminism in the psyche" carries many implications: that there is a level of mystery that cannot be "answered" through scientific method; that the nature of "psyche," a word which I distinguish from "mind," is not reducible to the brain or any other physical state of being; and that ultimately what we call "consciousness," cannot be isolated or defined mathematically and is therefore beyond the reach of physics.

The Psyche-Left-Behind

My reference to "the Psyche-Left-Behind," refers to the fact that in the beginning of the Genesis myth Adam and Eve were in an original state of at-one-ness with Nature, prior to their sin and subsequent expulsion. We have forgotten that our species was connected to a psychic state of at-one-ness with Nature before the Expulsion. Adam and Eve were expelled. However, that *pre*-expulsion psyche was not. And although the path out of the Garden of Eden has led to the kind of *Logos* left brain dominant Western psyche that we know, another dimension of psyche was "left behind" – and is still there, so to speak. This is the basis for Jung's term "dissociation" when referring to the "western world." Might Jung have been referring to the Western psyche's dissociation or split from the Psyche-Left-Behind, or what Dr. le Mouël refers to as "the wisdom of nature?" I believe that the Psyche-Left-Behind lives on in the surviving indigenous tribes, communities, *and* individuals in the wake of Western culture's genocide toward indigenous peoples. Is it Euro-Americans' intuitive sense that Native Americans carry a lost part of their own psychic roots that results in their projection of mana onto Native Americans?

Jung expressed it this way, "*We have been that mind, but we have never known it. [Through scientific understanding] we got rid of it before understanding it*" (1961, para. 591).[1]

In my view the collective unconscious, in a compensatory response to the crisis of Global Warming, appears to be pushing the Western psyche toward re-engagement with its psychic roots in Nature. What does that mean and how can we participate in bringing that about? One of the things that results from this re-engagement is the emergence of what I call "Border*land* consciousness." It is the latter that is the link for a re-engaged dialogue between the Western psyche and the "Psyche-Left-Behind." This chapter will focus on the nature of Border*land* consciousness and how it can bridge the Western psyche's dissociation leading toward a more consciously sane attitude and reparative approaches with regard to Global Warming.

Border*land* Consciousness

A somewhat exaggerated depiction of the dissociation of "the western world" that Jung refers to might look like this. As depicted here, the Western ego construct has no mediating transpersonal dynamic to hold in check its inflation, no spiritual force to communicate that it, the Western ego, did not give birth to itself.

In Figure 2.2 we see an ego that is being brought back into connection with the Self, *in spite of itself*. The two vertical arrows on the left, one ascending, one descending, depict a dynamic *that is in process* on a collective basis, not one that has happened and is complete. I wish to reiterate that this process is being *forced* onto the ego we saw in Figure 2.1 as an evolutionary compensatory response to the threat of annihilation of our species. The resultant new kind of consciousness is what I have called, Border*land* consciousness.

In May 2014, scientists in the Netherlands have proved the transference of quantum information from one physical space to another without moving the physical matter to which the information is originally attached (Pfaff et al., 2014).[2] In quantum physics, this process is known as "entanglement" and by extension provides a quantum portrayal of what I am referring to as the dynamic of

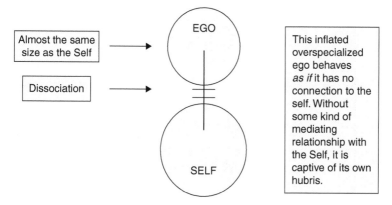

FIGURE 2.1 Dissociated ego–self relationship result in an ego that has become over-inflated and suicidal

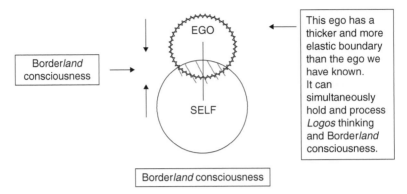

FIGURE 2.2 Emergent ego–self relationship resulting from the ego's reconnection with nature: Border*land* consciousness

Border*land* consciousness where an evolving and emergent ego can simultaneously hold and process *Logos* thinking and awareness emanating from what I call the Psyche-Left-Behind.

Because the language of Border*land* consciousness is that of <u>both</u> the *pre-* and *post*-expulsion psyche, I, as a post-expulsion member of our species, am stuck with speaking to you only in the language of *Logos* in this chapter. Therefore, rather than try to describe Border*land* consciousness in words, I think it would be better to *see* what one form of it looks like. A good portrayal of someone functioning in a state of Border*land* consciousness can be seen in the person of Anna Breytenbach in the video titled "The Animal Communicator." Readers are strongly encouraged to find a means of viewing the video in order to fully understand this chapter. The video is 52 minutes long, and the clip that is integral to this chapter begins at minute 8:12 and runs through to minute 12:40.

What I want you to notice is what Border*land* consciousness actually looks like on the face and body of someone while they are functioning in that psychoidal dimension. Also, notice Anna's explanation of how she enters that realm and the scientist's explanation of his understanding of the Border*land* realm. The voice that you hear first is that of a professional environmental reporter who is narrating the film.

This video portrays Border*land* consciousness between humans and animals. Ultimately, the critical transformative test will be human-to-human connection and dialogue between humans with all of Nature enabled through Border*land* consciousness.

Border*land* consciousness is not new on the individual level. It is thousands of years old, going back to the at-one-ness in the mythical *pre*-expulsion Garden of Eden. In more recent times, Border*land* personalities were seen as witches and heretics and burned at the stake. In today's world, many are seen as psychics or highly intuitive individuals; many are seen as neurotic, or even crazy. Border*land* consciousness becomes a relevant, and in my mind, an indispensable word and concept because it appears to be taking place on the collective level. Indeed, I believe that Border*land* consciousness will be the predominant form of human consciousness by the end of this century. Evolution of the psyche takes place at a much more rapid pace than biological evolution.

At the same time, this does not mean that by the end of the century everyone will be capable of what is shown in the video clip. Anna's is a cultivated skill derived from her growing awareness that she was capable of entering the psychoidal realm. The most important implication of Border*land* consciousness is the possibility of re-connection with Nature in its natural state, not the one that Western philosophy and science desacralized coming out of the seventeenth-century Cartesian Enlightenment.

On August 2, 2010, an astonishing and courageous article by two environmental scientists was published on the front page of *The Los Angeles Times*. The title of the article is, "The Earth Has Its Own Set of Rules." It reads, in part:

> The Earth has its own set of rules … solidly grounded in laws of physics and chemistry … Our anthropocentric economic model for interacting with the world ignores and is proving to be incompatible with Earth's rules, and is therefore on a direct collision course with them. To achieve a more accurate model of our relation to nature, we need to see ourselves as *part of nature*, governed by nature (not economics), beholden to nature for ecosystem services and subject to nature's disturbances. We need to view our existence in nature as dependent on numerous functions we are unable to perform ourselves, and without which we could not survive. Shortsighted anthropocentrism disrupts these functions to the degree that Earth will become uninhabitable for us.

The authors, however, do not tell us *how* to go about these life-saving adaptations they propose, beyond saying that the central task of ecology is to understand these conditions, processes, and rules and thereby understand the qualities and dimensions of this steady state. [Read more at: http://phys.org/news186859821.html#jCp]

On the one hand, they are correct, of course; on the other hand, their solution calls on our species' anthropocentrism to see and correct the errors of its own ways. The authors, however, have already asserted that it is our characterological anthropocentrism that is the source of the problem.

The pathological agent in the struggle for survival between Earth and our species is the Western ego construct's over-inflation. Unlike our lungs or kidneys, our ego construct is our only organ of consciousness. According to Jung and others, it is "disoriented and dissociated," a serious and potentially deadly pathological state. How can we rely on a dissociated ego construct to make our species submit to the rules of nature? After all, is not that how we arrived at this crisis in the first place?

Structure of Language and its Relationship to Psychic Structure

I have been emphasizing that the structure and character of the Western psyche is fundamentally different from that of the Native American psyche. One profound difference is the structure of the language characteristic of each psychic form. Western languages are *Logos*-based, binary, rigidly based in reason, linear and, importantly, *noun dominant*. As a result, these language structures tend to abstract experience and deal primarily with ideas and analysis. This puts space between the one speaking and the intended connection of the communication. It interposes abstract concepts and ideas in place of imaging and somatic understanding.

Oral Traditional Native American languages are metaphoric in structure, speak images, and are *verb dominant*; they are psychoidal in that they reflect and speak to archetypal dynamics, and reflect relationship with all of life. These characteristics of each psychic form are endemic to the languages themselves. Gregory Cajete, a Tewa Indian and Assistant Professor at the University of New Mexico's College of Education, in his book, *Native Science: Natural Laws of Interdependence*, speaking of the character of Native languages, writes the following:

> Language is more than a code; it is a way of participating with each other *and* the natural world ... At the deeper psychological level, language is sensuous, evocative, filled with emotion, meaning and spirit. Meanings are not solely connected to intellectual definition but to the life of the body and spirit of the speaker. In its holistic and natural sense, language is animate and animating, it expresses our living spirit through sound and the emotion with which we speak. In the Native perspective, language exemplifies our communion with nature rather than our separation from it.
>
> (Cajete, 1999, p. 72)

In a moment I will present some experiences to which Dr. Cajete refers. Before I do that I would ask that you read again the quote, but read it not with your mind. Read it with your body ...

And then, as I write the next few lines, read them with your sensuality and let them vibrate in your cells. Try not to think about meaning. Let the images that they generate be their meaning. Let yourself *experience* your experience.

> **How is your peace?**
> **Your culture is in the language**
> **Your voice is your medicine**
> **"Love" translates literally as: You are in my body and I am in your body**

The above lines are literal translations of Mohawk Indian expressions. Some of you, I am sure, were moved by, even pierced by, some of these phrases. I imagine that most of you did experience something on a bodily level and even beyond that, on a transpersonal level, perhaps even an experience of "ensoulment." For most of us, being touched by the Psyche-Left-Behind, is a powerful and an opening experience.

Before we get carried away, however, by the sensuousness of being touched by the Psyche-Left-Behind, I want to remind us that the subject of focus here is even more serious business – nothing less than the survival of our species.

So let us remember that Jung's specific observation in 1960 was "*Through scientific understanding* the western world has been left with a worldwide dissociation," (emphasis added). We are coming to learn in the twenty-first century that it is that same scientific understanding, co-opted by what other scientists refer to as "our anthropocentric economic model," that has played a central role in our species' dissociated suicidal behavior through our response to the Global Warming Crisis.

Global Warming Crisis

In this Age of the Global Warming Crisis, we are counting on that same scientific understanding to pull us back from the brink. Scientific understanding is both the source of the problem and simultaneously indispensable to its resolution. It is as if the latter is ignorant of itself as a major source of the crisis. Such can be the nature of dissociation. It is my proposition that resolution of the Global Warming Crisis is not possible alone by a profoundly dissociated ego construct. This is what two scientists, Mahall and Bormann, were saying in their article, "The Earth Has Its Own Set of Rules" (2010). So how does one go about healing a dissociated ego on the collective level?

In sharp contrast to the theme and tone of the article on Nature's Own Set of Rules, on May 2, 2015, an Op-Ed article titled, "Our Lonely Home in Nature," authored by Alan Lightman, a physicist who teaches Humanities at M.I.T., appeared in *The New York Times*. Apparently, Dr. Lightman's piece was provoked by the UN's International 5th Panel Report on Climate Change released earlier this year (2014). Many scientists refer to the conclusions of that report as "dire." Dr. Lightman ends his article with the following statement:

> In reacting to the report, we should not be concerned about protecting our planet. Nature can survive far more than what we can do to it and is totally oblivious to whether Homo sapiens lives or dies in the next hundred years. Our concern should be about protecting ourselves – because we have only ourselves to protect us.

The piece as a whole holds together, including Dr. Lightman's conclusion quoted here, when viewed primarily through the lens of a *Logos*-based psyche, with one exception.

Earlier in the piece Dr. Lightman asserts that we, Western civilization, have, and I quote him, a "… strongly felt kinship and oneness with nature …" Here, in this quote, is what dissociation looks like. "Kinship" does not include rape of the land; cutting down tropical rain forests in the name of building a new stadium to hold the World Cup competition; or polluting the air to the point where one cannot see from one corner to across the street; or blowing off the tops of mountains and suffocating the fish in the sea. Indeed, these practices are the very antithesis of kinship.

I want to be clear here, however: I am not making a clinical diagnosis of Dr. Lightman, whom I have never met. I am making a clinical diagnosis of the Western psyche and the prevailing scientific attitude. In Dr. Lightman's case, the dissociated and disoriented psyche of which Jung spoke, is speaking through the proxy of a particular scientist. Again, *my essential point here is psyche.*

Continuing in the same vein, Dr. Lightman goes on to say;

> Nature is purposeless. Nature simply is. We may find nature beautiful or terrible, but those feelings are constructions. Such utter and complete mindlessness is hard for us to accept. We feel such a strong connection to nature. But the relationship between nature and us is one-sided. There is no reciprocity. There is no mind on the other side of the wall. That absence of mind, coupled with so much power, is what [I find so frightening…]
>
> (Alan Lightman, *The New York Times* 5/2/14)

Inherent in my theory is the notion that *pre-expulsion* there was one psyche which was at-one with nature. That psyche most manifests in today's world through the Native psyche.

Post-expulsion, there were two – the Western psyche, and the Psyche-Left-Behind. The Western psyche was born at the cost of being cleaved and cleaving itself from at-one-ness with Nature. However, both are connected on a deep unconscious level in what Jung refers to as the collective unconscious. And central to my theory and ongoing and proposed research is that the Western psyche is seeking re-connection with the Psyche-Left-Behind by way of healing its dissociation and in the doing saving our species from suicide. How might this be done?

For the past several years I have been learning from a Navajo traditional medicine man, and from Frank Morgan, who is a colleague and "Navajo Cultural Translator." I have also enlisted the participation of Dr. Jeanne Lacourt, Professor of American Indian Studies at St. Cloud State University in St. Cloud, Minnesota. Jeanne is a Menominee Indian. She is also completing training through IRSJA to become a Jungian analyst.

Out of my forty plus years of dialogue with Hopi and Navajo people, the following idea emerged: If we could take statements regarding Global Warming made by Western scientists and politicians who appear to speak from the Western psyche's dissociation, and then filter those statements through the Oral Traditional Language structure of Native languages, then perhaps such an exercise could make connections between the two psychic dimensions. Some of you may have experienced what I am suggesting here with the earlier Mohawk translations that you read.

Recently I took specific excerpts from Dr. Lightman's Op-Ed piece quoted above and sent them to Frank Morgan and Dr. Lacourt, with the following request of each: First of all, I would like to know how … the paragraphs I suggested translate to your Native ears. I know you understand what he is saying in *Logos* language, but as a native, imagining even that you spoke no other language than your oral traditional language, what do you hear him saying and what does your internal response to what he is saying do to you? ... What does one do with that kind of attitude? Is there any hope of dialogue? And, most importantly, what would you say to him out of your traditional orientation, relationship with, and your own dialogue with Nature? (I am here thinking of the Menominee ceremony of feeding the language, [feeding the words]. What if you shared with him about that ceremony? What do you imagine his reaction would be?)

The second part of the experiment is: "What does your traditional self hear Earth and Nature as a whole saying to him through oral traditional language, expressed in English of course since we have no other common language? And, what do you hear him saying in response as part of dialogue – not who is right or wrong, but an honest exchange?" I report some of their responses:

Responses of Dr. Jeanne Lacourt and Frank Morgan

Dr. Lacourt to me: I think about how the elders on the reservation would simply thank him and not engage him further. To talk about the differences in the way we understand nature would require a meeting of minds and hearts. It would mean being open to another way of being in the world and to a deepening and changing in oneself, and in oneself with others ...

Now, if Lightman were actually engaged with members of the tribe and showed a genuine interest in learning, an open-ness, then another conversation is possible, but I would say the "conversation" might be less a dialogue and more an experiencing. By this I mean, we would take him into the woods and let him be there to listen, to hear, to be open, to be affected. We would invite him to social gatherings where he would hear people's stories of their experiences that illustrate relationships with animals and with nature, that describe living in accordance with her ways, that explain our living dialogue with nature ...

I am not sure that words alone could adequately convey what experience can. If I were to actually have a conversation with Lightman, I am afraid the academic in me would take over as a way to talk to him in his own "language" in the hopes that he'd more readily "get it." One can never underestimate the power of a dominant language, and here, I acknowledge that I would be mistaken. I imagine that Lightman would not take me seriously were I to say something about listening to how the birds change their song when the weather changes, or even describing a ceremony to feed language. So, I would have to use English and recognize that it is not adequate and does not really say what Menominee can.

One is reminded here of a quote from Vine Deloria, Jr.:

> Western science, following Roger Bacon, believed man could force nature to reveal its secrets; the Sioux simply petitioned nature for friendship.
>
> (Frontispiece: C.G. Jung and the Sioux Traditions: Dreams, Visions, Nature, and the Primitive)

When you say that nature is mindless, why is it important that nature [have] a mind? Is this the only way you know to connect with nature? Can you imagine that the mind is not in charge? What about letting the mind go and being open to a different way? Can you imagine that? It requires more of you; more than just your mind. It requires trust, humility, being vulnerable. Nature has her own way, her own language. We have to learn it, be open to another knowing, be respectful and thankful in the process, and respond. This is gift. We are not in charge.

Frank Morgan to Dr. Lightman: It is the human beings who are destructive. They have placed dangerous materials between earth and sky. They have set off powerful explosions in the earth and above the earth. They have taken part of the earth that was forbidden – it is called yellow earth[3] ... They do not ask for permission. They level mountains to get at black earth ... There is just no end to the kinds of things that are done by the people that is hurtful and damaging to nature.

Dr. Lightman is correct: there is reciprocity in the people's relationship with nature. Considering what people do to nature what *should* be expected in return. What have the people given to nature that is good? People who study and research often state when you put junk into computers it gives you junk [back]. I also listen to medicine men who treat patients affected by the spirit of earth. They say that the earth is extremely stubborn. When there is a conflict with earth, it does not forgive unless one offers the required exchange of valuables ceremonially. She is unforgiving.

Mr. Lightman says that nature is mindless, does [not] have mind, it has no way to think. It is not our friend and it is not harmful or helpful. Many human beings have placed themselves away from nature, and do not accept the consciousness and living entities with nature. Everything is conscious and this reality is not acceptable to them. They have a feeling that there is consciousness but they deny it. When things in the natural world interact, they do so according to a pattern no more, no less. They have laws for how they exist and produce things. Things are energized and there is movement like all the cycles in nature including water, earth, seasons, day and night, and all of these things are consciousness. Without consciousness there is no movement.

People are not betrayed. We did not follow the principles of harmony and relationship with everything and there are severe consequences now. The writer is looking at this from emotions only and it has no thinking or reasoning.

Dr. Lacourt to me: You asked what my internal response to what he is saying does to me? Does it make me angry, dismiss him? When I read his words, I have mixed feelings. First I feel sadness and then a desire (a responsibility) to share with him some stories. I can imagine asking him to come visit the reservation. I can imagine saying to him that his is one way of thinking about nature and there are others too, and that maybe the others have their truths to consider. I would want to tell him the story about my father and what happened to him because he killed his brother, the bear. I would want to tell him about a time in our tribe's history when tornados hit only non-Indian houses, I would want to tell him more stories about my relatives' experiences with animals and have him see how my mother's current husband talks to animals, how they listen, how birds land on his shoulder and head and how squirrels tell him when they are hungry. I would want to tell him about how my grand mother knew bird songs and what they seemed to be saying. I would want him to hear the loons on the lake and see if he could distinguish them from one another … I would like him to hear how the language sometimes mesmerizes. I would like to show him special places deep in the woods that take you to another dimension. I would like for him to hear the drum.

I asked both Frank and Jeanne to imagine how the Earth might respond if they were to inform it of what Dr. Lightman wrote in his article. Their respective responses follow:

Frank Morgan: I communicate with the Earth in a way I would not talk with a human person. I would state a prayer at dawn to introduce myself and give an offering of corn pollen. I would say in my prayer that a man, a Bilagaana, says that nature has not been kind and beneficial to the people living in the North American continent. He says nature betrays the people and causes them harm that they do not deserve. Show me what I can explain to him, Earth, my mother. You are the mother of living things on your physical body. You give us life and sustain us. Life is a sign that is inscribed on your being. I want peace and harmony. Harmony is endowed upon all things.

Earth communicates by visual and audible signs. I close my eyes and wait. Soon there is a vibration coming from all four directions. The vibrations turn to audible sound. It is a moaning sound as if it was coming from a wounded person. Now Earth is visible to me and she has sharp things like claws made of powerful elements growing from her surface …

The visions and sounds stop. I hear a bluebird and scream of an eagle. I open my eyes and I am still standing with my corn pollen bag. I am thinking about this vision. How do I interpret them? My mind focuses on Hózhó. Everything goes to equilibrium but at the cost of things being eliminated, the harmful elements are taken away, far away to the north never to return. In the meantime all things maintain [a] blessed state on Earth.

Dr. Lacourt: I imagine nature saying to him:

> "You need to get to know me. Right now you are far away from yourself."
> I can imagine his response would be one of confusion. He might not even
> know how to respond to this or what to do. He might just dismiss the idea.
> But, just *maybe* he would wonder and be intrigued with understanding how
> knowing nature is linked to knowing himself. He might ask what that means
> … I might share a story about my having learned about "seeing" from watch-
> ing beavers in the lake and that learning about seeing helped me see myself in
> relation to others. I'd wonder just how far away from himself he is? Is he so
> far away that even taking in other peoples' stories would be dismissed? Would
> he simply write off our stories as mere primitivism? Is there any opening in
> himself to relate? Maybe he has a story to tell *that can be listened to in another
> way <u>and told back to him differently — through a native lens?</u> Perhaps we can meet in
> our stories?*

These last statements from Jeanne summarize the goal of our research: that is for the *two psyches* to meet, touch, and be touched by one another, through their stories. Earlier I had quoted the Mohawk saying, "Your culture is in the language." I would add to that saying that psyche is in the language as well.

The goal here is healing a collective dissociation and disorientation. To provide a ground, a language, an image, a hearing of oneself through lost spirit, and to be opened to the possibility of re-connecting with a part of our soul left behind. Then perhaps we, Western civilization, can begin to hear some of Earth's rules as well as, *not instead of*, our own.

The Nature of Polemic

My intention in this research is to bring together the two psyches for, in Jeanne's word, a conversation, and ultimately an *experience* of what the Psyche-Left-Behind looks and feels like, and most particularly what openings may occur for healing of our dissociated ego construct. That, of course, means bringing together Global Warming deniers and Natives; physicists and environmentalists and ecopsychologists who sometimes can be as rigid as the deniers; educators, the media, politicians, venture capitalists, and corporate hierarchy. *Webster's Revised Unabridged Dictionary* defines "polemic" as: Gr. warlike, fr. war: cf. F. polémique and as:

- Polemic: an argument or controversy.
- Polemic: of or pertaining to controversy; maintaining, or involving, controversy; controversial; disputative; as, a polemic discourse or essay; polemic theology.

I am talking here about research and about influencing and transforming the *nature of polemic.* "Polemic," in today's world is not benign; it is too often deadly. It results in starvation and the death of tens of thousands of people; it paralyzes governments and starts wars. "Polemic" threatens the very survival of our species.

We do not know the outcome or even if the hypotheses of the research are feasible. There is only one way to find out and that is to *do the work.* That is the next phase in our effort, to find the funding to do this work.

The exercise described above wherein Frank Morgan and Jeanne Lacourt began a filtering of Dr. Lightman's words through the indigenous psyche and oral traditional language structure was a beginning. The research model contemplated would perform several iterations of such filtering of the subject's words so that polemic would be *distilled out* – not deleted – of their verbatim statements. The "end product" would be the meaning-*experience* of the concept being conveyed, absent the disputation which obscures both meaning and experience. For example, one would be left with the notion of "kinship" rather than the arguments around kinship that Dr. Lightman makes in his Op-Ed piece. The outcome – *filtered through an oral traditional psychic frame – would take one to an exchange around the meaning-experience of "kinship" as understood/experienced through the indigenous psychic frame and thus reinfusing the concept with eros and spirit, similar to the experience of the Mohawk expressions referenced above. The research objective would be to ascertain how and in what way such a process/exercise would impact the writer(s)/discussants and the initial polemic.*

Research requires outcome measures. There are many ways to assess differences that result from applying the research model outlined above. If outcome measures do show differences through behavior, then my expectation is that some of those differences would also show through brain wave studies.

Conclusion

I will conclude now with a quote from Alan Lightman's article:

> With the recent work of the Kepler spacecraft, searching for planets favorable for life, we can estimate that only about one millionth of one billionth of 1 percent of the material of the visible universe exists in living form. From a cosmic perspective, we and all life are the exception to the rule.

Dr. Lightman's statement leaves me dumbstruck with awe and a profound sense of humility and responsibility. From the perspective of the Psyche-Left-Behind, I imagine its response to Dr. Lightman's statement would look like this:

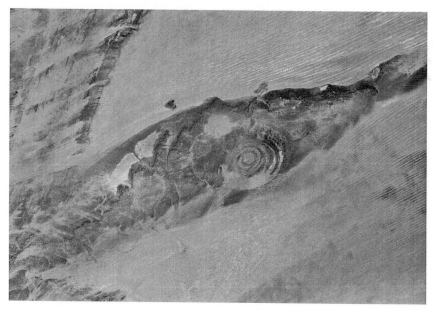

FIGURE 2.3   NASA/GSFC/MITI/ERSDAC/JAROS, and US/Japan ASTER Science Team

This formation is known as "The Eye of Africa." It is a natural formation in what is now Mauritania. It is 31 *miles* in diameter. Only with the advent of sub-orbital space flight in June of 1965 was it perceptible as Earth's eye *peering back at Man*. It would seem that the Eye both demands reciprocity and sparks it within the observer. It is as if the Eye poses the question: "What is it about your species that you think you can ravage me as if I were lifeless, as if I had no spirit, as if it did not hurt, as if it did not matter?

"It does."

Notes

1   Also see, "Participation Mystique in Peruvian Shamanism" by Deborah Byron in *Shared Realities: Participation Mystique and Beyond*, edited by Mark Winborn (2014) for a similar view through the lens of South American Shamanism.
2   John Markoff, *The New York Times*, May 30, 2014, page B3, "A Step Toward Winning a Dispute with Einstein."
3   The reference to "yellow earth" is to "a type of uranium obtained from leach solutions, in an intermediate step in the processing of uranium ores" (Wikipedia).

References

Byron, D. (2014). "Participation Mystique in Peruvian Shamanism," in M. Winborn (ed.), *Shared Realities: Participation Mystique and Beyond*. Carmel, CA: Fisher King Press.

Cajete, G. (1999). *Naïve Science: Natural Laws of Interdependence*. Santa Fe, NM: Clear Light Publishers.

Deloria, P.J. (1999). *Playing Indian*. New Haven, CT: Yale University Press.

Jung, C.G. (1961). "Healing the Split," in *Collected Works*, Vol. 18, *The Symbolic Life* (2nd edn). London: Routledge and Kegan Paul, 1993.

Le Mouël, C. (2014). "Self and the Paradox of Free Will," in *Psychological Perspectives, A Quarterly Journal of Jungian Thought*, Vol. 57, No. 1, Philadelphia, PA: Taylor and Francis.

Lightman, A. (2015). "Our Lonely Home in Nature," in Op-Ed. Article, *The New York Times*, May 2, 2015.

Mahall, B.E. & Bormann, F.H. (2010). "The Earth Has Its Own Set of Rules," in *Los Angeles Times*, March 2, 2010.

Markoff, J. (2014). "A Step Toward Winning a Dispute with Einstein," in *The New York Times*, May 30, p. B3.

Pfaff, W. et al. (2014). "Unconditional Quantum Teleportation Between Distant Solid-State Quantum Bits," in *Science*, Vol. 345, No. 6196, pp. 532–535. Washington, DC: Science Journals.

3

SEEING THE FOREST FOR THE TREES

Birthing Symbolic Life

Jeanne A. Lacourt

Author's Note

This chapter weaves a personal and cultural story with Jungian concepts in an attempt to share with readers my sense of living a symbolic life grounded in nature and community. I presented this chapter at the International Conference, *Rebirth and Renewal*, of the International Association of Jungian Studies in June, 2014 in Phoenix Arizona. At this presentation it was important to me that the audience actually sees images of the forest and the reservation, those places that gave, and continue to give, birth to my living a symbolic life. I incorporated a variety of pictures and short movie clips throughout the presentation that brought the audience to the reservation and directly into the forest with me. While this chapter cannot accommodate the many photos and movie files I displayed, the readers are, nonetheless, invited to imagine their own "inner forest" (or other landscape) where they can go to better know their own inner lives.

Introduction

About a year ago in a conversation I was having with a colleague, she uttered the phrase "living the symbolic life." These words played over in my mind like a song that just would not leave. I found myself asking what this means *to me*, to be living a symbolic life. Pondering this idea, I instinctively knew I would come back to it again and again as I continue to delve the depths of psyche. As an indigenous woman I recognize that living the symbolic life asks me to be open to another way of living and being in the world. For instance, following the Menominee kinship system, because my father was born into the bear clan, I too would follow this line and the bear would be considered my brother. Jungians might argue that the bear *symbolically represents* my brother, and many anthropologists and other scholars will argue this as well, but to the Menominee the bear is, quite literally, our brother. We are related. This familial relationship brings with it particular responsibilities whereby tribal members will declare: "The people who come from the Bear and the Bear's brothers are responsible for protecting the earth. This is not an individual responsibility" (Davis, 2000, pp. 51–53). Marshall Pecore, a head Menominee forester, elaborates this connection the Menominee have with the earth when he writes (1992, pp. 12–16) "It is said of the Menominee people that the sacredness of the land is their very body, the values of the culture are their very soul, and the water is their very blood." So living a symbolic life isn't *just* symbolic. We are summoned to accept responsibility for our place, for ourselves, and for our other non-human relatives. Our future, our survival, depends on knowing our connection with earth, place, animals, and those with whom we live and build relationships.

Reflecting on the theme of the IAJS conference, *Rebirth and Renewal*, and the place where the conference took place: Phoenix, Arizona, naturally the image of the phoenix rising from her ashes to start life anew came to mind. At the same time, I could not help but wonder about the other animals that inhabit the desert-like land of the southwest. There are stories that live there, that have been birthed there, and that are reborn into our lives with their every retelling. I questioned who was there to tell the stories that live in that place. Vine Deloria, Jr. (1999a, p. 252) reminds us that "every feature of a landscape has stories attached to it." Having not grown up and learned the teachings born to a dry, hot, desert-like climate, I instead turn to that place which informs me: the forest. For me, it is in the forest and on the rivers and lakes, where teachings and instructions abound. It is here, in this place, where I am reborn with each visit.

We are the Forest

Jung (1947, Vol. 1, p. 479) wrote, "Why not go into the forest for a time, literally? Sometimes a tree tells you more than can be read in books." Following Jung's advice, I invite you to journey with me into the forest, the deep woods that the Menominee Indian Tribe of Wisconsin has ministered to for countless generations. These are the woods that have sustained us through our hardest times and continue to be our home today. We are the woods. It is in these woods and in this place that I come to know myself more deeply. It is to these woods and to this place that I turn for guidance and instruction, and it is from these woods and from this place that I am renewed and transformed.

The journey into place, be it forest, desert, plains, coastal, or other area, is demanding and requires time. It compels us to be open to another way of being in the world, a way that asks us to slow down, to listen, to pay attention, and to be willing to be changed. Ultimately, it transforms. Jerome Bernstein (2005) eloquently captures the sense of what it takes to be attentive to place when he states, "We see and hear what we are open to noticing."

To the Menominee the forest is our special place. It gave birth to our origin story. This story describes how the bear and other forest animals transform to become the first Menominee people and establish our first clan systems. The story (Davis, 2000, pp. 50–51) relates how,

> At a special place, Mi'nika'ni se' pe (Menominee river), Masha' Ma'nido (Great Mystery) created numerous beings called manidos or spirits, giving them forms of animals and birds. Near a spot where the river's waters run into the Bay-In-spite-of-itself, Awaehsaeh, a Great Light Colored Bear emerged from underground and started traveling up the river. When Masha' Ma'nido saw that the Bear was still an animal, he determined to allow the Bear to change his form. The Bear was pleased at what Masha' Ma'nido was going to grant him. So Bear changed into a human and became the first Menominee, though keeping his light skin.
>
> The Great Ancestral Bear traveled along the river and after awhile found that he was alone. Looking up to the sky, he saw a great Golden Eagle, Kine'u, circling overhead. He decided to call to the Golden Eagle and said: "Kine'u, come down and be my brother." Thereupon Kine'u descended, changed into a human, and became the brother of the Bear.
>
> The two Brothers then traveled together. While they continued traveling up the river, they pondered on whom they would call upon next to become their Brothers. While considering, they saw a Beaver approaching. When they met, Beaver requested to be taken into the totem of the Thunderer. But, being a woman, was called Nama'kukiu' (Beaver Woman), and was adopted as the younger Brother of the Bear. As Beaver woman, she was equal to all her brothers.
>
> As the journey continued the Bear saw a stranger, Noma'eu (Sturgeon) and adopted him as a younger brother. Bear, fatigued, sat near a waterfall and from beneath emerged Moqwai'o, Wolf, and Mos, and from the sky flew Ota'tshia, Crane. All changed into human form. One day the Bear told his brothers to go on separate journeys. Through their travels, each met other animals and birds and each adopted some of them as younger brothers. These younger brothers changed into humans, and all together became the first Menominee people.[1]

Whether it be our orators and protectors of the earth (bear), our fighters for freedom and justice (eagle), our teachers of hunting and gathering (wolf), our builders and artists (crane), or the guardians of our community (moose), these animals and the forest they live in are significant in Menominee history and culture and have been physically and symbolically present throughout my life. Animals and our shared environment are crucial to how I live in the world and how I make sense of my life. Stories of these animals and how I experience them connect me to a life larger than my own.

Transformation

Jungians are likely to recognize the theme of transformation in the Menominee origin story. The great ancestral bear is accorded the *privilege* to change its form from animal to human, as are the other manidous (spirit beings). This transformation ultimately creates the first five major kinship clans of the Menominee Nation. They instruct our social order, our duties to the tribe, and our relationship to one another:

> from the Eagle to the Beaver Woman to the Wolf, all became brothers to the Bear – to earth. Thus, the Menominee have a special relationship with the earth. Almost without exception tribal members see themselves, even if their circumstances are unpleasant and destructive, as a people who protect the earth, the forest, and its creatures. If they fail in this duty, then they have failed as Indians, as human beings.
>
> (Davis, 2000, p. 102)

This act of transformation places spirit in the center of life, referred to as "soul" or "anima" in Jungian psychology; as that inner self-regulating movement that changes of its own volition, in its own time. In a sense, it is nature presenting itself to the world in a form that best suits its environment. Tribal elders and those living a more traditional *mythos* would agree with Deloria (1999b, p. 102) when he explains, "there is no essential spiritual/intellectual difference between people and animals." In fact, many elders in Indian communities are quick to add that "of all the createds, of all our relations, we two-leggeds alone seem to be confused as to our responsibility toward the whole" (Tinker, 1996, p. 158).

Being raised on the reservation and in the woods allowed me to see how connected we are to one another and how transformation occurs naturally. By assisting in hunting and gatherings and attending cyclical rituals and ceremonies, I came to gain an understanding of my relationship to place and to others. "Historically, Indians believed that they lived between the physical and spiritual worlds ... [songs, dances, and] ceremonies were supposed to help keep the people attuned to the rhythms of the spiritual world" (Deloria, 1999a, p. 102). When we dance, we dance in the woods. Keeping in step with the rhythm of the drum, and in that attunement the dancers become the bear, become the wolf, and become the butterfly. In ritual and ceremony the beat of the drum connects us with the natural rhythms of the earth. When we celebrate, we pray among the trees and other spirit beings. Some of our oldest ancestors are standing there, tall and proud, watching over us. Our relationship to ourselves, to our place continually emerges and is always in process. We transform into becoming. We are living our spirit.

Gregory Cajete, a Tewa scholar, (1994, p. 83) writes "Indian people traditionally understood the human psyche and the roots of human meaning as grounded in the same order that they perceived in Nature." In the small village where I grew up, we were reminded of our relationship to the natural world everyday. For instance, there are signs throughout the reservation reminding us of our relationship to animals, trees, water, rocks, and other life forms. We refer to the animals as our brothers, the trees our ancestors, the rocks our grandfathers, and other life forms our relatives. One of our legends tells of a young Menominee man who became a rock, "Spirit Rock." Very briefly, the story tells that a young man *dreamed* he and seven friends went off in search of Mä'näbus (a culture hero). When they found him, they were each granted a request. Six of them asked to be successful hunters, warriors, and leaders; but one asked for eternal life, which angered Mä'näbus. Mä'näbus then turned the young man into a stone telling him his people would last as long as the stone. This stone is now an "historical marker" on the reservation. At one time it stood more than 5 feet tall. Today Spirit Rock is not quite 12 inches. People place offerings on Spirit Rock with prayers that the Nation will continue. Spirit Rock reminds us to take our dreams seriously, to be humble and not ask for too much, to recognize our limitations, and to think ahead for our future generations yet unborn. It also speaks to a universal desire for immortality and an archetypal fear of death. We are the philosopher's stone, worked on and worked through, always in the process of becoming.

The nicknames we carried as children also reminded us of our connection to the natural world. These names were often based on attributes seen in nature or in animals. In my family, we called my brother Moose, my sister Turtle, and I honored the name Turkey. We understood that we were not above nature. We were reminded in our names, in the places we went, and in our stories, that while we are *on* the earth, we are also *of* the earth. It is not only the Menominee who understand this. Lame Deer suggested that, "as the Sioux get older their faces begin to reflect the landscape on which they live, the wrinkles of their faces resembling the rolling plains and Badlands of the Dakotas" (Deloria, 1999c, p. 270). Like alchemists who cultivate a relationship with their work in metals, Native people intimately relate to their homeland: they become the land. It should therefore come as no surprise that "those who have the deepest cultural connection to American soil would be among those most deeply affected by the modern, technological devastation of the land" (Tinker, 1996, p. 153). One need only see the ill effects the Navajo suffer from the uranium mines on their lands, the increase in diabetes among the Pima and Tohono O'odham, in part, from clean waters being channeled away from their lands. Native people seem to suffer from health issues in similar ways as the land suffers from neglect. I would not be surprised to learn if a correlation exists between the loss and destruction of our natural spaces with the increases we see in mental illness and other health issues.

The Menominee have always been known for the great care they take of the trees of the forest. Unlike our European farming neighbors, who indiscriminately clear cut acres of trees, home to countless species relying on what the forest provides, the Menominee adhere to a cyclical pattern that follows the sun's path when determining which trees can be taken. Elder Joseph Frechette would instruct:

> Start with the rising sun and work toward the setting sun, but take only mature trees, the sick trees, and the trees that have fallen. When you reach the end of the reservation, turn and cut from the setting sun to the rising sun, and the trees will last forever.
>
> (Spindler, 1971, p. 201)

This respectful method works so well that the Menominee are known worldwide today for their sustainable forestry. In fact, we have more timber in our forests today than we did over 100 years ago. Our forest, our relationship with the trees, has sustained us for generations. In the 1950s when the US government passed the Termination Act, a policy that devastated the tribe, it was our trees and our mill that carried us through that very hard time. We knew our place well and knew that we had enough resources and diversity of resources that they would sustain us. The one restaurant we have on the reservation is called "Forest Island," owing its name from the *island of trees* that starkly contrasts with the surrounding farm fields when the reservation is seen from an aerial perspective.

Differentiation

Knowing a place well requires one to be able to differentiate: to sort out this from that. Jung pointed out that "tribal peoples as yet unadapted to industrialized society retain certain highly differentiated sensitivities no longer available to Western man" (Spindler, 1971). Learning to differentiate in the forest takes skill, keen observation, and heightened sensitivity. In the woods, one needs to be able to tell the trees apart from one another. We know our hemlock from elm, our Norway from spruce and pine. We know which burn fast, which burn long, and which burn hot. We are able to distinguish their unique smells. We understand when to take their bark without killing them and note which barks to use for baskets and which are best for strong ties. We recognize those trees for building houses from those for building ships. One comes to know which plants grow in the dense forest and which flourish in open areas. We distinguish plants for healing from those that will kill us with their poison.

Samuels, Shorter, and Plaut (2007, p. 45) write that differentiation "is a natural and conscious psychological undertaking, … a person dependent on his projections has little recognition of *what* he his and *who* he is." Much like knowing the woods well, analysts too come to know how to differentiate their analysand's unique complexes from their transference, their persona from projection. The analyst ultimately determines if what they say is likely to heal or wound. They pay attention to detail. Without this fine-tuning and sensitivity to differentiation, an analysand can get confused and frightened. Lost even, if we are unfamiliar with our environment or the landscape in which we work. Sometimes knowing your place in the woods requires you to retrace your footsteps in order to take you back from where you've come. Other times it might require creating a mental map you can call upon when in need. Clinically this might look like revisiting our past to better know ourselves in the present or "sticking with the image," as archetypal analyst James Hillman would insist. Keen observation and differentiation are necessary processes when our environment is constantly changing. Psyche, like nature, demands our continual attentiveness.

When you are raised near the forest one of the first teachings you learn is NEVER go into the woods alone. This makes sense. "The forest is a place of loneliness, entanglement, healing, regression, loftiness, and obstruction, spontaneous growth and continuous decay" (Ronnberg & Martin, 2010, p. 118). In fairy tales, the forest is often viewed as the unconscious, a place one best not go into alone. Children in fairy tales live at the edge of the forest and wander into it as if caught in a daydream … and so the story begins. It is all too simple to get lost in the woods. You can lose your bearings and not find your way out, losing yourself. When in the forest it is easy to feel small and young and vulnerable. It can feel as though there is no end to the forest, that it is eternal. In the forest everything is alive. Animals are everywhere, often not seen unless you know how to see them. Sounds abound, a snap of a branch, the rustling of leaves, and sounds that cannot be named. These can call forth our deepest fears, those shadowy places we dread to know. Even Artemis wasn't alone in the forest. She traveled with her band of nymphs and hunting dogs and carried bow and arrow for protection. In literature and myths, forests are both enchanted and dangerous, places of refuge and places where monsters and witches are encountered. The hero enters the forest bravely, has challenging adventures, finds his way through, albeit with difficulty, and comes out transformed.

Analysts courageously go with their analysands into their forest. They do not let them go there alone. Together they meet witches and wolves and wicked winds; they form relationships with fairies and monsters who lurk in the deep, dark shadows of their own inner woods. They assist their clients in differentiating fear from anxiety, aggression from assertiveness, madness from sanity. Ironically, forest fires are necessary for new growth to occur and analysts are challenged to become alchemists who must tend the fire with knowledge and delicate care. Psyche, like forest, is richly diverse. If we can be keenly observant to how our inner creatures respond to life of their own volition, in their own rhythm and cycles, we will know our wild forest within. Not everything needs taming. The forest does not need to be made into organized farmland.

Direct Relationship

I recall a time when I became acutely aware of how trees and forest deeply influenced me. It happened one day when I was walking to class as a graduate student at the University of Wisconsin-Madison when I painfully realized how integrated trees were in my psyche. As a struggling student, I did not own a car and so I walked two miles to campus every day. One particular day while walking, I noticed that city tree crews were out trimming the trees that lined the streets and sidewalks. Rows of healthy full branches lay lifeless on the sidewalk where I was walking. For blocks I had to carefully step over these limbs and when I looked up at the trees, I saw clean shaved off spots where branches used to be. The trees looked wounded. By the time I reached campus I felt sick to my stomach. In class, I recall having a discussion on the book *How Institutions Think* by Mary Douglas (1986) and how we were discussing the nature of institutions, their 'natural' structure in relation to human knowledge. I remember asking a question about our understanding of the nature of Douglas' theory and having my question, like a dead branch, fall on deaf ears. So still and silent was the classroom that day that even the professor looked uncomfortable and not knowing how to proceed. All day long I just was not myself. By the end of the day as I was preparing to walk back to my apartment, I instinctively chose another route to take. I recall thinking to myself that this was quite a curious thing I was doing by taking an alternative, *longer* route home. I was tired and hungry. It was not until I crossed one block, looked to my left, and saw again the row of branches lying on the ground that it hit me. These branches were like my relative's limbs lying in pieces before me. There was no respect to this method of cutting, as I had grown up knowing. Dismemberment is what I saw. I became overwhelmed with a sadness so acute that it can come back today as powerful as the moment when I first experienced it. Much more, I painfully understood in that moment that "the language of home," my natural, instinctive way of communicating, did not translate well outside of the reservation. In a split second, I saw with great clarity the disconnectedness I had been experiencing since I left the reservation. The words of Zitkala-Sa (1959, p. 97) flooded my thoughts, she said:

> Like a slender tree, I had been uprooted from my mother, nature and God. I was shorn of my branches, which had waved in sympathy and love for home and friends. The natural coat of bark which had protected my oversensitive nature was scraped off to the very quick. Now a cold bare pole I seemed to be, planted in a strange earth.

On each block, alongside the dismembered trees were bare telephone poles supporting long wires to connect us "when long distance is the next best thing to being there." What a contradiction, I thought, that a tree now void of its ability to communicate naturally should be used as support for lines of communication for we two-leggeds. The imposed outer transformation of these trees cut off how they naturally communicate, denied the spirit within to transform of its own volition. Likewise, I too felt I was experiencing a transformation that seemed to deaden my lines of communication. Jung (1921, para. 781) might have explained this phenomenon as "participation mystique," as a

> particular kind of psychological connection with objects, and consists in the fact that the subject cannot clearly distinguish himself from the object but is bound to it by a direct relationship which amounts to partial identity.

Jerome Bernstein (2005, p. 9) would suggest that I am a Borderland personality and explain that I personally experience and feel the plight of the trees who are no longer permitted to live according to their own rhythm and who survive only in controlled states.

This *Borderlander* does indeed have a direct relationship with trees; it goes far back into the tribe's history. It is a relationship based on the understanding that the tree and I share life; however, how we come to naturally express our lived experience is dependent on the innate image we hold within, the relationships we cultivate and the transformation that unfolds. I would like to think that the alchemists would agree: that in order to learn from nature as she reveals herself, one needs to have a relationship with her. It is a process that requires patience, participation, respect, and reciprocity. Understanding my own nature means understanding the nature of trees. To see the forest through the trees is to be open to seeing the unseen and listening to an inner silence that speaks without using words.

Among Algonquin tribes (the Menominee are considered Algonquin), there is not a separate word for "nature" as if to distinguish something apart, or different from, ourselves. It is a distinction not recognized (Wall & Arden, 1990, 26). Here, there is no differentiation. Much later in life I came across James Hillman's "acorn theory" in *The Soul's Code* that eloquently explained that sense of inner transformation I carried from my tribe's origin story and from having lived in the woods. "I am answerable to an innate image which I am filling out in my biography … I am born with a character; it is given; a gift, the old stories say, from the guardians upon your birth" (Hillman, 1996, pp. 4–7).

Clinical Example – Beaver Woman

When I was younger I was fond of taking my dogs in the canoe in order to watch the beavers at work. In a secluded small bay of the lake, a beaver family had been working hard at constructing their lodge. I enjoyed visiting this area and counting the number of recently chewed trees and noting the underwater path that resulted when the beaver dragged the trees to their lodge. I admired the beaver. They were industrious, hard working, and seemed to go about their lives with determination. I learned that beavers are highly adaptable. They are equipped to live both above and below water, and at one time in beaver history they were not nocturnal, but have, over time, slowly adapted. Beavers have poor eyesight, and have a set of transparent eyelids that function much like goggles. They have keen senses of hearing, smell, and touch. When they want to signal danger, they slap their broad tails on the surface of the water, making a loud noise to warn others and then dip underwater, not to re-emerge for up to 15 minutes.

Last year, Beaver Woman from the tribal origin story helped me with a client. I had been working with a young woman, a student, but sensed that I had reached a roadblock. The client is considered legally blind but explained to me that she could partially see. She described being able to see shapes and shadows but could not make out the finer details of things. She presented with depressed symptoms, was often withdrawn and relied on others to initiate contact with her. She had difficulty making and meeting friends and she did not want others to know that she had a visual impairment. She often spoke of not wanting to bother others with asking them to do things for her, such as carry her lunch tray to the dining room table.

As a training candidate in the Minnesota Seminar of Jungian Studies, I attended a special weekend workshop that focused on transference/counter transference. A Freudian-trained therapist led us through a series of writing exercises in an effort to bring to our awareness some of the ways in which we work with our clients. In one such writing exercise she asked us to imagine ourselves as an animal and how we work with our clients. Here is what I wrote:

> I am beaver woman. I live between two worlds, the land and water. Knowing when to be in one or the other place depends on what is required. Above land I look for materials to build my home, under water I construct the home, and this is all done in the dark. Sometimes in a restful state I can float in the water and see both worlds at once. My tail is my muscle and power, my bones my medicine.

And then I added this short line afterward, "When I am with Mary (not the client's real name), the light does not allow me to see." Beaver Woman provided me another perspective with which to envision my work with Mary. "Light," in this instance, did not make things any clearer. It did not "illuminate" our work together. In fact, Beaver Woman suggested that I needed to explore the dark more, that place where Mary spends most of her time. I had been working so hard at trying to get Mary to "see" her issues from another perspective, that I too had become blind. Beaver Woman helped me understand that I needed to enter her shadowed, blurred world, and adapt to what it looks like as if from underwater. In one of my next meetings with Mary, part way through the session, I closed my eyes as we talked. At first, it was awkward, but as I eased into the darkness and focused on her voice, I was able to tune into her story more discriminately. I heard how lonely she sometimes feels, how she sometimes needs to make noise to be noticed. I heard that she tries hard and when discouraged, retreats into her lodge not to emerge for days. Toward the end of the session there was a noticeable shift in how we related. Mary said something that brought a smile to my face and I recall telling her, "Although you cannot see this, I am wearing a large smile right now," to which she replied, "I do not need to see it, I can hear it in your voice." Our work began anew.

Conclusion

Growing up near the forest and having spent much time in the woods provides me with a range of ways to better know myself. Whether it be from Awaehsaeh who transforms to human and is responsible to earth, Spirit Rock who reminds me of my own desire for immortality and fear of death, our Ancestors, the trees, who communicate an eloquence without words, or Beaver Woman who lives in two worlds and teaches me to explore the dark; these animals and this environment, when left to their own, transform in ways that are true to their innate nature. This way of being in the world allows me to better understand my own natural and innate process of individuation, helping me to become who I am meant to be.

Note

1   Accessed at www4.uwsp.edu/museum/menomineeClans/origin/

References

Bernstein, J. (2005). *Living in the Borderland: The Evolution of Consciousness and the Challenge of Healing Trauma*. New York: Routledge.

Cajete, G. (1994). *Look at the Mountain: An Anthology of Indigenous Education*. Durango, CO: Fulcrum Publishing.

Davis, T. (2000). *Sustaining the Forest, the People, and the Spirit*. Albany New York: State University of New York Press.

Deloria, V. Jr. (1999a). "Reflections and Revelation," in J. Treat (ed.), *For this Land: Writings on Religion in America*. New York: Routledge.

Deloria, V. Jr. (1999b). "At the Beginning," *In Spirit and Reason: The Vine Deloria Jr., Reader*. Golden, CO: Fulcrum Publishing.

Deloria, V. Jr. (1999c). "Introduction to the Vision Quest," in *Spirit and Reason: The Vine Deloria Jr., Reader*. Golden, CO: Fulcrum Publishing.

Douglas, M. (1986). *How Institutions Think*. New York: Syracuse Press.

Hillman, J. (1996). *The Soul's Code: In Search of Character and Calling*. New York: Warner Books.

Jung, C. G. (1921). "Definitions," in *Collected Works*, Vol. 6, *Psychological Types* (2nd edn). Princeton, NJ: Princeton University Press, 1971.

Jung, C. G. (1947). *C.G. Jung Letters*, Vol. 1, 1906–1960. G. Adler with A. Jaffé (eds.). London: Routledge and Kegan Paul, 1973.

Pecore, M. (1992). "Menominee Sustained Yield Management," *Journal of Forestry*, Vol. 90, No. 7, pp. 12–16.

Ronnberg, A. & Martin, K. (eds.) (2010). *The Book of Symbols*. The Archive for Research and Archetypal Symbolism (ARAS). Köln, Germany: Taschen Verlag.

Samuels, A., Shorter, B. & Plaut, F. (2007). *A Critical Dictionary of Jungian Analysis*. New York: Routledge.

Spindler, G. & Spindler, L. (1971). *Dreamers Without Power: The Menomini Indians*. New York: Holt, Reinhard and Winston, Inc.

Tinker, G. (1996). "An American Indian Theological Response to Ecojustice," in J. Weaver (ed.), *Defending Mother Earth: Native American Perspectives on Environmental Justice*. Maryknoll, NY: Orbis Books.

Wall, S. & Arden, H. (1990). *Wisdomkeepers: Meetings with Native American Spiritual Elders*. Hillsboro, OR: Beyond Words.

Zitkala-Sa. (1959). *American Indian Stories*. Lincoln, NE: University of Nebraska Press.

Website Addresses:

Menominee origin story and images of clans in half-human, half-animal forms
www4.uwsp.edu/museum/menomineeClans/clans/bearClan/bear.aspx
www4.uwsp.edu/museum/menomineeClans/origin/

Image of Cheyenne face (neighbors to the Great Sioux Nation) reflecting rolling plains landscape
www.flickriver.com/photos/griffinlb/3360968072/

Aerial view of "Forest Island," the Menominee Indian Reservation in Wisconsin
www.americanforests.org/magazine/article/menominee-forest-keepers/

PART III

Synchronistic Symbols as Liminal Place/Space

4

THE BURDEN OF MODERNITY

Three Takes on the Snake and Recombinant Visionary Mythology

Thomas Singer

Introduction

The archetype of death and rebirth, the initiatory rites of passage of ancient tribes, the cultures of contemporary indigenous peoples and the modern individual's search for meaning are all mixed up in the Jungian tradition. In fact, these themes are mixed up everywhere in contemporary society as is the wholesale promise of transformation through joining religious groups, political movements, or through the purchase of every imaginable consumer good from soft drinks to hard porn.

The Jungian flavor of transformation and rebirth remains a rare, handcrafted brew that grew out of the emergence and convergence of anthropology, archeology, mythology, and psychology with their magnificent flowerings at the end of the nineteenth and beginning of the twentieth centuries. Our modern myth of individuation draws heavily from a syncretistic blending of the knowledge of ancient cultures and their mystery traditions with twentieth and twenty-first-century psychologies that are used to enhance individual development. Stepping back a bit from our tradition, it is a rather remarkable conceit to believe that the story of a whole civilization's understanding of itself might provide a mythic framework for the individuation of a single modern person. Such a conceit is a double-edged sword that can encourage whopping inflations and cultism on the one hand and a potential boon for deeply humanizing experiences in individuals and even whole cultures on the other hand. In such a process, we tend to idealize the indigenous, ancient mind while devaluing the modern rational mind as one-sided.

This chapter tracks this primal mixing of ancient and modern wisdom traditions by looking at three examples of transformative encounters with the snake, all of which demonstrate the tendency to take elements of various myths and stories from different times and cultures and put them together in new ways.

Part One: The Snake and the Transformation of Energy

The first example focuses on a mythopoetic drawing by one of our founding elders, Joseph Henderson, that illustrates how ancient tales of death and rebirth were woven into a modern initiatory journey. In the fall of 1929, Joe Henderson, a young native of Elko, Nevada, arrived in Zürich by way of Princeton University and San Francisco for a year of intensive analysis with C.G. Jung. During that year, he also attended Jung's Wednesday morning Dream Seminar, which was made available to selected English-speaking analysands. The seminar followed the case of a Swiss businessman, one of whose dreams contained a powerful image of a large cauldron filled with metal objects, some of which were crosses and some of which were crescents (hauntingly resonant today with the conflict between the West and Islam). To teach the method of amplification, Jung divided the participants into two groups, instructing each to research the dream's archetypal symbols. Half of the group was assigned the crescent and the other half the cross. Dr. Esther Harding was appointed the leader of the crescent group, which included the young Joe Henderson. Dr. Harding's work on the crescent symbol awakened her interest in women's rites of initiation, which eventually bore fruit in her classic study *Women's Mysteries* (1972). The dream seminar also stimulated Henderson's interest in male initiation, which ultimately led to his seminal study *Thresholds of Initiation* (1967). In this early Jungian cauldron of seeking psychic reorientation from old myths, deep links were established between the study of dreams and the ancient and indigenous.

The result of Henderson's initial work with Jung led to his decision to move to England to take up a course of premedical studies with the goal of attending medical school and becoming a doctor who would carry on the Jungian tradition. All went relatively well until Henderson was taking his final premedical exams. On consecutive nights, he had powerfully disorienting dreams that led him to want to visit Jung again to get his bearings.

Before discussing the dreams and the visit to Zürich, however, I want to place Henderson's personal journey in the broader cultural context of the late 1920s and 1930s that ultimately led to the outbreak of World War II. In order to understand what attracted Jung's early followers to Zürich, it helps to put oneself in their mindset, mood, and cultural context. The world as they knew it was already falling apart following the outbreak of World War I and the Great Depression. World War II was looming on the not-too-distant horizon. The promises of the Enlightenment and the Industrial Revolution had not delivered the hoped-for benefits of the rational mind and its capacity to understand and adapt to the world. Rather, the impact of Freud, Darwin, and Marx on the human being's place in the cosmos had pretty much destroyed any sense of safe haven in the world for those sensitive to the deeper currents of the *cultural unconscious* (a term coined by Henderson). Indeed, by the middle of the twentieth century, only the Existentialists seemed to have a timely read on the state of being in the world, that it was an absurd place, without a god, in which, as Sartre put it, "existence precedes essence." This replaced Descartes' "I think therefore I am," both of which have unfortunately been replaced by "I consume therefore I am." All of this contributed to what we can think of as the burden of modernity, a Sisyphean weight in which the wonderful boons of technology, mass production, modern medicine, high-speed communication and transportation, and all the paraphernalia of our everyday lives can turn into Frankenstein monsters even while appearing to make our lives easier or better.

The Existentialists' answer to the burden of modernity was quite different from the Jungian response, which was to pivot (as they now say) to the wisdom of older traditions in a search for renewal rather than to declare the universe and our place in it absurd.

So a handful of people gathered around Jung in the late 1920s and early 1930s to forge a tiny beachhead of potential psychic reorientation based on a belief in the profoundly transformative powers inherent in wisdom traditions and within the psyche itself: hence, the early Jungians' strange brew of interest in initiation, in ancient myths, in indigenous peoples, all with the goal of discovering a psychic reorientation for modern men and women and even culture as a whole.

Joe Henderson was one of those who gathered around Jung in the late 1920s and, after a year of analysis, undertook a premed course of study in England. After two big dreams on consecutive nights in the midst of his premed exams, Henderson contacted Jung. In much of the narrative that follows, I will use Joe's words of his visit to Jung and Zürich as he told me the story over the course of a year-long series of interviews in his 101st year.

> The dreams made me think I needed an analytic hour or two to talk to Jung. I booked travel to Zürich as soon as I could, and I went to see Jung in the early summer of 1931. Jung was not very helpful. All he said was that he was leaving in a day or so for his summer vacation.

To put it mildly, Jung was not there for Joe when he needed him.

> I went to Zürich because I was in trouble. I needed to talk to Jung about myself. I needed someone. So, I decided to interpret the dreams myself and do this drawing which took about three weeks. At stake was whether or not to go to medical school.

Here is the drawing:

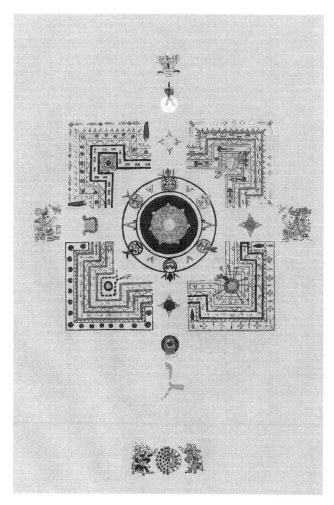

FIGURE 4.1 Joe Henderson 1931 drawing (see http://aras.org/sites/default/files/docs/00038Singer.pdf to view this figure in color)

Joe's drawing is a wonderful example of the early Jungian tradition of initiation through a death and rebirth ordeal that emerges out of a deeper layer of the psyche, an ordeal most familiar to the indigenous tribes of today and earlier cultures.

I have come to think of the drawing as a psycho-spiritual map that anticipated and guided Joe's journey, a kind of inner compass or gyroscope. The inner core of the drawing was actually the first thing that Joe painted in this drawing after going to an art supply store in Zürich and carefully picking out a piece of parchment on which he could work comfortably. He started drawing in the center using gold, coral, and turquoise. Joe told me that drawing the center first "put it all in motion." Just beyond this core of brilliant light that centers the drawing is an area of intense black about which Joe said the following:

This is the black obsidian mirror of Tezcatlipoca. I was very taken up with Mayan and Aztec art and archeology when I was drawing this. It is said that if you look into this mirror, you can see your essential Self.

Tezcatlipoca was the Aztec god of war. He carried a magic mirror that gave off smoke and killed enemies, so he was called the "god of the smoking mirror." Whoever gazed into this black mirror of obsidian might perceive the meaning of his soul. Joe said to me: "Looking into the black obsidian mirror symbolizes the ability to focus on the inner life."

Directly encircling the black mirror are a series of masks, some of which brought to my mind Donald Kalsched's archetypal defenses of the personal spirit. But Joe noted particularly the one at the top: a hermaphroditic figure with feathers in the hair representing the fullness of life and the one opposite to it at the bottom, a skull figure that represents death. The first of Joe's big dreams follows.

Dream One: Eagle and Horse

FIGURE 4.2 Dream 1: Joe Henderson 1931 drawing (see http://aras.org/sites/default/files/docs/00038Singer.pdf to view this figure in color)

A white horse is running along the surface of a gray sea. An eagle flies down from the sky and bites the horse in the back of the neck where there is an exposed artery. Blood spurts up from the pierced artery and the horse dies. I awoke and knew that I was going to fail my premed course exams on the following day.

Even as we look at the image of the dream, as it appears at the top of the drawing and in the detail shown here, the spurting blood seems fresh, as if it just happened this instant, which underlines the timelessness of archetypal reality. To some, the outer events and circumstances of Joe's life at the time of this dream might not suggest an ordeal, but to those who know the reality of the inner world, this dream, and its symbolic representation in the drawing convey grave danger and the onset of an ordeal.

Dream Two: Depths of the Ocean

Dream Two is represented in the drawing near the bottom and is shown in detail in this image:

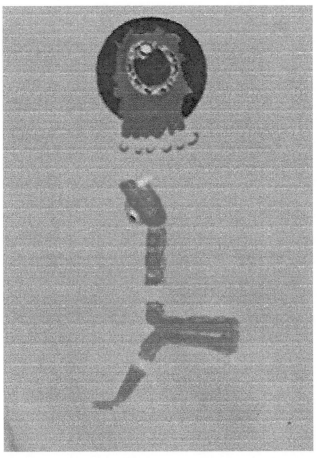

FIGURE 4.3 Dream 2: Joe Henderson 1931 drawing (see http://aras.org/sites/default/files/docs/00038Singer.pdf to view this figure in color)

The second dream is set in the depths of the ocean.

A snake with a red head comes up from below — from the depths — and bites a flat, black fish. The snake bites the fish in exactly the same way that the eagle bit the horse on the back of the neck the night before.

Joe elaborated on the meaning of the dreams in the following way:

The dreams seemed very complicated to me. The eagle bite (Dream One) was a bad one, a killer. It said to me that I was going to fail my examination on the next day. The red-headed snake bite of the second night (Dream Two) suggested a renewal of life. It felt life giving rather than death dealing. That surprised me and suggested that I was going to pass the examination somehow, but I didn't know how. The dreams seemed to be two pairs of opposites and I knew I had something to work on: There was the snake coming up from below, biting the fish. And there was the eagle coming down from above, biting the horse. The pair of opposites from above was matched by a pair of opposites from below. It presented to my eye a double vision, or two pairs of pairs.

A friend suggested to Joe that his dreams were about Joe's dreading the whole process of becoming a doctor. Following this line of thought, Joe said the following:

In that sense, the eagle was the medical profession itself. I was putting myself through something that was a trial of strength. The white horse symbolized my natural enjoyment of life and my not wanting to inhibit it. The serpent with the red head symbolized life energies coming from below and bringing new life. The flat fish lying on the bottom of the sea was like inertia itself, just heavy and unable to move. So there was a threat from above and a bite from below. In medical school my body was heavy, like the fish on the bottom of the sea. I had to kill my inertia and the wish to remain a white horse instead of a red snake. I had to give up my passive identification with heroic youth (white horse). Both the inertia (the flat fish) and the passive identification with the heroic phase of life and its enjoyment (the white horse) needed to die. The white horse carried natural instinct and the enjoyment of life, which in the process of becoming a doctor needed to die or be sacrificed.

I came to think that the bite of the eagle showed my fear of failing; that's why it was so negative to me. Not just failing the examination, but failing at the whole process of becoming a physician. I was afraid that I would be unable to go through with a medical career.

The first dream said that I was convinced I had failed. The second dream suggested that there could be a positive meaning to this failure. The snake dream was hopeful to me, that I might still be able to proceed. The hope for renewal really came from the snake bite from below.

The drawing was a wonderful initiatory link between my premedical world and my plunging into medical school. As in the drawing, medical school brought me into the presence of death and its opposite, rebirth. Initiation in medical school brought about both the feeling of being small and insignificant and of being large and part of an important world. I felt very small and yet part of a big tradition. Of course, those feelings of being big and small go along with the archetype of initiation because there is the experience of one's personal puniness in the presence of something big, important and meaningful. One is very small and *IT* is very important.

Between the two dreams, beyond the golden, turquoise, and coral core, and beyond the black obsidian mirror and then beyond the encircling ring of ritual masks, the central drama of this initiatory tale is played out in a progression of four panels that move, in a counterclockwise rotation, from the lower-left quadrant to the lower-right quadrant to the upper-right quadrant to the upper-left quadrant. These four panels tell the story of the snake's journey and/or of the transformation of the psyche's libido.

One can think about what happens to the snake in these four panels as being a picture of a transformative process along the instinctual-spiritual poles of the psyche. Joe never told me if he considered himself a member of a snake clan, but the esoteric narrative of this drawing is told through the snake's development. The snake at the lower left is, as Joe said, "Ok with itself – at rest."

> Joe said, "Its movement hasn't happened yet in reality, but it signifies the beginning of the initiatory process of snake undergoing a whole new cycle of transformation." The ordeal begun by the white horse being killed by the eagle above and the renewing serpent with the red head emerging from below to kill the flat, black fish hasn't yet mobilized the snake at the bottom left. But, Joe went on to describe the snake at the bottom right as "manic, chaotic, agitated."
>
> Joe explained, "He's really being worked over!! He's in motion (the red balls) and he may be suffering." The snake's ordeal has begun. The snake in the upper-right quadrant comes up and, according to Joe, "Out of itself into a new spiritual place and takes on the form of a plumed serpent."

I asked Joe if the plumed serpent in the upper-right quadrant was a coming together of the feathers from the eagle of his first dream (at the top of the drawing) with the red-headed snake of his second dream (at the bottom of the drawing) and that out of this coming together of feather from above and snake from below there emerged the figure of the plumed serpent. Joe agreed with this as a possible origin of the plumed serpent, but said that putting the feathers of the eagle together with the serpent biting the fish to make the plumed serpent was not something he thought about consciously when he made this drawing. Joe said that the upper-left quadrant showed the resolution of the initiatory ordeal in a mandala that takes the form of a plant.

What is most important to note in this story is that Dr. Henderson describes this as the "snake's transformation"; he doesn't say "my transformation." By speaking of the snake's transformation, he is saying that the instinctual energy at the deepest level of the psyche, symbolically embodied in the snake, is transformed: it goes through a process of death and rebirth; it is renewed.

Without much help from Jung on the occasion of his urgent visit to Zürich, Joe returned to London at the end of the summer of 1931, renewed and initiated from within. He was permitted to retake the premed exams in botany and physics that, as his dream predicted, he had, in fact, failed the first time around. He was not required to take all the courses over again. He passed the exams and entered medical school at St. Bartholomew's in the fall of 1931.

Part of the architecture of initiation that Joe was to later sketch in *Thresholds of Initiation* was what he experienced personally in returning to London and entering medical school. An essential aspect of the archetype of initiation is to rejoin the world in a new way as a natural expression of the initiatory experience to get, as Joe put it, "more connected to life and the social order." Joe found himself developing an outer relatedness, which was particularly difficult for someone as naturally introverted as he had always been. Put most simply, the snake's transformation led to a new life for Joe Henderson.

Part Two: The Snake and Healing

My own snake/initiatory story is the second of the three takes on the snake that I wish to offer as examples of Jungian ways of adapting to the burden of modernity. In the fall of 1965, I enrolled as a first-year student at Yale Medical School, having just returned from a year of teaching in Greece following graduation from college. The year in Greece had been one of glorious discovery and the awakening of a thirst for life. It was like being in a state of mild (and sometimes not so mild) intoxication for a year.

You can imagine how I felt when I returned to the United States and moved into the medical school dorm in New Haven. The newly acquired taste for life vanished almost instantaneously, and, as if imprisoned, I felt a dreary dread settle over me, just as Joe described in his associations to the dream flat fish. I was one of those majors in the humanities that medical schools say they like but often tear apart and spit out in no time at all. Yale was enormously forgiving and, unlike any other medical school in the country, had almost no exams for the first two years. They had the strange idea that the students they admitted would find their way and didn't need to be sadistically tortured into becoming good doctors. So I found myself desperately struggling to catch up in the first two years but not flunking out because we had no tests or grades.

The third year is when we began our clinical rotations, and all of my efforts to stay afloat failed when I was actually tested for the first time. It was as if I had landed from another planet. I had no sense of belonging, and whatever identity I had consolidated to date began to crumble almost immediately. Wherever my psyche was living, it was not at medical school, although I worked as hard as I could to catch up. In this frame of mind, I began my internal medicine rotation, and within the first day or so, I was assigned to examine a man who had just been admitted to the ward with a stroke. When I entered the room, he was surrounded by a family in great distress. Whatever primitive medical and human skills I had begun to develop deserted me. I fumbled through taking a history from the family and performing a physical exam on an elderly man who was comatose. For me, it was an agony of incompetence and being overwhelmed with fear and doubt.

Shortly after that, I was called to join our rounds of all the patients on the ward. Rounds included the resident, interns, medical students, and an attending physician, a virtual sea of white coats swooping into hospital rooms at what are often the most difficult moments in peoples' lives. The attending asked us, perhaps asked me directly, how one could tell the difference between a midbrain stroke and one that had occurred higher up in the brain. I froze, I only knew that the man I had tried to examine couldn't talk and didn't respond to any stimuli. I also knew that he was breathing and his heart was beating. I did learn in those rounds that someone with a midbrain stroke is staying alive with only the so-called vegetative functions intact, respiration and heartbeat. After the rounds, I simply walked off the wards, went back to my dormitory room, closed the door and didn't come out for two or three days. Eventually, the resident phoned and asked what had happened to me. I said that I couldn't come back. I went to the Student Health Department and began to talk to a kind resident psychiatrist and within about six weeks, found myself meeting a Jungian analyst for the first time. My first visits to the Jungian brought some relief in talking to someone who took my pain and my humanity seriously. Psychologically, I felt I was a midbrain preparation with only my vegetative functions intact.

I was able to tell the analyst about my time in Greece and my childhood. In the context of becoming a medical student, one childhood memory kept recurring with a surprising poignancy. I remembered throwing a rock at a friend and drawing blood from his forehead when I was eight years old. I was competitive but not combative. At the time, his father was my mother's doctor, and my mother was suffering severe ulcerative colitis that required major abdominal surgery and the removal of a large portion of her small intestine. As a result of the disease and surgery, my mother lost twins with whom she was pregnant at the time. I didn't understand any of this as an eight year old; I only knew that I had drawn blood from the son of my mother's doctor.

Often in driving to those first sessions with my analyst, I would experience excruciating migraine headaches as I began to reflect on how I had ended up in medical school. I began to remember and draw my dreams, and I began to think symbolically about my life experiences. In 1969, I had one of the big dreams that came to me at that time.

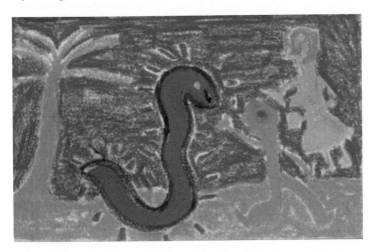

FIGURE 4.4 Author's snake dream (see https://aras.org/sites/default/files/docs/Amplification%20with%20images%20and%20ARAS%20conclusion.pdf to view this figure in color)

I stand face to face with a large "circus" snake. I don't know how I know it is a "circus" snake or even what a "circus" snake is. The name simply announces itself to me in the dream. I know that I want to flee from the snake. My mother stands behind me and insists that I stand my ground. The snake stands as tall even taller than I and is glowing and radiating energy. We look one another straight in the eye, and I sense that its intentions toward me are not malevolent. They might even be good.

Snake as phallus, snake as healer, snake as kundalini, snake as the mystery of death/rebirth and immortality, the living symbol came alive in me, although I knew nothing of the multiple symbolic meanings of the serpent at the time of the dream. They all accrued to the dream in the process of amplification over many decades.

In my first reactions to the dream, I really only knew that I was facing something terrifying that my mother was insisting I face head on. Two associations presented themselves to me at the time of the dream: first, I had literally run from the medical wards in the horror of seeing a dying man and his grieving family, propelled by my own feelings of utter inadequacy. My analyst-as-mother helped me begin to face more squarely the mysteries of life and death that were terrifying me and from which I was trying to flee. Second, my own mother had actually done pretty much the same thing on another occasion that actually came the summer before my meltdown on the medical wards.

I had just finished my first two years of medical school and taken the first part of the national boards. I had the summer off and had arranged to travel to Bolivia with a close friend whose father was stationed in La Paz, Bolivia, as part of a US Aid program. We were going to work with a medical missionary in the sparsely populated lowlands of Bolivia, which were just being opened up for settlement by Indians from the 11,000-foot Altiplano in a program sponsored by the Bolivian government.

Before traveling to Bolivia, I went back to St. Louis, Missouri, to make a brief visit with my mother and father. I especially wanted to see my father who was scheduled for a complicated neurosurgical procedure because of cervical osteoarthritis. My father's surgery was scheduled for a few days after my planned departure. On the appointed day I said my goodbyes, went to the airport, boarded the plane, and before we had even begun to taxi away from the gate, the man sitting in the seat next to me died almost instantaneously of a heart attack. He was laid out in the aisle, and I just remember looking at his short, black socks, and the white, hairless skin above them. The flight was delayed, of course, as the body had to be removed from the plane. The thought of my father about to undergo neurosurgery and the corpse lying next to me were enough to make me insist on exiting the plane. The airline officials were reluctant to let me disembark, but I would not take no for an answer and left the plane with the body.

When I arrived home by taxi, my mother was surprised. I told her what happened. Her seemingly heartless response astounded me. She said that I could only stay home for 24 hours and then I would have to leave. I later came to realize that she did not want me to stop my life just as it was beginning in the fear of losing my parents. She was fearful that I would be trapped in the guilt and mutual dependency of caring for ill parents, which had been a significant part of my father's fate in having to look after his father who lived until the age of 99. She had seen life itself stop in the fear of death. She, like my dream mother, wanted me to take a firm stand in facing the mysteries and realities of illness and death head on and to embrace its painful truths by affirming life. It was a brutal lesson. These were among my personal associations to the dream of the glowing and radiating serpent.

FIGURE 4.5 Image of boy, great mother, and serpent from Jane Harrison's *Themis*

Only years later would I stumble across this image of boy, snake, and mother in Jane Harrison's *Themis*, written in 1913 at just about the same time Jung had begun to talk about archetypes. In the pre-patriarchal, matriarchal era of the earliest Greeks, about 1500 BCE (or some 3500 years ago), the Greeks knew of the snake as a sacred consort of the Great mother, not as a destructive force of nature, but as a healing link to the earth and underworld, as an agency of the rebirth and transformation that it embodied. Like the very ancient Greeks, my dream of the snake began my initiatory journey into the psyche and the healing potential of unconscious, non-rational forces. Over time, the snake led me to the magnificent *Hymn of the Kouretes*, which was inscribed on an ancient stone that was uncovered in Crete. It became my initiatory song of rebirth and celebration of life. Again, modern psyche finds a source of renewal in ancient mythic traditions.

Part Three: The Snake That is Not a Symbol; the Snake That is not a Cigar

We have taken a look at how the burden of modernity led Jung and his early followers to seek the mystery of renewal, transformation, and rebirth in the mysteries of long-gone civilizations or in the traditions of contemporary indigenous peoples who sometimes live close to the wisdom of their elders. We also took a brief look at my own initiatory encounter with the snake. But what of the contemporary indigenous peoples themselves and how have they fared with the

FIGURE 4.6   Rod Moss, *The Interpretation of Dreams*

burden of modernity? Our Jungian tradition has been enriched by their wisdom, but have their traditions been enriched by living in the boundary between their quite old ways and our quite new ways? How does the modern world appear to contemporary indigenous peoples? Rod Moss's painting of the *Interpretation of Dreams* (Figure 4.6) sums up a jarring shift in perspective that would be required to see what our world looks like to the aborigine. Moss' wonderfully humorous and provocative painting puts Freud – and all modern psychoanalytic tradition by association – on the couch in the able hands of an Aboriginal elder. Perhaps we need a bit of help from the aboriginal elders, even as our modern world has dismembered their culture.

Among the indigenous peoples of the world, the Aboriginal experience of disintegration and negative transformation is the rule, not the exception. It seems that those who at one time knew so much about transformation and rebirth have found that the forces and burden of modernity have overwhelmed their capacities for renewal for their own people. I would like to focus on the work of Craig san Roque, a Jungian analyst who has lived and worked with the aborigines in the area of Alice Springs, in central Australia. I have collaborated with Craig on several projects over the past 15 years, including the book *Placing Psyche*, a study of cultural complexes in Australia.

This leads me to my third take on the snake, an aboriginal image of the snake as healer, of transformation and rebirth. Created by Andrew Spencer, a Warlpiri senior man renowned as an intercultural negotiator and social/cultural healer, this snake tells the story of healing from the perspective of Australia's indigenous people. Craig has worked closely with Andrew Spencer over the years and insists that we not think of the aboriginal snake as a symbol because that word can make too abstract what is, in fact, a living reality.

FIGURE 4.7 Andrew Spencer Japaljarri, *Wana Jukurrpa.* Photographed by Graham Prichard. Image from the Jungarai Wanu story by permission of Japaljarri Spencer and Dr. Craig San Roque, Alice Springs, 2015 (see http://aras.org/sites/default/files/docs/00075SanRoque.pdf to view this figure in color)

Here is what Craig has to tell us of Jungarai, the traveling snake:

> This is the story of travelling Jungarai a snake. He leaves a place where two men are sitting [signified by horseshoe shapes, the imprint they leave on the sand] and he is going to a place where many men are sitting. They are waiting for him. Well perhaps they have gathered to remember the story and acknowledge him. Along the way men are watching him. Who are those men? They are Ngangkari, traditional healers. Why are they shown sitting there? This is because the travels of the ngangkari snake have deep meaning for the healers who are part of this ngangkari story. This is their profession story, their training manual.
>
> (p. 11)

Spencer suggests:

> This story doesn't live only in the mind; it lives in the land. It moves in my ... body. The snake passes through many experiences. You can see him travelling along. He is attacked. He is injured. His skin is torn from his body. His guts are dragged out and dragged across the country. His heart is taken. He is rolled in the salt of a dried-out salt lake. Many things happen to this snake but he keeps going.
>
> (p. 11)

Spencer states "these things are happening in the present time":

> The ngangkari snake carries the pain. He carries the pain. He passes into that place in the west, that water hole that you see there. Deep inside that hole after a very long time his spirit (*kurunpa*), his power (*mapanpa*) changes. He becomes the spirit support to the ngangkari (the indigenous healers) who follow in his line. Ngangkari call upon him. They call on him. They use him to heal sickness of body/spirit. He becomes a spirit being. He carries "*mapanpa*" healing power. You see him there in the shape of a snake.
>
> (pp. 11–12)

Craig further expresses the following:

> This is how I understand it when Spencer tells this story. The snake, Jungarai Wanu, is a spiritual power that helps the doctors. They call on him. He carries pain for people. He takes the pain upon himself. He takes the suffering of the person who the doctor is attending. The suffering passes through the doctor and into the snake who carries it away. That is how healing takes place. The men sitting looking at the snake are singing to him, they love him. They know his story. They are a part of him. He is them. They are a part of him, that snake, They are him. They know how this works. That is the story that this scene is telling you.
>
> It would be more accurate to say that in the mind of the Warlpiri or Pintubi custodians of the story these snakes are real beings; they are not symbolic of anything conceptual, abstract or other than themselves.
>
> The snake, then – as I have seen it spoken of by Spencer as a felt presence – it emanates its own being, much as a real animal snake does – it has its own vitality and purpose – a life of its own. Independent of human mental constructions, it moves along its geographic track from site to site across several 1000 km of country and in so doing enacts a story that exemplifies the experiences of various forms of pain and dismemberment and restoration that a traditional healer may expect to pass through in an active way in his own human terms while training.

So this is a contemporary take on the snake that is also deeply rooted in time and memory. Craig insists that we not think of this snake as a symbol or (jokingly) "as a cigar." As he says, "One has to be careful about saying 'ah this snake is symbolic of …? The activities of these snakes symbolize …'"

As part of his ongoing work with aboriginal peoples in transition, Craig is now following the snake in its healing work by adapting one of the oldest myths of the Western world, the myth of Demeter and Persephone, in collaboration with Aboriginal and non-indigenous people working to help both sides of the black-and-white modern cultures appreciate the difficulties Aboriginal Australians might have in making the transition from a hunter–gatherer society into agricultural and industrial-monetized systems of food gathering, that is to say, into modernity. The Demeter and Persephone story shows the difficulties encoded in myth as revealing experiences in Europe five to ten thousand years ago. It is a useful cautionary tale for the specific group of indigenous Australians (with whom Craig is connected), struggling with similar transitions into the modern way of managing hunger, food production, and economic distribution of wealth gained from mining.

Many interpret the Demeter and Persephone story as an early tale of the transition from a hunter–gatherer to an agricultural people. It embodies the Greeks' early understanding of the mysteries of the annual renewal of agricultural cycles. The aboriginal cultural law has no account of making such a transition. Yet there are propositions and projects that suggest that the future survival of the central Australian (hunter–gatherer) Aborigines depends on their being able to allocate land under their control for managed economic development: this includes farming in some regions and adaptation to the procedures of agriculture on their land. This is a complicated and fraught transition that may or may not be possible.

Many practical economic managers and politicians insist that indigenous Australians must "get with the program," but as a psychologist Craig suggests "the program is in the thinking. Transitions into modernity implies transitions in mentality."

> The Jungarai snake story reveals how indigenous doctors configure the process by which a man becomes fit to heal others. It is a way of pain suffered and healing capacities internalised and turned to useful effect, backed up by custodians and mentors of that particular path. Singer's story shows a western doctor on a similar trek, backed up by the researches of his mentors and custodians. As individual practitioners there is valuable cultural interchange taking place in the psychomedical domain. There are psychic similarities under the skin. But for all of us caught up in massive transitions of this contemporary world, we the hunter gatherers, we the nomads, we the farmers, we the industrialists, we the fodder of the global marketeers … what will become of us?

Conclusion

One can see from these three takes on the snake that some facing the burdens of modernity look to the deepest levels of the psyche, rooted in the oldest tribal memories of the world's cultures, in seeking initiation, transformation, renewal, and rebirth. These ancestral wisdom traditions are often reworked to suit contemporary needs in what I think of as *recombinant visionary mythology*. I have chosen this term as I sometimes think of the modern world and its multicultural psyche as being engaged in a process similar to the biology of recombinant genetics in which parts of DNA are shuffled around to create new DNA. The material I have presented in this chapter, the three takes on the snake, all represent recombinant visionary mythology at work, in which bits and pieces of archetypal material from different cultures are reshuffled by various individuals and groups to create new mythologies that will hopefully lead to renewal and rebirth.

Author's Note

In the three separate takes on the snake, I have relied on text from other articles and chapters I have written and, in Part Three, on material from Craig san Roque. In Part One, I have adapted material from my chapter, "In the Footsteps: The Story of an Initiatory Drawing by Dr. Joseph Henderson," in *Initiation: The Living Reality of an Archetype*, edited by Thomas Kirsch, Virginia Beane Rutter, and Thomas Singer (Routledge, 2007). In Part Two, I rely on my chapter "The Circus Snake: A Numinous, Initiatory Calling from Below," in *Being Called: Scientific, Secular and Sacred Perspectives*, edited by David Bryce Yaden, Theo D. McCall, and J. Harold Ellens (Singer Praeger, 2015). Finally, in Part Three, with his permission, I quote from Craig san Roque's "Living People, Living Language, Living Symbol," *ARAS Connections* 4 (2014): http://aras.org/sites/default/files/docs/00075SanRoque.pdf. I also refer to his chapter "The Kore Story: Persephone's Dog," in *Ancient Greece, Modern Psyche: Archetypes Evolving*, edited by Virginia Beane Rutter and Thomas Singer (Routledge, 2015).

References

Kalsched, D. (1996). *The Inner World of Trauma: Archetypal Defences of the Personal Spirit*. London and New York: Routledge.

san Roque, Craig. (2014) "Living People, Living Language, Living Symbol," *ARAS Connections*, No.4. Online. Available at: http://aras.org/sites/default/files/docs/00075SanRoque.pdf (accessed 3 December 3, 2015).

Singer, T., san Roque, C., Dowd, A., & Tacey, D. (eds.) (2011). *Placing Psyche: Exploring Cultural Complexes in Australia*, New Orleans, LA: Spring Journal Books.

5

REBIRTHING BIBLICAL MYTH

The Poisonwood Bible as Visionary Art

Daphne Dodson

Introduction

In the commentary that follows the final chapter of *The Poisonwood Bible*, the author, Kingsolver (2005, p. 10), admitted that for years she referenced the seedling of the novel as "the Damn Africa book." She described its initial existence as bloated files stuffed into a tall metal file cabinet. I visualize it flourishing in the unconscious.

Primarily set in the early 1960s, *The Poisonwood Bible* is a story of the Price family. Written in first person using five first-persons, each female Price shares her own vivid memories as an American expatriate driven on a Christian mission to the Belgium-colonized Congo by the family patriarch, Preacher Nathan. Orleanna Price, the mother, introduces each book of the novel, offering hindsight perspective of the events narrated by each of her teenage daughters (first-born Rachael and the twins Leah and Adah) and her baby (the five-year-old Ruth May). Kingsolver (2012, para. 3) shared her conscious purpose in choosing to write in five voices: "In the four Price daughters and their mother, I personified attitudes crossing the spectrum from Orleanna's paralyzing guilt to Rachel's blithe 'What, me worry?' I wanted to create a moral conversation. That's what literature can do."

Perhaps, too, the novel required these five voices to better parallel the polyphonic narrative of the Bible, for, as I see it, *The Poisonwood Bible* is a metaphor of biblical stories. I argue it is a rebirthing of Judeo-Christian mythical imagery in a way that perceives the Bible not from a metaphorical *denotation* perspective, a literal interpretation by a given social order, but as the Bible in a most primordial sense. It is metaphor that invites a reading of the Bible not as allegory or absolute truth but as rebirthed *connotations* of creation and deliverance myths through what the psychologist Jung referred to (and I will later describe) as visionary art.

Rebirthed Mythical Imagery

The mythologist Campbell said

> the function of mythological imagery is to ... coordinate the energies of our body so that we may live a harmonious and fruitful life in accord with our society and with the new mystery that emerges with every new human being.
> (Mishlove, 1998, para. 6)

"Mythology has to do with guiding us" both in "society and the whole world of nature, which is outside of us but also within us" (para. 6). Campbell, who included religion as a form of mythology, asserted that mythology or religion evolves from and within a social construct. Thus, when one social order and its particular version of religion are incompatible with the next, they "come into collision with each other" (para. 10). Moreover, when explicit meanings of mythic images are dictated by a specific social construct, the myth is at risk of no longer being appropriately assimilated. Such dictates may be a product of the defensive ego where the ego drives conceptualization of non-ego images at the significant cost of value the image-proper would otherwise afford (Adams, 2008). Campbell reminded us that "mythology is a compendium of metaphors" (Mishlove, 1998, para. 64); thus, when each metaphor of the myth is embraced as mythic image and, therefore, invited to evoke connotations rather than reductionist denotations, the myth is opened to universal meaning and value.

Literary critic Coupe (2009, p. 100), in his book, *Myth*, raised a similar argument, tendering the term "radical typology" to describe the rebirthing of a myth through unique retellings where no one narrative form is privileged over any other version. "Myths remake other myths, and there is no reason why they should not continue to do so, the mythopoeic urge being infinite" (p. 100). As I see it, radical typology aligns with Campbell's perspective of newly connoted metaphor: mythology is rebirthed by encountering it through a contemporary lens and seeing it anew so that the mythic imagery is called into connotation against the backdrop of the current or emerging social order. Yet, what would spawn *The Poisonwood Bible* as rebirthed myth of the Bible?

Jung believed that art has the ability to be visionary in that it may, through symbol (similar to what Campbell described as mythical imagery), unconsciously bring into consciousness what is not yet known. Jung (1950a, para. 139) argued that visionary art is a complementary "mode of artistic creation" to psychological art, where the latter is derived from "the raw material of ... man's consciousness, from his eternally repeated joys and sorrows." To this end, Jung lamented, "There is no work left for the psychologist to do" (para. 139) because psychological artwork itself expresses what is already "clearly understandable psychology" (para. 140). Yet visionary art "is a primordial experience which surpasses man's understanding ... allow[ing] a glimpse into the unfathomable abyss of the unborn and of things yet to be" (para. 141).

In peering through Campbell's and Coupe's lenses, applying a Jungian eye of psychology and art, and close reading of the texts of both the Bible and *The Poisonwood Bible*, separating their narratives from their contexts, I argue this novel may be a visionary work of art in that it offers biblical metaphors rebirthed for a global, twenty-first-century social order. To be clear, I am not suggesting *The Poisonwood Bible* be interpreted as a new bible. Further, I am not suggesting an individual personal-experience interpretation of the novel for that would, according to Jung (1950a, para. 146), make such a visionary work inauthentic, even pathologic. Rather, I propose a reading of the novel as a visionary work that may leave us "astonished, confused, bewildered, put on our guard or even repelled" (para. 143) because we are not certain what to make of it, but we sense it is mythical.

A Renewed Approach to Biblical Text

To support my argument that *The Poisonwood Bible* is a renewal of biblical myth, I first explore the possibility that the Bible encourages a relevant interpretation of its text by each and every social order throughout time. I begin by sharing two verses from The Bible New International Version (NIV): "In the beginning was the Word, and the Word was with God, and the Word was God" (John 1:1); and "The Word became flesh and made his dwelling among us. We have seen his glory, the glory of the One and Only who came from the Father, full of grace and truth" (John 1:14). Biblical scholarship indicates that Greeks used the term Word to refer to the spoken and unspoken; it was the reason that governs all things; Jews, however, deemed Word as the sign of God (Barker, 1995, p. 1590). A Western culture denotation reading of John 1:1 and 1:14 indicates that Word is a man. This man, whom shall be known as Word, is unique and awe-inspiring, the embodiment of grace and truth. He has lived before humans were human; yet, paradoxically, this man, Word, came to dwell among humans as though humans existed before him. Radically, all encompassing, Word is reason, Word is God, Word is man, Word is beyond time, and Word is truth. Word is the product of Sky Father, the myth of a Western civilization that demands monotheistic worship of a patriarchal god, the spirit who reigns over all matter (Baring & Cashford, 1993; Eliade, 1958); a myth ostensibly compatible with the current or emerging social order at the birth of Judaism.

Word, moving forward several millennia, is understood as a component of language especially as considered through structuralism, a Western cultural theoretical lens rooted in the thinking of de Saussure, a turn-of-the-twentieth-century Swiss linguist. Structuralism posits that: first, words are arbitrarily assigned to that with which they are associated; second, words are relational, requiring other words to provide perspective of their meaning; and third, language not only describes the world, it creates the world. For example, we indiscriminately divide a continual year into seasons through the words spring, summer, fall, and winter (Barry, 2009, pp. 41–43). Historical Western culture has taken words to signify something, and, by this, we have given language intrinsic purpose making it *real*. In this way, words are Jungian signs as they represent what is already known (Jung 1950a, para. 105).

This reflects Coupe's (2009, p. 91) point that words are a metaphorical house of cards. "Text has other texts as its context, and this accumulation of 'con-texts' is not contained by an ultimate 'Text of texts,' so to speak, that would articulate 'the Truth.'" Arguably, he continued, "there is no Word which can explain the meaning of the world once and for all" (p. 91). In extending Coupe's thesis through the perspective seemingly tendered by both Jung and Campbell, we might take a new approach that understands when biblical text is denoted, it becomes too fixed to be meaningful. Conversely, connotations of biblical mythical imagery have the potential to be universal.

To this end, *The Poisonwood Bible*, seen as a biblical metaphor, demonstrates the elusive nature of language, thus opening a renewed reading of the "Word." The vain and simple-minded Rachael communicates through her malapropisms that words can mistakenly take on significant new meanings. Adah, the hemiplegic twin born paralyzed on one side, delights in seeing the world from a different perspective, including reading backwards. Through the passages that give voice to her time in the Congo, Adah often shares the palindromes she has scrawled into her journal: "Lived a tune, rare nut, a devil, Lived a devil! Lived a devil!" (Kingsolver, 2005, p. 360). In their warped, reversed orientation, Adah's palindromes are an example of what Coupe has suggested as "context," demonstrating the paradoxical "truth" that words can as easily manipulate as they are easily manipulated.

It is through the retelling of the Price father, Nathan, the missionary preacher whose voice is otherwise silenced in the novel, that the evasive qualities of Word are best exposed:

> "Tata Jesus is Bangala!" declares the Reverend every Sunday at the end of his sermon. More and more, mistrusting his interpreters, he tries to speak in Kikongo … Bangala means something precious and dear. But the way he pronounces it, it means the poisonwood tree. Praise the Lord, hallelujah, my friends! for Jesus will make you itch like nobody's business.
>
> (Kingsolver, 2005, p. 276)

As Adah shares in the above passage, the Kikongo language employs the same word to express many meanings. Through mispronunciation, Nathan associates Christ, Nathan's lord and savior, with a plant that will kill if the smoke from its burning branches is inhaled. His intense desire to conform the Congolese to Christianity, coupled with his mistrust of those same people, renders his efforts not only negligible but noxious.

Like her twin sister Adah, Leah encourages a nuanced approach to language. In the following passage, Leah, now middle-aged and still living in the Congo, reconciles the challenges of the Kikongo language by sewing a red thread through the words' woven connectedness:

> We worried over *nzolo* – it means *dearly beloved*; or a white grub used for fish bait; or a special fetish against dysentery; or little potatoes. Finally I see how

these things are related … precious as the first potatoes … precious as the fat-
test grubs … Only by life's best things are your children protected.

(Kingsolver, 2005, p. 505)

Leah and Adah demonstrate a risk posited by post-structuralism: assuming Word
as truth when it is narrowly defined on limited perspective. In the world of the
Kikongo, the words command meaningful relational meanings: they are the appropriate signs for the world *in which they are known*.

As previously stated, language is relational and creates the world; however, the
world it creates is inherently related to the world in which it lives. *The Poisonwood
Bible* thus challenges Western culture's historical and current denotations of biblical
verse as it demonstrates that no one language, no one culture, no one world, can
own the meaning of biblical text. Words are only signs for the culture in which they
exist. Thus, the verses John 1:1 and 1:14, prompted by the mythical imagery of the
novel, seem to connote the paradoxical concept that Word, whether interpreted
as reason, God, man, truth, or whatever meaning any culture might assign it, will
always remain, at its essence unknowable, just as a Jungian symbol (Jung, 1950a,
para.105). *The Poisonwood Bible* then helps to reclaim the myth of the Bible, demonstrating that the Bible has been, is, and will be rebirthed time and time again so
that it may serve, but never be subservient to, any given temporal or spatial system.

A Rebirthing of the Bible's Creation Myth

Having argued biblical myth as being open to renewed interpretation, let us consider what the Bible story of creation might mean to current and emerging societies
when it is re-visioned through a reading of *The Poisonwood Bible* as visionary art.

In the novel, the American missionary family is exposed to a new, astonishing
side of nature that had been purged from the Price's hometown of Bethlehem,
Georgia. This nature, the Congo, is beautiful yet dark: she gives; she takes away. The
Prices experience droughts then monsoons; they observe the withering away of
their sewn seedlings despite magnificent indigenous vines spontaneously overtaking
the same earth. Yet the family unequivocally comprehends nature's power by way of
an assumed inconsequential insect. Because of drought, all creatures of the Congo
are struggling to survive, including the ant. In one night, the small village is eaten
alive by an army of ants that drive the villagers into the river for protection while
the ants consume all that humans have left behind. Leah, the daughter who most
closely follows her father's preachings, is shattered by what she sees as Sky Father's
abandonment. Journaling her thoughts and dialogue with Anatole, an orphaned
schoolteacher who will later become her husband, Leah writes:

We were walking on, surrounded, enclosed, enveloped, being eaten by ants.
Every surface was covered and boiling, and the path like black flowing lava in
the moonlight … "Do you think this is the hand of God?" … "No." "Then
why?" "The world can always give you reasons. No rain, not enough for the

ants to eat" ... "God hates us" ... "Don't blame God for what ants have to do. We all get hungry. Congolese people are not so different from Congolese ants."

(Kingsolver, 2005, pp. 299, 308)

Anatole shares with Leah the way of nature: not a nature that is evil, but *Nature* who will protect herself against humans who do not see fit to live cooperatively with her.

Years later, Leah, having spent her adult life in impoverished Africa, has come to understand how Earth requires humans to make choices in order to survive. Here Leah speaks to Rachael, explaining an ancient ruin built of human bones:

So what looks like mass murder to us is probably misinterpreted ritual. They probably had ways of keeping their numbers in balance in times of famine ... You just can't assume that what's right or wrong for us is the same as what was right or wrong for them.

(Kingsolver, 2005, pp. 489–490)

This excerpt also illustrates how each society functions relative to its particular temporal and spatial system: a culture existing within a different system risks misjudging another's approach to life.

In another passage, Adah, who becomes a physician yet practices as an infectious disease epidemiologist, studying the bacteria and viruses that inhabit Central Africa, speaks to the same sense of balance, understanding that *Nature* seeks to survive:

In the world, the carrying capacity for humans is limited. History holds all things in the balance ... When Albert Schweitzer walked into the jungle ... he carried antibacterials and a potent, altogether new conviction that no one should die young. He meant to save every child, thinking Africa would then learn how to have fewer children ... Overpopulation has deforested three-quarters of Africa, yielding drought, famine, and the probable extinction of all animals most beloved by children and zoos ... For every life saved by vaccination or food relief, one is lost to starvation or war.

(Kingsolver, 2005, pp. 527–528)

Adah speaks for "other." She speaks for marginalized Africa and Africans who seemed once to have struck a balance, living out their own version of symbiosis, that is, before Western civilization pillaged Africa's resources and told Africans how to behave:

Poor Africa. No other continent has endured such an unspeakably bizarre combination of foreign thievery and foreign goodwill ... My church is the Great Rift Valley that lies along the eastern boundary of the Congo ... This is the story I believe in: When God was a child, the Rift Valley cradled a cauldron of bare necessities, and out of it walked the first humans upright on two legs. With their hands free, they took up tools and beat from the bush their own food and shelter and their own fine business of right and wrong ...

> They engaged a powerful affinity with their habitat and their food chain …
> It honors the balance between loss and salvation … God is in everything…
> God is a virus… God is an ant … If you could … rise up out of your own
> beloved skin and appraise ant, human, and virus as equally resourceful beings,
> you might admire the accord they have all struck in Africa.
>
> (pp. 528–529)

Coupe (2009, p. 195) argued from an ecocritical angle that art in the form of literature can function as symbolism manifesting a "power to change or intensify our sense of
responsibility to our natural environment." Coupe's perspective of art as symbol seems to
reflect Jung (1931, para. 118) in his posit that symbol in art is the "intimation of meaning beyond the level of our present powers of comprehension." Further, Coupe (2009,
pp. 200–201) cited Lovelock's "Gaia Theory" (an alternative term for "Earth System
Science") as the Earth being a "self-regulating organism" with a "dark side," warning
"that [humans] will very likely not survive the ecocastrophe to come," as it is "in the best
interest of the planet that we do not, so that Gaia can regain her balance once more."

Rowland (2012) has explored a slightly different yet complementary perspective
in that art (specifically as literature) is the act of nature creating knowledge. Her
argument begins by citing Wheeler's (2006) work regarding art as created by the
human enactment of animate nature and Polyani's (1967) posit that tacit knowledge
is the co-effort of body and psyche. It then weaves in Jung's (1954) perspective
of synchronicity (meaningful simultaneous occurrences of subjective and objective
happenings). What follows is the final tapestry of Rowland's (2012, p. 38) thesis: the
"unconscious is both nature in us, and specifically here, in synchronous acts, the
nature of the non-human world in us."

Thus, in a very Jungian sense, *The Poisonwood Bible* may be a visionary work
of art meaning that Kingsolver may have unconsciously surfaced what is not yet
known, compensating for ignored others to include Earth. If Africa is a representative microcosm of the greater health of the planet, we may see in Africa's deple-
tion the impending devastation of Earth. We may also see Earth's ability to rise up
against the one species, human, that forsakes all her others, just as Lovelock warned.

However, visionary art may also be a manifestation of the unconscious bringing
forth a mythology that guides us, as Campbell said, "in relation to the society and the
whole world of nature, which is outside of us but also within us" (Mishlove, 1998,
para. 6). Thus, in combining both Rowland and Coupe's perspective as supported
by Campbell and Jung, gleaning a reciprocal relationship between art and nature,
I argue that *The Poisonwood Bible* is a radical typology of Genesis, where nature is
rebirthing the biblical creation myth. With this in mind, I consider a renewed reading of Genesis 1:27 and 1:28 (NIV):

> So God created man in his own image, in the image of God he created him; male
> and female he created them. God blessed them and said to them, "Be fruitful and
> increase in number, fill the earth and subdue it. Rule over the fish of the sea and
> the birds of the air and over every living creature that moves on the ground."

"God created man in his own image." If seen through a lens of society's current English standards, the sentence reads, "God created man in man's own image," for the pronoun "him" must refer to the object to which it is most adjacent. If the same method is applied to the second part of Genesis 1:27, the line then reads: "In the image of God, man created himself." The line would finish as "male and female, man created other." Interpreted as rebirthed myth, man likens himself as the image of God and creates what Jung (1950b, para. 221) called a persona, the mask one metaphorically wears to hide one's true nature from himself and others. But this persona was only an image of God that man perceived he could possess, patriarchal and monotheistic. The byproduct of this creation was the feminine other that had to be cast aside from this monotheistic spirit. Along with the casting aside of the feminine went matter, including earth and body as Earth Mother (Baring & Cashford, 1993). God had been split between Sky Father and Earth Mother, and man had anointed Sky Father as supreme.

In Genesis 1:28, God, not the imaged monotheistic spirit possessed by man, but whole God, "blessed them," the other, "and said to them, 'Be fruitful and increase in number, fill the earth and subdue it. Rule over the fish of the sea and the birds of the air and over every living creature that moves on the ground.'" The other, then, as feminine matter, is told to care for herself.

When read in this way, the Bible as supported by the rebirthed biblical myth of *The Poisonwood Bible*, espouses the shared dominion and responsibility of Earth Mother and Sky Father: a coniunctio, a union of matter and spirit, of feminine and masculine. Western culture is called to see anew what is held as perfect in the eyes of the divine. In a mythical sense, the novel may renew our perspective of creation, calling us to embrace Earth and feminine not as "other" but as intrinsic parts of ourselves and our society. Perhaps then, the Bible, as myth, guides toward a path where human harmoniously exists within nature.

The Bible's Deliverance Myth Spoken Anew

So then if we embrace our connection to Earth and feminine, how might we get there? In this final area of discussion, I suggest that the novel as renewed biblical narrative calls us to re-vision our approach to what is heroic. I begin by sharing two quotes, the first from *The Poisonwood Bible* and the second from Genesis:

> I was blinded from the constant looking back: Lot's wife. I only ever saw the gathering clouds.
>
> (Kingsolver, 2005, p. 98)

> With the coming of dawn, the angels urged Lot, saying, "Hurry! Take your wife and your two daughters who are here, or you will be swept away" … "Flee for your lives! Don't look back" … But Lot's wife looked back, and she became a pillar of salt.
>
> (Gen. 19:15, 19:17, 19:26, NIV)

Exodus, book five of *The Poisonwood Bible*, is a rebirth of the deliverance myth as Orleanna Price portends when she likens herself to Lot's wife much earlier in the novel. Lot's story is also a myth of deliverance where Lot and his daughters escape God's wrath. Yet Lot's wife seemingly cannot help but to stare back to her home, the city of Sodom, thus she is reduced to a pillar of salt.

A denotative reading of these texts (*The Poisonwood Bible* and Genesis) implies that these women are weak, giving in to their personal fears and desires. Orleanna feels impotent in her inability to rise up against her husband and return her children to their American home. Lot's wife is literally rendered inanimate when she physically turns to witness the destruction of her homeland. Yet examining passages of the New Testament, the very salt in which Lot's wife is turned is associated with what is righteous: "You are the salt of the earth" (Matt. 5:13, NIV); "Salt is good" (Mark 9:50, NIV). A radical typology perspective might see the Gospel as rebirthing a Genesis deliverance myth, suggesting that Lot's wife is good, and, thereby, returned to Earth. In this way, we might envisage that Lot's wife is recreated by being set free from the unilateral domination of Sky Father to be embraced by the otherness of Earth Mother (cf. Hillman, 1982, and Marlan, 1995, for further explorations of salt in the alchemical process).

In the story of Orleanna Price, the tragedy of losing her baby Ruth May to the land of Africa at the hands of men who will stop at nothing to prove their command of God's will, emboldens Orleanna to rise from the depths of her darkness and deliver, from the Congo and from Nathan, her remaining daughters: "We only took what we could carry on our backs. Mother never once turned around to look over her shoulder" (Kingsolver, 2005, p. 389). Thus, we might connote a metaphor from these women's stories, that there must first be destruction before (re)creation. The psychologist Hillman (1999, p. 36) wrote, "The creating Gods are the destroying Gods. As Jung said, 'Creation is as much destruction as it is construction,'" adding that "the destruction of the soul is the counterpart of the creation of soul." For Hillman, soul-making, the development and relationship to our true selves through thoughtful reflection and deep mythical awareness of our lived experiences, naturally requires soul-destroying. He wrote: "the essence of creativity is that these aspects [destruction and construction] exist within each other *in every act*: that which builds at the same time tears down, and that which breaks up at the same time restructures" (p. 37). It is as if the texts of both the Bible and the novel mythically image that rebirth first requires some form of death.

This renewed myth of Lot's wife is also narrated in the stories of Adah and Leah, the twins that throughout the novel seem to reflect the contrasting yet relational properties of twins imaged in several creation myths (von Franz, 1972). Adah is delivered from Africa by Orleanna just as Lot's wife is physically removed from her home of Sodom. Yet, as Lot is never able to rescue his wife from Sodom, Adah will forever belong to Africa. Upon Adah's return to the States, she learns through the help of a neurologist to animate the paralyzed side of her body. It is through this regeneration that adult Adah recognizes she has left in Africa, the continent to which she now devotes her mind, what she perceives as the best part of herself, the person she refers to as the palindrome Ada:

Along with my split-body drag, I lost my ability to read in the old way ... How can I explain that my two unmatched halves used to add up to more than one whole? In the Congo I was one-half *benduka* the crooked walker, and one-half *bënduka*, the sleek bird that dipped in and out of the banks ... Tall and straight as I may appear, but I will always be Ada inside. A crooked little person trying to tell the truth.

(Kingsolver, 2005, pp. 492–496)

The rebirthed deliverance myth is also shared in Leah's adult story. Though Orleanna is able to extricate Leah from the Kikongo village, in the journey out of Africa, Leah is struck by near-fatal malaria that prevents her from leaving with her mother and sister. Leah is like Lot's wife in that she will never be rescued from Africa for in the weeks that follow Orleanna and Adah's departure, Africa captures Leah through love. It becomes the home of her husband, Anatole, and her mission. Leah, still shackled to her father's Christian canon that good must prevail over evil, is captivated by her idealism to see justice done in the Congo. Her father's righteous dogmatism ultimately transforms into Leah's personal hunger to see Africa, its ecosystem, and its people eventually embraced as holding their own essential purposes on Earth.

The Poisonwood Bible once again invites renewed connotation of the Bible by shifting the perspective of what we, in Western culture, have perceived as deliverance. In this novel, the damsels are re-animated. If Lot's wife's and Orleanna's stories are read from a metaphorical connotation perspective, we might see in the rebirthed narrative of deliverance that destruction is required in order to bring forth creation. Likewise, by remaining in Africa, Adah and Leah image the willful choice to embrace "other" rather than being rescued from it. In these ways, the deliverance myth regenerates, becoming *heroine* myth: these women boldly become salt of the earth, breaking free not just from their own past but from a historical Western cultural approach that seeks to be rescued from "other." They no longer function as pawns in a hero's myth that follows a pattern of battling and conquering that which is deemed alien; rather, they choose to commune with what is both of and other than themselves. Embracing the perspective that human and non-human nature are intrinsically parts of each of us opens a pathway toward wholeness. The novel is rebirthing biblical myth, compelling us to find and live out each of our own life-paths in a way that never need denigrate the path of any other of Earth's creatures because we understand all of Earth's creatures are part of our own selves.

In Closing, an Opening

The Poisonwood Bible is, in its own right, a beautiful story of the tragedy of colonialism and the tyranny of governments that will stop at nothing to marginalize others to better themselves. But in a renewed reading of the novel and biblical scripture, the narrative woven by Kingsolver is a radical typology of biblical myth. Rebirthing the myth of the Bible by inviting a new interpretation of the Word liberates biblical text from the shackles of Sky Father's monotheistic, patriarchal stronghold such that each social order might embrace the teachings of the Bible as a connection to the divine in the unique way that it consciously and unconsciously serves its own space and time. In rebirthing the Bible's creation myth as told in Genesis through the newly narrated myth of *The Poisonwood Bible*, we may come to appreciate that human does not reign supreme over nature, and while nature may be tolerant of human, Earth will stop at nothing to rebalance the ecosystem such to ensure her survival. Finally, in seeing the myth of deliverance anew, we are invited to renew our courage in accepting and fulfilling our own destinies to include a psychological and cultural rebirth with ourselves and our planet.

The Poisonwood Bible is a visionary work that beckons inhalation of a burning bush such that we may draw in the beauty of biblical myth, not as a toxic absolute truth, but as mythical imagery that may be narrated anew, time and time again. The novel opens the possibilities of rebirthed connotations of the Bible for those of us whom have long since lost connection with Sky Father but have not forsaken a desire to commune and live in harmony with what is both within and beyond ourselves.

References

Adams, M.V. (2008). "Imaginology: The Jungian Study of the Imagination," in S. Marlan (ed.), *Archetypal Psychologies: Reflections in Honor of James Hillman*. New Orleans, LA: Spring Journal, pp. 225–242.

Baring, A. & Cashford, J. (1993). *The Myth of the Goddess: Evolution of an Image*. London: Penguin Books.

Barker, K. (ed.) (1995). *The NIV Study Bible*. Grand Rapids, MI: Zondervan Publishing House.

Barry, P. (2009). *Beginning Theory: An Introduction to Literary and Cultural Theory*. Manchester: Manchester University Press.

Coupe, L. (2009). *Myth*. Oxford: Routledge.

Eliade, M. (1958). *Patterns of Comparative Religions*, R. Sheen (trans.). Lincoln and London: Bison Books.

Hillman, J. (1982). "Salt: An Essay in Alchemical Psychology," in (1982) J.S. Stroud & G. Thomas (eds.), *Images of the Untouched: Virginity in Psyche, Myth and the Community*. Dallas, TX: Spring Publications.

Hillman, J. (1999). *The Myth of Analysis: Three Essays in Archetypal Psychology*. Evanston, IL: Northwestern University Press.

Jung, C.G. (1931). "On the Relation of Analytical Psychology to Poetry," in *Collected Works*, Vol. 15, *The Spirit in Man, Art, and Literature* (2nd edn). Princeton, NJ: Princeton University Press.

Jung, C.G. (1950a). "Psychology and Literature," in *Collected Works*, Vol. 15, *The Spirit in Man, Art, and Literature* (2nd edn). Princeton, NJ: Princeton University Press.

Jung, C.G. (1950b). "Concerning Rebirth," in *Collected Works*, Vol. 9i, *The Archetypes of the Collective Unconscious* (2nd edn). Princeton, NJ: Princeton University Press.

Jung, C.G. (1954). "On the Nature of the Psyche," in *Collected Works*, Vol. 8, *On the Nature of the Psyche* (2nd edn). Princeton, NJ: Princeton University Press.

Kingsolver, B. (2005). *The Poisonwood Bible*. New York: Harper Perennial.

Kingsolver, B. (2012). Frequently Asked Questions: Previous Books. Available at: www.kingsolver.com/faq/previous-books.html#32 (accessed August 12, 2015).

Marlan, S. (ed.) (1995). *Salt and the Alchemical Soul: Three Essays by Ernest Jones, C.G. Jung and James Hillman*. Woodstock, CT: Spring Publications.

Mishlove, J. (1998). "Understanding Mythology with Joseph Campbell," in *Thinking Allowed: Conversations on the Leading Edge of Knowledge and Discovery with Dr. Jeffrey Mishlove*. Tulsa, OK: Council Oak Books.

Polyani, M. (1967). *The Tacit Dimension*. London: Routledge & Kegan Paul.

Rowland, S. (2012). *The Ecocritical Psyche: Literature, Evolutionary Complexity, and Jung*. Hove, UK: Routledge.

von Franz, M.L. (1972). *Creation Myths*. Boston and London: Shambhala, revised edition, 1995.

Wheeler, W. (2006). *The Whole Creature: Complexity, Biosemiotics and the Evolution of Culture*. London: Lawrence & Wishart.

PART IV
India

6

LIFE THREADS

C.G. Jung's 1938 and 1944 'Orissa' Awakenings

Evangeline A. Rand

Introduction

Following the germination of seeds already planted in *A Jasmine Journey: Carl Jung's Travel to India and Ceylon, 1937–1938 and Jung's Vision During Illness, "Something New" Emerging from Orissa, 1944* (2013), my chapter explores a minute jewel discovered in the Jung archival treasure house in Zürich – a new and tangible hint of a significant detail of Jung's experience with a particular family and their textile business in Madurai, the South Indian town of the great temple of Meenakshi, the ancient fish-eyed goddess. This 'clue' compelled me to locate and visit this family twice and also thread ever more deeply with textiles, the 'soul of India', incredible fabrics that have woven and coloured India's politics, history, culture, and spirituality. I also explore 'Orissa' awakenings of her interwoven arts and culture and some of her great temples in the towns of Puri, Bhubaneswar, Konark, and Cuttack, a *golden* triangle of ancient and contemporary pilgrimage and tourism.

In what appears as a seamless continuum of the evolution of what I call Jung's 'Vishnu-oriented genius' these revelations were woven into his later works. At the end of his life Jung was toasting not only the birth of the 'new and ancient woman' but also the birth of the voice of poetic tradition, the poetry of what we do. Furthermore, Jung's second 'Orissa' awakening placed him in what is now a *dark* triangle of current deepest ecological crisis on India's East coast, a critically polluted cluster/industrial area. These themes are developed through reflections of my two recent journeys in India during January/February 2013 and 2014, following in Jung's footsteps and employing an Indian popular tradition of picture storytelling.

Weaving an Indian Journey

Research for *A Jasmine Journey* (Rand, 2013) exposed aspects of Jung's fateful 1937–1938 journey to India and Ceylon[1] and his lifelong connections with India, revealing his Vishnu-oriented genius, his appreciation of emergent, story embedded creation as nature would have it. In the spirit of *Phoenix Rising*, my picture storytelling at the International Association of Jungian Studies 2014 conference journeyed to the fertile Orissa delta of eastern India – where Jung spent a few highly significant days and was my place of conception, birth, and early home.

The figures for this chapter, a picture story, may be accessed by requesting a password at www.evangelinerand.com/life_threads_orissa_awakenings.html.

(Figure 6.1) Pausing at a translucent doorway in Jaizelmer, northwest India, I am reminded that fully engaging with both story and narrative requires patience and a capacity for experiencing both embodied pleasure and even danger (Frank, 2004, 2012).

Setting up a Loom to Weave a Cradle Story

(Figure 6.2) Weaving a life myth on our given personal and societal warp requires long effort. Depth psychology's function is to assist to re-establish the movement of the weft shuttle if it gets stuck and even to perceive the order of warp threads. The effort requires Martial capacities of weaving rhythm with form.

The Sanskrit word *sutra* refers to an aphorism, or a collection of aphorisms, in the form of a text in Hinduism or Buddhism. Literally, it means a thread or a string that holds things together and is derived from the verbal root 'to sew'.[2] Probably the word originally referred to the texts inscribed on palm leaves and sewn together with thread. In Orissa **(Figure 6.3)**, I find an Oriyan rounded script gouged by hand into palm leaves and **(Figure 6.4)** a manuscript united with a central cord, the sutra.

Stein (2013, pp. 179–203) notes that *tantra*, with its emphasis on *shakti,* is derived from the root *tan* – to spread, or to weave and stretch – and the seeing of the world as a loom. Shakti is suggested as the hidden substance that pervades and activates everything as world soul. Shakti is sheer potential awaiting its awakening through conscious action.

In exploring 'cultural synchronicities' and the idea that space and time take on a 'more interactive mode in the democratic world', Cambray (2009, p. 89) notes two evocative metaphors from archaic Greece: hitting the mark through true aim and strength in archery and passing the shuttle through openings formed through the warp threads.

(Figure 6.5) Since 1968, I have lived mostly on the western Prairies, although born and raised in a variety of locations in India until I turned 15. My latter life has been full of pilgrimage. Though I had no impulse to return to India for 55 years, my interest in a well-known Indian style of rigorous yogic practice (as described by Goswamy, 2013) has encouraged me to make the journey: a continual weaving requiring challenging, assiduous presence, and Martian discipline, yet not time driven.

My last two India journeys, in 2013 and 2014, were enlivened by my research into Jung's fateful few weeks in India and Ceylon in 1937–1938. Except for Cuttack and Angul, I had never visited the places referred to here. This journey is not about going home in the sense of reminiscing; rather, I am discerning the spirits of my time that give depth to the creation of my life.

(Figure 6.6) This map shows Jung's journey in India and Ceylon, which I had exhumed in the spring of 2012 from an *Eidgenössische Technische Hochschule* (ETH) Zürich archived brochure. The map had been prepared for the group with whom Jung travelled (Rand, 2013, p. 4). In finding the map, surprisingly I dreamt of seeing a living and rooted tree trunk in the process of being garlanded and decorated.

(Figure 6.7) About 20 years ago, I painted a long sequence of big 'picture stories' illustrating sections of Jung's last great work, *Mysterium Coniunctionis*. I have presented picture stories in all my IAJS presentations since 2006. My missionary father was well known in India as a travelling picture and flannel-graph storyteller in numerous isolated villages in the 1930s and 1940s, walking, travelling by horseback, and fording rivers.

Unbeknownst to me 20 years ago, this style of picture storytelling hearkens back to Bengal. Jung's grand imaginative story and the original oral Bengal picture story have surprising parallels.

To illustrate, in Bengal 2,500 years ago, a monster came out of its cave every night and ate people. The people survived by showing the monster his mirror image. He rushed at it head on, breaking the mirror into thousands of pieces. Seeing the fragments, he dissolved in tears. His picture, and his demise, were painted on a large leaf and taken from village to village by the storyteller (Ghosh, 2013).

Perhaps today our vitalizing story would tell of a monster that bangs its head on a holographic plate that scatters to reveal an interwoven and unfolding Goethean scientific revelation that 'here is everywhere and everywhere is here', and that 'no part is independent of the whole' (Bortoft, 1996, pp. 5–7).

(Figure 6.8) Here is my picture storytelling concerning re-birth:

1. Something has died …
2. Enduring the emptiness in my dark cave, I cradle death.
3. A new child begins to take shape …
4. with that marvellous umbilical cord, that spiral connecting pathway between mother and child.
5. Don't forget the placenta. In ancient Egypt it was revered as the child's twin. Seeing the lurid reddish-purple glistening placenta can be a visual shock greater than seeing the baby.
6. A newborn baby.

(Figure 6.9) Indeed, a new baby with ten fingers, ten toes, a good sucking reflex, and a healthy umbilicus memorial spot.

I am weaving a 'cradle story', elaborating, embroidering, and emphasizing a process in the individual psyche that seeks its own goal independently of – and sometimes in spite of – external factors. Jung described this 'forming of itself according to itself', the recognition of a 'larger, greater personality maturing within us … *as nature would have it*', [emphasis added] (Jung, 1950a, para. 235) just weeks before the outbreak of the Second World War, a year after his return from India. Jung's description becomes more and more extraordinary in our only causal world. Yet this independent process is Life! (Bortoft, 1996, p. 268)

A life-based cradle story, a 'rhizome story', is discerned and disclosed with progressive immanence. It cannot be grasped as a merely external object. Without the continual birthing of a life story, we are lost in mere fantasy (Kane, 1989) – cut off from our rhizome, cut off from true imagination, and unavailable to take a personally sustained and vital stance in the world.

Late in Life Journeys to India: 2013

(**Figure 6.10**) India reveals unparalleled beauty – with ancient roots and practices and unbelievable sights of chaos and global garbage. (**Figure 6.11**) How to digest such chaotic complexities and beauty? India is the world's biggest democracy with 1.27 billion people, 17 official languages, and hundreds of mother tongues. Built uniquely into the constitution is the recognition that a strong sense of identity and freedom from colonialism must include respect for the human hand.[3] This is palpable on Republic Day (January 26) as representations from all over the Indian Republic pour through that memorial gate of the honoured dead revealing something of India's vital, rhythmic, ongoing, Martian nature married to a finesse of creative heritage and staggering and sensual beauty.

(**Figure 6.12**) During deep and chaotic illness, I experienced an eruption of Mars' Arithmetica and Jupiter's Geometrica in my own psyche, initially infuriating me and requiring a lot of hard work to re-approach deliberations on primary number, time, and space,[4] and to realize Mars as a strong part of my astrological beginnings! My journals began to change in character. Through this new learning and ordering, I framed what I call Jung's Vishnu-oriented genius.[5]

(**Figure 6.13**) I arrived in Delhi in January 2013 amidst the furore of the previous December 16 gang rape and murder – a very complicated matter. I landed right in my experienced professional field (Kane, 1989). And (**Figure 6.14**) I brought with me a 1936 parental photograph of the Delhi First World War Memorial designed by British architect Sir Edwin Lutyens to commemorate the thousands of Indian soldiers who lost their lives in Europe and the Middle East on behalf of the Empire of the British Raj. This is a Delhi sight Jung would definitely have seen on Christmas Day in 1937.

World Wars and Dream Threads

(**Figures 6.15 and 6.16**) During four previous research journeys to the First World War Somme battlefield of Normandy,[6] I had discovered the Indian Memorial, while recognizing Osiris in the suffocating coffin. I was also drawn to the wonderful damp moisture and the 'dense skies of Normandy',[7] under which Guillaume de Conches was born and which were reflected in his twelfth-century Chartrian teachings. His particular style of language read the world on the page and in the sky, his appreciation of the presence of 'world soul' as 'inwoven in the cosmos' (Ellard, 2007, p. xix and ch. 7). He influenced Paracelsus, and through him, Dorn, whose work accompanied Jung to India – an important but unvalued sutra thread.

(**Figure 6.17**) Visiting the site of the Second World War's Normandy pre-dawn Pegasus Landing on D-Day, 1944, it is hard to imagine the dramatic character change on the leaf of this storyteller. Indeed, a transformation of archetypal Pegasus occurred for Jung at the end of his life, as we shall note. But now you know something of the warp of my loom and I can begin to weave the weft threads.

(**Figure 6.18**) Into all these ruminations comes a dream of comfortably crouching, gazing into an empty rectangular dish in northwest India, sensing I was close to a great and flowing river. Perhaps it was the Indus? I had never been there. It is historically a place of many ancient civilizations and of a particular unity – prior to the traumatic 1947 political division. From the beginning, my home has been – and is – full of India. Yet this dream reveals an emptiness in the rectangular, riverside vessel.

Embroidered Fingerprints

A 1938 ETH-archived Tamil business card led me on a difficult search in Madurai, South India – close to the great Meenakshi temple of the fish-eyed goddess – to find a family of fabric sellers whose grandparents had met Jung. I have visited them twice; they spontaneously noted 'synchronous' happenings around my arrival and were self-described Vishnavites. They were delightedly enthusiastic that I would mention them and their family connection with Dr. Jung. The husband is descended from the original six brothers whom Jung visited while they worked in their adjacent homes. A small textile-trading moment is perhaps a significant thread in a Jungian world. Bear in mind that, unlike Germany, the imperial worlds of Britain, Portugal, and France intersected with India for trade, primarily in textiles.

(**Figure 6.19**) My own love of textiles, threads, and ornamentation shows through one of my embroideries[8] that took many years to incorporate collected and much-loved miniatures. Inspired by Allan Watts' 1963 book *The Two Hands of God*, each petal of flame is hand sewn and turned inside out. (**Figure 6.20**) The whole scene is woven into my fingerprints and lines of fate.

(**Figure 6.21**) We see a Winnicottian deep appreciation of the human thumb – the development of the child's transitional and functional movements into playful imagination. On this poignant detail, I pause to remember a horrendous aspect of British imperial rule. Greedy for the success of British Lancashire mills, Indian fabric skills were essentially stolen, and the thumbs of many Bengali weavers were literally cut off. Paradoxically, in the seventeenth, eighteenth, and nineteenth centuries, the British did some of the best documentation of Indian artisan practices, including their crafts and tools (Chatterjee, 2009).

Village Artisans: Living Through Creation

(**Figure 6.22**) Travelling in the expansive and profound educational impulse of Maiwa Handprints,[9] amongst the Kutch desert artisans in the little town of Bhujodi, a wonderful meal is shared. Then there is the showing of masterpieces and, of course, buying and selling. (**Figure 6.23**) Two of the five weaving brothers of a family studio, Shamji and Rajiv, show a masterpiece woven after the recent Kutch earthquake. Recovering from horrendous disaster, they learned that they must work as a community: this weaving represents a new design, they tell us. (**Figure 6.24**) We immediately see its inwoven four-fold design.

(**Figure 6.25**) All in the presence of the cow and her new calf, we learn that in the springtime, (**Figure 6.26**) men take their sons out into the desert to find the bulbs they need for their dying work and (**Figure 6.27**) that the indigo dye pot is a living process. It takes tremendous skill and ancient knowledge – kinship participation combined with seasonal insights – to keep this process alive. Even harvesting the indigo plant is very time specific and requires as much planning as a wedding.

Jodhpur: Marriage Preparations and Mehrangah Museum

(**Figure 6.28**) Wandering around Jodhpur early one morning in a garden by myself, I came upon wedding preparations everywhere (**Figure 6.29**) that even included hanging sparkling mirrors from the trees. (**Figure 6.30**) Jung's overwhelming eight-sided Ravenna Baptistery experience (Rand, 2008) was differently ornamented than this eight-sided overflowing, flowery expression of exuberance.

Then I heard a quiet voice asking me if I would like to see the cows. Absolutely! I was unaware there were cows in this wedding preparation compound, and I was graciously escorted to see them. I was asked if I would like my picture taken with the cows. What a splendid idea! (**Figure 6.31**) I've never looked as radiant as a bride, I'm sure!

(**Figure 6.32**) I come to charming museum cradles for royal babies, (**Figure 6.33**) this one presided over by Vishnu in his Krishna form leaning against his beloved cow Lakshmi. (**Figure 6.34**) Leaving the sandstone Mehrangah Museum, I begin to recognize a cradle of wandering – standing in thresholds and wondering. This is not the blood, sweat, and tears of extracting meaning: trying to understand and creating interpretations full of intention (Lockhart, 2014). No, this is the essential order of nesting, a required capacity for the emergence of a wholeness that is not the sum of the parts emerging in a linear fashion.

(**Figure 6.35**) I had only one dream during my 2013 journey in India. Feeling completely at ease I was standing under a huge cow, reaching up with my left hand to one of its udders. Some months later, back on the Prairies, I used my photo of a wonderfully appealing shopping bag to help coagulate and hold that one dream.

Yoni–Lingam Wholeness: Jung's Genius Seen Afresh

(**Figure 6.36**) Wandering further, I recognized a yoni–lingam beside a central tree – a common sight all over India. (**Figure 6.37**) Exploring Jung's eight-decade relationship with India, I introduced *A Jasmine Journey* (Rand, 2013, pp. 5–7, figs. 3–5) with photographs of a museum lingam obviously abducted from its matrix, the yoni – its physical, social, and cultural base. Symbols uprooted from their embedding origins call forth no psychological effort and result in no psychological rejuvenations. They cease to be symbols; they become simply signs of modernity.

Though the Sanskrit word *lingam* has no directly erotic connotations, it stands for a male principle. The Sanskrit word *yoni* means lap, womb, or origin. Some academics refer to yoni as a vagina[10] or even a stylized vagina (Beltz, 2011, p. 215, fn 26), with lingam placed in this said vagina. I am interested in womb, origin, and vulva – a reality that can slide away from discourse.

Jung's earliest remembered dream, when he was three or four (Jung, 1963, p. 11; Rand, 2013, pp. 2–4) shows him enthusiastically running towards a frightening mystery that oriented most of his life. Deep in the earth, pushing aside a brocade curtain, approaching by a blood-red carpet, little boy Jung saw an abstract, enormous tree trunk, 'ithyphallically enthroned'[11] in the darkness of a stone-lined rectangular hole in the ground. Jung later refers to it as an underground ritual temple, his initiation into 'the secrets of the earth' where he stayed buried for some time and where his 'intellectual life had its unconscious beginnings'. His lifelong engagement with this awakening, even terrifying, image reveals what I have called his Vishnu-oriented genius.

In India, I think of such an imaginative yoni–lingam scene as bearing a potential of life emergent, with its origins, surrounded and treasured through many rituals – the transitional activity of play and celebrations of creative emergence.[12]

(Figure 6.38) From 1918, Jung continued to develop his notion of *Pan Eros*, preferring it to Freud's definition of sexuality, right through to the 1960 arrival of *Pegasus as mare nursing a new and ancient woman* whose emergence through stone was to displace the king Jung had previously seen there. This is a staggering reversal of meanings from the pre-dawn D-Day *Pegasus* landing. Through his chiselling on stone, Jung toasted this new arrival of Pegasus nursing the new and ancient woman (Jung, 1975, paras. 615–616; Lockhart, 1987, pp. 72–79; Rand, 2013, pp. 109–114) – daughter of the mare, respectful, worshipful, openly desiring, reaching forward with her hand to receive and create real and volatile milk.

Jung's last great work written over the course of a decade, *Mysterium Coniunctionis: An Enquiry into the Separation and Synthesis of Psychic Opposites in Alchemy*, was finished in his 80th year. Jung highlights the synthesis of the *Shulamite* with *Parvati*, who in solitude realizes 'the secret immanence of the divine spirit of life in all things' (Jung, 1954a, para. 622). This is the realization of *Pan Eros*. John Dourley (personal communication, 22 March 2014) suggests that this 'sacred pantheism is at the core of the contribution Jung makes to our understanding of nature and human nature'.

Six months before his death, in two letters, Jung shows himself deeply engaged in the reception of Peter Birkhäuser's painting *Pegasus Arrives* (1980). Entwining Birkhäuser's painting and dream source with his own recent illness and dream, Jung includes a fourth factor: the evolution in time, a Vishnu task recognizing that everything becomes seen as full of life's inwoven realities and enterprise. To borrow Don

Fredricksen's (2014) phrase, Jung was stepping ever more fully into an ongoing 'synchronic liminality'.

Jung's relationship with acts of creation in time was further highlighted by the first and last time he penned a preface in a 1960 herald for a purely literary work by Miguel Serrano, *The Visits of the Queen of Sheba*, revealing his ongoing engagement with the ever-extending space and immeasurable depths of time of aesthetic experience.

Their relationship revolved around India: Serrano was probably the last visitor from abroad to visit Jung before his death. (Jung died on the 1961 anniversary of the June 6th D-Day.) Amongst other things, Serrano noticed a painting of Shiva on the summit of Mount Kailash, the mythological place of Shiva's abode with Parvati. (**Figure 6.39**) I recall that it takes the strength of the adoring bull Nandi to bear the combined weight of Shiva and Parvati.

Confrontation with Orissa: 2014

(**Figure 6.40**) I was glad for encounters with Nandi during my 2014 solo journey down the east coast of India. Visiting Orissa (Odisha), I focused particularly on the Puri–Bhubaneswar–Konark delta triangle of my own conception (in the jungle area of Angul), my 1943 birth, my early home (Cuttack), and my becoming-rhizome, placental re-conceptions of myself as I enter the eighth decade of my life.

(**Figure 6.41**) Jung briefly visited this delta area in January 1938. From Switzerland, Jung had arranged that he and Fowler McCormick would leave the main group of visiting scientists in order to travel from Calcutta to South India by themselves – including a few days in this delta area. Jung's overnight steam train would have pulled into Cuttack in the early morning – its particular light, sounds, and smells very familiar to me.

Entering Orissa, Jung would have carried within himself his appreciation of Richard Wilhelm, with whom he had originally produced *The Secret of the Golden Flower* in 1929 and from whom he deemed he had learned more than from any other man. They had met in 'the field of humanity beyond the academic boundary posts…There lay their points of contact; there the spark leapt across and kindled a light that was to become one of the most significant events of [Jung's] life' (Jung, 1931, paras. 74–76). Earlier, for Wilhelm's memorial service, Jung wrote that he had found Wilhelm's mind to be a 'rare, receptive and fruitful womb, a mind capable of giving re-birth to what might seem like a foreign spirit … a great and therefore "simple" medicine for the "keenness of western consciousness and its harsh problems."'[13] Sengupta (2013) hints that Orissa may have offered Jung more of the experience of wholeness that his own psychology sought (pp. 184–187). Orissa and its arts are often called the soul of India.

A later vision during illness reminded Jung of this Bay of Bengal field. He was to come back down to earth and find the people to whom he really belonged (Rand, 2013, p. 122). This vision was precisely on the fourth day of the fourth month of 1944. Rather a profound Number Four experience (Rand, 2013, ch. 4) two months before D-Day! Engaging with Jung's vision precipitates us into the golden Orissa delta pilgrimage triangle, so deeply associated with Lord Juggernath (also known as Vishnu), his brother Balhabadra, and the little sister Subhadra.

But we also fall into what has emerged as the dark triangle of a 'critically polluted cluster/industrial area' (Padel & Das, 2010), spiralling out from southern and middle Orissa. This is a natural bauxite/alumina-enriched area, now being corporately, internationally, plundered and ravaged, and entwined with the complex and bloody history of the aluminum industry at the heart of the global military–industrial complex. For many years I have located Jung's initial work with the 'realm of the dead', his effort to resuscitate deep, imaginative humankind values, as if emerging from a similar area of bauxite fertility and plunder in Provence, France (Rand, 2013, ch. 11). Only at the end of 2012 did I realize the similar enriched fertility and exploitable geological substrata of Provence and Orissa.[14]

Entering Orissa in January 1938, Jung brought in his trunk two documents: Rutherford's *Imperial Science* (Rand, 2013, ch. 7, pp. 70–72)[15] and, complete with envelope, Subramanya Iyer's *Wholeness in Truth*. Given that Jung was burdened by the demise of a truly living alchemy, these challenging documents hint at a tension Jung carried. No wonder he had to sink into profound containment as the journey ended.

To enter Cuttack is to enter what had been a busy port for many hundreds of years, and was the state capital when Jung visited. Its artisans are still renowned for their capacity to take lumps of raw silver and **(Figure 6.42)** create the most delicate filigree artifacts.[16] **(Figure 6.43)** The cross my mother was given at my birth was made at a nearby leper colony (Rand, 2013, fn. 208).

(Figure 6.44) Across the street from the present silver connoisseurs, I discover an infernal muddle, reminding me that Jung placed the terrifying Western muddle as the frontispiece to *C. W. Volume 13, Alchemical Studies* (Jung, 1967), that paradoxically opens with *The Secret of the Golden Flower*. **(Figure 6.45)** Fortunately for me, diagonally across the road are wonderful woven baskets for everyday use and traditional geometric–yantra invitations drawn daily at the threshold.[17]

Puri Temple and Puri Potters

(Figure 6.46) Arriving in Puri, the city of the Temple of Lord Juggernath, I am thankful to find yoni–lingam and adoring Nandi right outside my door, freshly attended each day.

Prior to my Indian journey in 2014, when attending *Yoga: The Art of Transformation*, I had noticed a large stack of *Temple Potters of Puri* (Cort & Mishra, 2012). **(Figure 6.47)** With help, I was able to obtain a copy.

(Figures 6.48 to 6.57) I found the potters – men, and women with their daughters – their homes and close communities immersed in the making of thousands of simple clay vessels for the great Juggernath temple feedings of pilgrims. I can think of few other life experiences of such a quiet authentic whole, a total immersion, no generalizations from a counterfeit whole (Bortoft, 1996, p. 69), no standing back. Jung may have had the air knocked out of him at Konark,[18] but there is no record of him visiting the Puri potters. In awe and appreciation, I saw multiplicity in unity, uniqueness without a felt fragmentation – an authentic community revealing itself, thousands of mirrors reflecting its basic organization. There is no separation between the primal phenomenon and its instances: 'There is no underlying reality *behind* the experiences, only the intensive depths of the phenomenon itself' (Bortoft, 1996, p. 233).

(**Figure 6.58**) With enormous courtesy and generosity of spirit, I had been taken across a threshold, one treasured and adorned with daily ritual. (**Figure 6.59**) I had an inkling of the necessity for the close presence of Nandi the bull.

Weaving Orissa: A Living Myth

(**Figure 6.60**) A potter's wife wearing a handwoven sari with ikat borders (Crill, 1998, p. 82, pl. 65) illustrates how potters, weavers, dancers, and poets are threaded together, inwoven with the land, culture, and geography. (**Figure 6.61**) Both warp and weft are ikat dyed and then woven in this silk sari (Crill, 1998, p. 82, pl. 65) revealing the motif of Vishnu's wakening conch shell and the Puri stepped triangular temple pattern.

(**Figure 6.62**) We know Jayadeva's Govinder-inscribed textiles were being created in Nuapatnam in 1719. (**Figure 6.63**) Today we still see rolls of handwoven silk ikat fabric outside the home studio. (**Figure 6.64**) One complete warp, tied and dyed, is placed so that the sun can fix the process.

(**Figures 6.65 and 6.66**) Inside the studio, I am shown an award winning ikat tenfold mandala of Vishnu's manifestation, complete with inwoven Oriyan script.

(**Figure 6.67**) 'Would you like to see a Lakshmi ikat wedding sari?' (**Figure 6.68**) 'Look – the couple is greeting each other with joy,' the weaver tells me. (**Figure 6.69**) I see Lakshmi's footprints in the eightfold mandalas. This is all eye-opening for me.

Love Through Aesthetic Experience

Both the warp and weft of Oriyan culture are a poem sung throughout Orissa and vitally alive all over India. Jayadeva's dramatic, medieval, lyrical poem *Gitagovinder* (Miller, 1970/1984) celebrates the intricacies of love between Krishna and Rhada joyously 'evoking the essence of existence' (Goswamy, 1986, p. 204). (**Figure 6.70**) This is a recently created painting using traditional, natural colours.

Jayadeva seemed to write for those sympathetic to an enjoyment of Krishna's love through aesthetic experience – a dramatic miracle. The poem arouses the audience to explore and engage fully with the poignant mood of the lovers when separated, particularly the eight moods of Rhada, and then to witness the center of existence – Krishna's ecstatic reunion with Rhada – in the forest thicket in the springtime. Such a scene suggests the lacuna in a Christian myth as many in the West have heard it and which, in the last 30 years, seems to have contributed to the furore of popular and scholarly interest concerning Mary Magdalene.

Jayadeva's Rhada is neither a wife nor a worshipping rustic playmate. She is an intense, solitary, proud female who complements and reflects Krishna's mood of passion (Miller, 1970/1984, p. 26). It is Rhada who brings Krishna home to the forest, the secret place of their divine love (ibid., p. 17). There are even hints that this aesthetic miracle would be a cure for our cosmic age of darkness. The legendary marriage suggests Jayadeva's initiation into the appreciation of Vishnu whose power is expressed through his consort Lakshmi. This is the foundational essence of *odissi*, Oryan dance, perhaps the oldest classical dance in India, developed through the religious art of temple dancers – known as the maharis – great women, the devadasis. Though profoundly affected by Kathakali dancers in Kerala, Jung would not have seen the great women of odissi, since their performance was prohibited by the British until India's independence.

Jayadeva's passionate *Gitagovinder* was first translated into English in 1792, but it was Edwin Arnold's translation of 1875 that was called *The Indian Song of Songs* (Miller, 1970/1984, p. x). With his Vishnu orientation, and unlike his father,[19] Jung was involved with the 'Christian' *Song of Songs* until the end of his life, attempting to further Dorn's work of bringing forth Sophia of the Gnostics that had become lost in Physis (Jung, 1954a, para. 592, 1954b, para. 699[20]). Why? So that man could be assimilated into the archetype of nature and to a love that is the process of mutual individuation where the archetypes become known as living forms of life.

Recent scholarship suggests Jayadeva was born near Puri. Though Jayadeva is known as a wandering poet, *Gitagovinder* may well 'have taken shape in the richly syncretic environment in Puri in the twelfth century' where, under the auspices of Juggernath, 'the Lord of the World', Jayadeva found sanctuary. Subject to much academic debate, everything about the worship, practices, sacraments, and rituals of Lord Juggernath does not conform to classic Hinduism.

(Figure 6.71) Offering his own Vishnu attributes to the creative endeavour, and recognizing and celebrating ten evolving aspects of Vishnu as a source of wonderment, Jayadeva's poem opens with an eloquent homage to the true nature of Krishna, who is none other than Vishnu – the profound and evolving nature of primal and cosmic man (Goswamy, 1986, p. 253). This devotional scene delicately and accurately places inscription on the far wall for the ten incarnations of Vishnu (Sei-Nainsukh, 1730).

(Figure 6.72) Ambling along to the Puri temple of the Juggernath, his brother, and his little sister, **(Figure 6.73)** I am remembering Jung's postcard from Puri and his accompanying journal notes regarding Wisdom's Western house (Rand, 2013, p. 77). **(Figures 6.74 and 6.75)** Puri is famous for its yearly celebration when the three gods are drawn out of the temple and taken across the square for a short holiday to a nearby temple. The pilgrim crowds are phenomenal, even everyday crowds. **(Figures 6.76 to 6.78)** We see pilgrim treasures and snacks, and are alerted to the street birth of a calf.

(Figure 6.79) We view the Puri temple and its kitchen – the biggest temple kitchen in the world – from the library opposite. Jung too had to view the temple from the outside only.

The Temple of Konark

(**Figures 6.80 to 6.86**) Along the coast, the Temple of Konark also draws many tourists and is approached by a large and beautiful road. In the twelfth century, this was a living temple, full of the wholeness of life, inwoven sexuality, astrological implications, dance, music and mandala wheels to adore the sun's uprisings. It astonished Jung and many other earlier European visitors and in the past its isolation seemed to add more appeal.

Puri and Cremation

Back to Puri in the evening, (**Figure 6.87**) wandering through town, I come to the burning grounds where bodies are openly cremated. There is that cow snitching garlands again, whenever she can, alongside the consuming flames, which are devoutly, quietly, and respectfully attended. (**Figures 6.88 and 6.89**) Crossing the road, I am in the beach-market, and (**Figure 6.90**) 50 yards further are the returning fishermen. Everything is woven together seamlessly. I feel as if I am walking in a very familiar dream.

On my last evening, I am taken to a place full of folk sculptures of mythological stories. (**Figures 6.91 and 6.92**) Astoundingly, as I enter, I am faced with an image propelling me back into the only dream of my 2013 India journey: there is Baby Krishna who reaches to nurse on the great cow! I never heard of such Baby Krishna happenings. He is even reaching for the same udder as I was, though he is using his right hand.

Bhubaneswar: Mercurial Threads

Bhubaneswar is a huge, busy, industrial city, also known as the City of 500 Temples. Shamdasani (2012) reveals some of the sketches of temple carving Jung made in his short visit. I developed some thoughts about Bhubaneswar and Jung's connections with Mercurius (Rand, 2013, pp. 105–108) as a thread of added complexity that Jung wove into his post-India mature work.

(**Figures 6.93 to 6.98**) Walking in the early morning through the city's quiet and contemplative compounds, I find that some temples date from the seventh century. (**Figure 6.99**) A priest is washing out his rice pot; I am told that later the fish will come for the rice grains. (This reminds me of Jung putting his porridge pot into the lake for the waiting fish at his Bollingen maternal hearth.) The fish expect this. (**Figure 6.100**) I am shown a daily-attended threshold honouring seven luminaries: the sun, the moon, and the five planets. At this small Bhubaneswar temple threshold, two eclipse figures are added to the seven: that which swallows the sun and that which swallows the moon. In a completely different style, Jung chiselled the seven luminaries on his special cube at Bollingen, honouring little Telesphorus who travels the world (Rand, 2013, pp. 115–118).

(**Figure 6.101**) There is further yoni–shakti insight into Jung's appreciation of Wilhelm's womb-like mind, 'a plant-like spontaneity, a language of living expression, the language of a living culture … a language that had remained alive (in China) … teachings that carried the delicate perfume of the golden flower' (Jung, 1931, para. 92). (**Figure 6.102**) There must be something in the way she moves! (**Figures 6.103 to 6.107**) Now I can appreciate the little logo sprinkled through Serrano's *The Visits of the Queen of Sheba* (1960/72, pp. 8, 27, 53). (**Figures 6.108 to 6.110**) In Bhubaneswar, Jung could have met a 'sculpted' odissi temple dancer of the threshold, but not a living, ritual dancer.

Personal Placental Threads

But what about my personal placental weave, my place of conception, close to Angul? (**Figure 6.111**) Road signage is an ever-present reminder of Lord Juggernath. (**Figure 6.112**) As night settles upon us alongside the great Mahanadi River, the old cowherd, always with his orange scarf, gathers together his beloved cows.

Where might I likely have been conceived? Old photos show a small and simple house with a thatched roof. (**Figure 6.113**) Is this a similar house? (**Figure 6.114**) I admire such care of handmade farming tools and excellently maintained and mudded walls. (**Figure 6.115**) I am entering the home courtyard of two brothers and their families, so welcoming. 'What are you doing?' I eventually ask. They are making a cradle; there is a new baby. (**Figure 6.116**) Her name is Lakshmi Priya.[21] I swear she has a halo! (**Figure 6.117**) This home is a cradle woven full of implication.

(**Figure 6.118**) An expansive post-Second World War connection here is Jung's reflection on Hildegard von Bingen's painting of a fourfold, square placental quickening of the child in the mother's womb (Jung, 1958, paras. 589–824; Jung, 1952, para. 656). Noting Jung's comments, Mathew Fox (1985) develops Hildegard's images as not only about our first birth, but also about our second – our renewal and regenerated life, a 'dynamic struggle to set up a holy tent', a 'gradual unfolding and unfurling of the tent of Wisdom in our lives, whatever be the struggles and obstacles' (pp. 54–57).

Conclusion: Interwoven Threads

Jung spent significant days in the Orissa delta of eastern India. During subsequent deep illness (1944), much of Jung's visionary experience, unfolding within the ambience of India's east coast synthetic fertility, enlivened and added complexity to his late in life 'diamond writings' (Rand, 2013, ch. 10). My woven picture story hearkens back to the fundamental roots of an ancient democracy[22] with vibrant, contemporary relevance for ecological struggles within the heart of global industrial–military complexity (Rand, 2013, ch. 11). When describing the living processes of the psyche, Jung 'deliberately and consciously [gave] preference to a dramatic and mythological way of thinking and speaking' (Jung, 1950a, para. 1, 1950b, para. 25).

Participating in a still evolving picture story, we see how Jung's travels to India, and his later East Coast India visions during deathly illness, precipitated him into the focal point of his Vishnu appreciative life – into a beginning recognition of Lakshmi and 'womb origins', into community to which he felt he belonged, and into the very territory that reveals the violent intrusions of a global military–industrial complex, into the depths of 'root' and self-sustaining people.

(Figure 6.119) Furthermore, and most significantly for my *Life Threads* now, appreciating Shakti's fusion of spirit and matter and the creative inwoven and ancient authority, teachings, and dance of the great women of Odissi, I recognize a pillar, rising from a lotus womb origin, emerging every day at noon from the lake at the centre of the universe.

Notes

1 'Ceylon' and 'Orissa' are used, as at the time of Jung's 1937–1938 travel. 'Something new', arising from the East Coast of India's Bay of Bengal, was Jung's description of aspects of his 1944 vision during illness (Jung, 1963, p. 290).
2 See Wikipedia for 'Sutra', and 'Pali'.
3 See Chatterjee, 2009. Working with hands is at the centre of India's ongoing struggle for freedom, and yet in her 1,618 tongues, there is no overarching word for 'handicraft.' Along with visionary and Nobel Prize winner Rabindranath Tagore, Ghandi, always in search of the indigenous roots of India's culture, learned a great many of the crafts of India before settling on spinning, designing a spinning tool that he could take with him when travelling and when imprisoned.
4 See Jung, 1946, para. 454: Jung engages fascism's greed for power, an absolute imposition of control, and the loss of Nature's own order.
5 See Rand, 2013, ch. 10, pp. 116–117.
6 My research was for the double purpose of (a) discerning more of the madness that transpired whilst Jung was wrestling with the First World War and 'Jung's own experience of "professionalism"'s encroachment', upon himself, developing *The Red Book* as an antidote, and (b) to inspect more of Canada's nation-forming war history, particularly the bloody Easter Monday Vimy Ridge battle.
7 'The moist substance stands for the basic material of the cosmos, being caught in the sphere of the fire.' See von Franz, 1980, p. 85.
8 Engaging with skills, threads and colours, my mother taught many Indian women to sew and embroider and to earn their own living. I have inherited my mother's sewing box, hand-carved in South India.
9 See Kwon et al., 2005, and www.maiwa.com.
10 See also Collins and Molchanov, 2013, p. 25: 'Noteworthy is the similarity of the central image of Jung's (initial) dream to the Indian symbol of the Siva lingam (a stylized erect phallus of the god *set in the vagina* [emphasis added] of the goddess, sometimes, but often not, obviously phallic).'
11 Jung describes it as a 'real fairy-story king's throne'. The displacement of 'the king' by a 'new and ancient woman' – the departure from fantasy towards embodied imagination – was still unfolding at the end of his life. See Rand, 2013, pp. 109–113.
12 In no way do I wish to abduct Indian cultural fullness and place it in the theoretical constraints of Western psychological frames.
13 Jung had penned these lines for the memorial service of Wilhelm in Munich, May 1930. See Jung, 1931, paras. 74–96.
14 See Padel and Das, 2010, ch. 2, p. 30. Aluminum's secret history is that it is a 'gateway through which polarities are equalized in every way'.
15 This document is the keynote speech to have been delivered in Calcutta by the President Elect, Lord Rutherford, at the 25th celebration of the Indian Science Congress

Association, in conjunction with the British Association for the Advancement of Science. At Rutherford's untimely death, Sir James Jeans took over the role. It is not known whether he read aloud Rutherford's already printed document.

16 I have no indication that Jung had any direct relationship to Cuttack's ancient silverwork. Of course, he makes many references to silver in the alchemical individuation process. See Jung, 1954c, para. 181, fn. 322.

17 Jung (1958, paras. 803–804) discusses *yantras* as 'instruments with whose help order is brought into being'.

18 In a letter to Dr. Mees, 15 September 1947 (Jung, 1973, pp. 477–479), Jung writes that he was 'profoundly overawed and the black pagoda of Bhuvaneshvara took all the air out of me'. Compare Sengupta (2013, p. 188). We can suggest that the experience of the temple of Konark winded or deflated Jung. (Fn. 11 (Jung, 1973, p. 478) shows some confusion regarding site(s) and Jung's conversations.)

19 Jung's father abandoned his earlier passionate dissertation on the Arabic form of the *Song of Songs*. See Rand, 2013, pp. 105–108, fns. 331 and 332.

20 See also Jung, 1968, pl. 232, and Jung, 1959, ch. 5.

21 Priya is the name of my first grandchild. The first Devali card I made her was, of course, about Lakshmi!

22 Sen (2005) highlights that the West has been engaged with India's religious richness at the expense of honouring her ancient and contemporary work in such areas as science, mathematics and the development of democratic and economic principles, even before CE.

References

Beltz, J. (2011). 'The Dancing Shiva: South Indian Processional Bronze, Museum Artwork, and Universal Icon', *Journal of Religion in Europe*, Vol. 4. pp. 204–222.

Birkhäuser, P. (1980). *Light from the Darkness: The Paintings of Peter Birkhäuser*. Basel: Birkhäuser Verlag.

Bortoft, H. (1996). *The Wholeness of Nature: Goethe's Way of Science*. Edinburgh: Floris.

Cambray, J. (2009). *Synchronicity: Nature and Psyche in an Interconnected Universe*. College Station, TX: A&M University Press.

Chatterjee, A. (2009). *From Ghandi to Globalization: Craft and Human Development*. Available at: www.maiwa.com/documentaries/pc_chatterjee_pt1.html (accessed August 18, 2016).

Collins, A. & Molchanov, E. (eds.) (2013). 'Churning the Milky Ocean: Poison and Nectar in Carl Jung's India. Jung and India', *Spring Journal of Archetype and Culture*, Vol. 90, Spring, pp. 23–75.

Cort, L.A. & Mishra, P.C. (2012). *Temple Potters of Puri*. Washington, DC: Smithsonian Institution.

Crill, R. (1998). *Indian Ikat Textiles*. London: Victoria and Albert Museum.

Ellard, P. (2007). *The Sacred Cosmos: Theological, Philosophical and Scientific Conversations in the Twelfth Century School of Chartres*. Scranton, PA: University of Scranton Press.

Fox, M. (ed.) (1985). *Illuminations of Hildegard of Bingen*. Santa Fe, NM: Bear.

Frank, A. (2004). *The Renewal of Generosity: Illness, Medicine and How to Live*. Chicago, IL: University of Chicago Press.

Frank, A. (2012). 'Reflective Health Care Practice: Claims, Phronesis and Dialogue', in E. Kinsella & A. Pitman (eds.), *Phronesis as Professional Knowledge: Practical Wisdom in the Professions*. Boston, MA: Sense, pp. 53–60.

Fredericksen, D. (2014). 'Fellini's 8 1/2 and Jung: Narcissism and Creativity in Midlife', *International Journal of Jungian Studies*, Vol. 6, No. 2, pp. 133–142.

Ghosh, P. (2003). 'Unrolling a Narrative Scroll: Artistic Practice and Identity in Late-Nineteenth Century Bengal', *The Journal of Asian Studies*, Vol. 62, No. 03, August, pp. 835–871.

Goswamy, B.N. (1986). *Essence of Indian Art*. San Francisco, CA: Asian Art Museum of San Francisco.

Goswamy, B.N. (2013). *Inward Journeys: Yoga and Pilgrimage*. Lecture conducted from Panjab University, Chandigarh, India, November.

Jung, C.G. (1931). 'Richard Wilhem: In Memorium', in *Collected Works*, Vol. 15, *The Spirit in Man, Art and Literature* (2nd edn). Princeton, NJ: Princeton University Press, 1966.

Jung, C.G. (1946). 'Fight with the Shadow', in *Collected Works*, Vol. 10, *Civilisation in Transition* (2nd edn). Princeton, NJ: Princeton University Press, 1970.

Jung, C.G. (1950a). 'Concerning Rebirth', in *Collected Works*, Vol. 9i, *The Archetypes and the Collective Unconscious* (2nd edn). Princeton, NJ: Princeton University Press, 1969.

Jung, C.G. (1950b). 'The Ego', in *Collected Works*, Vol. 9ii, *Aion: Researches into the Phenomenology of the Self* (2nd edn). Princeton, NJ: Princeton University Press, 1959.

Jung, C.G. (1952). 'Answer to Job', in *Collected Works*, Vol. 11, *Psychology and Religion West and East* (2nd edn). Princeton, NJ: Princeton University Press, 1969.

Jung, C.G. (1954a). 'Adam and Eve', in *Collected Works*, Vol. 14, *Mysterium Coniunctionis: An Inquiry into the Separation and Synthesis of Psychic Opposites in Alchemy* (2nd edn). Princeton, NJ: Princeton University Press, 1970.

Jung, C.G. (1954b). 'The Conjunction', in *Collected Works*, Vol. 14, *Mysterium Coniunctionis: An Inquiry into the Separation and Synthesis of Psychic Opposites in Alchemy* (2nd edn). Princeton, NJ: Princeton University Press, 1970.

Jung, C.G. (1954c). 'Personification of the Opposites', in *Collected Works*, Vol. 14, *Mysterium Coniunctionis: An Inquiry into the Separation and Synthesis of Psychic Opposites in Alchemy* (2nd edn). Princeton, NJ: Princeton University Press, 1970.

Jung, C.G. (1958). 'Flying Saucers: A Modern Myth', in *Collected Works*, Vol. 10, *Civilisation in Transition* (2nd edn). Princeton, NJ: Princeton University Press, 1970.

Jung, C.G. (1959). *Collected Works*, Vol. 9ii, *Aion: Researches into the Phenomenology of the Self* (2nd edn). Princeton, NJ: Princeton University Press.

Jung, C.G. (1963). *Memories, Dreams, Reflections*, A. Jaffé (ed.), R. & C. Winston (trans.). New York: Random House.

Jung, C.G. (1967). 'Alchemical Studies', in H. Read, M. Fordham, G. Adler, & W. McGuire (eds.), *The Collected Works of C.G. Jung* (Vol. 13). Princeton, NJ: Princeton University Press.

Jung, C.G. (1968). 'Psychology and Alchemy', in H. Read, M. Fordham, G. Adler, & W. McGuire (eds.), *The Collected Works of C.G. Jung* (Vol. 12). Princeton, NJ: Princeton University Press.

Jung, C.G. (1973). *C.G. Jung Letters* (Vol. 1, 1906–1950). Princeton, NJ: Princeton University Press.

Jung, C.G. (1975). *C.G. Jung Letters* (Vol. II, 1951–1961). Princeton, NJ: Princeton University Press.

Kane, E. (neé Rand, E.) (1989). *Recovering from Incest: Imagination and the Healing Process*. Boston, MA: Sigo Press.

Kwon, C., McLaughlin, T., Vonn, M., Balfour-Paul, J., Bilgrami, N., & Böhmer, H. (2005). *Indigo: A World of Blue*. Vancouver: Maiwa Productions.

Lockhart, R.A. (1987). *Psyche Speaks*. Wilmette, IL: Chiron.

Lockhart, R.A. (2014). 'The Fictive Purpose of Dreams: Part IV Encounters with the Inquisitor', *Dream Network Journal*, Vol. 33, No. 3, pp. 29–31.

Miller, B.S. (1970/1984). *The Gitagovinda of Jayadeva: Love Song of the Dark Lord*. Delhi: Motilal Badarsidass.

Padel, F. & Das, S. (2010). *Out of this Earth: East India Adivasis and the Aluminium Cartel*. New Delhi: Orient Black Swan Private.

Rand, E. (2008). 'Carl Jung and Ravenna Baptism: Bittersweet Anti-dote through World Wars I and II', Paper presented at the IAAP-IAJS Joint Conference, Zürich, Switzerland, July.

Rand, E. (2013). *A Jasmine Journey: Carl Jung's Travel to India and Ceylon 1937–1938 and Jung's Vision During Illness, 'Something New' Emerging from Orissa, 1944.* North Vancouver: The Mentoring Store.

Sei-Nainsukh. (1730). 'The Gods and Sages Beseech Vishnu to Incarnate Himself', [Painting]. Bhagavata Purana from the family workshop of Sei-Nainsukh (Series No. 46, No I-28). Chandigarh Museum, Chandigarh.

Sen, A. (2005). *The Argumentative Indian: Writings on Indian Culture, History and Identity.* London: Penguin Books.

Sengupta, S. (2013). *Jung in India.* New Orleans, LA: Spring Journal Books.

Serrano, M. (1960/72). *The Visits of the Queen of Sheba.* London: Harper Colophon Books.

Shamdasani, S. (2012). *C.G. Jung: A Biography in Books.* New York: W.W. Norton.

Stein, L. (2013). 'Jung and Tantra. Jung and India', *Spring Journal of Archetype and Culture*, Vol. 90, pp. 179–203.

von Franz, M. L. (1980). *Alchemy: An Introduction to the Symbols and the Psychology.* Toronto: Inner City Books.

Watts, A. (1963). *The Two Hands of God: The Myth of Polarity.* New York: Collier Books.

7

PARAMAPADA SOPANAM[1]

The Divine Game of Rebirth and Renewal

Sulagna Sengupta

Introduction

Traveling through the remote corners of the Indian subcontinent in 1938, Carl Jung discovered an archaic scroll in the temple alleys of Tamil Nadu in southern India (Sengupta, 2013a, pp. 200–202). The scroll contained a ritual game, traditionally used by devotees of Vishnu (one of the three gods of the Hindu Trinity) for nightlong play and worship during Vaikuntha Ekadasi, an auspicious Hindu festival.[2] In a civilization more than 75,000 years old, religious rituals form an intrinsic part of everyday life in India (Thapar, 2002, pp. 270–279). Rumblings of a new economy and a general irreverence to tradition notwithstanding, pockets of contemporary India continue to engage with the world of sacred rituals performed around popular deities at prominent temple sites. My chapter weaves this cultural and religious backdrop in its examination of Jungian ideas, offering a personal context to our understanding of psyche and spirit. It dwells on the symbolic nuances of an ancient matrix that Jung located in India during 1938. The mythical characters in the matrix symbolize opposites of all kinds. They represent the opposition inherent in the psyche that is vital for its maturation and growth.

Vaikuntha Ekadasi

A central myth associated with the game is the myth of Vaikuntha Ekadasi found in the ancient Indian religious text of Padma Purana. Vaikuntha (heaven) illustrated in the final square of the matrix is mythically known as the abode of Vishnu. Story reveals that the gods were frustrated with a demon named Muran and asked for Shiva's help. Shiva directed the gods to Vishnu and soon a battle ensued between Vishnu and Muran. During the battle Vishnu realized that Muran was not easy to

FIGURE 7.1   Image of Goddess Ekadasi in a South Indian temple

Source: Public domain

overpower and a new weapon had to be created to destroy him. He retreated inside a cave that belonged to Shiva's wife Parvati to contemplate on this task. Muran seized the opportunity then to attack a sleeping Vishnu. But a female form arose from within Vishnu and using her fierce glare turned Muran into ashes. Awakened and pleased with the help given by this figure, Vishnu named her Ekadasi, asking her to claim a boon for herself. Ekadasi did not seek anything for herself but asked instead that all Vishnu's devotees who fasted on that day be absolved of their sins (see Figure 7.1).

This is how we encounter Ekadasi in the game of Paramapada Sopanam. Ekadasi is not an independent goddess and there are not many temples in India dedicated to her worship. Born out of Vishnu's meditations, she is his life-giver and ally. Myth has it that her wish was granted and that devotees ritually fast on Vaikuntha Ekadasi as they wait near the temple doorway for a glimpse of Vaikuntha. The desire for divinity in his devotees has a transformative effect on Vishnu. He is believed to have opened the doorway even for the demons that fought against him. Thus Ekadasi personifies Vishnu's idealized anima – vigilant, selfless, and benign.

Paramapada Sopanam

In Hindu religious practice, the notion of god-image is important. Myths translate this notion variously and sometimes a whole experience of divinity is conveyed through a myth. Ephemeral and imaginary contact with gods through ritual worship in the manner of participation mystique is not uncommon. Inner divinity is projected on god-images, myths are narrated to rouse religious feelings and divinity is invoked. Jung implied this when he stated (1911–1912/1952a, para. 129), "I am therefore of the opinion that in general psychic energy or libido creates the god-image by making use of archetypal patterns and that man in consequence worships the psychic force active within him…" However, interpreting religious symbols for psychological analysis and understanding is not common in India. Narration of myths is popular as myths are sculpted on temple walls and evoked through rituals but they take on a different hue altogether when they are deliberated upon psychologically (see Figure 7.2).

The embodied characters on the matrix are spread across 132 squares that include thirteen serpents and ten ladders. The serpents are spread randomly on the board while the ladders lean toward the center, pointing upwards, toward Vishnu. The final squares lead to Vaikuntha and are preceded by images of Mayashakti and Parashakti (squares 128 to 132), forces that are believed to facilitate a devotee's passage to heaven.[3] There are squares that show Janmarahitam, meaning end of the cycle of ceaseless births and Janmaravaatham, meaning rebirth, implying that death and rebirth are necessary steps before one reaches Vaikuntha. This motif is implicit in the game and in the play of symbols. In Hindu religious worship, cessation of births is sought after a tussle between forces of good and evil. The plea is to transcend suffering and allow superior consciousness to emerge. The last square is preceded by eleven squares illustrated with the Tamil language letters of Paramapada Sopanam; they highlight the significance of Vaikuntha for the Hindu devotee. Psychologically, rebirth implies the death of old and dysfunctional attitudes and the birth of new consciousness. Renewal of consciousness may be brought about through radical events in one's outer life when one endures painful severance from old ties and witnesses new beginning from the remains of all that has disintegrated. In this process of dying and dissolution one confronts the dark aspects of the psyche through a willing immersion in its contents. This engagement with the dark regenerates consciousness and renews possibilities for psychic wholeness. Jung named this process individuation; it is often compared to the Hindu religious goal of *nirdvandva* (Jung, 1961, p. 276) but is not similar to it.

The game involves a test of fortune. The dice can throw up numbers that dodge the serpents and reach the ladders, giving the player much needed relief. Of course, that rarely happens. Encounters with the serpents are inevitable and the player surrenders himself to the synchronicity of these movements. Believing the ritual to be indicative of higher truths, the player undergoes a cathartic release of emotions during his ascent and descent on the board following images that are deliberately juxtaposed to emphasize archetypal polarities. Nature and animals

FIGURE 7.2 Paramapada Sopanam – Jung collected this scroll from India and preserved it in Zürich

Source: Jung Family Archive, Zürich

serve as sacred metaphors in Vedic texts and this matrix is also no exception. There are images of the sacrificial fire, holy men, plants, and animals symbolizing oppo-sites of all kinds. Images of holy men are placed adjacent to warriors, as are rival birds and animals. For example, the eagle is an archetypal foe of the serpent in Indian mythology but they are found in close proximity in this matrix. This sug-gests how myths and religious symbols depict the pervasive and inherent nature of the forces of opposition.

Looming over the twelve vertical and eleven lateral rows on the board are gigan-tic serpents representing mythical figures from the oldest Vedic texts. While the lower rows portray animals and humans, the uppermost row depicts images of holy structures and sites suggesting psyche's progression from its instinctual origins to the realm of the spirit. The upper squares illustrate only symbols showing how concrete, physical objects seen in the lower squares change into subtle, intangible expressions as the psyche journeys upwards nearing Vaikuntha.

The game is of Vedic origin but its genesis is obscure as literary and religious material belonging to this period was transmitted orally, long before recorded his-tory originated. Therefore the matrix is pre-historical. The term "Vedic" denotes consciousness, as Veda means knowledge derived from the root *vid*, which means "to perceive, to know, to regard, to name, to find out, to acquire, and to grant," (Campbell, 1962, p. 189). Jung emphasized that (1911–1912/1952b, para. 501) "The moment of the rise of consciousness of the separation of subject and object, is indeed a birth." Symbolically, consciousness is engendered when the player enters the square inhabited by a snake and confronts his enemy. He battles the enemy and when he succeeds in subduing this dark other, he moves forward or upwards. Moving upwards implies a rising, a deepening of consciousness through an engagement with the other. For the religious devotee this ascent often evokes in him a feeling of closeness with god. However, every ascent is followed by a quick descent and the matrix plays out this paradox, until the end.

The Play of Opposites and Their Psychological Relevance

The highest square in the game denotes Brahman. The notion of Brahman in Hindu religious discourse is moral perfection or a state of complete self-illumination. Dasgupta states (1967, pp. 80–81) that this is acquired through intuitive knowledge (*prajnana*) that is distinguished from cognition (*jnana*), implying that mere cognitive knowledge does not engender consciousness. Jung (1938, para. 69) echoed this when he expressed,

> My psychological experience has shown time and again that certain contents issue from a psyche that is more complete than consciousness. They often contain a superior analysis or insight or knowledge which consciousness has not been able to produce. We have a suitable word for such occurrences – intuition.

The Upanishad or sacred texts of India state that this insight or superior knowledge can be attained through tapas or contemplation; in analytic process this means turning inwards (introversion) with the intent of observing the psyche. *Brahman* from a root *bṛh* "to swell, expand, grow, enlarge" (Campbell, 1962, p. 205) is a dynamic connotation that denotes unfolding possibilities for the self – a boundless and all-encompassing whole (Dasgupta, 1967, pp. 50–57). For Jung, the fully integrated psyche is one that has assimilated its split-off complexes and is illumined through knowledge of its dark and fragmented parts. This enlightened self resembles the Hindu notion of Brahman. Yet it is different because the journey of becoming conscious is based on an individual's peculiar psychic make-up, making individuation a unique psychological process for all. This psychological nuance is not implicit in the Hindu religious notion of Brahman.

The central myth of Ekadasi brings us another view of Brahman. According to Campbell (1962, pp. 204–205), Vedic literature says that the goddess Adishakti holds the knowledge of Brahman. Myth has it that she taught Brahma, Vishnu, and Shiva the secret of Brahman, which made them superior to the other gods

FIGURE 7.3   The marriage of Shiva and Parvati solemnized by Vishnu

Temple iconography at Madurai temple, Tamil Nadu.

Photograph: Author

because they were the first to receive this knowledge. The mysterious figure that arises from Vishnu is a vestige of that original goddess, bearer of divine, life-enhancing powers. Ekadasi rises in a cave alluding to birthing in a womb. Her emergence from Vishnu's meditations in this womb-like cave personifies the birth of his anima, an inner figure that is stirred from the unconscious. It must be noted here that the sculpted panels of Madurai from where Jung collected this scroll shows an ancient pairing of Parvati and Vishnu as siblings. It shows Vishnu giving Parvati's hand to Shiva, as a brother gives his sister's hand in marriage in Hindu tradition. This symbolizes that mythically Parvati is Vishnu's brother, his soul imago. This archetypal pairing explains Ekadasi's appearance in Parvati's cave. In her humble and diminutive form, she seeks no special privilege for herself. Brilliant in her own entity, she is the bearer of an infinite life source, without whom Vishnu would not have overcome Muran and been rejuvenated to new life (see Figure 7.3).

In the Brihad-Aranyaka Upanishad, Brahman is described as pure knowledge: knowledge that spans mind, breath, seeing, hearing, earth, water, wind and space, energy and non-energy, of desire and non-desire, of anger and non-anger, of virtuousness and non-virtuousness and is made up of every kind of contrariness. Thus Brahman is *"made of this, made of that"* (Dasgupta, 1967, pp. 52–54). Vedic religious discourse has placed the knowledge of Brahman as an all-encompassing truth, knowledge that is beyond ordinary speech, sense perceptions, and thought. How is this Brahman to be realized then? The scroll portrays many opposites and suggests a journey through opposites as a way of approaching Brahman. It involves an engagement with the nature of opposites in the psyche, an experience that transcends ordinary perceptions and thought.

In his writings on India in *Memories, Dreams, Reflections* (1971) Jung noted that the Indian spiritual goal is *nirdvandva*, a state of being free from all moral conflict. The oldest Vedic concept of Brahman illustrated in this matrix shows a movement between heaven and hell as a path to reaching the Brahman or consciousness. This movement between opposites is further symbolized on the game board through the dyadic pairing of man and animal. Jung (1911–1912/1952c, para. 460) stated that,

> The cross, or whatever other heavy burden the hero carries, is himself, or rather the self, his wholeness, which is both God and animal – not merely the empirical man but the totality of his being, which is rooted in his animal nature and reaches out beyond the merely human towards the divine. His wholeness implies a tremendous tension of opposites paradoxically as one with themselves, as in the cross, their most perfect symbol.

The matrix demonstrates this tension of opposites and shows how the devotee undergoes numerous ascents and descents, confronting deadly serpents before he reaches Vaikuntha. Knowledge of the dark becomes imperative in pursuing one's higher goals. Jung (1911–1912/1952d, para. 106) expressed that

> Ethical decision is possible only when one is conscious of the conflict in all its aspects. The same is true of the religious attitude: it must be fully conscious of itself and of its foundations if it is to signify anything more than unconscious imitation.

The unconscious contents of the psyche are thus expressed in the images of serpents. The serpents take us to the oldest Puranic myths. They represent the instinctual forces of the psyche and personify our animal nature. They are hard to transform as they are constantly pulled downwards to their instinctual origins. This is shown in the game through the frequent descent of the serpents into lower squares that are inhabited by other animal figures. During the game, the player falls from a higher, morally elevated spot to one of the lower squares inhabited by an ordinary animal; inflation is necessarily reined in. The fall happens by chance as there is no particular way by which the dice can be thrown to dodge the serpents. The chance element signifies the inescapable nature of the conflict. Once thrown down the player finds himself in close proximity to an animal until another chance takes him forward or upwards. When pushed upwards, the psyche is confronted again with heightened moral demands. We see an emphasis on holiness on the board in the images of penance, abstinence, austerity, and asceticism. These can be overwhelming for an ordinary devotee. Burdened with the prospect of attaining something higher than what he or she is prepared for, the psyche regresses into its instinctual state. It is from this state of unconscious regression that the individual has to arise and move forward through a long and circuitous route, searching for a meaningful relation with the other. Without a close understanding of the forces of the dark that brings him down through the serpent's innards into his present death-like slumber, the player is unlikely to be able to forge a link with the unconscious and fulfill his journey toward enlightenment.

In this context, I recall a dream recounted to me several years ago. In it, the dreamer, a man, is looking down from the sky as he watches his young son play in the river. Suddenly a huge crocodile attacks the child. The crocodile's jaws have gripped the boy's feet and he is about to be eaten up. The man sees this from above and rushes down to save his child. Through some quick and bold moves he is able to extricate the child from the animal. He then flies back into the sky with the boy. The child has no real injury on his body. The dreamer feels that he has saved something integral of himself through this act.

The dream shows a characteristic hero motif and his battle with the forces of the underworld, reflected in the player's downward movement on the game board. We see that the self, represented in the young boy, is on the verge of being devoured by a crocodile. This animal represents the dark, archetypal mother who in her unconscious possession can overwhelm the child's psyche. The battle between instinctual and spiritual forces is symbolized in the duel between the young boy and the crocodile. The man has to free himself from this oppressive inner mother and a corresponding mother complex if his psyche has to evolve and mature. The father, representative of the ego, rushes to rescue the child from this threatening monster. The child is separated from the animal and is released upwards to a new life. It is a significant turning point in a hero's journey as also possibly in the dreamer's psyche. Jung (1911–1912/1952e, para. 396) stated that, "The father is the representative of the spirit, whose function it is to oppose pure instinctuality. That is his archetypal role which falls to him, regardless of his personal qualities." Fighting the dark forces of the unconscious, the man awakens to his own heroic potential, realizing that his differentiated thinking has helped him discern the danger. It is the ego's function to be vigilant when the self feels threatened by forces from below. Separating himself from the unconscious forces that threaten his survival, the hero invests himself with new life through this act and ascends skywards with his son.

Psychic conflicts that are of a moral nature can surface in life and death encounters in dreams, calling our attention to the task of adaptation. Adaptation is difficult when an individual is confronted with the demands of life that are far beyond his abilities. An essential link between the conscious life and the unconscious is severed. Jung (1950, para. 213) expressed … "One feels like lead because no part of one's body seems willing to move, and this is due to the fact that one no longer has any disposable energy. This well-known phenomenon corresponds to the primitive's loss of soul." The individual often abandons his heroic journey then and surrenders to the forces of the unconscious. His personality narrows. But when he frees himself from this deathlike entanglement and forges a link between his instinctual and spiritual nature, he sees a glimpse of his superior self. This psychological progression symbolizes a renewal of life for him and a symbolic rebirth.

Serpent Symbols and Serpent Myths

The game abounds in allusions to serpents. References to the cult of serpent worship are found in ancient Indian Yajurveda. The post-Vedic eclipse demon Rahu is said to be a serpent. In Hinduism the snake is associated with Shiva as it coils around Shiva's matted hair. The serpent is a symbol of both creation and destruction. Indian mythology places great significance on the symbolism of serpents. This is true especially for Vishnu who is seen reclining on the Seshanaga or the cosmic serpent in a state of mystic contemplation. Vasuki, another serpent, churns the milky ocean in the myth of Samudra Manthana (Sengupta, 2013b, p. 211).

The serpent king, Naga, is widely worshiped in the temples of India. Vishnu's mount Garuda, the eagle, is an archetypal foe of the Naga serpent. The Bhagwata Purana tells us about the myth of Krishna, the child god of Hindu pantheon who subdued the serpent Kaliya in the holy river of Yamuna. Serpent myths are common in rural India. In Karnataka, in the outskirts of Bangalore where I live, rural folk pray to the snake goddess. She is believed to be a protector of life, household, farm, and agriculture. The cult of serpent worship is ancient and is found in almost all sub-cultures of India. The snake is believed to have links with ancestral spirits. As it sheds its skin periodically it is considered to be a symbol of renewal.

The serpents loom large over the board, rising above the matrix in all shapes and sizes. When the psyche is no more able to hold the tension between opposites, the (serpents) images break from the squares like archetypal complexes split off from the psyche. These breakaway complexes take the form of extraordinary mythical characters on the game board embodying attributes of hatred, anger, jealousy, lust, pride, and arrogance. Thus the ordinary snake in square 26 is Ravana, the ten-headed demon king who abducts Rama's wife, Sita. However, Ravana is not just a demonic figure. He is a scholar of astrology, medicine, and politics and also an accomplished musician and devotee of Shiva. As the son of a Brahmin father and a demon mother, he has mixed lineage. This explains his dual character. His inflated psyche is personified in his ten heads. Myth explains that when he sought a boon from Shiva, he prayed that none from among the gods and demons would kill him. Being conceited he did not count the ordinary mortals as dangerous. Thus Rama has to be born as a mortal prince and as the seventh avatar of Vishnu to destroy Ravana in the story of Ramayana. The two characters Rama and Ravana symbolize a psychological pair of opposites. Ravana's superior self is personified in Rama, who, although noble, is flaw-ridden and morally imperfect. Jung (1954, para. 407) explained this idea when he stated,

> The psyche is made up of processes whose energy springs from the equilibrium of all kinds of opposites. The spirit/instinct antithesis is only one of the commonest formulations ... So regarded, psychic processes seem to be balances of energy flowing between spirit and instinct.

The serpents take the player downwards to squares that are inhabited by animals. Ravana's descent into square six is marked by the presence of a dog. The dog is an instinctual being; the Indian stray dog is highly adaptive. Coming in contact with the dog indicates possibilities for psychic adaptation and renewal. However Ravana's character barely undergoes this change in Ramayana. When the psyche projects its shadow unremittingly onto the other and fails to withdraw these projections, it prevents its own transformation. Ramayana depicts the tale of Rama's flawed heroism and the failed individuation of its two protagonists.

There are other mythic figures on the board that personify psychological complexes of various types. The serpent in square 47 represents Bakasura, a cannibalistic demon who preys on innocent villagers. He personifies an unconscious greed that is difficult to contain. When the five Pandava princes are called to surrender to Bakasura, Bheema, the mightiest of them and of demon lineage himself, challenges him to a duel. He kills Bakasura, and using his own demonic instinct devours him, destroying Bakasura's bestial hunger and greed. This is an intriguing example of how powerful complexes are seen disempowered in myths and fables.[4] Its psychological parallel as dismantling a complex by employing the elements that make up the complex is far-fetched but not inconceivable.

Square 59 represents Rama's father, King Dasaratha from the epic Ramayana. Dasaratha is besotted with his second wife Kaikeyi. When she schemes to have her son Bharatha crowned as the king of Ayodhya, sidestepping the first-born Rama, Dasaratha obliges her, blinded by his lust for the queen. Bharata's coronation is preceded by Rama's exile into the forests. Dasaratha is devastated by the turn of events and dies subsequently. Kaikeyi, symbolizing Dasaratha's anima is an important catalyst in Ramayana. Personified as a serpent, she represents a complex that has overwhelmed the king's consciousness. The anima is as much a figure of transformation as it is a symbol of the dark unconscious. Dasaratha's fall to square eight is supported by an image of a frog. The frog is not an ordinary creature. Its transformative qualities are found in Grimm's fairy tale "The Frog Prince." The frog symbolizes the undeveloped Eros in a man's anima (von Franz, 1970, pp. 84–85). The king has to discover for himself a genuine relatedness with his queen rather than be blinded by shallow and superficial lust. This self-realization could lead a player upwards from the frog's square to one that illustrates a higher, more integrated psychic symbol.

The serpent in square 55 is Duryodhana, the Kaurava prince who fought his cousins the Pandavas, for the throne of Hastinapura in the epic Mahabharatha. The serpent here personifies envy and greed, attributes that lead anyone to fall. The player falls from here to the image of a butterfly. This insect of family Lepidoptera (in Greek psyche also means butterfly) is characterized by its dual nature – life and death. As a symbol of self and of individuation, the butterfly symbolizes metamorphosis through death and rebirth. As the psychological other, this symbol underlines the long and difficult transition Duryodhana has to make to render himself fit for Vaikuntha.

Serpent Dreams and Working Through Opposites

Jung believed that the concepts of complex psychology are not intellectual formulations but ideas that become meaningful only when they are experienced within the psyche. Archetypal symbols appear in dreams encapsulating an inner psychic experience, giving us a closer insight of our psyche. Dreams thus become a vital link to the unconscious. The following dream came to me several years ago when I was trying to understand the nature of psychological complex.

In the dream I am attending a group program. In the actual program that I am attending, I have presented a theme about parental complexes. In the dream, I come out of the building where the program is being conducted and enter an open quadrangle paved in gray stone. At one corner of it, outside the edge on the right is an anthill that has grown out of the earth. It is reddish brown in color. I am inside this anthill coiled in a serpentine position, rising out of its bottom. The ground below is the earth. The mouth of the anthill is open and I am rising very slowly and moving upwards. But before I can come out, I hear the sound of barking dogs. Their barking is fierce and I am transfixed to my position. The dream ends.

I can see how the uncanny sight of a coiled human emerging from an anthill has agitated the dogs. In India stray dogs normally act as watchdogs. They guard territories and are vigilant of territorial infringements. I have no personal association with anthills but in Karnataka where I now live, anthills are common. This is how an anthill is described in a report by Irwin (1982, pp. 339–360; see Figure 7.4):

> Ethnographical reports of the last hundred years suggest that anthill worship is an ancient cult that survives in many parts of India up to the present day. The cult once occupied a central place in Vedic and Hindu religion, and from at least as early as the first millennium B.C., and probably earlier, it has figured prominently – if somewhat incomprehensibly – in rituals associated with all the critical events of human life, including birth, marriage, sickness, and death. Anthills have also played an important part in the consecration of temples, the warding-off of evil, ritual destruction of an enemy, calling divine witness, and securing material prosperity.

The anthill was a powerful image in the dream; it was infused with a life force of its own. Jung (1911–1912/1952e, para. 676) explained that

> The snake symbolizes the numen of the transformative act as well as the transformative substance itself, as is particularly clear in alchemy. As the chthonic dweller in the cave she lives in the womb of mother earth, like the Kundalini serpent who lies coiled in the abdominal cavity, at the base of the spine.

In the dryland region of the Deccan Plateau in India, anthills are considered sacred because it is believed that snakes lie at the bottom of anthills. The association

FIGURE 7.4   Image of an anthill in rural India

Source: Public domain

between snakes and anthills is ancient. Threads are tied around anthills to protect them and sometimes an entire temple is dedicated to an anthill. I had not understood the significance of anthill worship in India until I encountered the sacred anthill in my dream and took it up for analysis. The barking dogs reminded me of the critical voices of members in the program. They or the dogs would not let me emerge out of the anthill. Protecting this structure, especially the coiled serpent-like figure inside, seemed important. The anthill and the serpent symbolized for me the psyche and its inhabiting complexes – the structure denoting a deep underground place where complexes are housed. As vital elements of the psyche's growth and evolution, complexes need to be watched over so that their raw force does not erupt outwards. The interior is an important place for the psyche's regeneration and growth. Vishnu had retreated into a cave when he needed to introspect about Muran and gather his strength. As all instinctual forces have inherent opposing tendencies, the coiled serpent has an impulse to emerge from the sheltered interior. The barking dogs counteract this, showing how the dream holds this tension of opposites, infusing it with vitality and feeling. Jung, (ibid., para. 615) clarified that "Snake dreams always indicate a discrepancy between the attitude of the conscious mind and the instinct, the snake being a personification of the threatening aspect of the conflict."

The dream surfaced a psychological motif underlying an ancient rite practiced in India, one that a straightforward literary explanation of anthills had not conveyed to me before. It is through this symbol drawn from the dream that the psychological idea of a complex became clearer to me in a culture where analysis of dreams is not a dominant practice.

The second dream that I narrate here involves several snakes, a cat, and a dog. In the first scene of the dream, I am on the upper floor of an old house and am entering a small room that is dimly lit. On a bed sits my father and before him is a small table on which there is a plate of food. My father is eating this food. The food is not traditional but something from contemporary cuisine that my father may have never liked in real life. However, here he is enjoying it. He looks lively and vital as he talks to my Jungian friend who has entered the room with me. She is introduced to him and my brother who is not my own brother. He is a stranger who is introduced as my brother. We leave the room and enter the adjacent room where my friend hands me a brown cardboard box. It is full of snakes, black, small, and many in number. I place the box anxiously under a table at the end of the room and stand waiting at the entrance of the room. After a while, a brown puppy comes out of the box, shrugs itself, and trots away. I am surprised to see how unruffled the little dog is. When I move closer to the box, I see that it is open and a cat is lying inside with the snakes on its body. It is thinking that it has to eat the snakes gradually as they are poisonous and they have to be destroyed. But there is no anxiety or urgency in the cat as it contemplates this.

The animals show extraordinary adaptation skills around the snakes, compensating my own inferior attitude. The snakes represent all that is vile and repulsive for me, my psychological shadow. In the dream they are gifted to me, suggesting that I need to befriend the instinctual side of my personality. The superior adaptive skills of the two animals are shown as an example. The dog is unruffled; the cat is aware that destroying the snakes is a task that has to be accomplished, but it is not overcome with anxiety in contemplating this. Strangely, this act of killing is not an act of violence and bloodshed but a symbolic ingestion of the dark contents of the psyche. The diet of snakes is an unconventional one for the cat, much like the food that my father is seen consuming in the next room but this food had vitalized him. Figuratively, eating is to chew on something, which means to think, understand, and engage with. Chewing leads to chemical breakdown of food that helps in its assimilation back into the body. The dream shows how engaging with the other is possible in figurative and metaphorical ways and how these can have transformative effects on the psyche.

Conclusion

I would like to conclude with a story from Mahabharatha to show how animal symbols are used to signify psychological notions in the myths in India. When the battle between the Pandavas and Kauravas end and the five Pandava princes and their queen Draupadi prepare to journey heavenwards (Mahaprasthanika Parva), a dog joins them on their journey. He is none other than Dharma, the high god ritually worshiped in India. When the Pandavas fall one by one enroute and are unable to ascend the steps of heaven due to their earthly sins and misdeeds, the dog remains with the oldest Pandava, Yudishthira. At the doorway of heaven, Yudhisthira is asked to leave the dog before he enters heaven. He refuses saying that the humble dog has been his loyal companion, so he would not leave him. Yudhisthira and the dog are both allowed inside the gates of heaven. The ordinary dog becomes a superior being transcending all barriers between spirit and instinct. Both man and animal become equally deserving of a place in heaven. Everything stands aligned in this transformative moment. The illumined self is not the personal self alone, but one that holds the seed of all other beings who have participated in this journey of gaining consciousness, sometimes even acted as archetypal adversaries and propelled the psyche's movement forward. Such a journey mediated through a psychological play of opposites is portrayed in this ancient matrix that Jung chanced upon in 1938 in India.

Notes

1   Paramapada Sopanam – Sanskrit, meaning Steps to Heaven or Pathway to Heaven.
2   Ekadasi is the eleventh night of the Indian lunar calendar. The Hindu lunar calendar of twelve months is based on the two phases of the moon for each month and aligns with the twelve zodiac signs, determining the exact time of a month's beginning. This occasion is celebrated in the temples of India that are dedicated to Vishnu.
3   In Vedic discourse, Mayashakti and Parashakti are linked to Adi Parashakti. Adi Parashakti is the supreme goddess from whom other goddesses are born. She teaches the gods divine secrets.
4   Bheema was known to be greedy and devouring. When he failed to enter the gates of heaven, this attribute was cited as a reason for his failure to enter heaven.

References

Campbell, J. (1962). "The Mythologies of India," in *Oriental Mythology, The Masks of God*. London: Souvenir Press, 2000.

Dasgupta, S.N. (1967). *Hindu Mysticism*. New Delhi: Motilal Banarsidass Publishers Pvt. Ltd, 2009.

Irwin, C.J. (1982). "The Sacred Anthill and the Cult of the Primordial Mound," *History of Religions*, Vol. 21, No. 4. Chicago, IL: University of Chicago Press.

Jung, C.G. (1911–1912/1952a). "The Song of the Moth," in *Collected Works*, Vol. 5, *Symbols of Transformation* (2nd edn). Princeton, NJ: Princeton University Press, 1990.

Jung, C.G. (1911–1912/1952b). "The Dual Mother," in *Collected Works*, Vol. 5, *Symbols of Transformation* (2nd edn). Princeton, NJ: Princeton University Press, 1990.

Jung, C.G. (1911–1912/1952c). "The Battle for Deliverance from the Mother," in *Collected Works*, Vol. 5, *Symbols of Transformation* (2nd edn). Princeton, NJ: Princeton University Press, 1990.

Jung, C.G. (1911–1912/1952d). "The Hymn of Creation," in *Collected Works*, Vol. 5, *Symbols of Transformation* (2nd edn). Princton, NJ: Princeton University Press, 1990.

Jung, C.G. (1911–1912/1952e). "Symbols of the Mother and of Rebirth," in *Collected Works*, Vol. 5, *Symbols of Transformation* (2nd edn). Princeton, NJ: Princeton University Press, 1990.

Jung, C.G. (1938). "Psychology and Religion," in *Collected Works*, Vol. 11, *Psychology and Religion: West and East* (2nd edn). Princeton, NJ: Princeton University Press, 1989.

Jung, C.G. (1950). "Concerning Rebirth," in *Collected Works*, Vol. 9i, *The Archetypes of Collective Unconscious* (2nd edn). Princeton, NJ: Princeton University Press, 1990.

Jung, C.G. (1954). "On The Nature of the Psyche," in *Collected Works*, Vol. 8, *The Structure and Dynamics of the Psyche* (2nd edn). Princeton, NJ: Princeton University Press, 1981.

Jung, C.G. (1961). *Memories, Dreams and Reflections*. Recorded and edited by A. Jaffé. London: Vintage Books, 1989.

Sengupta, S. (2013a). *Jung in India*. New Orleans, LA: Spring Journal Books.

Sengupta, S. (2013b). "Samudra Manthana, Reflections on an Ancient Indian Myth," in *Jung and India*. New Orleans, LA: Spring Journal Books.

Thapar, R. (2002). *The Penguin History of Early India*. New Delhi: Penguin Books.

von Franz, M.L. (1970). *Interpretation of Fairy Tales*. Revised edition. Boston, MA and London: Shambhala, 1996.

8

RESPONSES TO A FILM ABOUT INTEGRITY

John Beebe

Introduction

Let me begin with what I said to the people in attendance at my session at the IAJS conference in Phoenix, whose organizers had invited me to show and discuss scenes from a "film from India."

John Beebe: I've decided to do something a little different today. I've been writing about film, teaching film for a long time. My first film seminar was in 1979 at the Jung Institute of San Francisco. It was titled "Film as Active Imagination." In those days I was bringing together the auteur theory of film and Jung's active imagination, and discovering that they fit like a hand in a glove. I was also trying to show people what I go through as an analyst every day. The reason I hit on sharing film is that I wanted a group of people to experience, in an encapsulated way, the emotional sequencing that occurs over a much longer time in the course of an analysis. With the shaping vision of a film auteur, you get not only the conscious situation, you get fantasy, you get dreams – sometimes literally and certainly imaginally.

I was shocked by how successful it was. I'd never done a seminar like that, and didn't know if it would work. I showed two Hitchcock films that weekend. One was *Notorious* (1946), the other was *Shadow of a Doubt* (1943). It launched in me a process of learning depth psychology from film. So an awful lot of what I've written about since I have learned not from Jung or Freud but from watching film.

Today I'm going to give you a big sample of a film that I have learned from and ask you to just immerse yourself in it. It's going to be quite a long period of film-watching. You're going to experience the internal heart of a film that works on many levels: personal, cultural, and historical. It's called *Monsoon Wedding*, by Mira Nair (2001).

To provide the context of the long clip you are about to see, I'd like to offer the essay-review I wrote about *Monsoon Wedding* when it first came out, which

I adapted somewhat for subsequent publication in my book, co-authored with Virginia Apperson, *The Presence of the Feminine in Film* (2008). Each of the chapters of that book had been designed to offer a different aspect of that presence as evoked in a particular film. I titled the chapter on *Monsoon Wedding* "Integrity," because I find that to be one of the most important ways that I experience a feminine presence in film. Many, many writers have noticed that there's something about the feminine, the feminine image, the female body, which is used to symbolize integrity, a subject that is otherwise almost invisible in art. Very rarely is integrity depicted directly, but indirectly through the feminine image. Marina Warner, in her masterpiece of cultural analysis, *Monuments and Maidens* (1985), has demonstrated clearly the relationship between *integritas* and the way a woman's body is depicted in public art, which of course raises the question of what that depiction does to women. This is a subject I have also touched on in my book, *Integrity in Depth* (1992).

As the woman's body figures largely in what is shown, I want to be sure you know that the film is directed by a woman auteur, Mira Nair, working from a screenplay by a wonderful first-time screenwriter, Sabrina Dhawan, who was a student at Columbia at the same time Mira Nair was there teaching film. Ms. Dhawan did a beautiful job with her shooting script, which you can find online.

Alas, my review, written in the style of academic thinking that we in the IAJS are used to engaging in, doesn't finally enable one to feel the topic anywhere near as powerfully as the film itself does. Nevertheless, here it is, as it appeared in *The Presence of the Feminine in Film* (pp. 155–158).

A Review of the Film

On the morning of September 11, 2001, citizens of New Delhi awoke to newspaper articles celebrating the news that a film by one of their own daughters about upper middle class Punjabi life had won a Golden Lion for the best picture at the Venice Film Festival. It was the first time a woman director had ever claimed the award, and for a film that seemed to have been thrown together in no time at all – just in time, in fact, to capture the happy spirit of international, postmodern, postcolonial culture before a new round of paranoid anxiety about the viability of that very culture would start to poison the party. Seeing *Monsoon Wedding* now, one can only marvel at the celebratory spirit of the pre-9/11 time that Mira Nair's movie recalls and preserves for us, like a jam made from summer fruit to get us through a prolonged winter.

The film, as the title makes clear, belongs to the genre of movie known as "wedding pictures," and Nair, a Professor of Film Studies at Columbia, knows her Vincente Minnelli, Robert Altman, P.J. Hogan (who found gold in this genre twice), and Ang Lee well enough to have created a classic to stand beside *Father of the Bride* (1950), *A Wedding* (1978), *The Wedding Banquet* (1993), *Muriel's Wedding* (1994), and *My Best Friend's Wedding* (1997) – and to trump

her predecessors in getting at the deeper meanings of the marriage archetype. This motif, known to students of analytical psychology by its alchemical
name, *coniunctio*, the "chemical marriage" of male and female opposites, is
described by Jung in two charmingly arcane, if deeply clinical, works, "The
Psychology of the Transference" (1946) and *Mysterium Coniunctionis* (1954),
but in such intuitive-thinking terms that it is possible to read these texts, with
their endless symbolic explications, without ever grasping that what is being
discussed is an emotional event. It is part of the achievement of Mira Nair's
film to have delineated the *coniunctio* in feeling-sensation terms, so that we can
experience the way it transforms lives.

That her own film comes together, grants Nair the authority to instruct
us on so deep a psychological matter, but she never neglects the surface in
her approach to her *prima materia*, which is simply a Punjabi wedding. The
director and producer has admitted that she wanted to capture on film what
in New Delhi is called *masti*, "the singular life-loving spirit of Punjabi culture," and in this she succeeds handsomely. But the *masti* is also accompanied
by *musti*, a spirit of mischief that subtly plays through the film like a trickster
insinuating itself into the loving animus of the movie.

The convergence of these forces is symbolized at the outset of the film
by an odd-couple marriage of convenience between incompatible characters
who must cooperate in bringing the wedding off. The cost-conscious, upper-
middle-class householder, Lalit Verma, is intent on seeing that his daughter's
arranged marriage to Hemant, a Houston-based engineer, is celebrated properly as a suburban June wedding. To decorate the garden and set up tents that
will protect the party from the impending monsoon downpours, he has hired
the dubious P.K. Dubey, an extraverted intuitive tent contractor from the
city who is trying to pass himself off as a wedding planner. Already, though,
the marigold bower is disintegrating, and all *tentwallah* Dubey wants to do is
munch on the falling marigolds while blandly insisting to the increasingly
doubtful Lalit that everything will be all right.

Neither man seems at all close to any feminine figure at this point: Lalit's
wife, Pimmy, has to hide her smoking from him, and Dubey has not yet
noticed how Lalit's lovely young maid, Alice, is shyly eyeing him while she
goes about her tasks in the background. But these less than animated face-offs
are nothing to the estrangement that looms at the heart of the arranged marriage itself. The bride, who in modern style has, like the groom, veto power
over the arrangement if it proves to be unsatisfactory, has elected to marry in
this traditional way only because the man she really loves, her married ex-
boss, shows no sign of leaving his wife for her despite the unbroken intensity
of their ongoing affair. Everywhere we look, a discordant note is struck. Only
the bride's younger brother, plump, androgynous Varun (played with enormous charm by Mira Nair's own sixteen-year-old nephew, Ishaan) seems to
sense the degree to which things are not as they should be – and his solution,
to the exasperation of his conventionally homophobic father, is to want to

cook and dance, as if to summon in his own body the feminine element that is missing in this heartless wedding.

The comedy of the wedding that is out of step with the *tao* (to import yet another language into this polyglot movie filmed in English, Hindi, and Punjabi) is a convention of the genre of wedding picture, which belongs to an even larger class of films that the philosopher Stanley Cavell (1981) has called comedies of remarriage. The scenarios in such films move from lesser, unsatisfying conjunctions to greater, more permanent, ones, as if to suggest that at some point the false arrangements have to give way to authentic feeling, or there will be no individuation in our lives. Nair takes up this suggestion with surprising force in *Monsoon Wedding*, so that when the rains do catch up with the wedding party, they have been preceded by an inner alchemical *solutio*.

The film takes care of us throughout with an extraverted sensation panorama of contemporary India as it is, inviting us into the extended family of a vibrant emergent middle class. Although it makes no concessions to a colonial standpoint that would require a first-world audience to bear a burden of guilt for the continuing underdevelopment of yet another third world country, it does not lack a critical perspective in regarding its apparently privileged subjects. This goes beyond the documenting sociological contemplation with which Nair observed the suffering of India's homeless children in *Salaam Bombay*. In *Monsoon Wedding*, her scriptwriter Sabrina Dhawan has deepened her vision, for the film seems to be seen through the silent eyes of an author's introverted feeling. This point of view concerns itself, not with the inappropriate distribution of wealth and power, but with taking responsibility for what one has.

An insistence on integrity pervades the film, and is given a vivid personal face in the bride's cousin, Ria, who has lived since childhood in Lalit's house because her own father, Lalit's brother, has died. Ria, an aspiring writer who is still unmarried, bears the twin resentments of the early loss of her father and the memory of subsequent childhood traumas. Her watchfulness qualifies the action of the film with hidden reservations – hidden, that is, until she suddenly challenges the conduct of a family elder. At this point, the film moves into extraordinary emotional territory. As head of the house, Lalit must decide what to do, and predictably, his first care is to maintain the appearance of harmony. But this is not a solution, and it does not hold. What seems to shift him is intimate contact, when he cannot sleep that night, with his wife Pimmy's body.[1] When Ria, the next day, sees her paternal uncle finally choose integrity over continuity, her eyes burn with amazement. This is not the scenario feminism has prepared the modern woman for! The blaze of Ria's initiatory vision forges a new understanding of the patriarchal animus.

Around this spine established between the introverted feeling niece and the extraverted thinking uncle, the rest of the plots swirl into the kind of satisfying resolutions that echo the MGM musicals reprised in *That's Entertainment*. Aditi, the "bride with the guy on the side," comes clean to her groom, and they enter a truly enchanted space of love, while in the charming subplot P.K. Dubey courts Alice, who turns out to be just witchy enough to face down his tricksterish defiance and release his sincerity. She even succeeds in transforming his lemur face into a lover's ennobled visage. Dubey's assistants, puerile men who have been stealing a glance at Alice while she tries on some of her mistress's jewelry, end up apologizing to her. (This is a sly assertion by filmmaker Nair of the reform politics of the "gaze" in feminist cinema, which allows her to glance repeatedly throughout her film at the beauty of men.)

During one of the New Delhi street scenes, we get a glimpse of a statue of Shiva, the paradoxical Hindu god who brings both destruction and integration, so that in the religious background of the movie this god is presiding over the regeneration of the family. As the monsoon hits, and P.K.'s tent proves inadequate, the guests happily continue their dancing in the soaking mud, a dark fertility in which they have found their footing. Lalit asks his maid, now Mrs. Dubey, to dance, and with this union of high and low the comedy of integrity completes its revitalization of Ria's world. As Nair's expansive film comes to its buoyant close, it is as if India has taken the lead in getting the world's act together.

Hopefully my piece gives you some sense of what it can be like to take in the film as a whole. Today, I'd like you to watch 45 minutes of this film with me, and see how many images or symbols of integrity you can spot. Notice the film's ways of depicting the intangible quality that we call integrity, the touching state of being untouched by corrupting influences.

If this experiment works, I will have convinced you that there is much to learn about depth psychology from film. You will also see, I hope, that Jungian psychology does not violate, but in fact can open up, the spirit of filmmaking. In this experiment, the movie watching will be the most important part. The rest of the time will be used just discussing what each of you has seen for yourself.

To orient you to the part of the film you will be watching, *Monsoon Wedding*, though in English, concerns an event in a Punjabi family in New Delhi. Like many Hindus, the elders in this family had to relocate as a result of partition. The middle-aged father, when he moved to the territory of Delhi, was helped greatly by his brother-in-law who was already established there. This brother-in-law, later in the sequence that I'm showing, becomes a more problematic character, but he has historically been instrumental in getting the family launched in the Delhi upper classes.

Now the father is an upper-middle-class textile merchant, successful enough to have arranged a marriage between his beautiful daughter, who works at a television studio, and a good looking Indian engineer who works in Houston, Texas. She's 24, he's 32. They are going to get married in Delhi in the traditional way. Though it is an arranged marriage, the two of them have already met each other and consented. Everything would be fine, except for the fact that the young bride-to-be has been having an affair with a married man at her television studio. Even though already engaged, she had to have one more fling with the married man to prove that their affair cannot go further. As the part of the film we are going to see starts, she's finally broken off that affair. Now she's got a dilemma as to what to say about the fact of it to her fiancé.

In a parallel subplot, the *tentwallah* who organizes the wedding, P.K. Dubey, has fallen madly in love with Alice, a maid at the house of the bride, but he and the men setting up the wedding tents have done a very stupid thing: they have secretly watched as Alice, cleaning up the bride's room, tried on the bride's wedding garments. When the men revealed themselves to her, they teasingly implied that perhaps Alice was stealing the jewels. As a consequence, she stops speaking to all the workmen, including their boss, the love-struck wedding organizer.

Those two stories are not the only subplots that will emerge, but they are already in the mind of the audience as the part of the film I am going to show begins. I think you'll find yourself feeling like you are part of this family. You may get a bit lost trying to specify for yourself their exact relations, but even that is like families, for as *Monsoon Wedding* knows, families are mixed up things in which people are both intimate to each other and don't know each other very well. I think you will enjoy that aspect of the film. It may remind you of events you've seen in our country as well. (For the reader who wants to watch the 45 minute film clip seen in Phoenix before reading the discussion that follows, which came after the showing, I would suggest obtaining the Widescreen DVD.[2] Start with Chapter 11, "Troubles," and watch for 45 minutes, until the end of Chapter 15, "Ria's Accusation.")

A Discussion of the Excerpt from *Monsoon Wedding*

What follows is an edited transcript of the discussion I had with the audience members after the excerpt of *Monsoon Wedding* was shown:

> *John Beebe:* First of all, do you agree with me that this is about integrity? I would submit that the images I've shown you touch on the theme of integrity rather consistently, yet our psychology has not taken this level of imagery seriously. We miss opportunities to help patients build integrity in a psychological way, proceeding from their own imagery of it. Yet working with images psychologically is a method that Jungian psychology generally knows a great deal about. As I see it, we need to be more attentive to the moral agenda of the individuating psyche. If you just look at this film text, almost every image has something to say about integrity. I am grateful because that sort of imagery, native to psyche, has been on my mind for 30 years. When the bride's father Lalit says "I'm falling" and we've heard earlier in the script that "you have to be someone to fall" how can one miss the play on the traditional theme of the Fall from grace? But when Lalit says, "I'm falling," we're supposed, psychologically, to begin to realize he is falling *into* his actual integrity, from the prideful position of merely persona integrity. This, as a way to achieve real integrity in a psyche, is a move I explored in my book, *Integrity in Depth*. James Hillman thought that

I was on the wrong track when, in our symposium on the Red Book in June, 2010 at the Library of Congress[3] I said that Jung's movement towards Salome was down, a fall toward his inferior function, thereby establishing an integrity in depth. Jim didn't think that the inferior function had anything to do with integrity. "What is added," he asked me backstage, "by bringing in typology?" I would say that the answer is right in the script to *Monsoon Wedding* when Lalit finds he needs to keep positioning himself *behind* the body of his wife and in this way make adequate contact with a female body that can give body to his own integrity as a man. He finally figures out that what he's going to do, he can't do by being someone on top, in the superior position. He has to take an inferior position, suggesting getting into his inferior function, at least to me. For Lalit, as an extraverted thinker, that would be his introverted feeling. To continue, though what did you see? What images spoke to you of integrity in this text? I find that this long 45-minute sequence is one of the most sustained passionate sequences in all filmmaking. It's beautiful in a way I can't imagine a male filmmaker doing this well.

Audience Member 1: I agree with you that practically every scene was about integrity, but I'll narrow it down a little. What really affected me, as a male, was two different scenes where the courage and integrity of the female standing up brought out the integrity of the nurturing and protective male.

JB: Excellent. Tell me which ones.

A1: I can't remember the character's name – the bride to be – who was afraid that she would risk losing her relationship if she told her fiancé the truth, that he would dismiss her as a slut. She went through with it, which was a great act of courage and integrity. It took him a little while to get it, but the fiancé came around and stepped up with integrity of his own. The second scene was where the bride's cousin, Ria, had the courage to out the abuse that was happening and inspired the father to finally do what I thought was a very high act.

JB: And this was actually not her own father, but the bride's father, Ria's uncle. Her father is the man in the picture on whom she places that red mark, that wonderful looking Hindu man, who died young.

A1: I was a little confused on the characters.

JB: It's a marvelous touch, that photograph! It's a signifier of lost integrity. Whenever you study integrity, you always come up against the nostalgia for when there *was* integrity, going all the way back to the Catholic idea of the Fall, articulated in the High Middle Ages by Aquinas, which makes us mourn for that Eden in which *integritas* or moral wholeness belonged to our First Parents, Adam and Eve, simply by the grace of God. Cicero we think, may have created the word integritas while Julius Caesar was still alive, making an abstract, ideal noun out of a very popular Roman adjective of the time, *integer*. Integer, as used by the poet Horace and others, meant ethically whole. It was a value that everyone thought Romans used to have in the early days of the Republic, before the country became rancid enough to need a leader willing to assume the role of dictator. So ever since the word integrity was coined, it has always referred to something the people around us used to have, and so it is in this family. We hear the bride's father say to her cousin, I can't possibly live up to your father, I can't replace your father. The cousin's father, from his picture, looks like he might have belonged to the intellectual India of people of the past, and to the purity of Ramakrishna. He represents the integrity of an earlier India, before the partition. Now we have an India that though independent, is filled with the compromises that enable affluence.

Audience Member 2: One of the symbols that really struck me was when one of the characters went home and his mother was upset because he was walking around in underwear.

JB: P.K. Dubey, the wedding planner. Yes.

A2: He went out and sat on the patio and looked out over the city and it struck me as feminine in an Athenian sense. The city was solid and looking back at him, and he seemed as if he had made a decision to follow his own integrity and to approach Alice.

JB: Yes. Integrity and the naked emotion of shame. The integrity is integral for the feeling of the latter. He doesn't even argue with his mother who is berating him for going around in his underwear. He doesn't acknowledge her in any extraverted feeling way. Yet his body language says, "How could you possibly say this? You're my mother and I love Alice with all my life and you tell me I have no interest in women!" In that twilight time of his sitting on the balcony, you can sense the introverted feeling of his body to an amazing degree.

Audience Member 3: John, I appreciated the scene where the uncle went to Ria and asked her to come home and said, don't talk. What I loved is that he conveyed his confusion. He didn't have any answers, he didn't make false promises, he didn't get up on his high horse. He presented her with his confusion and I really admired that.

JB: Right. I have never yet found integrity in anyone who was certain. [Laughter]

A3: I noticed the groom when he thinks out what he really wants to do about the bride's confession.

JB: It was wonderful to watch his evolution. It reminds me of how, when we first started talking about the issue of integrity in psychotherapy, it got raised around boundaries and boundary violations. Andrew Samuels pointed out to me that when you focus on boundaries, integrity gets "moralistic in a flash." He starts there, but real integrity is more liminal than that. There is a funny moment when the motorcycle is leaning against the groom's car and he tells those guys to move the motorcycle off. They don't move it immediately and he knocks the motorcycle off. He gets very righteous and indignant. This is an obvious displacement of his rage at his intended bride's transgression. Of course, there's been a terrible boundary violation on her part imposed on their relationship. There is that moment when she walks away, and he grasps that he can't just be moralistic, that the situation is more ambiguous than that. Then he reveals that he has had a relationship too. It's a tremendous move out of that righteous indignation which in all of us, is a first pass at integrity, but that is not very authentic, coming from defensiveness. Perhaps the groom is an introverted thinking type. It seems it's hard for him to get down to his feeling. It was beautiful watching him get to it.

Audience Member 4: This is an observation, really. During the film, there are lots and lots of hand-held shots.

JB: Yes.

A4: And to me, this has the effect of inviting us into the film to participate with the family.

JB: I hope you can speak for what it's doing to us to have the film made this way.

A4: I'm still asking a question in a way because we become one of the characters as we look into it, so our own integrity is there and we are challenged to reflect on those parts of us that can identify in uncomfortable ways with the agony of the characters, and what do we do with that?

JB: Well, integrity is hand-held (audience laughter). You've got to call it like you see it, you've got to hold the camera a certain way. I mean, everyone else wasn't actually seeing what was happening in plain sight, the older man coming on to the little girl. He was all over her, right down to the beret she didn't want in her hair, he was kissing her on the head. Anyone watching could have seen it, but members of the family weren't seeing it, and so one's noticing integrity is like a hand-held camera that allows you to change the angle of your vision just enough to be able to see the thing that's hiding.

Audience Member 5: John, I would offer that also many women in this room saw it.

JB: Of course, immediately! But the women in the film were acting like they didn't see it, so *their* convention was it's there, but you don't see it. I mean, the persona's view, the fixed camera angle of that family photography, that still, arranged picture, is so different from that hand-held thing, the liminal view that belongs to integrity.

A5: I was instantly proud of the little girl for taking the flower out of her hair.

JB: Oh, yes.

A5: I didn't even know the story yet, but I was just suspicious of that.

JB: Yes.

Audience Member 6: Thank you for those moments.

JB: The women's faces seeing is the integrity and then the question is, is there going to be room for that integrity?

Audience Member 7: Well, that scene you may have covered already where he (the groom) walks away from the car and they are maybe a few blocks away and he kind of rushes to her in the car. It's a moment that was overcoming a huge amount of cultural male pride, so of course that's integrity. I mention that because there's a men's movement that I think Hillman was part of for a while called the Mankind Project. We hold each other accountable to that kind of integrity on a weekly basis. It's great to see it portrayed pretty vividly.

JB: One thing that took me the longest time to see but that women viewers have seemed to relate to instantly is that the dance *itself* is integrity. The music has created some kind of whole that brings everyone together as part of one body, so that the violation of the body of one vulnerable member becomes more awful. And how beautiful the feminine body can be as a uniting thing, and therefore how terrible it is to desecrate that and kind of stick your tongue in it.

Audience Member 8: John, it's been a long time since I've seen this film, but my memory was it started really frantic, it felt very solar-dominated, and Lalit seemed really distracted, angry. It's hard to like him. I remember the scene just before the ones you showed today, where he sees Ria and her cousin, Aditi, lying asleep in the moonlight with a copy of Tagore between them. He says something like, "I love them so much, I would die for them." At that moment, I had a deep affection for Lalit. He became that kind of lunar integrity.

JB: So we're back to the idea that he had at least positioned himself in some way as the defender of the family. Then he can take the fall he needs to take – from defending the *persona* integrity of the family, with all the money he'd taken from that brother-in-law – to be able to humiliate himself to the degree that he would bite the hand that fed him in that sense, in the name of another value. He took that idea on, and then he finally lives it in a way that he could never have imagined.

Audience Member 9: I was struck when the wounding was happening. It was something we had to know, but it was all hidden.

JB: Yes: what I say in *Integrity in Depth* is that we scarcely know we have integrity until it's been violated. That's when we find out. It was his ability to feel the pain to his family. When he's crying in bed and turns to his wife, it's touching.

Audience Member 10: I'd like to suggest that Ria's integrity may not be about hand-holding. It may be about her standing up and walking forward, away from where she was, where handholding has been proposed, I was very struck by the heroine, one of the heroines walking down that avenue: she was not going to compromise her position. I thought that was a very profound image. It isn't always about falling. For many of us it's about standing.

JB: Oh, it's exactly about standing for something, in fact the idea of spine and standing for something is at the very heart of what integrity is. We each have to hold our integrity, no one can do it for us, and it has to be a stance of our whole person. For me, the most powerful image of integrity in the entire film is Ria's eyes, and never more so than when she sees her uncle Lalit doing what she imagines he could never do. The actress' eyes burn with a combination of gratitude and amazement. And to me, the thing that makes integrity so exciting as a subject is it's always utterly amazing when you see it. And you really don't expect you're ever going to see it. There are so many reasons not to: we see so much compromise of integrity. We live with that. We are that. So the look in Ria's face is unforgettable, and it links together all of the other gazes that have taken place, that belong to women's faces rather than the woman being the object of the gaze, something that has been criticized so often, particularly by feminist film critics, starting with Laura Mulvey's 1975 essay, "Visual Pleasure and Narrative Cinema" (2009, pp. 14–27). Here in Mira Nair's film the women get the gaze, but that doesn't mean that the women don't have something to learn. Yes, you've seen it all before, but Ria sees something she never thought she'd see and there's integrity in accepting that. It's easier to just look and decide men are bastards and make a silent look about that. It's another thing to see when men are not bastards and to accept that you didn't know that was coming. It's a very touching series of helpful humiliations.

Audience Member 11: I'm curious about the people who are from India here. I notice the integrity of place, and so like when they were decorating the car, you get a sense of the village, and when you go into their homes, you get a sense of their homes, that these weren't Hollywood-constructed places, but that it looked like the place itself had integrity. And in the same way, of the uncle's place in the family, as well as the daughter's place in the family and that relationship. That there's a sense of integrity of what that role means to be the uncle who replaced the father.

JB: Well, you people from India could probably comment. We've had a lot in the news about India.

Audience Member 12: Well, I think Mira shot this film in Delhi very close to her own family home, so it was the place she grew up. You know some of the actors are her very close friends, and so it was really done in a family kind of setting. The three pools where the water was taken out and where the dancer danced was, I think, her brother's house, so this was really something very close in for her and you can see the whole flavor of that in the film. I think integrity is also something very personal: if it doesn't come from there, you can't make a film like this.

JB: It's where we're at home and where we're not at home. It's exactly that and you know, the 15-year-old is her nephew, the probably gay son, and it's so marvelous because there's the father, who's having such a hard time being a man, trying to get his son to man up, when he's the one that needs to man up. I'm hoping that you'll go on thinking about this sequence and maybe see the rest of the film because it has a lot to teach us. Thank you.

Conclusion

What was not addressed in this discussion was the suitability of using a fiction film, created primarily for its entertainment value, as a basis for psychological insight. *Monsoon Wedding*, is, after all, a comedy of marital manners whose moral underpinning adds to the pleasure we might expect to find in any wedding film when the good in human relatedness has been rewarded and the shadows attending sexual love and courtship are overcome. Is it asking too much of this film to take it as a text from which to learn about marriage as a symbol of integrity?

From the depth and richness of the participants' comments, I would say it is not an inappropriate use of the film. These viewers verified how many ways the theme of integrity spoke to them from within the film and was part of their experience watching it. The audience's reflections on integrity gained in clarity and cogency through the participants' associations to specific moments in the part of the film they had watched. The film made possible a coming to consciousness of the integrity in depth we all have, our own willing "sensitivity to the needs of the whole," (Beebe, 1992, p. 125) enacted by our detailed responses to the whole of this impressive film.

Not that we exhausted the subject. Elizabeth Brodersen, who had asked me to lead this discussion, shared her own reflections later, in (unpublished) written comments that she called "Moments of Integrity in *Monsoon Wedding*." She prefaced her remarks with this observation, which I think has much to say about what happens to us as we watch the film:

> I interpret integrity as moments of honesty when one is forced to confront a truth which has been kept hidden or half-hidden from oneself and from significant others. It bursts forward into a moment of self-awareness, transforming the self and the other(s) with its revelation.

She mentioned the problems posed for integrity by an arranged marriage, which tests the bride to be honest about her own previous compromises of the virgin archetype that is so glibly assumed to be inviolate in patriarchal marriage, and brought up as well a related shadow, patriarchal violations of the incest taboo, which raise questions of both the 'missing' and the 'false' father. Brodersen asserted that because such compromises were honestly faced within the scenario, they actually enhanced our sense that integrity, and marriage based on integrity, can survive them. After exploring in detail how this theme is dramatized in *Monsoon Wedding*, she added a note on "The 'flower' as a symbol of integrity," making sense for the first time how the decorative marigolds that Dubey keeps eating serve as a living symbol of the integration of integrity as a value that is the warp and woof of watching this film. Brodersen wrote:

> The yellow flower is an image of the healing joy of love. Experience of sexual abuse prompts Aliya to remove the flower from her hair but it is (as it were) replaced by Dubey who restores Alice's innocence and Aliya's by association. One could even say that Alice now eats and digests the flower that Aliya tears out of her hair earlier with the consequence that both are healed.

I would add only that many of us in the conference session were healed, in our attitude toward what integrity makes possible, by watching and talking about this film.

Notes

1   Pimmy has come from dancing with other women and some of the more venturesome, feminine-oriented men, a scene Virginia Apperson rightly emphasizes in *The Presence of the Feminine in Film* (2008, p. 170). It seems to be a rallying of the libido of the feminine for what will eventually be a defense of the feminine body against masculine aggression.

I am also indebted to Ann Alkire for first pointing out to me the importance of the scene of the women dancing, which speaks particularly to women viewers; it is indeed the key to the moral movement of the film.

2   Universal Studios, DVD #22284, 2002.

3   Available on YouTube at www.youtube.com/watch?v=SAURpBfGA1I (accessed August 19, 2016).

References

Apperson, V. & Beebe, J. (2008). *The Presence of the Feminine in Film*. Newcastle: Cambridge Scholars Publishing.

Beebe, J. (1992). *Integrity in Depth*. College Station, TX: Texas A & M University Press.

Cavell, S. (1981). *Pursuits of Happiness: The Hollywood Comedy of Remarriage*. Cambridge, MA: Harvard University Press.

Jung. C.G. (1946). "The Psychology of the Transference," in *Collected Works*, Vol. 16, *The Practice of Psychotherapy* (2nd edn). New York: Pantheon Books, pp. 163–323.

Jung, C.G. (1954). *Collected Works*, Vol. 14, *Mysterium Coniunctionis* (2nd edn). Princeton, NJ: Princeton University Press.

Mulvey, L. (2009). "Visual Pleasure and Narrative Cinema," in *Visual and Other Pleasures* (2nd edn). New York: Palgrave Macmillan, pp. 14–27.

Nair, M. (Director) (2001). *Monsoon Wedding*. [Motion picture].

Warner, M. (1985). *Monuments and Maidens: The Allegory of the Female Form*. New York: Athenaeum.

PART V

Primordial Archetypal Feminine

9

REMEMBERING EVE'S TRANSGRESSION AS REBIRTH

Vanya Stier-Van Essen

Introduction

Remembering Eve

Eve's transgression, as she listens to the council of the serpent and takes from the forbidden tree in the Garden of Eden, is a pivotal moment in the Eden story. The Eden story (Genesis 2:4–3:24) has served as the predominant creation myth of the Western world and, therefore, holds special significance in the development of our worldview. I suggest that at this critical historical moment, as we collectively grapple with the effects of having lived for so long primarily in a style of consciousness that denigrates the female, seeks dominion over nature, and relegates to the feminine and to matter (body, earth) all that it considers unacceptable, Eve and her transgression should be remembered.

Von Franz (1972, p. 5) wrote, "Creation myths are the deepest and most important of all myths." She asserted that creation myths are different from other types of myths, writing, "They refer to the most basic problems of human life, for they are concerned with the ultimate meaning, not only of *our* existence, but of the existence of the whole cosmos" (ibid., p. 5). In other words, creation myths have an instrumental and dialogical relationship with our ways of being in the world, interacting with and informing our conceptions about our daily struggles and our imagination around the nature of reality. Since the image of Eve's transgression is a pivotal point in the predominant Western creation myth, we could say that it has had an instrumental role in the shaping of Western consciousness. Tarnas (1991, p. xiv) wrote, "Today the Western mind appears to be undergoing an epochal transformation … I believe we can participate intelligently in that transformation only to the extent to which we are historically informed. Every age must remember its history anew." This inquiry seeks to remember Eve anew.

Although this inquiry is based on a religious image, it is a psychological exploration, not a theological one. What I mean by this is that the goal of this research is not to make metaphysical claims about the nature of God or religion, but rather to explore the terrain of our psychological experience. In order to more deeply understand our lives and the world in which we live, we must explore the dominant images shaping our consciousness (Neumann, 1954, p. 105).

The Image of Eve's Transgression

Here, I refer to images not exclusively as visual data but as carriers of psychic energy or as units of psychic experience. Jung (1938, para. 75) asserted, "Everything which we are conscious of is an image" and boldly stated, "image *is* psyche." We experience the world and psyche in and through images. Jung broke the confines of the visual image and recognized image as the currency of our consciousness. Furthermore, Jung (1923, para. 127) concluded that our unconscious psyche (the aspects of the psyche and psychic experience of which we are not aware in our waking ego-lives) consists of images that express universal principles he called archetypes. He asserted that if we closely examine these images they give form to innumerable typical experiences that constantly reoccur throughout history, offering us a "picture of psychic life" (ibid., para. 127). Therefore, according to Jung and post-Jungians, such as Adams (2008, p. 226), not only does our consciousness exist in images, our unconscious psyche also consists of images. Images, then, can be understood as the building blocks of the whole psyche, like the cells of our psychic body, each building block a portion of psychic experience. Therefore, the images we carry and the way in which we carry them, even unconsciously, shape the way we live out our lives.

The Problem of Eve

In this creation myth, we find Eve and Adam living peacefully in the Garden of Eden. They are visited often by their creator, Yahweh, and have been given one rule: they may not eat from the tree of the knowledge of good and evil or they will surely die (Genesis 2:17, NIV). However, on the fateful day of her transgression, we find Eve standing in the middle of the garden admiring the tree and listening to the counsel of the cunning serpent.

The serpent offers her a different perspective. "You will not surely die," the serpent assures Eve, "Your eyes will be opened, and you will be like God, knowing good and evil" (Genesis 3:4–5). Despite strict warning from Yahweh that she should never eat from the tree in the middle of the garden, Eve trusts the serpent and her own intuitions. The biblical account states, "The woman saw that the fruit of the tree was good for food and pleasing to the eye, and also desirable for gaining wisdom" (Genesis 3:6). In a world-shattering moment, Eve reaches for the fruit, brings it to her lips, and takes a bite. She then offers the fruit to Adam, who also partakes in the fruit from the forbidden tree. Later, upon discovering their transgression, Yahweh pronounces an angry curse, which includes the subjugation of women and an antagonistic relationship with the land (Genesis 3:14–19). After covering their shamed bodies, Yahweh casts Eve and Adam out of the garden forever.

If this image is taken literally, *woman* holds humankind's fall from divine grace in her guilty hands. Animal life must be silenced, the body must be hidden, the Earth is cursed, and Eve is shamed, guilty, dependent on men, and subjugated. Here in the predominant creation myth of the Western world lives an image that, if taken literally, infuses our consciousness with the view that woman is inferior. Moreover, in its concretized state, this image suggests that listening to the animal voice is dangerous, that gaining wisdom from nature is destructive, and that the Earth should be understood as an adversary.

This literal interpretation appears congruent with the proposed intentions of the author of the Eden story. In the book, *Mythology of Eden*, George and George (2014, p. 7) built a strong case arguing that the author of the Eden story was most likely a scribe from Judah referred to as "J," who wrote the story in the mid-900s BCE. Using detailed historical and archeological evidence, they asserted J wrote the story with overt anti-Canaanite political intentions, which depended largely on establishing the supremacy of Yahweh as the only deity of Israel. This, in turn, necessitated the suppression of the pagan and Goddess traditions (ibid., p. 72). The worship and veneration of the Goddess, mostly recognized in the region at this time as Asherah, was widely practiced in Judah and Israel at the time J authored the Eden story (ibid., p. 72). By associating Eve's transgression with established Goddess symbols, specifically the serpent, the sacred tree, and the garden, J was sending a clear message to his readers that engaging with the Goddess was dangerous and would have severe consequences (ibid., p. 237).

Therefore, while maintaining and strengthening the etiological basis for the subjugation of women already existing in Hebrew culture, J went further and sought to not only subjugate but to eliminate the Goddess. Put another way, we could say he went beyond subjugating the female gender into denigrating the feminine principle of the psyche, represented by the Goddess Asherah. This, of course, would reflect and perpetuate a patriarchal paradigm that denigrates and negates all that it considers feminine and relegates to the feminine all it considers unacceptable.

Jung's (1936, paras. 119–120; 1940, para. 296) recognition of a contra-sexual principle in each person opened up an opportunity for a deepened understanding of these archetypal principles. With this foundation, we can begin to distinguish the feminine and masculine principles from literal gender and understand them as counterbalancing archetypal energies that exist in every person regardless of biological gender. We could say that the Eden story was a perpetuation of the patriarchal urge to subjugate the female and, furthermore, to suppress and even eliminate the archetypal feminine principle. Within the framework of power, in order for Yahweh to rise, Asherah had to be pushed down.

While it seems that in the West we have indeed enacted the conscious aspects of the myth, we can still inquire into what remains unconscious in the myth. That is to say, while J and his audience may have been conscious of the general meaning of these symbols, symbols are living entities. Jung (1923, para. 116) believed that true symbols rise up from the womb of the creative psyche and point us toward the unknown, like "bridges thrown out towards an unseen shore." Remembering the image of Eve's transgression and exploring what remains hidden or unconscious arises as an imperative, for what remains unconscious in the images living through us remains unconscious in our ways of relating to ourselves and to the world. To remain literal would be to petrify what is conscious in the myth; to move into imagination and archetypal exploration is to seek what is hidden or unconscious in the image of Eve's transgression. Hillman (1979, p. 4) called this movement of deepening into an image and returning it to its "imaginal background" an "epistrophe." In that sense, this chapter is an epistrophe of the image of Eve's transgression.

An Epistrophe of Eve's Transgression

While Hillman (1997, p. 218) asserted that the Eden story established a framework for male primacy and subjugation of the female in Western consciousness, he also reminded us that "Eve was required" in order for new life to begin (2005, p. 196). In other words, he recognized Eve as an archetypal necessity. Hillman recognized that Eve was far more than a disappointing wife and daughter; he recognized her archetypal potentialities for the creation of consciousness. Likewise, Jung (1939, para. 56) equated Eve with the awakening power of the soul. He wrote, "She is full of snares and traps, in order that man should fall, should reach the earth, entangle himself there, and stay caught, so that life should be lived: as Eve in the Garden of Eden could not rest content until she had convinced Adam of the goodness of the forbidden apple" (ibid., para. 56). Jung seems to be offering a radical view of Eve's transgression as a courageous act, with Eve as representative of a disruptive and necessary energy of the psyche. As we begin to imagine Eve as an essential and awakening force in the psyche, we can begin to remember her transgression anew.

Transgression and Knowledge

In the traditional interpretation, this transgression resulted in the original curse, the fall of humanity. Within this understanding, Eve's rebellious act is understood as cause for great human suffering, shame, and painful separation from the divine. However, a deeper inquiry reveals a different perspective.

Certainly, Eve's betrayal did not come without profound grief and loss. Once she had eaten of the fruit, she had to leave. To stay in the garden after *knowing* would have been to live covered in fig leaves; it would have been to live ashamed. When Eve left the garden, she lost the safety of Yahweh's approval and protection, the innocence of not knowing, and the ease of not having to live by her own inner law. Eve lost the quietness of an unquestioned life; she lost the only way she knew of being in the world. The transgression did indeed result in destruction and death. However, her transgression also resulted in extraordinary new life.

George and George (2014, pp. 249–250) concluded that the knowledge Eve and Adam gained in the garden consisted "*of understanding how this divine cosmic dynamic of order (good) and chaos (evil) operates in the world and the role that humans play in this dynamic*" (emphasis added). It had mainly to do with the ability to distinguish, discern, and differentiate. Therefore, rather than a debased act of irrevocable sin (a word which was never used in the Eden story), the transgression actually resulted in the "*elevation* of humans above their prior state … sharing to some extent in divine understanding" (ibid., p. 248). In other words, it created new consciousness. Jungian analyst Neumann (1954) highlighted the significance of moments of transgression to the emergence of consciousness, particularly in creation myths.

Neumann (1954, p. 121) described this mythic act of separation as a reverberating "No" to the World Parents, "To become conscious of oneself, to be conscious at all, begins with saying 'no' to the uroborus, to the Great Mother, to the unconscious … To discriminate, to distinguish, to mark off, to isolate oneself from the surrounding context – these are the basic acts of consciousness." Consciousness is created with a move beyond unconscious unity into differentiated relatedness, "a qualitatively different unity" (ibid., p. 116). Consciousness emerges out of transgression. While Neumann emphasized that this is a courageous and creative act, he also reminded us that the separation is experienced by the ego as suffering and guilt, and is often experienced as "original sin, a fall" (ibid., p. 114). The Eden story carries this sense of guilt and has been imagined by many traditional Christian theologians as the original sin that contaminated all of humanity, Augustine being a primary example of this kind of thinking (Pagels, 1989, p. 99). Perhaps because this myth has been used for political gain and to perpetuate a patriarchal paradigm, the underlying mythic meaning has been largely missed. With most of the attention given to the guilt, the archetypal significance of the transgression remains largely unfelt and unseen. In a story potentially meant to give the powers of creation and fertility over to Yahweh (George & George, 2014, p. 232), on a mythic and archetypal level Eve emerges as the creatress of new consciousness.

After they ate the forbidden fruit, Adam named Eve the "mother of all the living" and Yahweh declared that she and Adam had become like the gods, "knowing good and evil" (Genesis 3:20–22). Since the phrase "mother of all the living" was historically used in reference to the Goddess, it is likely that J used this phrase to strengthen Eve's association with the Goddess, therefore tying the Goddess to Eve's downfall (George & George, 2014, p. 227). However, as we look beyond the surface of this image, we can discern the echoes of humanity's elevation into consciousness as they moved into knowledge that had previously belonged only to the divine, that is, the ability to differentiate and discern between opposites (ibid., p. 250). A close look at the myth reveals that they were not cast out of the garden simply because they had become vile or impure. They were cast out of the garden because they knew too much. While on the surface Eve was shamed in her association with the Goddess, below the surface we witness Eve rising into her divinity through the Goddess as she is named mother of all.

The Serpent, the Tree, and the Goddess

Continued close attention to the image reveals a crucial aspect of this moment of transgression: Eve did not enact this revolt alone. At the moment of her transgression, she was with the serpent and the tree. Again, although on the surface these Goddess symbols may have been intended to turn the reader away from the feminine principle (i.e. Asherah), looked at now as we remember this image through an archetypal lens, we find Eve being led out of unconsciousness and servitude precisely *through* the feminine principle. Beneath the patriarchal polemics we find the force of feminine transgression leading Eve beyond unconscious obedience, from what Neumann (1954, p. 113) called "uroboric unity," into new consciousness.

An ancient association exists between the serpent and the Goddess (George & George, 2014, p. 51). Archeological evidence reveals this strong and ongoing connection and suggests that the Goddess has been associated with the snake as early as the seventh millennium BCE (Gimbutas, 1989, p. 122). In fact, in ancient temples the Goddess was often identified and referred to as "Serpent Lady" (Stone, 1976, p. 207). The serpent was associated with wisdom, divination, and prophecy (ibid., p. 199). In a twist of archetypal irony, at the heart of a story meant to warn the reader to stay away from serpent-knowing associated with the Goddess, we find the energy and wisdom necessary for the move out of unconsciousness and into consciousness coming precisely from this kind of feminine knowing.

The serpent was not the only link between Eve and the Goddess traditions. The sacred tree was also an ancient symbol associated with the Goddess (George & George, 2014, p. 51; Stone, 1976, p. 214). Often in archeological discoveries, the Goddess and the sacred tree are presented together and are "*interchangeable in iconography*" (George & George, 2014, p. 71). Further demonstrating the link between the tree and the Goddess traditions was the common practice of passing a branch around a circle and partaking of the fruit of the tree as a form of communion with the Goddess, "To eat of its fruit was to eat of the flesh and fluid of the Goddess" (Stone, 1976, p. 215). Eating as part of the creative process of destruction toward consciousness is a common mythical motif. Neumann (1954, p. 124) expressed it thus, "The formation of consciousness goes hand-in-hand with a fragmentation of the world continuum into separate objects, parts, figures, which can only then be assimilated, taken in, introjected, made conscious – in a word, 'eaten.'" To eat is to destroy in order to create. It is to make something a part of who we are. By eating the fruit, Eve made the tree a part of her body; she partook in the flesh and fluid of the Goddess. Through this intimate communion with the Goddess, Eve moved out of unknowing into knowing.

It is a tragedy that this image, surrounded by impoverished imagination, has contributed to the denigration of nature. In its literalized form, this image implicates the female and the earth with evil and casts them into the dark. The unconscious concretization of this image results in a consciousness that blames the female for the dark and takes out its hatred on matter. However, remembering the transgression through an archetypal lens, we find Eve moving into knowing through profound

collaboration with more-than-human nature. Eve did not find her voice and courage in a void; she found it in communion with nature. She relied on the wisdom
of animals and on the nourishment of trees. The wildness of nature mirrored her
wild intuitions and gave them voice; communion with the natural world broke the
spell and her eyes were opened. The very act of her betrayal was an act of taking the
Earth into her body. Eve found her voice in the hiss of a snake and in the rustling
of the trees.

Adam

Another significant aspect of the image that must not be overlooked is that when
Eve reached for and ate the fruit, Adam was present and Adam participated. The
male, here, is a necessary element of the transgressive move. Although a deeper
look at the complicated world of gender relations is far beyond the scope of this
chapter, I recognize that the image reminds us that our battle against a patriarchal
paradigm is not simply a fight between male and female (for treatments of this myth
in relation to gender considerations see Daly 1973, Grimke 2009[1838], Plaskow
2009[1979], Stone 1976, Pagels 1989). Furthermore, Jungian analyst Woodman
(1993, pp. 30–31) reminded us that although patriarchy has been associated with
maleness and masculinity, the power-oriented framework of patriarchy is a gross
distortion of the masculine principle as well, and these distortions could be enacted
equally by matriarchal systems. A patriarchal paradigm abandons the true archetypal
masculine and feminine principles and seeks to usurp reality with power.

The image of Eve's transgression, which for so long has been associated with
this power paradigm, suggests that the problem belongs to both the masculine and
feminine principles and that the way through requires their union. Woodman and
Dickson (1996, p. 208) emphasized the need for this collaboration as we seek new
consciousness, calling the move beyond the Rule of the Father "the third sacred
dream." A paradigm that disparages the feminine, female, and nature, and relegates
to those all that it considers unacceptable or undesirable, distorts both the feminine
and the masculine; both must transgress.

Eve stands at this juncture. Although used to justify and perpetuate patriarchal
values, she is deeply associated with the Goddess, that is, the sacred feminine principle of the psyche. With a muddy sense of belonging, her loyalties have been continually questioned. However, in light of Woodman and Dickson's admonition, Eve
may emerge as a crucial mythical figure now, as she moves beyond both matriarchal
and patriarchal paradigms into something new and yet unknown.

An Interlude: Eve's Moment

Eve stirs in us every time we have to choose between knowing and unknowing;
every time we have to choose between the safe and the dangerous; every time
the deepest longing of our hearts threatens worlds; every time we have to choose
between the sterile safety of civilization and the wildness of animals and trees. In

that quiet and dark moment between inhale and exhale, the moment between worlds, between creation and destruction, between death and life, Eve shows us the way.

Eve calls us to do more than know in our darkest heart, she asks us to act. Eve does not allow one to revolt in secret; she demands material involvement; she demands the implication of the body. Eve's betrayal was neither ideological nor theoretical. It involved reaching hands, vigorous muscles, the sensuality of taste buds, and inglorious digestive juices. Eve calls us into a posture of perpetual creative transgression as we seek to move into new consciousness. We need Eve's insight, courage, and strength to walk out of the quiet, acceptable life into the wild riot of our own voices.

Conclusion

A return of Eve's transgression to its imaginal and archetypal background reveals Eve as a necessary awakening force of the psyche. Although on the surface her association with the Goddess was meant to subjugate the female and elimi-nate the feminine, on an archetypal level her intimate bond with the Goddess suggests the creation of consciousness precisely *through* the feminine principle. Furthermore, standing between Asherah and Yahweh, between the archetypal feminine and the archetypal masculine, Eve and the image of her transgression may have more to show us regarding a move beyond patriarchal and matriarchal paradigms into something new, beyond power into more equitable differentiated relatedness.

Eve shows us a kind of consciousness and discerning knowledge that is gained not only through differentiation but also through communion. As she takes in the flesh and fluid of the Goddess into her body and as she communes with more-than-human nature, she is transformed. She finds separation, differentiation, and discernment through integration and unity. Her transgression emerges as a myste-rious move into consciousness through simultaneous separation and communion. Through her transgression, Eve is reborn.

References

Adams, M.V. (2008). "Imaginology: The Jungian Study of the Imagination," in S. Marlon (ed.), *Archetypal Psychologies, Reflections in the Honor of James Hillman*. New Orleans: Spring Journal, pp. 225–242.

Daly, M. (1973). *Beyond God the Father: Toward a Philosophy of Women's Liberation*. Boston: Beacon Press.

George, A. & George, E. (2014). *The Mythology of Eden*. New York: Hamilton Books.

Gimbutas, M. (1989). *The Language of the Goddess*. New York: Thames & Hudson.

Grimke, S. (2009). "Letters on the Equality of the Sexes and the Condition of Woman," in K. Kvam, L. Shearing, & V. Zeigler (eds.), *Eve and Adam: Jewish, Christian, and Muslim Readings on Genesis and Gender*, pp. 340–343. Indianapolis: Indiana University Press, 1838.

Hillman, J. (1979). *The Dream and the Underworld*. New York: Harper and Row Publishers.

Hillman, J. (1997). *The Myth of Analysis: Three Essays in Archetypal Psychology*. Evanston: Northwestern University Press.

Hillman, J. (2005). "Betrayal," in G. Slater (ed.), *Senex and Puer*. Putnam: Spring Publications, pp. 193–213.

Jung, C.G. (1923). "On the Relation of Analytical Psychology to Poetry," *The Collected Works*, Vol. 15, *The Spirit in Man, Art, and Literature* (2nd edn). Princeton, NJ: Princeton University Press, 1966.

Jung, C.G. (1936). "Concerning the Archetypes and the Anima Concept," in *Collected Works*, Vol. 9i, *The Archetypes and the Collective Unconscious* (2nd edn). Princeton, NJ: Princeton University Press, 1990.

Jung, C.G. (1938). "Commentary on the 'Secret of the Golden Flower,'" in *Collected Works*, Vol. 13, *Alchemical Studies* (2nd edn). Princeton, NJ: Princeton University Press, 1967.

Jung, C.G. (1939). "Archetypes of the Collective Unconscious," in *Collected Works*, Vol. 9i, *The Archetypes and the Collective Unconscious* (2nd edn). Princeton, NJ: Princeton University Press, 1990.

Jung, C.G. (1940). "The Psychology of the Child Archetype," in *Collected Works*, Vol. 9i, *The Archetypes and the Collective Unconscious* (2nd edn). Princeton, NJ: Princeton University Press, 1990.

Neumann, E. (1954). *The Origins and History of Consciousness*. Princeton, NJ: Princeton University Press, 1949.

Pagels, E. (1989). *Adam, Eve, and the Serpent: Sex and Politics in Early Christianity*. New York: Vintage Books.

Plaskow, J. (2009). "The Coming of Lilith: Toward a Feminist Theology," in K. Kvam, L. Shearing, & V. Zeigler (eds.), *Eve and Adam: Jewish, Christian, and Muslim Readings on Genesis and Gender*, pp. 422–425. Indianapolis: Indiana University Press, 1979.

Stone, M. (1976). *When God was a Woman*. New York: Harvest/HBJ.

Tarnas, R. (1991). *The Passion of the Western Mind: Understanding the Ideas that have Shaped our World View*. New York: Ballantine Books.

von Franz, M.L. (1972). *Creation Myths*. Dallas, TX: Spring Publications.

Woodman, M. (1993). *Conscious Femininity: Interviews with Marion Woodman*. Toronto: Inner City Books.

Woodman, M. & Dickson, E. (1996). *Dancing in the Flames: The Dark Goddess in the Transformation of Consciousness*. Boston: Shambhala Publications, Inc.

10

SYMBOLIC RENEWAL; RENEWAL OF SYMBOLS, THE REBIRTH OF THE TRICKSTER GODDESSES IN MYSTERIES

Susan Rowland

> A symbol remains a perpetual challenge to our thoughts and feelings. This probably explains why a symbolic work is so stimulating, why it grips us so intensely, but also why it seldom affords us a purely aesthetic enjoyment. A work that is manifestly not symbolic appeals much more to our aesthetic sensibility because it is complete in itself and fulfills its purpose
>
> (Jung, 1922, para. 119).

Introduction

Jung's distinction here between the psychic potency of the symbol and aesthetic completeness is perhaps a clue to more than just his distinguishing between two kinds of images in art. For whereas he calls a "sign" those motifs that denote a single, straightforward meaning, he insists that "symbols" point to something mysterious, not fully understood and yet cannot be represented in any other way (Jung, 1922, para. 105). Given this dichotomy, symbols might be characterized by "incompleteness" for they represent an invitation to the psyche to *co-create* meaning.

Symbols invoke, they draw in, fascinate, and enchant. They are in culture and art the counterpart of what C.G. Jung posited about the psyche, that it was composed of inherited principles for generating images and meanings called archetypes (Jung 1947/1954, para. 394). Hypothetical and unrepresentable, archetypes are both body and psyche. They have a root in somatic instincts while reaching to the spiritual energies that Jung regarded as intrinsic to human functioning. Spiritual or religious impulses do not necessarily entail a supernatural realm of gods, but they also do not exclude it.

In our religions and our arts we find the product of these innate archetypes in archetypal images. As autonomous psyche drives, archetypes work *in* time, not outside of it. As embodied, they co-create images *with* the experience of individual historical and encultured lives. Archetypal images are always also participating in the here and now while not being determined by personal factors, the body, or by powerful forces within a culture. Such images span the potential of the archetype for transcendence and its root in our immanence, our gritty, ego-oriented, and located lives. So archetypal images manifest as symbols: images of the image-ination, or archetypal psyche, in words, paintings, photographs, music, architecture, film, etc. that reveal the autonomous activity of the archetype finding substance within human culture.

Such a perspective on the making of culture positions symbols as dynamic imagery. In turn this suggests their propensity to tell stories. Here symbols may be metonyms for myths where a metonym is a motif that is meaningful by being connected to something larger. Indeed, mythic stories to Jung were the psyche's way of managing the limits of consciousness, making coherence at the borders of the knowable or reasonable (Jung 1947/1954, paras. 412–415). In turn, conscious limitations may actually produce symbols to enable the psyche to incarnate that mystery. So for example, in a detective story set in a theater, *Freeze My Margarita*, by Lauren Hendersen, what is previously a Jungian sign, lighting evoking a moonlit night, becomes eerie, magical, an anticipation of unknown transgression; it becomes a symbol.

Here the enchanted setting invokes Artemis of the wild woods. The symbol of moonlight hints at the goddess of the hunt in a story in which an as yet unknown killer is about to strike. While the genre of detective fiction may lack the aesthetic completeness that Jung referred to in its adherence to formulaic rules, if it generates symbols and myths, then it arguably takes part in the psyche's everyday drama of making meaning from its images.

Such an account imbues the psyche's images in the symbols materialized by a culture to make an archetypal architecture of being. However there is more to be said about symbolic renewal in the context of how the creativity of the human psyche meets the creativity of non-human nature. Might symbols renew by undoing modernity's distancing from our bodily selves? Indeed, going further, might symbols return us to lives that are companioned by animals, plants, trees, and rocks?

The Ecocritical Psyche

In my book, *The Ecocritical Psyche* (2012), I offered two arguments about Jungian symbols that are germane to this chapter. In the first place, symbols are synchronistic while secondly, symbols are engines of complexity evolution and portals to non-human nature.

To take symbols and synchronicity first of all, Jung defined synchronicity as meaningful coincidence between something psychic and something material (Jung, 1952, para. 960). Psyche and matter unite when symbolic art is made, and the independent meaningfulness of the work has the capacity to affect audiences across time and space. This meeting of psyche and matter is the symbol: the material manifestation of archetypal patterning born in the psychic particularity of the artist and again, differently, in his or her audience. Therefore synchronicity denotes the symbol's capacity to connect immanence in particularity and transcendence in spirituality.

Synchronicity is when we feel connected to something outside or larger than ourselves with no rational cause for it. This is what symbols do.

However, before considering the specific molding of symbols and myth in detective or mystery fiction, I want to provide a broader notion of symbols and psyche in evolutionary terms. The new science of "complexity evolution" or "emergence" shows the Jungian symbol as capable of healing, by making whole, the wound modernity opened between human psyche and non-human nature. Art that invokes symbols would therefore become a *reciprocal* dialogue between humans and nature.

Complexity theory is a key modification of evolution after Darwin. Evolved nature is not so much a competition between competing species, as Darwin originally envisaged, but is more like successive, ever more interpenetrating environments. These Complex Adaptive Systems (or CAS) interact in ways so complex they cannot be mapped or traced with the usual linear cause and effect methodology (Shulman, 1997).

Rather, the interpenetration of CAS stimulates evolutionary change by the emergence of new "wholes" that appear to be more than the sum of their parts (ibid.). Such evolution has to be called "creative" in suggesting a kind of innate animation in non-human nature itself. That is, nature displays creativity in the emergent properties of Complex Adaptive Systems, including the human organism as a psyche-body matrix. Human beings participate in complexity evolution on an unconsciously embodied level with the non-human complex adaptive environments. Indeed, Jung had a name for just these kinds of unconscious creative processes: synchronicity.

Unsurprisingly, Jungians such as Helene Schulman (1997) and Joseph Cambray (2012) have developed Jung's identification of synchronicity and the collective unconscious in connection to the new theories of complexity or emergence. My own contribution in *The Ecocritical Psyche* is to suggest that complexity evolution occurs in the making and appreciation of art by means of the synchronous Jungian symbol as an evolutionary portal into the psyche. The symbol offers the return of an animistic sense of non-human nature. Symbols unite the human psyche to the animism of the non-human world. They are animistic, not metaphorically but in actuality.

It is time to consider the symbols and myths preferred by the un-aesthetically un-whole popular genre of detective fiction.

From Tricksters to Goddesses in Mysteries

In a previous work, I have suggested that the founding myth of detective fiction is that of the trickster, in which, most importantly, the tricky protagonist could stand for hero or villain or both (Rowland 2012). Indeed, if the trickster myth emerged from archaic times when humans learned to hunt and be hunted, then modern detective fiction preserves and exposes us to that elemental structure of consciousness.

Moreover detective fiction shares both its *modern* genesis (as a late nineteenth-century genre) and its ancient heritage in the trickster myth and symbols with the contemporary emergence of psychotherapy and psychologies of the unconscious. What links depth psychology to detective fiction is a similar sense of knowledge as a *problem* with tricky overtones, rather than something subject to wholly rational analysis. Both the detective and the psychoanalyst have to search for clues to a truth that is hidden from view. In both cases the truth sought for is of unknown extent. Both cultural forms additionally structure their quests in terms of seeking an ultimately narrative understanding of knowledge. This is to say that the revelation of "whodunit" is not enough; it is the *process*, the story of discovery that embodies the true knowing of the genre, as I shall show.

Reading a mystery book is to enter a *mystery* in which symbols connoting myths of goddesses return to extend the possibilities of being human and being connected to the cosmos.

However it is Jung who shows the way from the trickster myth of hunter/gatherers, to the return of the goddesses, in order to heal the modern psyche:

> Even [the trickster's] sex is optional despite its phallic qualities: he can turn himself into a woman and bear children … This is a reference to his original nature as a Creator, for the world is made from the body of a god (Jung, 1954, para. 472).

Here in Jung's work is the admission that the trickster is one image or figuration (figure) of the Earth Mother – his more capacious sense of the Freudian pre-Oedipal mother. For the trickster is the protean psyche, itself, as the origin, ground, and multiple possibilities of being. The trickster as pre-Oedipal entity makes a cosmos from her/his ungendered body. Earth Mother is a figuration of a very ancient mythical idea, according to Ann Baring and Jules Cashford in *The Myth of the Goddess* (1991). It is of the pre-monotheistic paradigm of the Earth herself as the sacred ground of being from whom all life is born and manifest in animistic religions. Here consciousness is based on connection and body, sexuality, matter, and nature are divine.

The rise of masculine monotheisms produced a binary countering of Earth Mother in Sky Father religions in which the god produced nature and humans as separate from himself. Inaugurating dualism, Sky Father models consciousness as separation, disembodiment, and transcendence. Myths such as the protean, plural gendered trickster preserve much of Earth Mother's multiplicity and ambiguity in an age beset by stark divisions of gender and the law. Therefore, I argue that the trickster's presence in the genre as a whole represents a psychic dynamism that manifests in differentiated divine symbols. Put another way, the trickster is rich earth for seeding symbols of goddesses and gods that pre-date the dominance of *one* disembodied Sky Father.

Central to my project of tracing these goddesses as symbols and myth in modern detective fiction is the work of James Hillman in converting Jung's multiple archetypes into a polytheistic psyche (Hillman, 2007). Even more germane is the work of Ginette Paris in *Pagan Meditations* (1986) on Hestia, Artemis, and Aphrodite in the modern woman and the rich exploration of psyche and gender by Christine Downing in *Women's Mysteries* (Downing, 1992). To Paris and Downing is owed so much of the insight into goddesses in modern culture in this chapter.

When following the subtle progress of goddesses in mysteries it is vital to bear in mind the overlap I am positing between symbol and myth. While the divine ancients are to be found in stories, their capacity to evoke numinosity from these tales gives them also a metonymic symbolic function. So the name "Aphrodite" stands for all the divine characteristics of the goddess that are invoked in the myths. For this reason the name is a symbol because it connects to an archetypal way of being that is not limited by our conscious capacities. Similarly the symbol "Aphrodite" reciprocally implies the myth: *her*stories.

It is time to look at the four characteristic goddesses of women's mysteries: Aphrodite, Artemis, Athena, and Hestia.

Reclaiming Aphrodite in Symbols

As Ginette Paris shows in *Pagan Meditations*, Aphrodite as symbol of feminine sexual energy and knowing was marginalized both by Plato and much later, Freud. Each reconfigures Eros to occlude her radiance. In the Greek pantheon, Aphrodite shares with Dionysus in giving "a central position to the spontaneity of the body and to sexuality" (1986, pp. 90–95). There the resemblance between more primordial and brutal Dionysus and civilizing Aphrodite ends. While Dionysus is ecstatic and savage, Aphrodite is beauty and seduction. Aphrodite is the arts of love while Dionysus provides instinctual energy frequently careless of human vulnerability.

Above all, Aphrodite is a virgin goddess; her divinity demonstrates sexuality as sacred. Put another way, Aphrodite is a form of knowing and being in mysteries. She is virgin in the sense of being self-contained, not to be regarded as defined by any one relationship to an-other. Significantly, she shares this virginity with Athena, Artemis, and Hestia, suggesting the importance of conceiving of the feminine in terms of a primary reality, not as a secondary product of an original masculinity.

On the other hand, the project of marginalizing the sexuality of divine feminine began early with Platonic philosophy. As Paris explains:

> Platonic philosophy marked the end of Aphrodite's predominance; it gave the myth of Eros precedence over that of Aphrodite, dissociated love from its corporeal aspect, and valued mostly the all-male relationships ... More and more Apollo controlled Dionysus ... Woman's body stopped being one of the paths to the sacred (Paris, 1986, p. 41).

Here Paris reveals Plato's move in replacing Earth Mother origins with Sky Father dualistic and patriarchal values. By elevating mobile Eros and discounting the somatic sacred of Aphrodite, erotic love begins on a path toward a divine devotion directly opposed to the pleasures of the body. Such a move is indivisible from a separation and privileging relation between genders. Moreover, Apollo, god of reason and order, starts to direct cultural preferences, rather than being a psychic capacity among other gods who are regarded just as highly.

In making Eros the *masculine* force of the psychic energy that Freud saw as fundamentally sexual, Freudian psychoanalysis compounds Platonic preferences. Hence the Freudian libido is masculine; Aphrodite and feminine sexuality as an ontological or primary reality is not offered as part of the Freudian tradition. This is clearly not the case for Ginette Paris's development of a Jungian notion of multiple archetypes, inborn psychic potentials which have all the possibilities of feminine or masculine expression. Hence the return of this goddess in mysteries is a move toward a greater embodied intensity of life. Aphrodite is not a ghost from the past but rather a renewal for our future.

So Aphrodite in mysteries is not an invitation to retreat from the present world. It is rather a way of re-connecting with human potentials that have been neglected in the Western psyche. If, as I have been suggesting, these goddesses and gods have returned in cultural forms such as mystery fiction, it might be worth exploring a little further what Aphrodite holds out to us. After all, if divine feminine sexuality is a civilizing force, then what about the sexual component of fictional crime? Might such an understanding of the knowing potential of the body aid a detective's quest?

Crucial to mystery fiction is Aphrodite's adulterous alliance with Ares, god of war. As Paris explains, today neither Aphrodite nor Ares are prime movers of war and soldiering to the detriment of psychic health (1986, pp. 79–85). Contemporary Apollonian dominance in technology and disembodied order has triumphed over the somatic aggression of Ares. What has largely replaced face-to-face combat is war fought at a distance through rockets and unmanned drones controlled from bunkers thousands of miles away.

Here I want to suggest that mystery fiction, born in its modern form in the mid-nineteenth century shortly before the First World War, is a trickily fictional attempt to link our ancient history of hunting and being hunted with our modern condition of war. Strategies of the hunter are developed even in modern technological warfare by the snipers and those who direct drones. Yet modern war is distinguished by its capacity to annihilate populations, not just those who choose to fight. It is therefore particularly traumatizing to human culture in threatening its very survival: when survival is at stake, the trickster surfaces.

I would like to propose that, as a whole, genre mysteries may be attempting to compensate for, or rebalance, the cultural psyche in a time when war seems to efface the meaning of an individual death. For above all, mysteries make death comprehensible in terms of being part of a known story, and therefore solvable at the level of fiction. Mysteries convert death, in all its many occasions – from old age, illness, accident, nameless acts of war, to conscious and preventable murder. They therefore return the deliberate killing of a human being to the individual, human, and embodied plane of Ares, lover of Aphrodite.

As a metonym is a figuration of language that works by being part of what it signifies, one could say that at some deep level mysteries are metonymic substitutions for war, for physically taking up arms against an enemy. In effect *they symbolize a war that then need not literally take place.*

In mysteries, symbolic Aphrodite is a trickster. She deceives and causes pain, yet her erotic bounty remains sacramental in uniting bodily desires with the survival of the soul. Whether it is in the capacity to heal the warrior to come *home* from battle, or to offer the fictional detective that instinctual *knowing* that similarly heals the realm of the mystery from continued killing, it is time for an example to explore her invigorating divine symbolic powers.

Symbols of Aphrodite Absent in *Trophies and Dead Things* by Marcia Muller (1990)

San Francisco Private Investigator, Sharon McCone is hired to find the mysterious heirs of a man whose Vietnam service links him to her boss, Hank. Trophies and dead things surface at the home of one of the heirs, all of whom prove to be connected to that war. Indeed the novel title refers to the loss of Aphrodite to more than just the investigator. War in which Ares is giving way to Apollo in Vietnam and is without a bond to Aphrodite's civilizing arts of love for so many veterans, proves behind so-called random snipings in the city. Far from being random, they are the crazed revenge of one who cannot escape his experiences.

Moreover, three of the four lost heirs from the 1960s have been wrecked by their inability to keep their ideals of a more just society in touch with Aphrodite's celebration of the life of loving bodies. Two of them, Libby and D.A. were imprisoned for attempting to bomb a military base. The third, the maker of trophies from the dead, was the planted government agent who betrayed them. The fourth heir proves to be his daughter with the woman he pushed into committing suicide lest his indiscretion impede his "vain ambition."

Aphrodite is multiply betrayed in the divorce of Ares from his lover as the conspirators lose touch with the value of embodied life, by the spy who destroys the joy of his relationship and pushes a woman to despair, and, of course, by a society that enforces control and war at the expense of attempts to connect erotically. Fortunately, Sharon's loss of the goddess is not her rejection of divine feminine sexuality. Her previous relationship with cop, Greg Marcus, ends with both of them respecting the *knowing* of the other so they are able to make an alliance in detecting.

Also, Sharon instinctively pays tribute to the polytheistic psyche. She says early on that she needs to know the truth – a statement that resonates with Jess, daughter of the suicide member of the 1960s conspirators. However the truth is not the same as the mere facts of the attempted bombing. For the truth only begins to emerge from the hidden fact that all the recent sniper victims knew each other in a bar in

Vietnam 20 years previously. This "truth" requires the presences of goddesses to be manifested.

Sharon needs to *figure* the depressive feelings of the departure of Aphrodite in her own life in order to see what the harsher rending apart of the goddess for Jess's mother could do. She, in her Athena mode of close working with men, also knows enough of the horror of Hanks' Vietnam to sense some veterans' desperate absence of Aphrodite too. It is this goddess who proves to symbolize the trauma of war-damaged psyches in her absence and also that knowing that might lead to renewal in averting further tragedy. Yet Sharon needs more than one symbolic goddess within to find the truth that might just heal. She has to be Artemis as well.

Hunting Symbols of Artemis in Mysteries

Goddess and feminine hunter, Artemis grants access to a wild and primitive feminine that is entirely independent of any other goddess or god. She symbolizes the feminine radically autonomous and self-sufficient. Artemis is an Earth Mother who connects all nature, positing humanity as creatures with a natural habitat of the wilderness.

Artemis is profoundly implicated in mysteries of life and death. By forbidding a hunter to wound an animal rather than kill it and end its suffering, Artemis brings death if it is required to sustain the primal purity of life she stands for. Although a virgin and never a mother, Artemis holds women in childbirth when death and new life are intimate with each other.

Therefore Artemis symbolizes the hunter's protection of instinctual life, a protection that includes the mysteries of death. She drives martyrs, suicidal heroism, and sacrifice, even human sacrifice in the deep archaic past as is suggested by the myths surrounding Iphigenia. In her myth, Iphigenia is a Greek princess sacrificed by her father, Agamemnon, to enable him to proceed with the war against Troy.

Yet Iphigenia is not simply a tragic and passive victim of patriarchal aggression. Paris shows that Iphigenia is associated with Artemis herself, not just as one sacrificed to her but also as containing some of her divine, primal energy (1986, pp. 120–124). Hence it is not so surprising that unmarried and childfree detective Victoria *Iphigenia* Warshawski, created by Sara Paretsky for Chicago's troubled streets, is indefatigable in defense of the vulnerable. She bears the scars of her own sacrifices on her body and psyche.

Above all, Artemis is a goddess symbolizing knowing through the feminine as divine and as independent of any other reality. As Paris puts it, Artemis enables a connection to a wild feminine beyond possibility of domestication and of being trapped in social conventions. Every fictional detective who steps outside those compromises demanded by an imperfect system of justice is an Artemis picking up her bow. The sleuth who needs to know in order to fit her nature to the nature she is connected to outside conventional bounds is Artemis who "know[s] the art of preserving within [herself] a force that is intact, inviolable, and radically feminine" (1986, p. 115).

So Artemis in detective fiction is one whose drive for purity of life is uncomfortable for those around her, yet forces her to penetrate the mysteries of life and death. This uncompromising goddess at work incarnates the need to know the truth about the murder; often not just who did it, but who and what set of circumstances was ultimately responsible. Like the Artemis who will bring death if that is what it takes to preserve wild primitive living, such an attitude on the part of the sleuth can be very dangerous to those around her. Sometimes an investigation directly causes further deaths.

Artemis inhabits a detective who must continue the hunt for the truth to the point where it satisfies a divine appetite for psychic justice in one who may bring death as part of her pursuit. For example, in *The Sugar House* (2001) by Laura Lippman, Tess Monaghan seems an unlikely Artemis, until her father confronts her over the smoking ruins of the family home and blames her persistence for the burning house and the dead body inside. Perhaps even more stark is the instance of Kinsey Milhone in *K is for Killer* (Grafton, 1994), who at the end of her hunt for the murderer of Lorna Kepler makes a phone call that leads to another murder.

Through her investigation, Kinsey and the reader get a sense of Lorna as a complex personality seeking a purity of life, and with a gift for friendship. Being beautiful, she incurs the jealousy of her landlord's pregnant young wife, who bugs her apartment. What the eavesdropper hears is Lorna telling her self-absorbed spouse to be understanding of a woman's burden with childbirth and caring for an infant. She tells him to help more in the house. Here is the Artemis woman who protects women around childbirth. Perhaps it is significant that Lorna is killed just before she was about to marry a man whom Kinsey is sure is highly placed in organized crime.

By dying before her marriage, Lorna distances herself from possible identification with Persephone, the daughter of Demeter who was abducted by Hades, god of the Underworld. Demeter obtains her daughter's release, but not before Persephone has ingested enough of the underworld to cause her to return there for part of each year as Hades' queen. Although Lorna certainly tastes the Underworld's fruit in her thriving one-woman escort service, she was not abducted or forced down into that world. She chose to go there and seems to have chosen to remain in marrying into the lucrative orbit of the mafia.

Such a position as Queen of the Underworld was not to be hers. Lorna has taken care not to let her various domains overlap. Yet a collision occurs when her boss from her day job becomes a client, and she and Danielle witness how corrupt he is. Lorna is killed; later Danielle is horribly beaten and dies of her injuries. Two moments link Kinsey to both murdered women in an intimacy that is of Aphrodite and Artemis. Visiting Lorna's night owl friend, Hector, and his dog, Beauty, who mourns Lorna, Kinsey seems to provoke an otherworldly despair in the animal. The dog howls as if she is transported to hell.

Kinsey has taken on Lorna's smell and this makes the bereaved dog experience hope followed by renewed despair. Beauty becomes a real character in this novel. Her relationship to Lorna and her depression at her vanishing is a vivid contribution to Kinsey's archetypal goddess-activated detection. Not only do Lorna and Kinsey embody Artemis in their primal relationship to Beauty, the dog's name also reminds us of the beauty of Artemis as primal feminine, virginal nature.

Crucially, this moment is one in which Kinsey, huntress for a truth that will restore a purity to her client's (Lorna's mother) life, and increasingly to the memory of Lorna, takes on Lorna's scent, in order to understand her in the sense of standing on her ground of being. Indeed, by literally inhabiting Lorna's body, Kinsey brings something of Lorna to rebirth.

Now it is time for a goddess symbolizing less likely qualities in a female detective: Hestia, guardian of hearth fires and the sense of home.

Symbols in Mysteries of Hestia's Hearth

Hestia is the goddess of the center; the center of the self, of the home, and of the Earth (Paris 1986, pp. 167–188). She is the hearth fire that makes a home. "Hestia" means both the actual goddess and the flames of the sustaining hearth at the center of the earth. Therefore Hestia is where the family makes its home. She also is a personal sense of center: the ability to be at home in our own bodies and souls.

Such a powerful *necessary* goddess of well-being lends herself to stillness, to creating the home that nurtures. So in what sense can Hestia be found in mysteries with their energetic quests for difficult truths? One answer lies in Hestia as protector of the stranger, for the hearth is sacred. Once a stranger is accepted at the hearth, he or she is under the goddess's protection.

Hestia is also patron of mysteries that center on the home and family, which is either itself threatened by the crime; or where someone, including strangers, accepted at the hearth/heart of the home is in danger. "Cozies" typically have a female sleuth who, although not professionally involved in law enforcement, is drawn into the quest because of concerns for family or the stranger at the hearth. Here we have Lucy Stone, wife, mother, reporter, and sleuth, from the pen of Leslie Meier (1991), or the bed and breakfast mysteries of Mary Daheim (1991), or Annie Darling, bookstore owner, whose passion for justice in her immediate family and community is drawn from the imagination of Carolyn Hart (cf. 1987).

Hestia's sleuths defend the family and the stranger at their hearth as the centering energy of the home. They *cannot* stand by when violence or crime threaten to destroy it. A particular subset of the cozy is the food mystery, in which the detective is primarily a cook and recipes appear in the book along with the quest story. So, unsurprisingly, food mysteries frequently involve a cook with a catering business who stumbles across dead bodies when her hearth, or catering event, is meant to enact Hestia for family and close knit community. Diane Mott Davidson's (1992) detective, Goldy Schultz, has a cooking enterprise run from her own kitchen; Katherine Hall Page's (1991) Faith Fairchild lives in a small New England town where she combines the role of mother, wife to a clergyman, and caterer; while Isis Crawford writes about catering sisters, Libby and Bernie, who live close to New York.

Joanne Fluke's (cf. 2003) very popular Minnesota series, with cookie-storeowner Hannah Swensen, perfectly illustrates how the Hestia sleuth is not confined to symbols of a traditional homemaker. A romantically minded spinster living alone, Hannah is nevertheless intimately bound up with family and community through the act of solving mysteries. Additionally, she is family-centered because her cooking is an enactment of familial connection extended into the community of significantly named Lake Eden. Moreover, her cookies and cakes become a material medium for drawing her into a murder, enacting the desires of those around her for sweetness. Sleuthing, for Hannah, restores Lake Eden to a mythological Garden of Eden by centering and discovering what is necessary for "home" to be reconstituted. Perhaps this accounts for the large dose of sugar in the portrayal of tensions within small towns named for paradise.

The powerful presence of Hestia in cozies does not preclude her divine energy from other mysteries by women writers. Centering a family, or a group making a new kind of family, is arguably innate to women's detective fiction. Even loner Kinsey Milhone has a familial relationship with Henry, her aged, yet still handsome, landlord. V.I. Warshawski and Sharon McCone each find many of their professional cases invoke Hestia for their clients, along with drawing familial dimensions of their own lives. So in *Trophies and Dead Things* Sharon takes on a project that appears only distantly linked to her friend, only to discover that the people she is most connected to, her new family, are in danger.

Above all, Hestia inhabits women's mysteries in the aspect of knowing, that finds the center in the solution to the murder. Finding the solution centers and re-ignites the hearth; the community is reborn, and the wasteland healed. Hestia here embodies the symbol, and is also the object of, the quest. The detective has to *know* through the Hestia symbol because only solving this crime will re-start the hearth fire. The stranger lies dead, and so the sacred fires need re-kindling in a heroic symbolic renewal of the home, of this person; or this group and this Earth-centered nature.

Now to the fourth goddess, Athena of the city sorely in need of her divine symbols.

Athena's Troubled Cities

Christine Downing, in *Women's Mysteries*, says that Athena calls on women to take on the male world in male terms, seeing everything in terms of the interests of the community. Athena is here embodiments of arts and insight: "the goddess of clear vision and artistic power" (1992, p. 175). So it is not surprising that Athena symbols are particularly well represented among detectives created by women writers in sex crimes prosecutor, Alexandra Cooper, for Linda Fairstein. She prioritizes the responsibility she feels for the city and those persecuted within it.

A lawyer dedicated to making the masculine-dominated justice system work, Alex Cooper is Athena, whose closest comrades are male cops. Where Alex differs from Athena is in the goddess siding with the patriarchy. Alex does not side with patriarchy in her work prosecuting the (mostly) male criminals who have raped or sexually assaulted (mostly) women and children. Indeed, *Night Watch* (Fairstein, 2012) opens with Alex imperiling her romantic relationship with a Frenchman, Luc, when he takes the side of a socially important man accused of rape.

Alex Cooper very precisely embodies such an exponent of skillfully woven words dedicated to stitching together the body politic of her city. Here also is her characteristic love of New York which is enacted in plots that explore and bring back to her ordering communal influence the city's deep fabric such as the water pipes beneath the streets in *Bad Blood* (Fairstein, 2007), or the literary legacy of Edgar Allen Poe in *Entombed* (Fairstein, 2004). In her concerned exploration of the history of New York she reminds us of Athena's devotion to Athens.

Athena remains virgin despite her intimacy with masculine order. Similarly, Alex, while erotically bound up with NYPD detective, Mike Chapman, places her professional relationship with him above its erotic potential. In fact she, most Athena-like, sees a love affair with Mike as threatening her power. If she becomes too close to Mike her boss would intervene, she would be removed from her potential to protect the city.

Alex chooses Athena over Aphrodite to be inside the patriarchal system where communal values of politics will take precedence over the personal integrity that marks her relationships with cops, Mike and Mercer. The reward for such sacrifice is for Alex to enact what Hillman describes as Athena's "institutional mothering" (2007, p. 67). Her nurturing and defense of vulnerable victims of sex crimes embodies the sacred mothering of the state or of the justice system. It is an Athena aspect bound up with her role as presenting the divine necessity of reason in Alex's skills and strategies as a prosecutor (Hillman, 2007, p. 66).

On the other hand, as Alex Cooper discovers, Athena's divine reason and skillfulness within the masculine system is no protection against surprises.

> So even in the realms where Athena and rational strategy are most called upon … there are obvious and tragic strategic failures because too many other dominants have been left out of the calculations (Hillman, 2007, p. 79).

These other dominants may include less rational qualities of ambition, greed, and desire. Given Athena's distinctive emphases, she needs to partner with Aphrodite's more flexible attitude to accuracy, Artemis's dedication to the hunt and Hestia's centering powers of consciousness and home. Together, I suggest, these four goddesses provide symbols of personal and collective psychic renewal in mystery fiction by women. We need to pay greater attention to their presence among us.

Conclusion: Renewal in Symbols

Above all, this chapter suggests that Jung's idea of the symbol, particularly as an image in words, has been undervalued and under-theorized. Jung's sense that writing can have similar impacts on the collective psyche that powerful dream images do for the individual, is an important lens for cultural analysis. In particular, arguing that the modern psyche is fragile because it has historically (in the west) suppressed so much that is other to rationality, Jung's insight into social, cultural, and historical structures implicitly implies a return of what has been hitherto marginalized as feminine.

Here the Greek goddesses can be regarded as symbols, not because they have been consciously reintroduced into the contemporary world, rather, the goddesses have re-emerged as changing social dynamics have made space for more flexible formations of gender. Put another way, seeing goddesses as Jungian symbols is to use their narratives to make visible their nuanced and complex feminine qualities that have remained shadowed and invisible in a patriarchal culture. If instead, these detective fictions were deliberately "about" one or more goddesses then these images would be stable signs, not mystery haunted symbols.

Goddesses as symbols are engines of psychic renewal because they focus and shape energies and anxieties around life and death, home, sexuality, nature and human nature, and violence. They convert psychic energy into meaning-making imagery so renewing being and knowing. Where these goddesses span the so-called human nature divide, they reveal the divide itself as a cultural boundary that needs transgressing. Hence, the symbol becomes an engine of complexity evolution, or, figuratively, goddesses such as Artemis, Hestia, and Aphrodite are re-stitching us back into the fabric of the cosmos as whole, as one system.

Symbols are the synchronous language of the deep psyche that unites knowing and being. Detective fiction is a microcosm of uncertainties about knowledge and identity in a 21st century of unstable divisions between the "city" and its "outside," nature and human nature, violence, and Eros. Seeing goddesses in detective fiction is then a metonym (part representing whole) of psychic renewal via the symbol as the image of what is missing, and what is to come.

References

Baring, A. & J. Cashford (1991). *The Myth of the Goddess: Evolution of an Image*. New York and London: Vintage.

Cambray, J. (2012). *Synchronicity: Nature and Psyche in an Interconnected Universe*. College Station, TX: Texas A & M Press.

Daheim, M. (1991). *Just Desserts*. New York: Avon.

Downing, C. (1992/2003) *Women's Mysteries*. New Orleans, LA: Spring Journal Inc.

Fairstein, L. (2004). *Entombed*. New York: Scribner.

Fairstein, L. (2007). *Bad Blood*. New York: Scribner.

Fairstein, L. (2012). *Night Watch*. London: Penguin Group.

Fluke, J. (2003). *Chocolate Chip Cookie Murder*. New York: Kensington.

Grafton, S. (1994). *K is for Killer*. New York: Henry Holt & Co.

Hall Page, K. (1991). *The Body in the Belfry*. New York: Avon Books.

Hart, C. (1987). *Death on Demand*. New York: Crimeline.

Henderson, L. (1998) *Freeze My Margarita*. London: Hutchinson.

Hillman, J. (2007). *Mythic Figures: Uniform Edition of the Writings of James Hillman*, Volume 6.1. Putnam, CT: Spring Publications.

Jung, C.G. (1922) "On the Relation of Analytical Psychology to Poetry," in *Collected Works*, Vol. 15, *The Spirit in Man, Art and Literature* (2nd edn). London and New York: Routledge, 1990.

Jung, C.G. (1947/1954) "On the Nature of the Psyche," in *Collected Works*, Vol. 8, *The Structure and Dynamics of the Psyche* (2nd edn). London and New York: Routledge, 1991.

Jung, C.G. (1952) "Synchronicity: An Acausal Connecting Principle," in *Collected Works*, Vol. 8, *The Structure and Dynamics of the Psyche* (2nd edn). London and New York: Routledge, 1991.

Jung, C.G. (1954) "On the Psychology of the Trickster Figure," in *Collected Works*, Vol. 9i, *The Archetypes and the Collective Unconscious* (2nd edn). London and New York: Routledge, 1990.

Lippman, L. (2001). *The Sugar House*. New York: Avon.

Meier, L. (1991). *Mistletoe Murder*. New York: Kensington.

Mott Davidson, D. (1992). *Catering to Nobody*. New York: Ballantine Books.

Muller, M. (1990). *Trophies and Dead Things*. New York: The Mysterious Press.

Paris, G. (1986). *Pagan Meditations: The Worlds of Aphrodite, Artemis and Hestia*. New Orleans, LA: Spring Journal and Books.

Rowland, S. (2012). *The Ecocritical Psyche: Literature: Complexity Evolution and Jung*. New York: Routledge.

Shulman, H. (1997). *Living at the Edge of Chaos: Complex Systems in Culture and Psyche*. Zürich: Daimon Verlag.

PART VI

Ancestral Memories: Familial Constellations of Rebirth and Renewal

11

ADAM AND EVE AS A KLEINIAN NARRATIVE OF INFANCY

Jeff Strnad

Part 1: Introduction

The story of Adam and Eve, as set forth in its traditional form as part of Genesis 1–3, and particularly the portion of the story involving "the Fall" and expulsion from the Garden of Eden, not only is foundational to two major world religions, Christianity and Judaism, but also, as demonstrated by Sanders (2009), is culturally pervasive in the United States, appearing prominently in major secular domains such as movies, songs, and books. From a Jungian perspective, one would suspect that such a persistent story reflects multiple inner, unconscious themes. Various scholars have suggested that the story, ostensibly a tale about the origin of humanity, reflects psychological aspects of infancy. The fact of childhood amnesia, that people are unable to remember most personal events and experiences from the first five to six years of life (Crain, 2011, p. 329), enhances the possibility that the Adam and Eve story may situate infant experiences lost to conscious recall. Given the Jungian presumption that myth and other archetypal material are reflective of unconscious aspects of the psyche, it is not surprising that among the scholarly works linking the story to infancy are prominent examples from Jungian theorists such as Edinger (1972) and Sanford (1974).

But the Jungian presumption arguably has broader reach. In a more extensive work (Strnad, 2014, available as a free PDF online) I explored the hypothesis that the Adam and Eve story reflects multiple and conflicting major conceptions of infant psychological development, including prominent ones arising from depth psychological approaches that do not include a strong role for myth and therefore have no inherent inclination to give the story theoretical weight. Because this hypothesis is difficult to test via statistical or experimental means, the approach in that work was to present various examples in which the story analogizes theories of infant psychological development, some in the existing literature and some new.

The work succeeds to the degree that the reader comes away with more respect for the hypothesis. One part of the work develops a single intensive example, demonstrating how closely the story of Adam and Eve matches Melanie Klein's narrative of infancy. Klein's depth psychology emphasized "a psyche filled with unconscious introjects, figures, structures, or functionaries that play an important role in behavior, development, pathology, and healing" (Strnad, 2014, p. 10), but material from mythological, religious, and cultural sources played little or no role in her scheme.

This chapter uses excerpts and summaries from Strnad (2014) to present an abridged but still deep version of the analogy between Klein's narrative of infancy and the story of Adam and Eve. Part 2 discusses applicable historical, cultural, and religious background. Part 3 presents the abbreviated version of the Kleinian analogy. Part 4 concludes with a discussion of a few cultural and religious implications of the more general hypothesis. The New American Standard Bible, a scholarly but readable translation readily available online, is the source for all the biblical quotes herein. Readers unfamiliar with the Adam and Eve story or those who have not read it recently might read Genesis 1–3 before going further, paying particular attention to Genesis 2:15 through Genesis 3.

Part 2: Some Cultural, Religious, and Psychological Background

As discussed in Strnad (2014), the plethora of cultural, religious, and psychological sources associated with the story of Adam and Eve is staggering. In this part, I consider a few cultural, religious, and psychological aspects that relate heavily to the development of the analogy in Part 3 between the story and Melanie Klein's narrative of infancy.

Augustinian Original Sin

The doctrine of original sin holds that Adam and Eve's sin was directly transmitted to their descendants (Pagels, 1988, p. 131), creating in them helplessness before physical death and a corrupt personal being characterized by a tendency toward sin and evil (p. 142). Adam and Eve's failure also resulted in the corruption of nature: "Thorns and thistles sprung up from the once fertile land," and "all nature was changed for the worse" (pp. 133–134).

Pagels (1988) noted that this interpretation of the Adam and Eve story was not inevitable but in fact rose to prominence only in the early fifth century, its strongest proponent being Augustine of Hippo (pp. 127–150). Augustine's most eminent opponents, Pelagius and later Julian of Eclanum, argued that nature was not affected by Adam and Eve's transgression (p. 133), that God did not curse future generations based on their transgression (p. 137), and that physical death is a natural event which "merely offers us the necessary transition to eternal life" (p. 138). For Julian, the Adam and Eve story was about the human response to limitation and suffering, and "the subjective experience" of one who responds sinfully (pp. 137–138). To that individual, nature seems "resistant, hostile, and the source of nearly intolerable frustrations and disasters" (p. 138), just what Adam and Eve experienced after their transgression.

The dispute between Augustine and his opponents was intense on both personal and social levels. Pagels (1988) noted riots that broke out in Rome arising from the divisions between partisans on either side of the dispute (p. 129). Augustine and Julian engaged in vociferous personal debate, which consumed much of the last 12 years of Augustine's life (p. 143) and led him to author six volumes entitled "Unfinished Work Against Julian," which Pagels characterized as amplifying his argument, an argument that he had been pursuing with "eloquence and fury" (p. 130). Something about the debate stimulated emotions of archetypal force in the participants.

Augustine prevailed as a historical matter. "After considerable controversy, the church of the fifth century accepted his view" (Pagels, 1988, p. 143), which became "the basis of Christian doctrine for [the ensuing] 1600 years" (p. 146). Despite having considerable support, including at one point the Pope, Pelagius finally was excommunicated and died shortly thereafter (pp. 129–130), and Julian ended up being considered a heretic (p. 143).

The Gnostic Wisdom Interpretation

The "Gnostic wisdom interpretation" of the story of Adam and Eve is ancient, although it definitely was a losing one within mainstream Christian thought. It sees the story as a positive account of the development of consciousness rather than a description of a fall into sin and depravity. The serpent is a hero, an instructor who led Eve, and through her, Adam, to the knowledge that triggered that development and that helped them to resist a jealous and ignorant god. Pagels (1979) collected and quoted Gnostic sources from the first few centuries of the Common Era (AD or CE) to this effect (pp. 29–31).

Two Stories, Two Gods

Hendel (2013) noted that from clues of grammar, style, and content, scholars have been able to identify three literary sources for most of Genesis ... known as the Yahwist (J), the Elohist (E), and the Priestly source (P)," which "were carefully combined by one or more editors" (p. 17). Two of the sources, J and P, are the basis for the first part of the book, including the creation story and the tale of Adam and Eve in Genesis 1–3. The creation account in Genesis 1:1–2:3 is from the P source, whereas the account in Genesis 2:4–3 is from the J source, a source that antedated P (Hendel, 2013, pp. 33–39). The God figures of the P and J accounts are strikingly different. The P source presents "a good world, created by a beneficent and omnipotent God" (p. 38). "The cosmos is both rational and moral, and in it humans have a noble place" (p. 38). "God is the prime mover of the desired state of order" within "a view of reality as an ordered structure in which all things have their place" (p. 23).

The God portrayed in P "is a transcendental God" (p. 23) who created a cosmos in which "nothing ... is random or incomplete" (p. 38).

The God portrayed in J is very different. He is "a deity with the human traits of regret, anger, compassion, and delight" (Hendel, 2013, p. 23). Hendel described him:

> [The J source] God is both gracious and punishing – he creates, feels compassion ("it is not good for the man to be alone"), makes clothes, and finally expels humans. We must fear and respect him. Yet he is not the transcendent and cosmic God of Genesis 1 [the P source God]. He walks and talks in the Garden, and even makes mistakes (remember that the animals are not the solution to Adam's loneliness, so God created Eve).
>
> (2013, pp. 43–44)

God in the J accounts is named "Yahweh," whereas in the P accounts he has names which in English connote "the generic title, God" (p. 19).

Being faced with two different God figures creates great difficulty for a literal reading of Genesis, but from a depth psychological perspective, it is an opportunity. The two figures in Genesis, the idealized, good God of the P source and the turbulent and often persecutory God of the J source may represent two different very significant inner figures. Rather than being a roadblock to explain away or omit, this feature is presumably revelatory, especially given the status of the creation story and the Adam and Eve story as major myths carrying archetypal themes.

Goldman: The Infant as Destroyer of Paradise

Psychotherapist Harriett Goldman (1988) wrote about "patients who experience ... a deep core sense of essential inner badness or defectiveness, which often borders on a feeling of being personally evil," accompanied by "an underlying and almost always unconscious fantasy of having been the wicked destroyer of a preexisting paradise" (p. 420). Each such person "unconsciously believes that before his or her conception and birth, there existed a state of paradisiacal unity and bliss between the parents and an essential goodness in the family situation" that was "ruptured by the child's advent and thereby irretrievably lost" (p. 420). This belief is "a specific way in which the child blames him- or herself for the pain and difficulty of a family structured by narcissistically deprived and damaged parents" (p. 420). Goldman saw the "resultant deeply-embedded sense of personal badness" as originating from "splitting and projective identification on the parents' part" (p. 423), the parent or parents "retaining the good side" while their child becomes "the living personification of the bad side of the split" (p. 438). Goldman also noted that in this splitting situation, there is "a parental injunction against knowledge, against having the power of understanding in order to sort things out and eventually extricate oneself by forming a different, independent world view" (pp. 425–426).

As Goldman (1988) observed, this picture matches up superbly with the Augustinian "Original Sin" reading of the Adam and Eve story that insists "that we are innately corrupt in our essence and guilty from conception" (p. 431). Under the Augustinian view that Adam and Eve's transgression corrupted nature as well as future humanity, the picture also reflects "the child's experience ... of a pre-existing paradise of perfection and wholeness which was spoiled by his or her coming into existence" (p. 431). The result for the child is a life of "constantly striving to make reparation or do penance for a vaguely perceived but irreparable Original Sin," which can

> run the gamut from a higher-level personality organization who compensates by becoming a psychotherapist or physician and spending his/her life taking care of others' needs ... to a highly-impaired narcissistic personality with all the life difficulties which that presents.
>
> (Goldman, 1988, p. 432)

The all-good God in the Augustinian view embodies the requisite splitting, and that God prohibiting Adam and Eve from partaking of the tree of knowledge matches the "parental injunction against knowledge" that Goldman cited (p. 425).

Goldman suggested that a much milder form of the pathological situation that she highlighted may be pervasive. Because "children are a captive audience" (p. 432), parents can "exploit this situation by using their children as repositories for their own split-off unrecognized 'badness'" (p. 433), and "it is possible that all parents are likely to do this to their children to whatever degree they have not recognized, accepted, and integrated various dissociated aspects of their own character" (p. 433). Goldman concluded: "The wicked destroyer theme is not particular ... to the ... patients presented here," but is "embedded in the human psyche, an archetype that was recognized and already being wrestled with by the narrator of *Genesis*, one of the great early explainers of human experience" (p. 448).

Part 3: Melanie Klein's Narratives of Infancy Embodied in the Story of Adam and Eve

Melanie Klein was "a key transitional figure between the drive/structural model [of Freud] and the relational/structure model [of object relations theorists]" (Greenberg & Mitchell, 1983, p. 121). Klein "greatly expanded" the "Freudian concept ... of 'internal objects,'" which in Freud's work was "limited to the super-ego, [parental and societal strictures] internalized during the resolution of the oedipal crisis" (Greenberg & Mitchell, 1983, p. 124). Klein depicted "a complex set of internalized object relations" and believed that "phantasies and anxieties concerning the state of one's internal object world are the underlying basis ... for one's behavior, moods, and sense of self" (p. 125). Klein used the "ph" spelling, "phantasy" instead of "fantasy," in order "to indicate that the process is unconscious" (Mitchell, 1986a, p. 22).

Klein's Basic Narrative

Klein believed that "object relations start almost at birth and arise with the first feeding experience" (1955/1986, p. 52). The "first object" is "the mother's breast which to the child becomes split into a good (gratifying) and bad (frustrating) breast" (Klein, 1946/1986, pp. 176–177). Splitting, beginning with the breast, is characteristic of the "paranoid-schizoid position," which Klein saw predominating during "the first three or four months of life" (1955/1986, p. 83). Klein explained the initial splitting as follows:

> The sensations experienced by the infant at birth and the difficulties of adapting … to entirely new conditions give rise to persecutory anxiety. The comfort and care given after birth, particularly the first feeding experiences, are felt to come from good forces … The infant directs his feelings of gratification and love towards the "good" breast, and his destructive impulses and persecution towards what he feels to be frustrating, i.e. the "bad" breast.
> (1952/1986, p. 202)

Normal development in Klein's scheme included a shift from the early predominance of the paranoid-schizoid position to the onset of what Klein called the "depressive position," prompted by the realization that both the good and bad breast are aspects of the same mother:

> Its own destructive feelings … make the baby very anxious. It fears that the object on which it vents its rage (e.g., the breast that goes away and frustrates it) will retaliate. In self-protection it splits itself and the object into a good part and a bad part and projects all its badness into the outside world so that the hated breast becomes the hateful and hating breast. Klein describes this as the paranoid-schizoid position … As developmentally the ego becomes able to take in the whole person, to see that good and bad can exist together in the same person, it continues to rage against the mother for the frustration she causes, but now, instead of fearing retaliation, it feels guilt and anxiety for the damage it itself has done in phantasy. This Klein calls the depressive position.
> (Mitchell, 1986a, p. 20)

I take up the depressive position later, associating its initial onset with the experience of the Fall.

Klein stated that "idealization is bound up with the splitting of the object, for the good aspects of the breast are exaggerated as a safeguard against the fear of the persecuting breast" (1946/1986, p. 182). In the case of the good breast, Klein believed that the idealization "also springs from the power of the instinctual drives which aim at unlimited gratification and therefore create the picture of an inexhaustible and always bountiful breast" (p. 182). A parallel picture is the limitless bounty and ease of Eden, in which "out of the ground the Lord God caused to grow every tree that is pleasing to the sight and good for food" (Genesis 2:9). The mother's breast is the first good object which the infant introjects and idealizes (Klein, 1946/1986, p. 184). Analogously, the largess of Eden is God's first good gift to humankind.

But there was another part of Eden, the tree of the knowledge of good and evil, which God withheld from Adam and Eve, threatening that "in the day you eat from it you will surely die" (Genesis 2:17). When Eve disobeyed, severe persecution followed: expulsion from Eden along with being condemned to a future of toil, pain, and hardship. Sanford (1974) noted that the extremely disproportionate nature of the punishment creates a paradox for a "traditional Christian" interpretation that rests on an all-good and omniscient God because "God created everything and placed it in the garden, serpent included," and "either he knew what the serpent would do, in which case he cannot place all the blame on Adam and Eve, or there was a failure in his omniscience, and he must be faulted for ignorance" (pp. 112–113). But it is not a paradox if one associates the fruit of the tree of knowledge of good and evil along with the negative, sadistic side of God with the bad breast, an exaggerated product of splitting which is carrying all of the infant's "persecutory anxiety" and the accompanying fear (Klein, 1946/1986, p. 182). The infant in Klein's scheme introjects good and bad objects into its inner world, "projects its own aggression onto … objects it feels … to be 'bad,'" and "conceives of them as actually dangerous – persecutors who it fears will devour it, scoop out the inside of its body, cut it to pieces, poison it – in short, compassing its destruction by all the means which sadism can devise" (Klein, 1935/1986, p. 116). Eve's act of aggression toward Yahweh and the forbidden tree (bad breast) triggered the expulsion. The expulsion scene, along with the persecutory side of God manifested at that point, partake deeply of the kind of phantasy that might be associated with the bad breast. If Klein's theories bear truth, these story aspects will resonate deeply and be very familiar, at least unconsciously, to all who hear them.

Klein believed that "the infantile depressive position is the central position in the child's development" (1935/1986, p. 145; 1940/1986, p. 150). The depressive position arises when the child comes to know the "mother as a whole person and becomes identified with her" (1935/1986, pp. 141–142), experiencing "feelings of guilt and remorse" along with "pain … from the conflict between love and uncontrollable hatred" directed toward what it now recognizes as a single object, its mother (p. 142). The infant "ego's unconscious knowledge that the hate is indeed also there, and that it may at any time get the upper hand" represents "the ego's anxiety of being carried away by the id and so destroying the good object," and "brings about the sorrow, feelings of guilt and the despair which underlie grief" (Klein, 1935/1986, p. 125). In this description is a picture of the Fall: Eve eats the fruit and obtains the knowledge of good and evil, her own. She can no longer disavow her aggressive tendencies, formerly split off and projected onto the tree of the knowledge of good and evil, the serpent, and the persecutory aspect of God.

Klein placed the "climax" of the ensuing "depressive feelings … just before, during and after weaning" (1940/1986, p. 147), and stated that "the object which is being mourned is the mother's breast and all that the breast and the milk have come to stand for in the infant's mind: namely, love, goodness and security" (p. 148). Adam and Eve have lost Eden and along with it God's seemingly unlimited and free nurture, a Fall that can only bring terrible grief.

Mirroring Conflicting Theologies

Despite the grief, pain, and loss associated with the initial onset of the depressive position, Klein saw it as a key step forward in development. The projection and splitting mechanisms, which are the "chief feature of the paranoid-schizoid position … must be overcome if the greater integration of the depressive position is to be reached" (Mitchell, 1986b, p. 175). Ultimately, the knowledge of good and evil is a blessing not a curse. The ensuing grief and guilt are salutary signs: "The synthesis between the loved and hated aspects of the complete object gives rise to feelings of mourning and guilt which imply vital advances in the infant's emotional and intellectual life" (Klein, 1946/1986, p. 178). Klein believed that "oral sadism reaches its climax during and after weaning," the same time as the initial onset of the depressive position (1932/1975, p. 128) and asserted that "only when the ego has introjected the object as a whole and has established a better relationship to the external world and to real people is it able fully to realize the disaster created through its sadism" (1935/1986, p. 124). One view of God's speech at the time of expulsion from Eden is not that it is the imposition of a sadistic punishment but that it is a delineation of a reality inevitably realized: that the cost of the birth of one's self as an individual is awareness that one will die and that the effortlessly available nurturance of Eden cannot persist. The real world of painful toil and childbirth beckons. This realization is linked with the "disaster" of oral aggression, eating the fruit, which triggered the awareness of Eve's own nature and separate will, that she is good and evil wrapped up in one package along with an ego that faces both aspects.

The fact that the onset of the depressive position indicates progress and growth toward individuation and psychological maturity creates a parallel with the Gnostic wisdom interpretation of Genesis. It even includes an evil, persecutory God whose commandment not to eat the fruit is an obstacle in the path of that development. Strikingly, the Klein narrative also picks up aspects of other, seemingly contradictory, views of the Adam and Eve story. Because Klein viewed the aggression that triggered the Fall as innate, a derivative of Freud's death drive, which she also held within her own theory, her narrative has an affinity with Augustine's original sin idea. Eve at the point of the Fall and the infant at the onset of the depressive position in Klein's scheme are simply recognizing a "bad" tendency that already was part of them. Before it was hidden behind the withheld knowledge of good and evil for Eve and, in Klein's theory, behind the splitting, projection, and ensuing denial of the "bad" tendency during the early months of infancy when the paranoid-schizoid position dominates.

Greenberg and Mitchell (1983) read Klein in a way that suggested a more general analogy to Augustine's original sin interpretation. They detected in Klein's theory "a tendency to see bad objects as internally derived, that is, arising from the child's own drives, and good objects as absorbed from the outside" (p. 135). This tendency "stemmed from her view of psychopathology as arising from internal, constitutional sources and her parallel minimization of the importance of parental anxiety, ambivalence, and character pathology" (pp. 135–136). Analogously, in the Augustinian interpretation, the Fall is due entirely to human failure, and humans emerge bad to the core in contrast to an *external, wholly good* (parent) God.

A Destroyer of Paradise Aspect

At the heart of the onset of the depressive position, Klein envisioned an experience similar to the one delineated by Goldman (1988) and discussed in Part 2: the sense that the infant is somehow a "destroyer of paradise" with respect to the infant's own family. Klein viewed the onset of the depressive position as being accompanied by "depressive anxiety" because, as "the infant increasingly perceives and introjects the mother as a [whole] person," the "infant's aggressive impulses and desires toward the bad breast (mother) are … felt to be a danger to the good breast (mother) as well" (1952/1986, p. 203). She went on to describe a "destroyer of paradise" aspect that extends to the infant's entire family:

> Depressive anxiety is intensified, for the infant feels he has destroyed or is destroying a whole object by his greed and uncontrollable aggression. Moreover, owing to the growing synthesis of his emotions, he now feels that these destructive impulses are directed against a *loved person*. Similar processes operate in relation to the father and other members of the family.
>
> (pp. 203–204)

The destruction of the mother, the bearer of the good breast, is tantamount to the destruction of Eden. The other object elements of the infant's world, the infant's family, are encompassed in the infant's phantasized destruction, analogous to the corruption of nature as a consequence of the Fall in Augustine's original sin interpretation. Thus, Klein posited a Goldman-like "destroyer of Eden" phantasy as an aspect of *normal* infant development.

The Resurgence of Splitting

In Klein's theory, the paranoid-schizoid and depressive positions are "structural" rather than "developmental" notions: "a 'position' is an always available state, not something one passes through" (Mitchell, 1986b, p. 116). The splitting and projection characteristic of the paranoid-schizoid position remains available to enable "a deflection of guilt from the self on to the other person" (Klein, 1946/1986, p. 187). Faced with the consequences of her aggressive act at the time of expulsion, Eve blamed the serpent; Adam, meanwhile, blamed Eve and also implicitly God: "The woman whom You gave to be with me, she gave me from the tree, and I ate" (Genesis 3:12–13). In a striking parallel to Adam and Eve's attempt to pass off blame for the Fall upon the serpent and God, Klein identified a resurgence of the splitting that is characteristic of the paranoid-schizoid position precisely during the onset of the depressive position:

> It seems that at this stage of development the unification of the external and internal, loved and hated, real and imaginary objects is carried out in a way that each step in the unification leads again to a renewed splitting of the imagos.
>
> (1935/1986, p. 144)

At the time of the Fall, Eve's aggressive tendency is exposed, she gains knowledge of her own good and evil, and Adam and Eve now feel naked, their inner being exposed, and consequently both cover themselves up with fig leaves and try to hide from God. Adam and Eve then disavow responsibility by blaming each other, the Serpent, and God, consonant with the resurgence of splitting which Klein identified at the time of the onset of the depressive position.

Sequencing and Nature of Objects

Klein believed that the very first incorporated object "at once assumes the role of a super-ego" (1932/1975, p. 127 n. 3), becoming "a vehicle of defence against the destructive impulses within the organism" (p. 127). Viewing the Adam and Eve story as descriptive of an inner psychological domain, God is the first introject, the first figure that appears in the story. Klein derived her concept of super-ego from Freud, for whom the super-ego "takes its form from an internalization of particular external injunctions and prohibitions, of the world's *thou shalts* and *thou shalt nots*" (Mitchell, 1986a, p. 15). In the story, it is God, the vehicle of defense against Eve's destructive impulses, who lays down the prohibition not to eat from the forbidden tree. Klein also mentioned that one result of the infant's "anxiety … evoked by his destructive instinctual impulses" is to "focus his fears on his *external* object … as a source of danger" after the development of reality testing leads the infant to "experience his mother as someone who can give or withhold satisfaction" (Klein, 1932/1975, pp. 127–128). The God of the Adam and Eve story has this very power, and like a mother with respect to an infant, birthed Adam and Eve.

Klein emphasized the role of idealization. During the predominance of the paranoid-schizoid position, "the infant's relative security is based on turning the good object into an ideal one as a protection against the dangerous and persecuting object" (Klein, 1952/1986, p. 202). "Idealization" is therefore a process that is "prevalent during the first three or four months of life," when "splitting processes are at their height" (p. 202). As discussed in Part 2, the early chapters of Genesis contain two creation stories and two corresponding God figures. The compiler of Genesis

put the story that developed later in history first. The God in this story is "beneficent and omnipotent," the creator of an orderly cosmos which "is both rational and
moral," in which "nothing … is random and incomplete," and in which "humans
have a noble place" (Hendel, 2013, p. 38). This God is certainly an idealized figure.
In contrast, Yahweh, the God of the second account, which includes the story of
Adam and Eve, is emotional, makes mistakes, and, in one aspect, plays the role of an
extremely harsh, punishing version of the super-ego. These two Gods in the story
are reconciled as internalized Kleinian objects within her view of the super-ego, the
topic of the next subsection.

The Super-ego in Klein's Scheme

Klein believed that the very first incorporated object, the mother's breast, immediately took on a super-ego role. The infant's phantasies of attacks on the mother's
body lead to a fear of retaliation, and therefore "the initial defences of the ego are
directed against the anxiety aroused by destructive impulses and phantasies" (Klein
1955/1986, p. 50). In particular, "the internalization of an injured and therefore
dreaded breast on the one hand, and of a satisfying and helpful breast on the other,
is the core of the super-ego" (pp. 50–51).

On the negative side, there is "the internalization of an attacked and therefore
frightening mother – the harsh super-ego" (Klein, 1955/1986, p. 49). Klein observed
that in analysands this introjected super-ego element enacted prohibitions which
"no longer emanated from the *real* mother, but from an introjected mother," who
"exercised a harsher and more cruel influence … than [the] real mother had ever
done" (1926/1986, p. 62). In Klein's view, the "ego falls under the sway of the super-
ego" at a time when "sadism is at its zenith," a time later identified with the onset of
the depressive position, the point of the Fall (Klein, 1929/1986, p. 87). This timing
accounts for the "sadistic severity" of the super-ego at that point (Klein, 1928/1986,
p. 71). We see God, in Yahweh, J source, guise at his most sadistic when he expels
Adam and Eve from Eden at the time of the Fall by imposing an extremely disproportionate punishment for an act of oral aggression which appears to have been
unavoidable based on the inclinations which God himself built into the two humans.

The good object also carries super-ego elements that can be severe. Klein identified an "urgent need to comply with the very strict demands of the 'good' objects"
(p. 123). These "strict demands serve the purpose of supporting the ego in its fight
against its uncontrollable hatred and its bad attacking objects, with whom the ego
is partly identified" (p. 123). The good God helps humans to be part of the good
and orderly but moral universe he created. However, "the stronger the anxiety is of
losing the loved objects, the more the ego strives to save them, and … the stricter
will grow the demands which are associated with the super-ego" (p. 123). Despite
the fact that early splitting is sharp and categorical, resulting in "a conception of
extremely bad and *extremely perfect* objects," including the highly idealized good
object, as time goes on, "since the ego cannot really keep its good and bad objects
apart in its mind, some of the cruelty of the bad objects and of the id becomes

related to the good objects" (p. 123). The idealized P source God at the beginning of Genesis blends into the capricious and sometimes sadistic J source God of the Adam and Eve story. Both carry Klein's super-ego.

Part 4: Some Implications

Strnad (2014) noted that research into personal experiences suggests that therapy and religious practice are often not very distinct. This result is not surprising if one believes, along with Jungian analyst Lionel Corbett, that there are common elements addressed by both:

> Like religions, contemporary psychotherapy also tries to deal with the sense that we are incomplete in some way, that there is something we need that is missing, or that something about us needs fixing. By offering its own solution to our feelings of incompleteness, psychotherapy can be thought of as a secular form of salvation, so that religious systems and psychotherapy offer alternative approaches to the same problem.
>
> (2007, p. 113)

Corbett went on to speculate, "in fact, one contribution to the waning of the power of religion in the last one hundred years may be the concomitant rise of psychotherapy" (p. 113).

Another possibility reverses the causality: Due to the historical path that mainstream Judaism and Christianity took, certain archetypal elements could no longer receive full expression within the churches and synagogues and thus bloomed elsewhere, including in the realms of psychotherapy and psychoanalysis. If the pervasiveness and persistence of the story of Adam and Eve arises from carrying central narratives of infancy, unconsciously clearly recognized, then if we removed it from history, it would reconstitute itself and be present again, perhaps with different names and a somewhat different structure. That is the meaning of archetypal. Similarly, if a religious version of the story became less accessible due to restrictive interpretations or a drop off in Biblical literacy or faith, then it should appear elsewhere. One possibility is that Melanie Klein and other theorists of infant development are telling stories resembling the Genesis narrative of Adam and Eve to people for whom psychoanalysis or psychotherapy have supplanted therapeutic or meaning-based roles that formerly resided in domains of religious practice. The loss of salience of the Adam and Eve story due to secularization meant that it came back in various secular forms.

The hypothesis that the Adam and Eve story reflects multiple, conflicting conceptions of infant psychological development also provides a potential explanation for the vehemence of the doctrinal dispute detailed in Part 2 above between Augustine and his allies on one side supporting the doctrine of original sin, and Julian of Eclanum, Pelagius, and their allies on the other side who argued that Adam and Eve's transgression did not corrupt nature, bring a curse upon future generations, or initiate physical death. If the parties had different infant experiences, then they would interpret the Adam and Eve story differently, and to each one, their interpretation would seem obviously correct. The infancies of Augustine and his allies, for example, may have been filled with the aspects described by Goldman (1988). As a consequence, their early history, perhaps the deepest part of them, would carry a "destroyer of paradise" theme, remaining potent, although unconscious, hidden behind the infant amnesia barrier, later to emerge consciously in the form of the doctrine of original sin. For the contesting parties, the church was the chief carrier of meaning and perhaps the major available vehicle for therapeutic healing. As a result, validation by the church of their own infant experiences would loom large, leading to riots in Rome, to the contesting parties spending years applying their prodigious intellectual and rhetorical talents to the dispute, and to the ultimate result for the losers being excommunication, removal from the community.

Narratives of our infancy are a deep and precious, although largely unconscious, part of each of us. A Jungian stance suggests that they will find expression in archetypal material, including religious stories and the narratives embedded in psychoanalytic theories. When old expressions fade, new ones will arise, and they will be salient both for individuals and for culture.

References

Corbett, L. (2007). *Psyche and the Sacred: Spirituality Beyond Religion*. New Orleans, LA: Spring Journal Books.

Crain, W. (2011). *Theories of Development: Concepts and Applications* (6th edn). Upper Saddle River, NJ: Prentice Hall.

Edinger, E.F. (1972). *Ego and Archetype*. Boston, MA: Shambhala.

Goldman, H.E. (1988). "Paradise Destroyed: The Crime of Being Born – A Psychoanalytic Study of the Experience of Evil," *Contemporary Psychoanalysis*, Vol. 24, pp. 420–450.

Greenberg, J.R. & Mitchell, S.A. (1983). *Object Relations in Psychoanalytic Theory*. Cambridge, MA: Harvard University Press.

Hendel, R. (2013). *The Book of Genesis*. Princeton, NJ: Princeton University Press.

Klein, M. (1926). "The Psychological Principles of Infant Analysis," in J. Mitchell (ed.), *The Selected Melanie Klein* (pp. 57–68). New York: Penguin, 1986.

Klein, M. (1928). "Early Stages of the Oedipus Complex," in J. Mitchell (ed.), *The Selected Melanie Klein* (pp. 69–83). New York: Penguin, 1986.

Klein, M. (1929). "Infantile Anxiety Situations Reflected in a Work of Art and in the Creative Impulse," in J. Mitchell (ed.), *The Selected Melanie Klein* (pp. 84–94). New York: Penguin, 1986.

Klein, M. (1932). *The Psychoanalysis of Children*, A. Strachey (trans.). Rev. in collaboration with A. Strachey by H.A. Thorner. New York: Delacorte Press, 1975.

Klein, M. (1935). "A Contribution to the Psychogenesis of Manic-Depressive States," in J. Mitchell (ed.), *The Selected Melanie Klein*. New York: Penguin, pp. 115–145, 1986.

Klein, M. (1940). "Mourning and its Relation to Manic-Depressive States," in J. Mitchell (ed.), *The Selected Melanie Klein*. New York: Penguin, pp. 146–174, 1986.

Klein, M. (1946). "Notes on Some Schizoid Mechanisms," in J. Mitchell (ed.), *The Selected Melanie Klein*. New York: Penguin, pp. 175–200, 1986.

Klein, M. (1952). "The Origins of Transference," in J. Mitchell (ed.), *The Selected Melanie Klein*. New York: Penguin, pp. 201–210, 1986.

Klein, M. (1955). "The Psycho-Analytic Play Technique: Its History and Significance," in J. Mitchell (ed.), *The Selected Melanie Klein*. New York: Penguin, pp. 35–54, 1986.

Mitchell, J. (1986a). "Introduction," in J. Mitchell (ed.), *The Selected Melanie Klein*. New York: Penguin, pp. 9–32.

Mitchell, J. (ed.) (1986b). *The Selected Melanie Klein*. New York: Penguin.

Pagels, E. (1979). *The Gnostic Gospels*. New York: Random House.

Pagels, E. (1988). *Adam, Eve, and the Serpent*. New York: Random House.

Sanders, T. (2009). *Approaching Eden: Adam and Eve in Popular Culture*. Lanham, MD: Rowman & Littlefield.

Sanford, J.A. (1974). *The Man Who Wrestled with God: Light from the Old Testament on the Psychology of Individuation*. New York: Paulist Press.

Strnad, J. (2014). "Adam and Eve as a Psychological Narrative of Infancy," (Master's thesis). Pacifica Graduate Institute, Carpinteria, CA. Available at: http://pqdtopen.proquest.com/doc/1508797800.html?FMT=AI (accessed August 18, 2016).

12

SYMBOLS OF CREATION IN MYTH AND DREAM

Directive, Orientative, Regenerative

Eileen Nemeth

What happened in the beginning describes at once both the original perfection and the destiny of each individual.

(Eliade, 1969, p. 142)

Introduction: Myth and Dream

The images found in the creation myths throughout the world visit us in our dream world, giving meaning to our personal journeys. If we emotionally connect to these images and symbols offered to us from the unconscious, we can move into life with renewed energy – an energy that through its creative potential orients and directs where we are going, who we might become, and what the meaning of life is, for both the individual and the collective.

The sense of being in the world, for which we have been created, must be constantly renewed as we physically, emotionally, and spiritually change our own inner landscapes, from infant to child, from adolescent to adult, and into old age. Additionally, the experience of being *welcome* in the world at all these stages of life is essential. We need to feel welcome for a fulfilled and deeply embodied experience of being. We experience this sense of being (being welcome) not only in the personal body but also, and necessarily, in relationship to the larger body of nature: animals, people, and earth, indeed, all forms of life. Myth and dream are invaluable sources for this essential ongoing renewal needed to keep the relationship of self and world alive and vital.

Belonging: The Longing to Be

One of the greatest forms of suffering we experience, which I often confront in my analytical practice, is the painful feeling of not belonging – to oneself, to others, to family, community, and world. Many years ago, a female analysand, 24 years old, brought in a dream that exemplifies this alienation. She was a small child on another world looking down at the earth, feeling alone and afraid. This dream keeps returning in our work as she struggles to feel welcomed and an active participant in our world, to feel her roots in earth's terrain and not on one distant and unknown planet, so that she belongs here and now.

Lucy Huskinson (2008, p. 2) writes:

> This tendency of feeling out of place within ourselves exemplifies a lack of *rootedness* of being, a tendency that is frequently lamented in discourses of continental philosophy and also by Jung. Thus, Heidegger, who asserts that we have lost our home in the world, seeks *Bodenständigkeit* ["rootedness to earth"], … a metaphysical relation or profound attunement to the earth as a place of dwelling. *Bodenständigkeit* is a relationship to the earth that acknowledges its hidden and concealed dimension; only when we are rooted to the earth as a source and ground of our being, can we find meaning within ourselves.

The creation myth, in all its forms (origin myth, emergence myth, etc.) is the myth of belonging, not only in a temporal and immediate way, but also opening us to the eternal and transcendental experience of being.

Temporal and Eternal

The temporal and immediate has to do with our bodily incarnation, our sensual relationship to form and matter, to the lived experience of being in the world. It is "… to incarnate our psychological life and recover that vital ecological sensibility that is the foundation of a meaningful existence" (Brooke, 1991, p. 62).

Our bodily incarnation always includes emotionality and physicality, with all the sensuous life that entails and, of course, the confrontation with our mortality. It is the physical and psychological reality of our humanness, moving in time, as well as, in space.

Too often this is forgotten, and the creation myth is seen as an awakening of consciousness, the origin of man's conscious awareness of the world. We must remember that our conscious awareness of the world is always a psychophysical experience. We can, through our growing consciousness, objectify the world around us, but we must always remain a subject in the ongoing dialogue between world and self. As Romanyshyn (1991, pp. xiii–xiv) so adroitly explains:

> For creatures of flesh the things of the world are not in space. They are, on the contrary, always a place, and as such their size matters in relation to the desires, intentions, motives, and interest of an embodied perceiver who in living in the world moves about within it. Moreover, for creatures of flesh which we are, these things of the world are never just objects over there … they are

things which solicit our gaze, or invite our touch, or appeal to us with their sensuous seductions, depending upon us, as the poet Rilke says, just as we depend upon them, for our mutual real-ization.

The eternal and transcendental is going beyond ego consciousness and opening to a larger reality, seeing ourselves held and contained in the greater truth of who we are. Addressing those profound questions: Where did I come from? Where am I going? What is my purpose of being? In a Jungian language we could say it is connecting/re-connecting to the dialogue between ego and Self. We cannot deeply connect to the Self unless we experience numinosity through our own living flesh. As Jung (1940, para. 291) has so succinctly stated:

> The symbols of the self arise in the depths of the body and they express its materiality every bit as much as the structure of the perceiving consciousness.

The Cultural Myth and the Individual Dream

In traditional societies, the creation myth is retold in moments of personal or collective crisis. It is read in order to heal illness or suffering, to put whatever is out of balance, back in balance. It is a return to the primordial totality, when the human was in balance with the spiritual and natural worlds. I would like to share a personal experience, the one that keeps me on this path, trying to understand the power behind these words and images of creation. A number of years ago I began reading the creation myths every morning and slowly I began to experience a centering within my body; a felt sense of order, more physical than intellectual.

I believe we search for "the beginning" in our own moments of crisis, in our "rites of passage" and through our process of individuation. If these are not experienced consciously, they are experienced in our unconscious, through dreams, or through other forms of expressive activities. There is, of course, the great danger that when our need to belong is not met in its positive form, in a movement toward life, relational and empathic; it can be answered in its opposite very negative and destructive form, through power and control. We must be constantly re-centering and re-creating ourselves, as we move through life. As Jung (1961a, p. 285) intimated, it is "the great process of being." To understand that process as fully as we can, we must go back to understand the present, and to move on into the future. We must return to the beginning, always a form of rebirth, in order to follow our destiny.

The dream is part of that "great process of being" (ibid., p. 285) or becoming. It wakes us up figuratively and literally, and offers us the wisdom we have inherited both through the cells of our body and the nature of the psyche. It is the source of connectivity between the temporal bodily states we occupy and awakens that sense of numinosity that goes beyond our physical boundaries, revealing age-old truths.

In Illo Tempore

For a moment, let us return to the beginning, *in illo tempore*, in that time, and open ourselves to the images offered, from one of the oldest creation myths recorded.

> *All was in suspense: calm, silent, motionless, and at peace: empty, the immensity of the sky. There was as yet neither man nor beast. There were no birds, fish, crabs, trees, rocks, caves, ravines, meadows, or woods: there was only sky. Not yet to be seen was the face of the earth, only the peaceful sea and a vast emptiness of sky. Nothing was yet formed into a body, nothing joined to anything else. There was nothing moving, nothing rustling not a sound in the sky. There was nothing upright, nothing but the peaceful waters of the sea, quiet and alone within its bounds. For nothing as yet existed. In the darkness, in the night, there were immobility and silence, but also, the Creator and the Maker, Tepeu and Gucumatz, those that engender, those that give being, alone in the waters, like an increasing light.*

This creation myth is the beginning of the Popol Vuh, the Guatemalan Sacred Book of the Quiché, and people of Mayan race. This creation myth dates back to ca. 300 BCE. Its first known written form dates between 1554 and 1558.

Here is a dream from an analysand, 49-year-old woman:

> *The world was destroyed, burnt, there was nothing, no life, and all was empty and barren. The sky was an orange color. I knew it was done by some evil force, evil men. But I knew about their plot, I had the proof, they knew I had the proof and were after me, as I was standing there pondering how to get the truth to others, to save the world, I saw the last tree, it was right in front of me, the evil people chopped it down so it would fall on me and kill me. I saw the tree fall and I knew I was going to be killed. It fell on me and for a moment all went dark. Was I dead? Then I picked myself up, I don't know how, brushed myself off and continued to try exposing the evil men and to save the world.*

These two, the creation myth and the dream, go on in more detail about how each of their world building or world saving continues. But, for my purposes, I will stay with these opening images, and explore the temporal and eternal in each. Jung often discusses the temporal and immediate and the importance of living with and in our bodily condition; that we experience emotions through the body. When image and emotion are simultaneous only then, "being charged with emotion, the image gains numinosity (or psychic energy); it becomes dynamic, and consequences of some kind must flow from it" (Jung, 1961b, p. 96). One of my favorite quotes from Jung (1934, p. 1316) on this aspect of dreams is as follows:

> If you just have a dream and let it pass by you, nothing has happened at all, even if it is the most amazing dream; but if you look at it with the purpose

of trying to understand it, and succeed in understanding it, then you have taken it into the here and now, the body being a visible expression of the here and now. For instance, if you had not taken your body into this room, nobody would know you were here; though even if you seem to be in the body, it is by no means sure that you are, because your mind might be wandering without your realizing it. Then whatever is going on here would not be realized; it would be like a vague dream that floats in and out, and nothing has happened.

All Was in Suspense

In the first creation myth from the Popol Vuh, there emerges from nothing form and matter. It emerges out of the eternal, the vastness of nothingness, emptiness, a cosmic pool, stirring and waiting, till the right time and right force, the right combination of forces, and then we are rewarded with the stirrings of life. Out of the darkness comes light, out of the two named gods we begin to feel differentiation and division, form and matter. It becomes a place to enter, to see, feel, and touch the world as it forms. We leave the eternal and enter at that moment the temporal. A psychophysical consciousness is born.

In the second instance, the woman's dream, we also begin with nothing, a return to emptiness because of the destruction caused by "evil" forces. A death, a symbolic death, must happen in order to live a more differentiated and autonomous life. Through this death by "evil forces" a rebirth takes place, one necessary in order that a separation from the primary source, or World Parents, is possible and the birth of an individual life unfolds. Or, in Mircea Eliade's words when describing the cosmogonic myth of the Ngadju Dayak of Borneo:

> The world is a result of a combat between two polar principles, during which the tree of life – i.e., their own embodiment – is annihilated. But from destruction and death spring the cosmos and a new life.
>
> (Eliade, 1969, p. 143)

My dreamer's struggle is the hero's journey (cf. Jung, 1911–1912/1952, paras. 251–259), "the longing of the unconscious, of its unquenched and unquenchable desire for the light of consciousness" (para. 299). It is the solar myth, the setting and rising sun, death, and rebirth. She must be ready to sacrifice her existence for a greater good. Darkness ensues after the last living structure is destroyed, the tree of life. Nothing, darkness and then a new beginning, dusting off, attending to her body, becoming embodied, knowing why she is here and what she must do, again the stirrings of life, the dawning of new consciousness. She falls into darkness and then reawakens to light and life. The dream ego, the dreamer, occupies the temporal space, she feels fear, anger, and determination, and these can only come from a bodily existence. In the dream she dusts off, aware of her physical boundaries. In both, dream and myth, we feel this creative impulse, supporting new possibilities, new beginnings, generating new energy and moving us forward, into life.

Unlocking the Doors of Matter

Let us turn now to the dream and mythological symbolism of the egg. For the alchemists, "That round thing was in possession of the magical key which unlocked the closed doors of matter" (Jung, 1938, para. 92).

> *In the beginning this universe was non-existent. It became existent. It grew. It turned into an egg. The egg lay for the period of a year. Then it broke open. Of the two halves of the egg shell, one half was of silver, the other of gold. That which was of silver became the earth; that which was of gold, heaven. What was the thick membrane, of the white, became the mountains; the thin membrane of the yolk, the mist and the clouds. The veins became the rivers; the fluid in the bladder, the ocean. And what was born of it was yonder Aditya, the sun. When it was born shouts of "Hurrah" arose, together with all beings and all objects of desire. Therefore at Aditya's rise and its every return, shouts of "Hurrah," together with all beings and all objects of desire, arise.*

The Chandogya Upanishad is one of the primary Upanishads, a sacred Hindu text, dating from the Brahmana period of Vedic Sanskrit before the eighth century BCE.

A dream from a 42-year-old, female analysand:

> *I am on a street. El (friend who was recently married) takes two big eggs, dinosaur size. She will hatch those eggs by her body warmth. I want to try and get two eggs. She put one of the eggs in the clothes so she looks pregnant. I am thinking; when will I start? I am heading to somewhere on the street so it's not a good place to start. However, I like the egg so much and wonder what will come out. I can feel my body is hotter. I could hatch this egg. I guess. I decide to put it against my back inside the clothes so I won't press it when I ride the bicycle. I reach the destination and see El. I jump from the bicycle. The egg on my back has fallen and is broken. I am shocked, staring at the fragment on the ground. El helps me to pick it up. Another egg of mine has a crack. El brings it to try fixing it. I walk in the house and see two big cups. One has some broken egg white and yolk, which belong to the broken egg. Another cup has the egg with a crack in it. I can see orange red egg yolk, like hard yolk. I am hoping it can be repaired, but I guess not. I am sad and admire El who can have a baby, she hatches a baby. I hope I can have one more egg.*

Desire

I will look again at the temporal and eternal elements in both, but as I explore the myth and the dream one important archetypal energy keeps drawing my attention, namely, desire. I immediately think of my analytical and psychotherapeutic work and am struck by the significance that desire plays in any creative act, be it in the birthing process or in any psychic movement. It is the fundamental motivation for all human activity. The lack of desire in a patient always leaves a dark and stagnant space in which no individual life can evolve. The fear to desire, to want, to hope limits any further exploration, perhaps it is the best expression of a deep fear of life itself, or withdrawal from life, a passive and not active participation-in-the-world. There is no sensuousness of being in the world, no desire to be here, now, and in relationship to the objects of the world. Perhaps this lack of desire is a non-emotional defense against knowing and recognizing oneself, with the fear that that existence will not be recognized by others and a deep sense of alienation fills its void.

As I desire to understand the importance of desire as an archetype per se I realize very quickly that I am stretching the boundaries of this chapter. However I would like to touch very briefly on the interconnecting statements on desire found in mysticism, philosophy, and psychology, that pertain to our psychophysical incarnation and the creation myth as such.

According to Jung, Lacan, and Hegel, "the soul is found in desire itself and not in the play of the objects of desire" (Drob, Blog, 2009). Through desire we open our hearts to soul and can find its expression in images, metaphors, mythology, poetry, and dreams. Through these we bring soul back into our lives and feel our aliveness, our uniqueness, and individuality. We can recognize ourselves. As Jung (1914–1930, p. 232) stated:

> He whose desires turns away from outer things, reaches the place of the soul … He becomes a fool through endless desire and forgets the way of his soul, never to find her again. If he possessed his desire, and his desire did not possess him, he would lay a hand on his soul, since his desire is the image and expression of *his* (my italics) soul.

Desire puts us back in touch with *our* subjectivity, and defines *our* personalities, separate and connected to the other objects around us. When seen as soul, it takes us beyond our knowing through ego consciousness but a knowing that arises in the depths of the body (Jung, 1940, para. 291), sensuous, emotional, perceptive, and connected to the seen and unseen worlds. The language of myth and dream, opening the doors of desire, and through the subjectivity it fosters, allows us to lead more soul-filled and meaning-filled lives.

The Sacred Marriage in Jewish mysticism, symbolizing the union of the feminine and masculine principles, contains the belief that everything in the world exists because of desire. It is desire that continues to create and recreate the universe. This concept underlines my previous statement that we, in our earthly existence, must feel welcome, here and now. If we are desired, we are most certainly welcome, and have an active part to play in the relationships of the sentient world. We play essential roles in the continuation of that divine creative energy.

Referring to Hegel's 1806 *Phenomenology of Mind* and the relationship to desire and the longing for wholeness, or completeness, Drob (2009, pp. 1–2) states:

Hegel understands humanity's most fundamental and primitive desire as the longing for a state of completeness, self-sufficiency, and non-disturbance.

Desire, according to Hegel, even in its most basic primitive form of necessity, seeks to fulfill and embody this essential merger of subject and object.

And most profoundly:

What the subject actually desires is *recognition*.

This deep longing, either for an original wholeness, or the egg as cosmic wholeness, supported through warmth and an open heart, is so beautifully expressed in the myth when Aditya, the sun, is born. "When it was born shouts of "Hurrah" arose, together with all beings and all objects of desire"; or in the dream when her body responds to the egg "I feel my body is hotter" and desire is felt with, "I hope I can have one more egg."

Desire is not one of our emotions, but is a physical longing that grows out of an absence. It is one of our strongest impulses for any creative activity. We sense its presence in many creation myths, be it a god, an animal, or an unexplained event; here we feel the desire either for a mate, for a sense of completion, for love, or worship. We also sense desire in creation myths for beauty and for a growing and abundant world. Desire, as felt in the dream above, is often a longing for a person, a place, an object, or a particular outcome to a life event. It brings with it an energy that leads toward action; it is the great motivational element in both collective myths and individual dreams. As Jung (1916, para. 567) has expressed:

All psychological phenomena can be considered as manifestations of energy, in the same way that all physical phenomena have been understood as energic manifestations ever since Robert Mayer discovered the law of the conservation of energy. Subjectively and psychologically, this energy is conceived as *desire*.

Is not one aspect of our work as clinical analytical psychologists to awaken and support this very psychophysical longing or desire/soul and bring consciousness to it? It is the archetype per se felt in myths and dreams that truly leads us on our path of individuation. It is only through our incarnation as physical, earth-bound beings that we can truly experience desire in its life sustaining and directive presence.

Defined Time

I would now like to return to the temporal element in both myth and dream, a clearly defined time. Most creation myths I have read either have one year in which to hatch the egg, seven days to create the world and the people in it, one moon phase to another to allow a circular rhythm, nine months to allow the new to form and be born. All organic growth needs its proper time, its proper place, and the right concentration. It needs, as Marie Louise von Franz (1972, p. 224) elucidates, a form of brooding, "to give warmth by meditative concentration."

Brooding is also connected to incubation, which is the process of maintaining a uniform heat in order to engender new life and of course, psychologically, new consciousness. Von Franz (ibid., pp. 230–231) aptly describes the process of brooding thus:

> As soon as the image of the egg comes up, it is associated with the idea of concentration: *tapas*, brooding, and the birth of intelligence … it does not mirror a primitive psychological state, for it is already the result of a certain amount of concentration of attention … the human being has, for the first time, a chance of reflecting upon himself … When the egg appears in the dream, then you know that this moment is approaching, that now the birth of consciousness, as an act of self-reflection, is at least possible, it is constellated.

Cosmos to Boundaried Space to Cosmos

The egg motif is significant as a symbol of wholeness in that it contains everything needed within its shell. It is the microcosm in all its completeness mirroring the macrocosm, in all its wholeness. And out of one must come two for the important step of division and movement. The egg symbol in both the Chandogya Upanishad and my dreamer's dream brings us once again back to the union of psyche and matter. Out of the chaos, the unformed potential within the egg, that primary substance, *prima materia*, comes form. It is the numinosity found within our form, or flesh, composed of the primary material, sometimes known as God, Atmen, Yahweh. Out of that primary substance develops body and soul, psyche, and matter. In the Chandogya Upanishad we are told how the entire world was contained within the egg, and how shell, yolk, white, membranes, and veins unfolded into the world we know. "In the beginning" they were all one.

We see division, or boundaried space, in the separation of yolk/yellow from white, silver from gold, top from bottom. It is always in the opposite, light from dark, good from bad, conscious from unconscious, that we begin to feel tension. This tension, when connected with desire, carries the potential for a differentiated consciousness, one not stuck in the polar opposites. It is when we closely differentiate terms such as "bad" that we find the fluidity needed to understand the complexities of life. Division is also psychologically important for the birth of ego out of the whole, the ongoing journey of individuation, becoming an individual in a collective world. As Jung (1940, para. 286) explained, it is a "new birth, … the most precious fruit of Mother Nature herself, the most pregnant with the future, signifying a higher stage of self-realization."

In the creation myth the two halves become heaven and earth, and the details of a completed world develop from there. In the dream the egg is broken and the two parts of yolk and white, psyche and matter, are revealed in one cup, the first step of division. The other egg is cracked and held in another cup. There is the question if it can be fixed or not. The friend, a positive feminine energy, more able to birth a new possibility, just might be able to fix it. Hope is always an awakening to new possibilities. It is an unlocking of closed doors, allowing in air, light, life, and with that desire.

This dream contains three creation myth motifs, the symbol of the egg, the marriage of opposites and the twin creators, who do not have to be twins, but both have the potential to create. The two creator motif in this dream expresses the paradox often found in any creative process, containing both the yes and no, the knowing and not knowing, conscious and unconscious. By accepting both, we can move into a new state of awareness and self-reflection.

This dream, bringing greater consciousness to the dreamer, also awakens her to her creative potential, and the physical longing of desire. This experience of body through her desire "I hope I can have one more egg," with all its sensuous and emotional possibilities, becomes a true gift from the unconscious, allowing a life containing both body and soul.

> In the last analysis the human body, too, is built of the stuff of the world, the very stuff wherein fantasies become visible; indeed, without it they could not be experienced at all.
>
> (Jung, 1940, para. 290)

Why Must We Attend to the Symbols of Creation in the Dream?

The symbols of creation in myth and dream touch on the very foundation of our human existence. The archetypal images and structures we encounter in both grounds us in nature, our own, and in the relationship to the world encompassing us. When these archetypal images are activated and emotionally engaged with (Jung, 1961c, paras. 578–593; Jung, 1921, paras. 814–829) we begin to feel that sense of being welcome, not only through personal relationships, but transpersonal as well, that experience of being held within something larger than ourselves. Through, and with the recognition of, our incarnation as psychophysical entities a relationship to all other matter – animals, people, and earth – is possible. Psyche and soma are then experienced as one. This sense of being part of a greater whole, welcomed, allows an acceptance of our individual particularities and we are able to be active members in the world we find ourselves, connected to the mysterium, our souls awakening to the numinous, contained in the smaller, personal body, and in the larger body earth. This is why we must attend to the symbols of creation in the dream, "in the beginning," and in our lives thereafter.

A return to the beginning is not a regression but redemption, redeeming what was there at the beginning and healing the split that keeps us separate from the ground of our being, and the ground on which we stand, in order to orient ourselves in the world. It returns us to wholeness, a psychophysical wholeness, not leaning more toward body or psyche but accepting they are one of the same, as Jung (1928, para. 195) expresses so well:

But if we reconcile ourselves to the mysterious truth that the spirit is the life of the body seen from within, and the body the outward manifestation of the life of spirit – the two being really one – then we can understand why the striving to transcend the present level of consciousness through acceptance of the unconscious must give the body its due, and why recognition of the body cannot tolerate a philosophy that denies it in the name of the spirit.

The creation myth, the myth of our incarnation, is the beginning of the ego-body/Self connection. In that, we begin to live in a particular place, with a particular form, and we become conscious of the world around us, knowing that this relationship is essential. We are not encapsulated within our own psychophysical boundaries, but these boundaries allow us to open to, and differentiate, the objects we encounter. It is the beginning of knowing we exist, are real, and belong here at this singular moment of time.

As we read creation myths we realize that our very existence has a purpose and came about through numerous actions on the part of Gods, or god-like beings. We are a product of these divine creatures, either human or animal, designed or thrown together; there is a reason for our being. There is the sense of being welcome here in our completeness, a sense of belonging to the whole, that whole being those spirit fathers and mothers and the incarnated form they have given us. This sense of belonging justifies our becoming active members in this world, our world, with the responsibility and care that that bestows on us.

Conclusion

Jung often called a psychological illness an imbalance in the psyche. The creation myth and the dream give us the possibility of restoring balance, knowing one's own center and being able to move in all directions available to us as embodied selves; up, down, right, left, forward, and back. Indeed, all the diagonals that come out of that structure are included, thus allowing a fluidity of motion in both body and mind.

These are the reasons why we must capture those dreams that bring us closer to both the temporal and eternal images found within the myths of creation. I do not believe we can heal any psychological suffering if the psyche is not embodied, with a rootedness in oneself and in the ground on which we stand, with "… a profound attunement to the earth as a place of dwelling …" (Huskinson, 2008, p. 2). That is why the archetypal stories of creation and the archetypal images in dreams can restore for the suffering of a soul that is alienated and desperately searching for home, a rootedness in oneself, in community, and in the natural world that embraces us all.

References

Brooke, R. (1991). *Jung and Phenomenology*. London and New York: Routledge, 1993.

Eliade, M. (1969). "Cosmogonic Myth and 'Sacred History,'" in A. Dundes (ed.), *Sacred Narrative*, Berkeley, Los Angeles, London: University of California Press, 1984.

Huskinson, L. (2008). "Introduction: Ordinarily Mythical," in L. Huskinson (ed.), *Dreaming the Myth Onward: New Directions in Jungian Therapy and Thought*. London and New York: Routledge.

Jung, C.G. (1911–1912/1952). "The Origin of the Hero," in *Collected Works*, Vol. 5, *Symbols of Transformation* (2nd edn). Princeton, NJ: Princeton University Press, 1976.

Jung, C.G. (1914–1930). *The Red Book*, Mark Kyburz, John Peck, Sonu Shamdasani (trans.), New York and London: W.W. Norton, 2009.

Jung, C.G. (1916). "Psychoanalysis and Neurosis," in *Collected Works*, Vol. 4, *Freud and Psychoanalysis*, Princeton, NJ: Princeton University Press, 1979.

Jung, C.G. (1921). "Definitions," in *Collected Works*, Vol. 6, *Psychological Types* (2nd edn). Princeton, NJ: Princeton University Press, 1977.

Jung, C.G. (1928). "The Spiritual Problem of Modern Man," in *Collected Works*, Vol. 10, *Civilization in Transition*, 1964/1970 (2nd edn). Princeton, NJ: Princeton University Press, 1978.

Jung, C.G. (1934). "Lecture V, 21 February 1934," in C. Douglas (ed.), *Visions: Notes of the Seminar Given in 1930–1934 by C.G. Jung*. The first version, transcribed from shorthand notes taken at the seminar meetings. London: Routledge, 1998.

Jung, C.G. (1938). "Psychology and Religion," in *Collected Works*, Vol. 11, *Psychology and Religion: West and East*, 1958/1969 (2nd edn). Princeton, NJ: Princeton University Press, 1977.

Jung, C.G. (1940). "The Psychology of the Child Archetype," in *Collected Works*, Vol. 9(i), *The Archetypes and the Collective Unconscious*, 1959/1968 (2nd edn). Princeton, NJ: Princeton University Press, 1977.

Jung, C.G. (1961a). *Memories, Dreams, Reflection*, recorded and edited by A. Jaffé, R. & C. Winston (trans.) Collins Fount Paperbacks.

Jung, C.G. (1961b) and M.L. von Franz, Joseph Henderson, Jolanda Jacobi, Aniela Jaffé, *Man and His Symbols*, C.G. Jung (ed.), (followed by M.L. von Franz after his death.) New York: Doubleday & Company Inc.

Jung, C.G. (1961c). "Symbols and the Interpretation of Dreams," in *Collected Works*, Vol. 18, *The Symbolic Life* (2nd edn). Princeton, NJ: Princeton University Press, 1980.

Romanyshyn, R. (1991). "Forward," in R. Brooke (ed.) *Jung and Phenomenology*. London and New York: Routledge, 1993.

von Franz, M.L. (1972). *Creation Myths*. Boston and London: Shambhala, 1995.

Online sources

Drob, S.L. (2009). "The Concept of Desire in Hegel, Freud, Sartre and Lacan, Margins Psychological Forum," January 26 (accessed October 17, 2014).

Drob, S.L. (2009). "The Red Book of C.G. Jung, Refinding the Soul," pp. 231–232, *theredbookofcgjung.blogspot.com/2009/.../refindin soul* ... October 18, 2009 – 7:41 pm. (accessed October 18, 2014).

13

TRICKSTER, TRAUMA, AND TRANSFORMATION

The Vicissitudes of Late Motherhood

Maryann Barone-Chapman

When a woman becomes aware at mid-life that time is causing the procreative option to pass her by, the goal of making a baby can become numinous as a sacred duty high in feeling tone. All other endeavors and relationships may pass into the darkness of lesser importance, demonstrating an *unconscious determination* (Jung, 1955a, paras. 355–406). Originally contemplated as a crucial part of regression in the transference for the purpose of individuation (Jung, 1946, paras. 445–449) it has become a *symbol of transformation* (Jung, 1911–1912/1952a, paras. 300–418) when "the libido that is withdrawn so unwillingly from the 'mother' turns into a threatening serpent, symbolising the fear of death – for the relation to the mother must cease, *must die,* and this is almost the same as dying oneself" (Jung, 1911–1912/ 1952b, para. 473). The symbol can no longer be said to apply to mothers and sons in the biotechnological age of late motherhood (Barone-Chapman 2014a). A "return to the mothers" is an opening to the unconscious, "a metaphorical way of saying that when ego development climaxes at midlife there is no further meaning in continuing to pursue the same old goals…" (Stein, 1998, p. 177). If the desire for a child in the second half of life carries a drive to conceive at all costs, we may become curious about what traumatic influences have previously caused a woman's desire to become pregnant to be split off until now (Jung, 1955b, paras. 203–229) attempting to re-integrate in a frantic gesture of repair with little concern for the addictive nature of repeated IVF (Barone-Chapman, 2007). Medical reproductive biotechnology is apt to be perceived, during a *pregnant pause* (Barone-Chapman, 2011) in a prior life narrative, as a benign form of patriarchal authority, a returning, mothering-oriented prodigal father coming home to give his middle-aged daughter permission to alter time. In the course of a woman's life sudden transformation raises the possibility an early relational disturbance, with an inhibiting or prohibiting affect, has been preventing "the trauma [to] be 'forgotten,' and 'remembered' instead of being always present" (Cavalli, 2012, p. 598). The term "trauma" in this chapter may mean "any experience that causes the child unbearable psychic pain or anxiety" (Kalsched, 1996, p. 1).

"In the mid-life search to seek procreativity, the opportunity presented by postponement, to integrate yin and yang energies, discover a self and begin to individuate, the project succeeds and fails in part if object and subject are in the wrong place" (Barone-Chapman, 2011, p. 189), because "a relationship of 'reverse parenting,' in which the child's unconscious belief is that his or her task is to contain the parents' anxieties and meet their needs" learns fear of relationship and love (Knox, 2007, p. 544). Bion's (1962; later in Cavalli, 2014) consideration of containment is the function of transforming infinite affect into the finite, which can be understood as a feeling. This capacity to contain one's own affect, to transform beta into alpha (op cit.) requires a lived experience where emotion and thought can be linked through mind and body. "Put in these terms the intercourse between mind and body could be seen as the realization of an archetypal potential that can only be constellated when, through interaction with another, enough capacity to bear affect has been established" (Cavalli, 2014, p. 33). When affect cannot find mind with a capacity to link (Bion, 1959), feelings go into the body and the body is attacked through somatization, in effect rendering the body as neglected and forgotten. This paradigm within the body parallels early interaction with caregivers, requiring an opening into understanding the dissociation between time (thinking) and the body (feeling) in a *pregnant pause*. What this psychosocial research has discovered is late motherhood has some reparative value regarding past traumatic events, though the actual child cannot on its own satisfy mother's narcissistic injury or her need of adult partnership. The process of affect transformation in Bion's (ibid.) terms, combined with Cavalli's (op cit.) contextualization, and the act of finding relationship with an*other*, are all part of a redemption motif within a pregnant pause.

Late Motherhood – A Field of Plenty

Persecuting and annihilating ambivalence, the longing for redemption, a second chance, and transmutation of suffering are ingredients I have likened to sulfur rising through a blackened body of trauma and shame (Barone-Chapman, 2014b). This putrefaction phase of an individuated journey extends consideration of alchemical processes to an aspect of the Anima Mundi to do with ongoing development of the repressed feminine at mid-life. *Late* desire for motherhood has both an inner and outer construction. It is as much about the fear of not becoming a mother as it is about not having an identity as a mother. Early childbearing has become a class identifier (Walkerdine et al., 2001, pp. 187–210), while delayed motherhood has been associated to selfishness (Smajor, 2009). Motherhood especially occupies a shadow place in popular culture as a personal sphere of influence (Walkerdine, 1997, pp. 165–189), as it is made up of complexes, born of "groups and classes of people as filtered through the psyches of generations of ancestors" (Singer and Kimbles, 2004, p. 4). Affects constellate through complexes, and include participants in this research showing up late or forgetting their appointment to participate in Jung's Word Association Experiment, which has its own large affective field.

A complex is identified through the structure of thought, language, affect, body responses, dreams, and in very serious cases, decompensating symptoms. Complexes do not exist in the mind, body, or unconscious, but in the totality of psyche where observed phenomena functions like Trickster. I will present case material in this chapter where Trickster went to great lengths to obscure attention to inter-subjectivity, repetitive patterns, highly charged affects – including time collapsing and lengthening. When a complex is strong the ego experiences little freedom to choose wisely. Complexes need human connection to manifest and heal. As unconscious processes they are compensations to conscious ego function for regulation of the self.

The arc of Jung's (1946, para. 452) work shifted perception of the unconscious from a warehouse of repression to a fountain of potential healing. Jung saw the collective unconscious as a part of psyche, formed through inherited "collective representations," a term he borrowed from Levy-Bruhl originally defined by Hubert and Mauss on the subject of comparative religion (Jung, 1938/1940, paras. 88–92). Jung claimed these representations to be "preconscious primordial ideas" (ibid., para. 89) pre-existing within everyone to synthesize conscious and unconscious elements. The archetype of the child, for instance, "paves the way for a future change of personality" (op cit., para. 278), becoming part of the individuation process, synthesizing conscious and unconscious elements. Late desire to create a child brings to the fore redemption and reparative motifs seeking transformation. Necessary to this are ambivalent creative processes, including Trickster's normative thieving ways, pointing the way toward the irrational third or transcendent function. Although he may be the master of double-binding manipulation and paradox (Beebe, 1981), Trickster is also the midwife and bearer of redemptive unifying symbols, foreshadowing the new king of consciousness.

"Trickster and trauma archetypes have large affective fields, as they can enact in the form of obstinate psychosomatic illnesses … until desire for the doting mother and latent desire for father unite in transference fantasies, including regression and incest, coming to awareness only to be worked through" (Hubback, 1988, p. 56). While conducting doctoral research in social science on late motherhood, two analytical engagements with the feminine came to my attention as evidence of a patriarchal bias toward the realm of womanhood (Barone-Chapman, 2014a, p. 41). Across affective fields and narratives on late procreative desire, buried in Word Association Tests and held in dream journals, was the memory of a male sibling who had enjoyed primacy of place in the parental home over the daughter (ibid.). The female body with a voice was missing, as it was in the one-sided perspectives of Freud and Jung on the subject of the feminine, and became evidence of patriarchy as background (op cit.). The affects before me at micro level were emerging into a macro view of how feminism emerged when the feminine could no longer quietly accept being thwarted to favor the masculine (Barone-Chapman, 2014a, p. 42). Like the Sumerian goddess Inanna [known as the "Evening Star, Queen of the land

and its fertility, Goddess of war, Goddess of sexual love, the Healer, Life giver, and Composer of songs" (Shaindel Senensky, 2003, p. 163)], participants had taken their procreative desire underground until the clamor of mid-life beckoned them to reclaim the right to enjoy an ordinary life (op cit.). When Inanna returns from the depths she rises with equal parts of wisdom and ruthlessness.

Researching Unconscious Processes of Late Motherhood

My focus in this chapter will be on one particular research participant, Mrs. Anyer, and her ambivalent relationship to becoming a mother, the lengths she went to, including changing her sexual identity, to create what she had missed from early life: a family. Trickster is a two-faced god who tests us through paradox, difficult choices, and mettle making conditions often involving sacrifice, before finding renewal and rebirth.

In the Middle Ages an identification with the complex went by another term – possession (Jung, 1948, para. 204). Jung pays considerable attention to the "unpleasant" nature of a complex, though they are "ubiquitous," they are not something "not to be met in the street and in public places" (ibid., para. 209). Possession of the ego by an autonomous complex was considered crucial to maintaining mental health (Jung, 1950, paras. 222–239) if the ego is capable of experiencing the possession without identifying with the unconscious. That is to say, a "battle of wills, of ego and unconsciousness, each trying to dominate the personality with its own monologue … ends with a reconciliation of the two, and the reinstallation of their creative dialogue" (Huskinson, 2010, p. 88). Unconscious processes manifest as affects in surprising ways and may be viewed as compensations to conscious ego function for regulation of the entire psyche, as:

- An invasion of feeling states
- Taking over ego function
- An intruder of our will
- Such that, time expands and collapses
- Affect occurs where adaptation is weakest
- Creating/arousing defenses of the self. (Fordham 1974)

Affects are sometimes seen as "enactments" of strongly held feelings, ideas, or beliefs. They are not always verbally expressed. Often they are *enacted* non-verbally, such as what can be seen in the void left by disappearance and avoidance. The void is empty on the outside to the unsuspecting viewer, but the combination of emotion and feeling together "begins to alert the organism to the problem … emotion has begun to solve … [giving] the organism an *incentive* to heed the results of emoting" (Damasio, 2000, p. 284), producing "*the feeling of what happened*" (ibid.), reactivated as what is happening in the present. Running away is part of the "fight or flight" response to avoid re-facing a shameful idea hooked into a history of shameful associations.

"Shame inverts libido. Jung emphasises libido's role in differentiating ego from Self. Introversion of energy is seen in self-destructive illness behaviour and sterile relationships" (Mathers, 2000, p. 88). These and other *generative anxieties* form a profile of shadow affects regarding gender and femininity in the age of medical biotechnology (Raphael-Leff, 2007) which in turn form the backbone of my observations that trauma to the feminine is not just a personal, cultural, or collective problem, it is an ancient longitudinal problem: "Shame is a powerful affect or emotion that functions to dampen or extinguish interest, pleasure and/or excitement" (Eurich-Rascoe & Vande Kemp, 1997, p. 103). While proto-shame occurs spontaneously in infants (Nathanson, 1987), in due course the child will learn to shut off pleasure to avoid the "adult's negating response" turning avoidance into the lynchpin that keeps out meaningful connection to an important adult (op cit.). From this early learning the primary caregiver becomes associated with self-criticism and doubt about survival (Gerhardt, 2004, p. 143).

The experience of a complex can be negative, positive, or both, but is only pathological if it is connected to personal conflict (Jacobi, 1974). These three regions, in the same order, have three qualities:

- A root, usually in the past outside of conscious memory
- A nature, how it displays in culture
- A mode of expression through the unconscious as phenomena.

In response I have mirrored these three qualities in a research design to include clinical epistemology of the inter-subjective field, Jung's Word Association Experiment and dreams journals kept before and after word associations. A three-layered funnel approach was designed to access "the wish for transcendence" (Beebe, 1993, p. 3), a lifelong goal of Jung's to cross-fertilize opposites, to find a *transcendent function*, where spiritual and "empirical reality of life ... together forms a whole ..." (Jaffé, 1970, p. 2). In a Jungian approach, respect for psyche makes it possible to find religious, aesthetic, philosophic, and social attitudes (Henderson, 1984, pp. 13–14).

The First Meeting – Mrs. Anyer

Phase 1 Phenomena of Affective Communication
> *Before we met*
> Participant Over One and A Half Hours Late for Interview
> *Within the first 25 minutes:*

- Explanation – Distracted by trying to find work – made more difficult since having baby at 41
- Difficulty due to move to area where people of mixed race poorly received in academia
- Graduate of top college at Oxford University

- Passion for social research in black and same sex communities
- Wanted to talk about her research/no notice of why she was there

From this highly affective field I wanted to discover what could be understood of her earliest experience that paralleled the earliest minutes of our meeting; what would it mean through my own feeling states? She was late, quickly communicating a working mother is limited, she used race as an issue, revealed non-hetero normative identity, and summarized by saying she didn't know why she was there. From this I found three layers of communication:

Affective Symptoms	Transf./CT	Super-ordinate Theme
Chaotic organization	Inferior woman-child	Narcissistic wound
Entitled	Not enough value	Compensation
Better/smarter Oxford	Poor Ph.D. student	Hard life for working mother
Never chosen	Induced Empathy	Wants to be in control
Wants to be seen	"Listen to me!"	Hunger for authority

The interview took on a pattern of repetition/disruption as a transformative process through a series of tone changing repetitions, and appeared to be Trickster's work, to keep me from learning something important about her. At first she wanted me to believe it was a simple matter, her desire for a baby – "*I was coming up to 40, I just wanted to have a baby.*" The pattern broke down into three phases, moving from repetition to disruption, repeating itself six times.

- "*I guess initially I always expected not to become an early mother because you know I come from that kind of middle-class family where they expect you to do other things with your life first, but it did go on a little bit partly because I was in relationships with women …*"
- "*When I look back on it now I can see that there were ways but I was kind of set up to take on partners that were not really very good at forming family relationships and that actually needed a lot of support, work, help and effort put into them.*"
- "*I wasn't really set up to establish good family relationships but also I was mainly in gay/lesbian relationships so I was never going to become a parent by accident …*"
- "*If you're going to fall pregnant in a lesbian relationship you're going to have to make a very conscious choice.*"
- "*… I wasn't in any sort of relationship but there was this little edge to it because I was part of the gay community so it was like I could have a family in a really different way and that would not only be personally exciting but socially revolutionary …*"
- "*I don't know, my family are weird, they are not a good family … they're just terrible, I mean really selfish … and self-centred and they remained that way …*"

Beginning with the personal collective, she moved into the culturally specific, sideways to the universal before descending to universal longing. I was left with highly ambivalent and anxious feelings. A transformative pattern emerged through the following three statements, foreshadowing what Mrs. Anyer was trying to tell me.

1. *"The whole world is very hetero normative"*
2. *"Difficult to live as a lesbian family"*
3. *"I think people hunger for that sort of closeness, support and warmth you get in a good relationship and basically good family"*

I could feel she was sincerely asking me to enter her world so she could discover if trust was possible. The interview process was successful in allowing me to ethically feel into her experience before commencing the Word Association Experiment. Mrs. Anyer's unconscious communication began to suggest dark historical information lurking in the shadows, which her child had helped to repair, although lingering thoughts of the past remained:

> *"My dad worked away from home a lot and my mum and I were not close … I had to really try to be a substitute support for my younger sister who was completely neglected by my parents."*
>
> *"You know I am his favourite, I always was his favourite and we used to get on really, really well."*
>
> *"Now that I've got my daughter I see that a lot of the things I tried to pour into family and other relationships were actually maternal but not really appropriate for those sorts of relationships."*
>
> *"…Life is very full, you know you just don't have that emptiness in your life, there's always somebody."*

The question in the air between us was what has maternal identity/pre-occupation been trying to repair? By the end of this first phase Mrs. Anyer was still ensnared by Trickster through creative use of ambivalence between her work in academia, fantasies of retaliation, and motherhood. The belief she did not fit into white middle-England academia kept her outside of achieving academic status. I began to wonder if her unconscious struggle represented an argument between thinking and feeling that left her outside of belonging anywhere. If she could only achieve procreative identity, it meant, in not doing so, only half of her was alive (Seligman, 1985).

> *"Mainly I fret about work at the moment and the way in which I behave inappropriately so I don't get jobs and people treat me inappropriately and don't offer them to me. Oh! The number of interviews where afterwards they had to make up some convincing reason not to appoint me! Good job I have a good sense of humor. Also I keep thinking one day I will write devastating journal articles out of all my hilarious experiences of racism and sexism and other -isms – or even better web blogs which lead to heads rolling, ha ha ha,"* (rubs hands with glee).

Jung's Word Association Experiment and Mrs. Anyer

Jung's original Word Association Experiment, (hereafter referred to as the WAE), was made available to all participants, with the invitation to keep dream journals in the week before and after. The synthesis of interpretive-phenomenological analysis (Smith, 2003), in concert with the WAE and dream journals is reported on in the Case Study presented below. The WAE tested the reliability of the discursive method in Phase 1. The three means of viewing complexes began to speak to each other, as if one was finishing the sentence of the former. Jung suspected it would be possible to view a complex by identifying how speech patterns were altered, *affected,* by unconscious disturbance. Through the Word Association Experiment (Jung, 1904–1907; Jung, 1918/1969; Meier, 1984) Jung found the basis upon which unconscious complexes could be identified as autonomous *splinter psyches* (1948, para. 203; see also paras. 194–219), as he witnessed fear and resistance guarding the road that lead to the unconscious. It was only then that he understood why Freud first conceived the unconscious as filled with immoral contents that needed to be repressed (ibid., p. 213). As a psychological instrument the Word Association Experiment bypasses rationale consciousness to more genuinely reflect what happens between two people engaged in dialogue, rather than an interview with questions and answers formed in sentences. "Reaction disturbances" in the form of large gaps of time, misunderstanding of words, falsification of memory, stumbling over words, changing the answer, playing with meaning, contrariness, and responses that are meant to be rhymes or opposites, such as "white" in response to "black" reveals another kind of *defense of the self* (Kalsched, 1996, pp. 41–42). Throughout, my researcher position was one of non-interference, purposely not analyzing their dreams so Psyche and Eros, if they wished, could release hidden trauma. Responses to the research experience ranged from remarkably transformative to an itch that couldn't be scratched immediately.

Affective Communication

The WAE seeks to highlight perseveration patterns, and other complex indicators such as lengthy reaction times, calculated into fifths to accentuate what is above and below the median of all response times. Mrs. Anyer's case material revealed a synthesis of phenomenological findings from the interview to be in concert with findings from the WAE and dreams. In Figure 13.1, within the first 50 words, we see Mrs. Anyer displayed very high response times to five words I have highlighted in bold text: TO PAY, TO ASK, COLD, LAKE, and SICK. Response times recorded in fifths, above the median, reveal a pattern of perseveration commencing with the 10th stimulus word "TO PAY" at 14. The response was "Bald" and later as "Salary." Mrs. Anyer said she heard "toupee" in the first instance, an example of a misunderstood word becoming what Jung (1918/1969, p. 135) called "the affective idea which fills up consciousness." Older men wear a toupee, or hairpiece, in the main. Further evidence of a perseveration appears with "TO ASK" producing "To Give" both times. "COLD" at 19 follows to produce "Warm." Further down with 17th word, "LAKE" produced "Ripples" at 14, followed by "SICK" slightly elevated at 11. "Lovely" is a word repeated several times during the WAE.

Word	Response	2nd Word	Time	Fifths
to pay	bald	salary	2.88	**14**
window	sky	sky	1.54	8
friendly	**lovely**	**lovely**	1.56	8
table	chair	chair	1.07	5
to ask	to give	to give	3.04	**15**
cold	warm	warm	3.1	**19**
stem	flower	flower	0.88	4
to dance	to sing	to sing	1.5	7
village	shops	shops	1.87	9
lake	ripples	ripple	2.78	**14**
sick	unwell	unwell	2.25	**11**
pride	lions	lions	1.53	8
to cook	**stew**	stew/casserole	2.05	**10**

FIGURE 13.1   Beginning of a perseveration

Notably below in Figure 13.2, Perseveration continued, Mrs. Anyer's response to "ANGRY" does not produce a response time above the median. "To Swim" registered higher as it resonates emotionally to her daughter's swimming lessons. "Blue" at 15 produces "Yellow" (opposites on a color wheel), followed by "LAMP" producing "Bulb" at 14, and was also repeated correctly. It is not until we reach "TO SIN" that we find the stimulus word with the highest charge to "Prayer" at 35. "BREAD" a seemingly simple association to "Butter" produces a response time value of 19. Response times suddenly drop under the median to produce "Poor" for "RICH" and "Leaf" for "TREE," telling us the perseveration of affect beginning with "TO PAY" in the first chart (Figure 13.1) is completed.

Word	Response	2nd Word	Time	Fifths
ink	green	green	1.65	8
angry	sad	sad	1.54	8
needle	thread	thread	0.81	4
to swim	lessons	lesson	2.2	**11**
journey	car	car	1.42	7
blue	yellow	yellow	2.97	**15**
lamp	bulb	bulb	2.87	**14**
to sin	prayer	prayer	6.99	**35**
bread	butter	butter	3.83	**19**
rich	poor	poor	1.05	7
tree	leaf	leaf	1.43	7

FIGURE 13.2   Perseveration continued

Taken together the pattern has its own narrative as stimulus words and associations relate to each other as if one is a problem and the other an empty space needing a remedial solution, such as a circumambulation of affect appearing as rings around a core (Figure 13.3). The corresponding narrative interpretation of this perseveration foreshadows what Mrs. Anyer would only reveal in the last meeting to review her WAE responses, and might be understood in this way:

> Do as you're told and you'll be paid. If you're asked you had to give.
> If the atmosphere in the family was cold, you provide warmth.
> The ripple effect upon a still lake from something penetrating
> is a strong image that stays and stays.
> If you're blue bright yellow can help.
> It's difficult to know what is happening in the dark
> if the lamp has no bulb in it.
> But when you know which side your bread is buttered
> you do what you have to do.

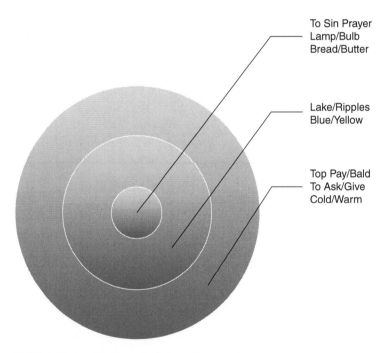

To Sin Prayer
Lamp/Bulb
Bread/Butter

Lake/Ripples
Blue/Yellow

Top Pay/Bald
To Ask/Give
Cold/Warm

FIGURE 13.3   Circumambulation of a complex

Through her associations and timed response to stimulus words, Mrs. Anyer was getting ready to tell me something important about what had happened to her, but it wasn't yet the time, there were still dreams to talk about. Later she told me she hadn't heard me say "TO SIN" but "To Sing," another way of saying performance was corrupted.

Fast and Slow Numbers Parallel High Feeling-Toned Dreams

Three words stood out in the second half of the WAE with very fast responses. The three words were "SAD" associated to "Happy," "HAPPINESS" associated to "Flowers," and "TO CHOOSE" associated to "Life." Mrs. Anyer couldn't reproduce "Happy" in response to "SAD." Flowers as a sign of "HAPPINESS" had a short stay in her mind. And though she chose "Life" through giving birth, there are too many other areas of life where she seemed to have no choice.

In the second half of the WAE, high numbers, as seen in Figure 13.4, began to appear, meaning it took longer for Mrs. Anyer to bring an associated word to mind as her internal processes had a larger amount of "data" to wade through.

Word	Response	2nd word	Time	Fifths
part	pieces	pieces	7.19	**36**
family	home	home	6.23	**31**
anxiety	blood running	rushing blood	14.56	**72**
to abuse	privileges	privileges	4.62	**23**

FIGURE 13.4 More high numbers

We may wonder if parting with former lovers, a way of life and her loss of family connection carry a feeling of "falling to pieces." "FAMILY" is associated to "Home," consistent with the first phase of research. Family has been important to Mrs. Anyer's well-being. Within it she could adhere to and later recreate subject formation as the mother. "ANXIETY," her highest response time, held the greatest amount of high feeling-tone as she recalled the memory of later multiple miscarriages. Mrs. Anyer didn't just want a baby; she wanted a home with several babies. Ending the WAE on the word "TO ABUSE" was a genius choice on Jung's part for research endeavoring to reach the repressed feminine. Her association to "Privileges," above, may indicate an arrangement that had gone too far. In reviewing other high–low numbers I found "FAMILY," "FRIEND," and "FEAR," an alliteration of "F" words to hold family, lovely, and loss. Mrs. Anyer no longer sees her family of origin but described them as once being very close.

Her description of "being very close" fits with displaced maternal pre-occupation in dreams before the WAE, to do with *a little boy* and *two little girls* she has looked after. The children are a way of describing what has been on her mind most of her life, having to be the mother for the family and one of the children. After the WAE, Mrs. Anyer's dream images appeared as a *complexio oppositorum* against her conscious attitude. The actual dream situation appears as a message to do with accessing and relating to the unconscious. The dream is followed by her own interpretation:

> *"I started going along a path up a hillside then I realised it was the wrong path to take, I needed to go down through an under path. As I came back down it became hard to cycle and I realised the small wheels of the bike had disintegrated."*
>
> I think it's significant that in my dream I was going the wrong way on this silly bike my father bought me then when I turned round to take the right route the bike broke. In real life I bought myself a bike with money I earned, this time I didn't depend on birthday money from family and friends … I think I might turn things around for myself in my career –

As we were nearing the end of our time together, Mrs. Anyer couldn't believe all that had come up about her family and siblings. She was able not only to face what had happened to her she also put her past trauma into the following context:

> As a survivor of childhood abuse it took a long time to get into an "appropriate" relationship. My daughter's father is the only partner I have ever had who has been decent to me.

It was a long while before I could read these words aloud without wanting to weep.

Metabolizing Trickster and Trauma

Between a personal complex and a complex of the collective unconscious is a meaningful mid-space organizing concept "that lies between the collective unconscious and the manifest pattern of culture" (Henderson, 1990, p. 103). Within this pattern (Kimbles, 2014, pp. 8–9) are three areas of experience at group level (family and in society): 1 – intergenerational processes; 2 – collective shadow processes; 3 – the role cultural complexes play in producing social suffering. Identification of these strands becomes useful to our understanding of shame and trauma as it is often the implicit and covert messages that arouse damaging affect.

Many of the women involved in this research had been groomed to feel inferior to the masculine, by being less considered, desired, and entitled than a male sibling, resulting in a view they might be less capable in life than a male (Barone-Chapman, 2014a). That most of the participants enjoyed engagement in the world of work long past their peers, until onset of pregnancy around the fourth decade, goes some way to suggesting how late motherhood resonates, at minimum, with having to prove something to themselves and others about their masculine value. Normative, predictive generative identity via motherhood was not possible until their masculine worth had been established. Uncannily, birth control, bio-technology, and a woman's right to choose when to reproduce has overturned Freud's (1933, p. 149) basis of femininity as "biologically given and thus 'bedrock' to the psychical field" (Hillman, 1972, p. 292), yet dichotomously has reproduced this new developmental twist on the creation myth, "first-Adam-then-Eve" (Barone-Chapman, 2014a, p. 47). When the principle of "masculine" and "feminine" is concretized as first Adam then Eve, we find a link to the alchemical subtle body becoming physically and psychically blackened, precipitating a sulfuric decay to rise so that the problem as it is felt can dissolve (Barone-Chapman, 2014b).

Many delayed motherhood narratives reveal how the female body was neutered into performance of patriarchal values for fear of becoming a mother. Compounding this union of personal and collective influences was the emergence of a transcendent space between a woman's personal mother and the mother she thought she must be. Most often this meant earlier maternal failures required her to be "the better mother." In this research it appears the relationship with the mother set the stage for how Eros, the masculine god and carrier of the feminine, manifested. An emotional cocktail of shame, regret, and stigma remained for many who became the mother they wished they had, but all too late in life. Ultimately this research sought to unpack archetypal imagoes of the symptomatic body that made motherhood appear as the ultimate redemption of earlier trauma.

In Neumann's (1955, p. 226) "Great Round" perceptions of how the feminine develops and transforms there is "the phenomenon of reversal" (ibid., pp. 75–83) along the axis of fertility and death, occupied by the archetypes of *Good Mother* and *Terrible Mother* respectively, polarities which are part of the ordinary mother. This includes the mother of maternal preoccupation, subjectivity, and ambivalence. Transformation can also be viewed as compensation, held by positive and negative poles conceptualized as the opposites, for example, Sophia and Lilith. In this intersubjective space between mother and daughter a "doer and done to" relationship (Benjamin, 1998), becomes accountable for the feeling of either/or choices, submission or resistance, to the demands of "other" (Ogden, 1994). Women who delayed motherhood described feeling that they had betrayed themselves in some way, as if ruined by Lilith, "the character of enchantment leading to doom" (Neumann, 1955, p. 81). In such an archetypal image we find a woman's inner conflict between worth and desire part of a feminist challenge to society's patriarchal values (Vogelsang, 1985, p. 149).

Siegmund Hurwitz (2009, pp. 31–32), finds the Lilith figure occupies an important place within the realm of demonic images, as the Terrible Witch Mother, an archetype documented across millennia in many cultures, unchanging until the Talmudic-Rabbinic and Greco-Byzantine traditions when her persona split into a dual nature. For women possessed by a negative mother complex, she arouses feelings of being faced with a demon mother trying to injure pregnant women and their babies. The evolution of the feminine in consciousness according to Hurwitz (ibid., p. 31) proceeds from the Great Mother as "a bipolar, archetypal figure, in that she contains the aspect both of the nurturing, caring mother and of the terrible devouring mother."

In parallel, Lilith earns her dualistic persona through the seduction of men as a "*divine whore*" for all time until the Day of Judgement (ibid.). In this context Lilith is the eternal home-wrecker who will not allow men to be faithful and women to bear and raise their children. Lilith as an archetype is therefore integral to understanding the archetypal power operating in delayed motherhood, longitudinally, from mother to a daughter who comes under a spell. The spell takes form through a belief it is not safe for her to feel fecund, yet it is this very fear under Lilith's influence that is projected onto men as the reason for their vagaries, making them appear unsuitable as partners and fathers. With Lilith we get both fear and fascination. When a woman has a father "who values the feminine and in his attitude reflects this regard, his attitude will counteract the influence of the collective … [but if father] does not participate in her life, she will be forced to deal with the collective conscious … *before* she can realise her shadow qualities" (Vogelsang, 1985, p. 156).

Trickster, who could be described as a soul in hell (Jung, 1954, paras. 456–461), is known for "transformation of the meaningless into the meaningful that reveals Trickster's compensatory relation to the 'saint'" (ibid., para. 458). Trickster is therefore the necessary but often destructive ingredient for metabolizing "death of time, death of language and death of narrative" (Connolly, 2011, p. 611; Cavalli, 2012, p. 598), transforming trauma originating in maternal disregard. As a messenger of the underworld, Trickster's methods include sacrificing naiveté, ego, and victimhood. S/he is uniquely placed to hold the negative and positive until the meaning and purpose of each woman's creation myth becomes installed as a psychic reality regardless of procreative result.

Conclusion

Mrs. Anyer is among a growing number of women choosing to pause from the world of work to become pregnant before more time passes, a patriarchal choice perhaps, to claim something of the missing, absent father. It is typically patriarchal to set the tone and agenda to what will most profit at various times in life, rather than let biology, the wishes and choices of others, set the bar for outcomes. Thus the former abandoned father's daughter follows on from making a career of her own to also make time for maternity with the adroitness of Trickster. She comes to it with *Logos* and determination the "time is now" for rebirth and renewal. There will be time to regress to the Eros of motherhood later. The new myths of creation, born of biotechnology are plural, outside of linear time, in perpetual preparation and reparation. This kind of mid-life change has become reclaimed "bedrock" of feminine transformation born from unconscious appreciation of Inanna's descent, as its own alchemical imagination, crucial for redemption of the Anima Mundi. When the feminine is equal in value to the masculine the children know.

References

Barone-Chapman, M. (2007). "The Hunger to Fill An Empty Space: An Investigation of Primordial Affects and Meaning Making in the Drive to Conceive Through Repeated Use of ART," *The Journal of Analytical Psychology*, Vol. 52, No. 4, pp. 389–541.

Barone-Chapman, M. (2011). "Pregnant Pause: Procreative Desire, Reproductive Technology and Narrative Shifts at Midlife," in R. Jones (ed.), *Body Mind and Healing After Jung: A Space of Questions*. London and New York: Routledge, pp. 174–191.

Barone-Chapman, M. (2014a). "Gender Legacies of Jung and Freud as Epistemology in Emergent Feminist Research on Late Motherhood," in L. Huskinson (ed.), *The Behavioural Sciences in Dialogue with the Theory and Practice of Analytical Psychology*. Basel and Beijing: MDPI, pp. 41–57.

Barone-Chapman, M. (2014b). "Sulphur Rises Through the Blackened Body," in D. Mathers (ed.), *Alchemy and Psychotherapy Post-Jungian Perspectives*. London and New York: Routledge, pp. 205–221.

Beebe, J. (1981). "The Trickster in the Arts," *The San Francisco Jung Institute Library Journal*, Vol. 2, No. 2, pp. 21–54.

Beebe, J. (1993). "Jung's Approach to Working with Dreams," in G. Delaney (ed.), *New Directions in Dream Interpretation*. Albany, NY: SUNY Press, pp. 77–101.

Benjamin, J. (1998). "Beyond Doer and Done To: An Intersubjective View of Thirdness," in *The Psychoanalytic Quarterly*, Vol. 73, pp. 5–46.

Bion, W.R. (1959). "Attacks on Linking," in *Second Thoughts*. New York: Jason Aronson, pp. 93–109.

Bion, W.R. (1962). *Learning from Experience*. London: Heinemann.

Cavalli, A. (2012). "Transgenerational Transmission of Indigestible Facts: From Trauma, Deadly Ghosts and Mental Voids to Meaning-Making Interpretations," *Journal of Analytical Psychology*, Vol. 57, pp. 597–614.

Cavalli, A. (2014). "From Affect to Feelings and Thoughts: From Abuse to Care and Understanding," *Journal of Analytical Psychology*, Vol. 59, No. 1, pp. 31–46.

Connolly, A. (2011). "Healing the Wounds of our Fathers: Intergenerational Trauma, Memory, Symbolization and Narrative," *Journal of Analytical Psychology*, Vol. 56, pp. 607–626.

Damasio, A. (2000). *The Feeling of What Happens: Body, Emotion and the Making of Consciousness*. London: Vintage.

Eurich-Rascoe, B.L. & Vande Kemp, H. (1997). *Femininity and Shame Women, Men and Giving Voice to the Feminine*. Lanham, NY and Oxford: University Press of America, Inc.

Fordham, M. (1974). "Defences of the Self," *Journal of Analytical Psychology*, Vol. 19, No. 2, pp. 192–199.

Freud, S. (1933). "New Introductory Lectures on Psycho-Analysis," *The Complete Works of Sigmund Freud*, 24 volumes. J. Strachey et al. (eds.). London: The Hogarth Press and the Institute of Psychoanalysis, 1953–1974; SE 22, pp. 3–182.

Gerhardt, S. (2004). *Why Love Matters: How Affection Shapes a Baby's Brain*. London and New York: Routledge.

Henderson, J. (1984) *Cultural Attitudes in Psychological Perspective*. Toronto: Inner City Books.

Henderson, J. (1990) "The Cultural Unconscious," in J. Henderson, *Shadow and Self*. Wilmette, IL: Chiron.

Hillman, J. (1972) "On Psychological Femininity," in *The Myth of Analysis Three Essays in Archetypal Psychology*. Evanston, IL: Northwestern University Press.

Hubback, J. (1988). *People Who Do Things To Each Other: Essays in Analytical Psychology*. Wilmette, IL: Chiron.

Hurwitz, S. (2009). *Lilith The First Eve Historical and Psychological Aspects of the Dark Feminine*. Einsiedeln, Switzerland: Daimon Verlag.

Huskinson, L. (2010). "Analytical Psychology and Spirit Possession: Towards a Non-Pathological Diagnosis of Spirit Possession," in B.E. Schmidt & L. Huskinson (eds.), *Spirit Possession and Trance: New Interdisciplinary Perspectives Continuous Advances in Religious Studies*. London and New York: Continuum.

Jacobi, J. (1974). *Complex, Archetype, Symbol*. New York: Princeton University Press.

Jaffé, A. (1970). *The Myth of Meaning in the Work of C.G. Jung*, R.F.C. Hull (trans.). London: Hodder and Stoughton.

Jung, C.G. (1904–1907). *Collected Works*, Vol. 2, *Experimental Researches Including the Work Association Test* (2nd edn). London: Routledge and Kegan Paul, 1992.

All further works listed by Jung are published by Routledge and Kegan Paul, 2nd edn.

C.G. Jung. (1911–1912/1952a). *Symbols of the Mother and of Rebirth*. CW 5.

C.G. Jung. (1911–1912/1952b). *The Dual Mother*, CW 5.

C.G. Jung. (1918/1969). *Studies in Word Association*.

C.G. Jung. (1938/1940). *Dogma and Natural Symbols*, CW 11.

C.G. Jung. (1946). *The Psychology of the Transference*, CW 16.

C.G. Jung. (1948). *A Review of Complex Theory*, CW 8.

C.G. Jung. (1950). *Concerning Rebirth*, CW 9i.

C.G. Jung. (1951). *The Psychology of the Child Archetype*, CW 9i.

C.G. Jung. (1954). *On the Psychology of the Trickster-Figure*, CW 9i.

C.G. Jung. (1955a). *The Aetiology of Neurosis*, CW 4.

C.G. Jung. (1955b). *A Review of the Early Hypotheses*, CW 4.

Kalsched, D. (1996). *The Inner World of Trauma: Archetypal Defences of the Personal Spirit.* London: Routledge.

Kimbles, S. (2014). *Phantom Narratives: The Unseen Contributions of Culture to Psyche.* New York & London: Rowman & Littlefield.

Knox, J. (2007). "The Fear of Love: The Denial of Self in Relationship," in *Journal of Analytical Psychology*, Vol. 52, pp. 543–563.

Mathers, D. (2000). *An Introduction to Meaning and Purpose in Analytical Psychology.* Hove, UK: Routledge.

Meier, C.A. (1984). *The Unconscious in its Empirical Manifestations*, Vol. 1, *The Psychology of C.G. Jung with Special Reference to the Association Experiment of C.G. Jung.* Boston, MA: Sigo.

Nathanson, D.L. (1987). *The Many Faces of Shame.* New York: Guilford Publications.

Neumann, E. (1955). *The Great Mother: An Analysis of the Archetype.* New York: Pantheon Books.

Ogden, T. (1994). *Subjects of Analysis.* Northvale, NJ: Jason Aronson.

Raphael-Leff, J. (2007). "Femininity and its Unconscious 'Shadows': Gender and Generative Identity in the Age of Biotechnology," in *British Journal of Psychotherapy*, Vol. 23, pp. 497–515.

Seligman, E. (1985). "The Half-Alive Ones," in A. Samuels (ed.), *The Father: Contemporary Jungian Perspectives.* London: Free Association Books.

Shaindel Senensky, S. (2003). *Healing and Empowering the Feminine.* Wilmette, IL: Chiron Publications.

Singer, T. and Kimbles, S. (2004). "Introduction," in T. Singer & S. Kimbles (eds.), *The Cultural Complex Contemporary Jungian Perspectives on Psyche and Society.* Hove, UK: Routledge.

Smajor, A. (2009). "Between Fecklessness and Selfishness: Is There a Biologically Optimal Time for Motherhood?" *International Library of Ethics, Law, and the New Medicine*, Vol. 43, pp. 105–117.

Smith, J.A. (ed.) (2003). *Qualitative Psychology: A Practical Guide to Research Methods.* London: Sage.

Stein, M. (1998). *Jung's Map of the Soul: An Introduction.* Chicago & La Salle, IL: Open Court.

Vogelsang, E.W. (1985). "The Confrontation Between Lilith and Adam: The Fifth Round," *Journal of Analytical Psychology*, Vol. 30, pp. 149–163.

Walkerdine, V. (1997). "Advertising Girls," in Valerie Walkerdine's *Daddy's Girl Young Girls and Popular Culture.* Cambridge, MA: Harvard University Press.

Walkerdine, V., Lucey, H., & Melody, J. (2001). *Growing Up Girl: Psychosocial Explorations of Gender and Class.* Basingstoke, UK: Houndmills.

PART VII

Eco-Psychological, Synchronistic Carriers of Rebirth and Renewal

14

ARCHETYPAL IMAGES IN JAPANESE ANIME

Space Battleship *Yamato* (Star Blazers)

Konoyu Nakamura

Introduction: Anime as a Full-fledged Medium of Expression in Japan

"Why Anime?" asks Napier (2001, 2005, p. 3). She proceeds to wonder whether anime is a high-culture artifact or a sociological phenomenon that should be seriously discussed. There are many answers to these questions; I will explore some of them here.

In the 1990s, Schodt (1996, pp. 21–22) who introduced Japanese *Manga* into the US, explained, "Japanese people have had a long love affair with art (especially monochrome line drawing) that is fantastic, humorous, erotic, and sometimes violent," citing as an example the twelfth-century *Chojugiga* (Animal Scrolls) by the Buddhist priest *Toba*. He also mentioned significant cultural differences: "American comic books are usually between 30 and 50 pages long, contain one serialized story, and are published monthly. But manga magazines, many of which are issued *weekly*, often have 400 pages containing 20 serialized and concluding stories" (ibid., pp. 22–23). This output is so prodigious that, "According to the Research Institute for Publications, of all the books and magazines actually sold in Japan in 1995, manga comprised nearly 40 *percent* of the total" (p. 19).

Drazen (2003, pp. vii–viii) has explained the wide-ranging focus of these by noting:

> The Japanese don't regard animation as a "children only" playground … Japanese animators …have also used animation to explore broader themes: love and death, war and peace, the historical past and the far future. Once these animators took the first giant leap away from the age and subject matter limitations of the West, they kept exploring, kept pushing the envelope to see what would happen next.

Drazen states that "their viewers are male and female, grade schooler and graduate student, housewife and businessman. The content can include raucous humor or theological speculation or horrifying pornography, or all three at once" (ibid., p. vii).

Napier (2001/2005, pp. 6–7) explains this comparison by stating: "Essentially anime works include everything that Western audiences are accustomed to seeing in live-action romance, comedy, tragedy, and adventure," yet with "psychological probing of a kind seldom attempted in recent mass-culture Western film or television."

Nakamura (2006, p. 21), an expert on mass media, points out five features of Japanese anime, including comics, films, TV series, computer games, and music, namely, a variety and differentiation of genres, a reliance on imported scientific techniques, a folkloric culture, a lack of borderlines between children and adults, and an ethos of Eros-violence. Thus they developed into "expressions for adults" (p. 18), which extended their reach across generations. In sum, anime suffuses Japanese daily life, subsuming history, science, religion, literature, and even educational materials. Therefore, Schodt (1996, p. 72) is correct to state, "Japan is the first nation on earth where comics have become a full-fledged medium of expression."

Acceptance of Japanese Anime Around the World

According to Levi (1996, p. 6), the first dubbed anime was Osamu Tezuka's *Tetsuwan Atomu* (the Mighty Atom), which appeared on American TV under the title *Astro Boy* in 1964. Since the 1970s, Japanese anime have become popular around the world, initially accepted by young, enthusiastic fans called *otaku* (cf. Macias and Mochiyama, 2004, 2006) as part of a sub-culture. In the 1980s, *Star Blazers* and *Robotech* were aired on American TV. However, American viewers did not know they came from Japan, since "they were heavily edited to accommodate American tastes and sensitivities" (Levi, ibid., p. 7). They were extraordinarily popular and spread rapidly to Asia and Europe in the 1980s (Nakamura, 2006, p. 31).

Drazen (2003, p. 11) mentions that during the 1990s, *Sailor Moon* and *Dragonball Z* were successes in Japan, the US, Canada, Poland, the Philippines, and Brazil. Napier (2001/2005, p. 18) states, "By the 1990s intellectually sophisticated anime were increasingly appearing. The two most important of these were Anno Hideaki's television series *Neon Genesis Evangelion* (*Shinseki Ebuangerion*) and Miyazaki Hayao's film *Princess Mononoke* (*Mononokehime*)." When Miyazaki's *Spirited Away* (*Sen to Chihiro no Kamikakushi*) obtained the Golden Bear Award from the *Internationale Filmfestspiele* in Berlin and an Academy Award in 2003, it ratified anime as a genuine art form of high quality, with compelling philosophical themes. Nakamura (2006, p. 30) points out that in 2002, 60 percent of TV anime around the world were made in Japan, and in Europe the figure was 80 percent.

Clearly, Japanese anime have become mainstream in the West, leading to innumerable studies in the fields of art, media theory, sociology, history, anthropology, psychoanalysis, and psychology (cf. Schodt, 1996; Levi, 1996; Drazen, 2003; Kelts,

2006; Napier, 2001/2005; Lamarre, 2009). As Napier (2001/2005, p. 4) has expressed, anime are "worthy of being taken seriously, both sociologically and aesthetically."

Japanese Anime and Analytical Psychology

According to Jung (1936–1937, para. 89): "The concept of the archetype, which is an indispensable correlate of the idea of the collective unconscious, indicates the existence of definite forms in the psyche which seem to be present always and everywhere. Mythological research calls them 'motifs.'" Jung also stated (1954a, para. 6): "Another well-known expression of the archetypes is myth and fairy tale," and noted that, "the essential thing, psychologically, is that they occur in dreams, fantasies and other exceptional states of mind" (Jung, 1929, para. 229). As Schodt (1996, p. 31) posits about anime, "Viewed in their totality, the phenomenal number of stories produced is like the constant chatter of the collective unconscious – an articulation of the dream world." Napier (2001/2005, pp. 24–25) also notes that, "animated space has the potential to be context free," and "anime is 'another world,'" quoting Mamoru Oshii, a famous Japanese animator. Consequently, anything can occur in anime over space and time, beyond the regulations in society, much as dreams or fantasies are delivered from our unconsciousness and perceived as "another world" by our consciousness. Thus, anime are clearly grounded in archetypal images.

Indeed, some Jungians have examined anime in Japan. Yokoyama (1995, pp. 13–16), for example, has discussed the feminine archetypes, using "a bitter nostalgic story" (Schodt, 1996, p. 203), *Akai Hana* (Red Flowers) by Yoshiharu Tsuge (1985). Yokoyama explores the feminine mystique of a young girl's transformation into a woman through menarche. Kuwabara (1999, pp. 149–164) has dealt with integration in female sibling conflicts in terms of a shadow archetype, interpreting a comic named *Hanshin* (Half God) by Moto Hagio (1985).

Recently, Portes and Haig (2013, p. 248) have discussed how anime have influenced young people in Brazil, in particular *Naruto*. They assert: "Analytical psychology and anime gained visibility in the same way." Thus anime are clearly suitable material for an examination of archetypal images today. The purpose of this chapter is to explore those in one popular anime, Space Battleship *Yamato*, in the social context of its time.

Why Battleship *Yamato*?

Space Battleship *Yamato* was a popular TV series, which began in 1974 in Japan and led to an abundance of related comics, movies, and sequels. "Star Blazers," the animated version of Reiji Matsumoto's *Uchu Senkan Yamato* (*Space Cruiser Yamato*), was groundbreaking, since it had a 26-week story-arc, dwarfing predecessors the way its namesake dwarfed other battleships (Drazen, 2003, p. 8). Levi (1996, p. 7) has stated, "At least, that was true until the 1980s, when Space Cruiser *Yamato* and *Macross* made their first appearance on American television," adding that their popularity was partly due to the way "they were heavily edited to accommodate American tastes and sensitivities." For example, as Levi explains, "The names of all the main characters were changed to make them less foreign and easier to remember. Thus, *Susumu Kodai* became Dereck Wildstar, *Yuki Mori* became Nova" and "Dr. *Sado*, the hard-drinking medical officer of the *Space Cruiser Yamato*, must have attended AA meetings before signing on as Dr. *Sane* of *Star Blazers*." Kelts (2006, p. 15) has elucidated the attraction of such anime: "The characters looked different and fresh," "their modes of transport had sleek yet believable shapes," and "adding to the visual titillation was the fact each character was defined by personal dilemmas, tics, and unpredictability."

In Japan, Inoue and Arai have dealt with Space Battleship *Yamato* in terms of the Japanese psyche, the culture and society, and even the economy. In short, Space Battleship *Yamato* is fertile ground for archetypal research, a story of the renewal of the earth.

Battleship *Yamato,* Some Background History

Before I discuss Space Battleship *Yamato*, I would like to briefly touch on the real battleship *Yamato* of the Imperial Japanese Navy, because I think that her tragic history essentially affects the anime. Before the Second World War, the Japanese believed in the invincibility of its battleships, after the victory in Tsushima against Russia in 1905. The belief drove the Japanese navy to build "the largest and strongest battleships in the world," including the *Yamato*, increasing international tension in the 1930s (Nagasawa, 2007, p. 63). Ironically, however, the Pearl Harbor attacks showed that she was an anachronism. *Yamato* did not actually play a significant role during the war, especially after Japan lost command of the air, and she was called the "*Yamato* Hotel," staying in the *Seto* Inland Sea. Near the end of the war, naval officials decided to send her to Okinawa to keep up appearances. Some, however, realized that the operation was suicidal. Indeed, in April 1945, *Yamato* was sent on a suicide mission, a so-called *Tokko*.

On April 7, attacked by nearly 400 planes for two hours, *Yamato* sank with her commander-in-chief, Sei-ichi Ito, and about 3000 crew members (Yoshida, 1952). As Drazen (2003, p. 205) notes, "This event marked the end of the Imperial Japanese Navy." Since, at the time, the existence of *Yamato* and this event were confidential in Japan, people learned about it much later from Yoshida's work, *Requiem for Battleship Yamato* (1952, Miner, 1985, trans.). Thanks to Yoshida's work, *Yamato*'s tragic history has become well known in Japan. The story tends to be referenced in terms of the grace of the "Japanese spirit." Thus, people sympathize with those who accepted their "meaningless" death and glorify their sacrifice. At the same time, this sentiment means Japanese do not examine their past faults and do not seriously learn from them.

The Story of Space Battleship *Yamato*

Against this background, Space Battleship *Yamato* has many different versions and sequels. To limit my discussion, I use only one text, the first comic by Reiji

Matsumoto (1975). In 2199 AD, the Earth is attacked by *Gamirasu*, a distant planet led by President Dessler, because they need a new home. The radiation from *Gamirasu*'s planet bomb forces everyone on earth underground. Captain *Okita*, age 52, the last star force commander, wages war against *Gamirasu* around Pluto, but he is defeated and loses all his battleships and soldiers, including his son, due to *Gamirasu*'s superior military power and technology. In this battle, *Mamoru Kodai* carries out a suicide mission, defying *Okita*'s retreat order. *Okita* loses his son in the battle, like the real-life Ito. With no escape from the radiation, all life on earth seems doomed to disappear in one year. Meanwhile, *Susumu Kodai*, age 18, who is on Mars as a trainee, finds a strange, beautiful woman, *Sarsha*, dead. She is bearing a message capsule from *Starcha*, queen of *Iscandar*, 148,000 light years away. In the message, *Starcha* invites people to use a device called the *Cosmo Cleaner*, which will remove radiation from the earth. She also supplies plans for a Wave Motion Engine by which they can travel to *Iscandar*.

Although *Susumu* has a conflict with Captain *Okita* because he thinks that *Okita* is responsible for the death of his brother *Mamoru*, he becomes a leader of Space Battleship *Yamato*. Thus the *Yamato* of the Imperial Japanese Navy is transformed into a space battleship loaded with the *Wave Motion Engine*. With key crew members *Yuki Mori*, age 18, a radar operator, and nurse *Daisuke Shima*, the same age, chief navigator, and Dr. *Sado*, age 47, a medical officer, the spaceship reaches *Iscandar* and returns to earth with the *Cosmo Cleaner* within one year. The earth is renewed. However, rejecting treatment for his radioactive illness, *Okita* shares confidences with the crew, except Dr. *Sado*, and dies just before her return (Matsumoto, 1975).

Okita as Hero in the Samurai Tradition

The comic's target is young boys: however, interestingly, the true hero of the story is Captain *Okita*, not *Susumu Kodai*. In US comics, films, and TV programs for children, the hero is typically a tough young man, a 52-year-old man being out of the question. Although *Okita* has no special fighting ability, he is called "a great brave man" (Matsumoto, 1975, p. 164), and "a great warrior of the earth" in the story (ibid., p. 203).

Levi (1996, p. 76) noted that Westerners cannot understand Japanese anime without learning first about Japanese culture, for example, about the tragic heroes of the "*samurai* tradition." She cites the example of *giri*, one of the *samurai* virtues, embodied in *Okita*. *Giri* means a "feudal concept of duty or obligation" (ibid., p. 160), and it entails the sacrifice of individual happiness and, if necessary, of life itself.

Arai (2010, p. 76) suggests that *Okita*'s name is taken from that of a young *samurai*, *Soji Okita* (1842 or 1844–1868), famous for his sword-fighting skills and loyalty to the *Tokugawa* Shogunate during the Meiji Restoration. Drazen (2003, pp. 104–116) has usefully explained that the *samurai* code of *bushido*, the way of the warrior, is based on stoicism, influenced by Confucius. This was the principle followed by the Japanese Imperial Army, as we see in *Requiem for Battleship Yamato*. It suffuses the plot of the anime, where "peace and the rescue of the earth" are carried out with an "elegiac mood" (Napier, 2001/2005, p. 13).

In Jungian psychology, the hero archetype is significant. Jung (1911–1912/1952, para. 251) notes that, "the finest of all the libido is the human figure, conceived as a demon or hero." Campbell (1953, p. 16) mentions in his work dealing with this archetype, that the hero is the man of self-achieved submission, but submission to what? His answer is that, "Typically, the hero of the fairy tale achieves a domestic, microcosmic triumph, and the hero of myth a world-historical, macrocosmic triumph ... the latter brings back from his adventure the means for the regeneration of his society as a whole" (ibid., pp. 37–38).

According to Arai (2010, p. 190), the *Yamato* story describes an apocalyptic situation, with elements of the plot of Gilgamesh in ancient Mesopotamia and of the Holy Grail legend of King Arthur. It also reminds us of the Golden Fleece, as the name of the battleship was altered to *Argo* in the American TV series. It is, thus, an essentially mythological story, like *The Journey to the West*, based on *The Great Tang Record on the Western Regions*, by monk *Xuanzang* of the *Tang* Dynasty in the sixth century, a story about carrying important Buddhist scriptures on a 16-year journey through savage wilds. Similarly, the crew of Space Battleship *Yamato* travel to the farthest reaches of space, where no one has ever been, to find the *Cosmo Cleaner*. As Jung (1954a, para. 72) expresses it, "Anyone who follows this horse comes into the desert, into a wild land remote from men – an image of spiritual and moral isolation. But there lie the keys of paradise." Seen in this light at the end of the story, Campbell states (1953, p. 356):

> The last act in the biography of the hero is that of the death or departure. Here the whole sense of the life is epitomized. Needless to say, the hero would be no hero if death held for him any terror; the first condition is reconciliation with the grave.

Thus *Okita*/Ito represents an ideal *samurai* and an archetypal image of a hero because he sacrifices himself.

In addition, the figure of the demon, in Jungian terms, can also be elaborated. The enemy of Captain *Okita*, President *Dessler*, is a handsome, gentle, and intelligent man, unlike the usual enemy in US comics. He is a competent governor. With his planet facing destruction, he tries to rescue his people from an apocalyptic situation.

On the other hand, it is often noted that *Gamirasu* is a modified version of Nazi Germany (cf. Saito, 2001, p. 158). Arai (2010, p. 174) notes that too much belief in science leads to Space Imperialism. The philosophy of *Dessler* expresses another figure who personifies a shadow aspect of the hero. Regarding this, Campbell (1953, p. 15) states:

> The figure of the tyrant-monster is known in the mythologies, folk traditions, legends, and even nightmares, of the world; and his characteristics are

everywhere essentially the same. He is the hoarder of the general benefit. He is monster avid for the greedy rights of "my and mine." [T]he inflated ego of the tyrant is a curse to himself and his world.

Interestingly, Captain *Okita* and President *Dessler* respect each other, and their covert communication implies a connection between positive and negative aspects of the hero, or between consciousness and unconsciousness. This gives dynamism to the story, touching psychic depths as it does so.

The Bildungsroman of *Susumu Kodai*

Susumu Kodai, age 18, is an average boy. Since *Yamato* is largely meant for boys, many important characters are young people, such as high school students in normal classrooms. Boys can identify with this story because it reflects the real state of the Imperial Japanese Navy at the end of the Second World War, and they can see how boys of their age were tragically sacrificed. This arouses both sympathy and nostalgia.

Susumu is lonely and hurt by his brother's death, so he argues with Captain *Okita*, struggling to find meaning in the war, making thoughtless mistakes in the process. His behavior is "unstable" (Arai, 2010, p. 202), like that of a typical adolescent. However, *Susumu*, which means "progress" in Japanese, grows up during the journey, assisted by the cool, rational *Daisuke*, his positive shadow, and his anima, *Yuki*. Thus Arai calls the story a *bildungsroman*. From this viewpoint, *Okita* functions as the wise old man, or, in Jung's terms, "the superior master and teacher, the archetype of the spirit" (Jung, 1954a, para. 74), leading *Susumu* to adulthood. For Arai (ibid., p. 99) *Okita* "symbolizes patriarchy" implying that the masculine Japanese collective consciousness is based on the *samurai* tradition. Campbell proposes that when a boy unifies with the father through initiation, he becomes a hero and succeeds his father's position. Thus, after *Susumu* compromises with *Okita*, he confronts President *Dessler* as the deputy Captain of the *Yamato*. Here we see another archetypal image, that of a young hero, who overcomes a father–son conflict.

Yuki as Eternal Virgin

However, women are also involved. Yokoyama (1995, p. 163) has studied their role in *samurai* society. According to him, after *Yoritomo Minamoto* (1147–1199) established the first *samurai* government in 1192, society was grounded on a strong patriarchal principle influenced by Confucianism. Women were forced to submit to men absolutely. Their status did not change, even after the Meiji Restoration (ibid., p. 171).

In light of this, it is interesting to examine *Yuki*, the heroine of *Yamato*. Levi (1996, p. 123) has expressed, "In Japan, women tend to go around sexist institutions rather than to confront them … *Yuki Mori* and *Misa Hayase* never seemed troubled by the fact that they were surrounded by men." Saito (2001, p. 160) has noted that

Space Battleship *Yamato* is typical of "the lone woman story." *Yuki* is the "only woman accepted into a patriarchal society," (ibid., p. 9) as she is always "young and pretty" (ibid., p. 49). Indeed, at the beginning of the story, Dr. *Sado* says to her, "You, a woman, are not supposed to look into an operating room," in spite of the fact that she is a nurse! Yet he tells another male crewmember, "She is brilliant, isn't she? I accept beauty alone in the medical area." Such bald sexism in anime for children merely reflects the real state of gender roles in Japan, and circumstances have not changed substantially.

According to Saito (ibid., p. 160), *Yuki* is a typical "workplace flower," more decorative than practical. She is engaged in radar operations and nursing, so-called "pink" jobs. Her interests are exclusively in erotic and romantic areas, her ultimate purpose to find a boyfriend (ibid., p. 161). At critical stages in the story, she acts only out of her love for *Susumu*. *Yuki* arbitrarily operates the *Cosmo Cleaner* to help *Susumu*, but she dies in an accident due to the device's imperfections (Matsumoto, 1975, p. 233).

The motif of women sacrificing themselves to achieve men's purposes is familiar to Japanese artistic expression from the time of *Kojiki*. Her Augustness Princess *Otö-tatibana*, a wife of *Yamatö-takeru-nö-Mikötö*, which literally means a brave hero of *Yamato*, drowns herself to help her beloved husband complete his eastern expedition, leaving behind a love poem for him. Her sacrifice is connected to Japanese national unification under the legendary Emperor *Keiko*, father of *Yamatö-takeru* (*Kojiki*, 1968, pp. 241–243). In this light, we can understand Inoue's (2004, p. 68) admiration for *Yuki*'s sacrifice, since it contributes to saving the earth.

Later, *Yuki* miraculously revives just before *Yamato*'s return to the earth (Matsumoto, 1975, p. 239). *Yuki* could personify the archetype of the eternal virgin. The name *Yuki* means "snow" in Japanese, which symbolizes her purity and chastity. At the same time, she is a mother figure, a caregiver for the crew. She, thus, functions as a highly idealized male projection, an erotic image of a virgin mother.

Starcha and *Yamato* Itself as Great Mother

In *Journey to the West*, it is Buddha who always supports the characters. Similarly, in Space Battleship *Yamato*, *Starcha*, queen of *Iscandar*, behaves like the Buddha. Although her planet is dying, she does not do anything to rescue it, unlike President *Dessler*. Instead, she sends *Sarsha*, her only sister, to earth, but she dies on Mars at the beginning of the story (Matsumoto, 1975, p. 20). Nevertheless, *Starcha* kindly offers to provide everything that people on earth need. When *Yamato* experiences crises, *Starcha* suddenly appears and helps, without any explanation about why she is so generous. Jung (1954b, para. 156) notes of such selflessness that, "Like any other archetype, the mother archetype appears under an almost infinite variety of aspects," adding, "Other symbols of the mother in a figurative sense appear in things representing the goal of our longing for redemption" (ibid., para. 156). *Starcha* symbolizes such a longing. Jung (ibid., para.158) continues, "The qualities associated with [the mother archetype] are maternal solicitude and sympathy." We see this in

Starcha's mercy which seems infinite, reinforced by the image of *Iscandar* as a beautiful planet mostly covered by the sea (Matsumoto, 1975, p. 217), since maternity and the feminine are so deeply related to water. *Starcha* is the lonely queen of a world where everyone has died (ibid., p. 221), but is also a cosmic mother. As Jung (1954b, para. 158) elucidates, "The place of magic transformation and rebirth, together with underworld and its inhabitants, are presided over the mother." When the masculine, represented by *Okita*, interacts with the feminine, embodied by *Starcha*, rebirth is achieved through their sacrifice.

Another important symbol of the mother archetype in the story is the space battleship *Yamato* itself. Like Noah's Ark, *Yamato* is a container and an incubator in which something new grows, which is cherished and sustained. *Yamato* is a battleship, but rarely uses her main weapon, the wave motion gun, to attack, but defensively, to withstand crises. Unlike her namesake of the Imperial Japanese Navy, which symbolized destruction, war, and powerful masculinity, and which became a huge coffin for young men, the renewed *Yamato* in the anime is a symbol of rebirth, peace, and generous maternity.

Nevertheless, there is a serious psychological problem in the story, namely that there are no negative aspects of the mother archetype. This means that *Starcha* is a projection of men's extraordinarily "ideal" feminine image of a virgin goddess and, necessarily, a reflection of the inflated collective consciousness of patriarchal Japan.

Space Battleship *Yamato* and Japan in the 1970s

Finally, I would like to mention the social context of the 1970s, when Space Battleship *Yamato* became popular. Napier (2001/2005, p. 12) discusses Japanese anime by categorizing: "I intend to look at the variety of anime in terms of three major expressive modes that I have termed the apocalyptic, the festival, and the elegiac." Arai (2010, p. 189) also mentions the apocalyptic, calling representations of the earth in ruins a popular sub-cultural motif. Regarding Japan in the 1970s, Inoue (2004, p. 58) states, "When Space Battleship *Yamato* was born it was a chaotic time turning into a quagmire with the oil crunch." Arai (ibid., p. 198) emphasizes the prevailing frustration, noting that the campus political movements of the 1960s generally ended in disillusion: "If the 1960s felt like a time something new was produced from destruction and confusion, the 1970s felt like a time when everything was getting worse. Belief in science declined and people indulged in irrational and mystic things."

I, too, have previously discussed the spiritual crisis of this period: "While Japan was recovering from its defeat in the war, at least economically, it introduced a Western democratic system. The traditional Japanese psychic identity, supported by conservative Buddhist or Confucian notions, became unstable" (Nakamura, 2014, p. 246). To summarize, Japan in the 1970s was in political, psychological, and spiritual crisis. Of such a situation, Jung (1927, para. 275) commented:

Today religion leads back to the Middle Ages, back to that soul-destroying un-relatedness from which came all the fearful barbarities of war. Too much soul is reserved for God, too little for man. But God himself cannot flourish if man's soul is starved. The feminine psyche responds to this hunger, for it is the function of Eros to untie what *Logos* has sundered. The woman of today is faced with a tremendous cultural task – perhaps it will be the dawn of a new era.

However, this is expecting too much of women; in the same vein, Hayao Kawai, the first Japanese Jungian analyst, asserted that Japan is a maternal society (Kawai, 1976). Regarding this spiritual crisis, I think that Space Battleship *Yamato* offers another perspective. Yes, Japan was defeated in the war, but in the anime, the Japanese (as represented by the crew of Space Battleship *Yamato*) can save the earth by virtue of the *samurai* spirit, while comforted by an archetypal mother figure. According to Arai (2010, p. 190), this is akin to Christian eschatology in its focus on rebirth and utopia.

Meanwhile, concerning the social situation of the US in the 1970s, Kelts (2006, p. 37) states:

> If manga and anime emerged as underground expressions of trauma in Japan, then their sudden popularity in the United States today means that we are finally voicing in our conversations about atomic bombs ... the cultural upheavals of the 1960s and 1970s, and the violence, the uncertainties and fears of the twenty-first century. Japan's popular culture is speaking to us in a visual and psychological language that we may find fresh and entertaining – but it may also be telling us something we need to hear.

Thus, the final victory over *Gamirasu* may have reminded Americans of their success against Nazi Germany, but the impetus was anxiety about their failure in Vietnam.

Conclusion

It is clear that Space Battleship *Yamato* is an expression of "universal themes and images" (Napier, 2001/2005, p. 10). We can understand the success of the ship as grounded in mythological motifs that are suffused with nostalgia and important archetypal images, such as the hero, father, wise old man, eternal virgin, and great mother, which are evoked by "external historical conditions" (Jung, 1954a, para. 49), namely the apocalyptic mood in the 1970s.

References

Arai, H. (2010). *Uchusenkan Yamato to 70 Nendai Nippon* [Battleship *Yamato* and Japan in the 70s]. Tokyo: Shakihyoronsya.

Campbell, J. (1953). *The Hero with a Thousand Faces*. New York: Bollingen.

Drazen, P. (2003). *Anime Explosion! The What? Why? & Wow! of Japanese Animation*. Berkeley, CA: Stone Bridge Press.

Hagio, M. (1985). "Hanshin," [Half God] in *Hagio Moto Sakuhin Syuu* [Collected Works of Hagio Moto, Vol. 9]. Tokyo: Shogaku-kan.

Inoue, S. (2004). *Anime Generation Yamato kara Gandamu heno Anime Bunkaron* [*Anime Generation: A Cultural Critique of Anime from Yamato to Gandamu*]. Tokyo: Syahakihyouronnsya.

Jung, C.G. (1911–1912/1952). "The Origin of the Hero," in *Collected Works*, Vol. 5, *Symbols of Transformation* (2nd edn). New York: Princeton University Press.

Jung, C.G. (1927). "Women in Europe," in *Collected Works*, Vol. 10, *Civilisation in Transition* (2nd edn). London: Routledge and Kegan Paul, 1991.

Jung, C.G. (1929). "The Significance of Constitution and Heredity in Psychology," in *Collected Works*, Vol. 8, *The Structure and Dynamics of the Psyche* (2nd edn). New York: Princeton University Press.

Jung, C.G. (1936–1937). "The Concept of the Collective Unconscious," in *Collected Works*, Vol. 9i, *The Archetypes of the Collective Unconscious* (2nd edn). New York: Princeton University Press.

Jung, C.G. (1954a). "Archetypes of the Collective Unconscious," in *Collected Works*, Vol. 9i, *The Archetypes and the Collective Unconscious* (2nd edn). New York: Princeton University Press.

Jung, C.G. (1954b). "Psychological Aspects of the Mother Archetype," in *Collected Works*, Vol. 9i, *The Archetypes and the Collective Unconscious* (2nd edn). New York: Princeton University Press.

Kawai, H. (1976). *Boseisyakai Nihon no Byori* [The Pathology of the Maternal Society of Japan]. Tokyo: Chuo Koron Sha.

Kelts, R. (2006). *Japanamerica: How Japanese Pop Culture has Invaded the U.S.* New York: Palgrave Macmillan.

Kojiki (1968). Donald Philippi (trans.). Tokyo: University of Tokyo Press.

Kuwabara, T. (1999). "Kyoudai Shimai" [Siblings], in Y. Yamanaka, Y. Hashimoto, & R. Takatsuki (eds.), *Shinema no naka no Rinnsyou Shinnrigaku* [Clinical Psychology in Cinema]. Tokyo: Yuikaku, pp. 149–164.

Lamarre, T. (2009). *The Anime Machine: A Media Theory of Animation*. Minneapolis, MN: University of Minnesota Press.

Levi, A. (1996). *Samurai from Outer Space: Understanding Japanese Animation*. Lima: Carus.

Macias, P. & Mochiyama, T. (2004). *Cruising the Anime City: An Otaku Guide to Neo Tokyo*. Berkeley, CA: Stone Bridge Press.

Macias, P. & Mochiyama, T. (2006). *Otaku in USA: Ai to Gokai no Yunyushi* [Otaku in the USA: A History of Love and Misunderstanding]. Tokyo: Ootashuppan.

Matsumoto, R. (1975). *Uchu Senkan Yamato, Volume 1, Daichohen SF comics*. Tokyo: Akitashoten.

Nagasawa, M. (2007). *Senkan Yamato to Nihonjin Senkan Yamato towa Nihonjin ni totte Naninanoka* [What is battleship *Yamato* for the Japanese?]. Tokyo: Kojinsya.

Nakamura, I. (2006). "Preface," in I. Nakamura & M. Ono (eds.), *Nihon no Poppower Sekai wo Kaeru Contents no Jituzo* [Japanese Pop-Power, Its Real Contents Changing the World]. Tokyo: Nihon Keizai Sinbunsha, pp. 15–22.

Nakamura, K. (2014). "Goddess Politics: Analytical Psychology and Japanese Myth," *Psychotherapy and Politics International*, Vol. 11, No. 3, pp. 234–250.

Napier, S.J. (2001/2005). *Anime from Akira to Howl's Moving Castle: Experiencing Contemporary Japanese Animation*. New York: Palgrave Macmillan.

Portes, G.P. & Haig, E. (2013). "Seeking a Methodology the Analysis of the Influence of Anime on Brazilian Youth: A Post-Jungian Approach," *Matrizes*, No. 7, pp. 247–262.

Saito, M. (2001). *Ko Itten Ron* [Theory of the Lone Woman Heroine Figures in Anime and SF]. Tokyo: Chikuma Shobo.

Schodt, F. (1996). *Dreamland Japan: Writings on Modern Manga*. Berkeley, CA: Stone Bridge Press.

Tsuge, Y. (1985). *Red Flowers*, *Raw* magazine, 7.

Yokoyama, H. (1995). *Shinwa no naka no Onnna-tachi Nihon Syakai to Joseisei* [Women in Myths Japanese Society and the Feminine]. Kyoto: Jinbun Shoin.

Yoshida, M. (1952, 1974, 1994). Senkan *Yamato* no Saigo [The End of Battleship *Yamato*]. R.H. Miner (trans.) (1985). *Requiem for Battleship Yamato*. Tokyo: Kodansya.

15

PROMETHEUS IN OUR MIDST

The Planet's Overdependence on Oxygen

John Demenkoff

Introduction as Personal Odyssey

"Take a deep breath please." With that simple request and a stethoscope's bell placed on the chest, I listen to air rushing in and out of my patient's lungs. These five simple words open doors not only to diagnosing a medical problem but they also serve as an entrée into the mysteries of life itself. I hear rales, rhonchi, and wheezes while visualizing oxygen molecules trickling down bronchioles, traversing alveoli, leaping onto hemoglobin molecules and finally disembarking at just the right destination. We need oxygen to live and in a real sense my entire professional life as a lung specialist has been dedicated to choreographing the balletic performances of this single molecule as it dances upon the human stage. I am fascinated by the supreme elegance of the lungs. As a pulmonologist, I have come to know firsthand how precious breath of life is and conversely how agonizing it is when lost through disease or neglect. One might say that my profession has given me a special and unique appreciation for the inherent tragic nature of life. Perhaps this is why I am so drawn to Prometheus who affirms and deepens such understanding.

The seeds of "Prometheus in Our Midst" were sown early. As a 25-year-old medical resident in a large Northwest teaching hospital, I saw many lives hang in the balance of our oxygen-dependent existence. Some survived and some did not. I have been reminded of the contingency and fragility of human life almost on a daily basis ever since. My interest in myth stems from the fact that it animates and amplifies the human response to life's limitations like no other modality. It was primarily for this reason that in 2007 I enrolled in the Mythological Studies program at Pacifica Graduate Institute. As I was about to begin my third year, however, in a moment of disquietude, I decided not to return to school. Over the course of the next several months, I began to regret my decision and literally pined for Pacifica. I assuaged my longing by reading Thomas Mann's mythopoetic masterpiece *Joseph and his Brothers* (Mann, 1943/2005). In addition, I immersed myself in the deep history of Planet Earth and read Lane (2002) *Oxygen: The Molecule that Made the World* and *Power, Sex, and Suicide, Mitochondria and the Meaning of Life* (Lane 2005). Here Lane skillfully spun a science-based narrative that tracked the evolution of Earth from a gas spewing orb to one spawning life that rivaled any creation myth I had studied at Pacifica. I also chanced upon an intriguing medical article titled "Oxygen in the Evolution of Complex Life and the Price We Pay" by Thannickal (2009).

If my readings were any indication, a titanic battle between the gods of science and myth were raging in my psyche. It was a battle I relished because intuitively I knew that deeply meaningful knowledge, no matter how it might be parsed, cannot be and moreover should not be hermetically sealed into separate magisterial domains. After all, I was a practicing physician dedicated to both the art and science of medicine, who in fact had always been moving seamlessly back and forth between the two. For me Pacifica, with its emphasis on root metaphor, analogy, and personification, reaffirmed affinities between the sciences and myth. To that list I hasten to add my personal experiences of wonder, fascination, and awe that science often evokes and myth inculcates. After four months, my psyche sufficiently transmuted by the alchemy of such diverse readings, I found my way back to Pacifica and ultimately graduated with a Ph.D. in mythological studies. Was not my sabbatical from graduate studies in fact a Promethean interlude, a visitation by the Titan himself? I think yes for I, like Joseph in Thomas Mann's exegesis, had emerged from a well renewed. The gods I have discovered can never be denied.

Renewal and Regeneration

The Promethean myth, apropos to the theme of the IAJS 2014 Jungian conference in Phoenix Arizona on Rebirth and Renewal, speaks not only to renewal but also to regeneration. The mythic narrative begins with the theft of fire by the Titan Prometheus from Apollo's lair atop Mt. Olympus. Humankind is the beneficiary of the god's largesse but counterbalancing this boon is Apollo's complaint of Zeus that sets in motion severe consequences. On Zeus's command Prometheus is summarily bound with chains and tied to a rock outcropping where a vulture pecks away daily at his eternally renewing and regenerating liver. Prometheus's ubiquitous presence throughout the course of human history prompted Kerenyi (1963) to label him as the archetypal image of human existence. For Jung, Prometheus symbolizes the renewing energy found deep within the psyche and becomes most apparent when an enantiodromia occurs.

> Psychologically, this means that the collective, undifferentiated attitude to the world stifles a man's highest values and becomes a destructive force, whose influence increases until the Promethean side, the ideal and abstract attitude, places itself at the service of the soul's jewel and, like a true Prometheus, kindles for the world a new fire.

> Jung (1923, para. 311)

FIGURE 15.1 Paul Manship's Prometheus perched above the skating rink at the Rockefeller Center. Note in his right hand the fire stolen from Apollo's liar on Mt. Olympus. Photo taken April 18, 2015 with author's iPhone 6 Plus

The centrality of this god in Western civilization is apparent even today. Tourists visiting the Rockefeller Center can see Paul Manship's sculpture of Prometheus poised prominently above the ice skating rink falling back to Earth clutching the stolen fire (Figure 15.1).

A god that survives in mid-town Manhattan can survive anywhere. Prometheus's theft has an audacity and boldness that rivals the New York City skyline. Indeed the god's renewing energy expressed in the phoenix-like structures arising from Ground Zero at the former World Trade Center site offers hope and succor to humanity. In a Darwinian sense the boon of fire guaranteed the survival of our species. Without this added source of renewing energy, we would have eventually died off, becoming a mere footnote among the many dotting an evolutionary landscape. Yes, Prometheus is in our midst; in the air we breathe, the water we drink, and the food we eat. He is part of our biology, psychology, and our physiology, our past, our present, and our future.

The eighteenth-century French chemist Anton Lavoisier (1743–1794) likened the Promethean archetype to a vital force, "the torch of life," whose ultimate source is the sun, "the fire stolen from heaven." He made copious use of myth and metaphor to explain his experimental results:

> The fire stolen from heaven, this torch of Prometheus, does not only represent an ingenious and poetic idea, it is a faithful picture of the operation of nature,

> at least for animals that breathe; one may therefore say, with the ancients, that
> the torch of life lights itself at the moment the infant breathes for the first
> time, and does not extinguish itself except at death.
>
> (Fruton, 1972, p. 262)

Since the time of Lavoisier, the paradoxes of life, death, renewal, and regeneration embedded within the Promethean *mythos* have launched a multitude of metaphors. Lives have been likened to candles blowing in the wind, easily snuffed out by the slightest breeze. In our busy day-to-day lives, we tend to burn the candle at both ends with often-times dire consequences. There is a price to be paid for our high octane existence. Besides its metaphorical meaning, "burn out" is a literal fact of life. In the end, as Lavoisier states, we merely flame out after a lifetime of incandescence that has amounted to nothing more than a very slow and steady burn.

What does the future portend for Prometheus? His mythic power of renewal will be most keenly felt in the fast growing field of regenerative medicine. It is unclear what the Greeks knew about the liver's capacity to regrow and regenerate. What is clear, however, is that an archetypal image emerged from the collective psyche of that culture to become a potent and transformative symbol across space and time. The resurgence of regenerative medicine may be a sign that we are now finally catching up with this myth. Perhaps myth has once again set the stage for the advancement of a novel science, stem cell biology being its most recent iteration.

The IAJS 2014 Phoenix conference tapped into this same zeitgeist, one that Hannah Arendt might have called a Promethean revolt (Arendt, H. 1958, p. 139). Presenters and attendees alike stole fire from the gods out of which new intellectual capital was minted.

Deep History, Mythic Time, and Time's Arrow

Given the remoteness of time and the sheer vastness of space, it has been left to scientists to hypothesize and conjecture about the deep history of Earth. One fact is certain, however, and that is for billions of years after the Big Bang planet earth's atmosphere was totally devoid of oxygen (cf. Lane, 2002, 2005; Thannickal, 2009; Falkowski, 2006, 2010; Raymond & Segre, 2005). How the first stirrings of organic life emerged from that initial gaseous abiotic abyss remains a mystery to this day. It would take evolution billions of years first to oxygenate the planet and then for sentience and sapience to eventually appear. Despite the constraints of the second law of thermodynamics, higher and higher levels of metazoan complexity appeared. According to time's arrow such complexification is a thermodynamic impossibility. Mythic time on the other hand, where order emerges from chaos, allows for fundamental paradoxes seen in the evolution of life forms.

To unravel this paradox, envision a spiral, unfolding in wider and wider orbs, that starts with our material origins and ends with the current state of sapience. Viewed along its central axis each 360 degree turn of the spiral expresses a leitmotiv, a variation of the original theme. The eternal return of the evolutionary spiral has an archetypal quality and is governed by mythic time. Viewed from the side, time's arrow presides as layers of increasing complexity are stacked one atop another along a vertical axis of historical time. The vulture eternally devours Prometheus's liver and is a symbol of mythic time whereas the theft of fire is a discrete event that brings to humankind the reality of time's arrow. That reality links the fullness of life with its denouement, death.

Beginning with the Big Bang, the complexity of life forms has increased exponentially, especially following planetary oxygenation 2.5 billion years ago (see Figure 15.2). While microbial life can easily live on without us we still remain dependent on the energy resources it provides through global catalysis and environmental transformations.

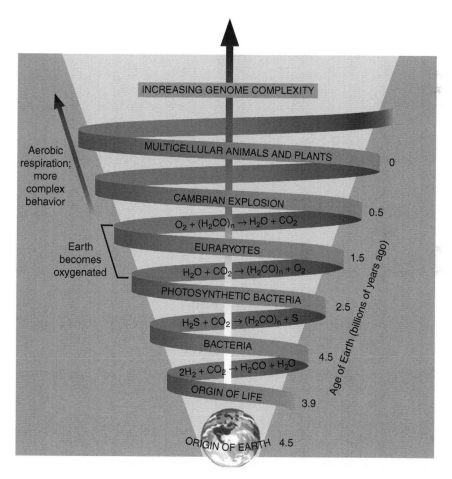

FIGURE 15.2 Beginning with the Big Bang, the complexity of life forms increased exponentially following planetary oxygenation that occurred 2.5 billion years ago

Image credit: P. Huey/Science

Time in both its mythic and historical forms is the defining feature of the lived world. We experience the latter as time's arrow, irreversible and inescapable, while the former, the mythic sense of time, is found in our memories, dreams, and imaginings. Travel between these two aspects of time is mediated by Prometheus who paid dearly for challenging the authority of the Olympic gods. By rebelling against Zeus and the hegemony of mythic time, he managed to link the sacred with the profane and in doing so provided a bridge between past, present, and future. In the final analysis, deep history is part science and part agreed upon myths. In the next few sections the overlaps of science with myth as reflected in the evolution of biological systems will be discussed in greater detail.

Myth and the Laws of Thermodynamics

Our lives are a recapitulation of the laws of thermodynamics whose first mythic iteration we find embedded in the amber of Hesiod's *Theogony* (c.700BCE/1991; Kerenyi, 1963.) From the second law of thermodynamics, we are told that in a closed system higher levels of chemical complexity such as DNA, RNA, and other macro-molecules are not possible. In closed systems, energy is conserved but entropy always increases and usable energy that is needed to construct increasingly complex molecules becomes depleted. Thus the ongoing synthesis of more complex macromolecules the hallmark of sentience and sapience, is stymied. Some other source of energy must be drawn upon to accelerate the chain of molecular complexity required to form the building blocks out of which life is hewn. Prometheus embodied such a force, one that provides biological systems and eventually the human race with enough energy to flourish and multiply. At the same time, he was a Titan, dialectically linked to the hegemony of the Olympic gods. Any challenge to their prevailing power structure would have, indeed did have, significant consequences. While Prometheus's heroism, the theft of fire, was a boon to humanity, there are consequences to relying on him as the primary energy source. In fact Prometheus's transgression has actually resulted in many medical maladies facing *Homo sapiens* today such as a whole host of degenerative diseases associated with the process of aging (Thannickal, 2009, 2010).

A central goal of this chapter is to unravel these medical paradoxes. First, I will review evolutionary studies that track the long and circuitous path that led to the emergence of planetary oxygenation. Second, I will present the pathobiology of aging and chronic diseases as an epiphenomenon of these very same evolution-ary pressures (Thannickal, 2010). In profound ways, the myth of Prometheus is intertwined with the very stuff of life manifesting both in the genesis of animated protoplasm and its ultimate demise.

Historical Accidents, Contingencies, and Opportunities

Some 3.5 billion years before Hesiod, the first traces of the Promethean myth swirled in the chaos of a newly born planet called Earth whose initial atmosphere was entirely devoid of oxygen. Given this constraint, any early life form had to have relied exclusively on non-oxygenic means for the production of energy needed for basic cellular functions. Electron donors and acceptors (manganese, sulfur, iron) unearthed from various geophysical phenomena (volcanoes, sand storms, earth quakes) sourced a primitive but robust microbiome (Falkowski, 2006; Falkowski, Fenchel, & Delong, 2008; Falkowski & Godfrey, 2008; Falkowski & Isozaki, 2008). Such raw materials were necessary for redox reactions that could generate proton gradients from which usable energy would be extracted (Falkowski et al., 2008). For the first billion years or so, these electrons shuttled back and forth across membranes of microbes in a process called non-oxygenic photosynthesis. With a series of incestuous lateral gene transfers the genomic infrastructure upon which this energy production was based continually diversified in response to changing microenvironments. Despite such evolutionary innovation the most abundant electron acceptor, water (H_2O), remained virtually untapped.

This changed 2.5 billion years ago when a single cell organism, a purple green bacterium called the cyanobacterium (Shi & Falkowski, 2008), cobbled together a genome that coded for not one but two interlocking photosystems. This genomic re-configuration gave rise to a system of macromolecules that could take photonic energy from the sun and split apart molecular water (H_2O). By the miracle of serendipity the elegant water–oxygen cycle was born and soon began to spin with more and more vigor, which ultimately led to what was called the Great Oxidation Event (Falkowaski, 2006). Abundant oxygen was now being released into the biosphere as a byproduct of oxygenic photosynthesis. What was stolen by Promethean macromolecules residing within the cyanobacter (aka green pond scum) was photonic energy, the mythic fire of the sun god Apollo. While oxygen from photosynthesis was a boon for planetary evolution, its combustible properties had a distinct Promethean taint, as I will explain.

Endosymbiosis

Moving ahead billions of years to the present, every cell of sentient and sapient beings contains an organelle that once was the regnant cyanobacter. Through an act of cannibalism eukaryotic cells phagocytized the cyanobacteria, which then morphed into the present-day mitochondria (Scheffler, 2008; Yang et al., 1985). It comes as little surprise that part of the highly conserved genome, one that codes for the macromolecules necessary for oxygenic photosynthesis, the *sine qua non* of the ancestral cyanobacteria, can be found today within mitochondria of each person.

With the incorporation of mitochondria and oxygen-based metabolism eukaryotic (mammalian) cells were able to evolve to higher levels of complexity. Paradoxically, though, such nanoscale combustion also sowed the seeds of cellular damage and eventual cell death (Allen, 2003; Scheffler, 2008; Thannickal & Fanberg, 2000; Ross, 2004). Buried deep within the churning energy centers of the mitochondria are proton gradients that are continually being generated and dissipated. The energy released from cascading protons is captured chemically in the bonds of ATP but the process generates toxic byproducts called free-radicals (e.g. super oxide anion, hydrogen peroxide, and hydroxyl radicals) (Fruton, 1972; Thannickal & Fanberg, 2000; Ross, 2004). Thus, the oxygen-based metabolic machinery bequeathed to mankind by the long sweep of evolution has toxic consequences of Promethean proportions. Our intracellular space, the cytosol, is perpetually bombarded by toxic/oxidative stress not unlike the vulture pecking away at Prometheus' liver. It is a wonder that we do not succumb to such oxidative stress much sooner than actuarial tables currently forecast. If it were not for the presence of a parallel system of endogenous anti-oxidants called the NADPH oxidase (NOX) system (Bedard & Karl-Heinz, 2007; Lambreth, 2007; Thannickal & Fanberg, 2000) we probably would all incinerate more rapidly than we currently do.

NOX and ROS: A Faustian Bargain

The genesis of the "Oxygen Paradox" arises from "Antagonistic Plieotropy" and "Disposable Soma," both of which are Promethean themes at play in the evolution of sentient beings.

The NOX system represents a family of anti-oxidant enzymes, namely superoxide dismutase, catalase, peroxiredoxins, and glutathione peroxidase (Bedard & Karl-Heinz, 2007; Lambreth, 2007; Thannickal & Fanberg, 2000). The potential damage done by free-radicals otherwise known as reduced metabolites of oxygen or reduced oxygen species (ROS) is counterbalanced by the NOX system (see Figure 15.3). In fact there appears to be a regulatory function of ROS such that a free-radical increase signals for NOX release. It is hypothesized then that vestiges of the NOX enzyme family must have predated aerobic metabolism thus protecting the cyanobacteria from self-destruction by its own ROS.

Indeed, the genome for NOX and its homologues is so highly conserved that they are implicated in a much broader range of cellular functions besides their role

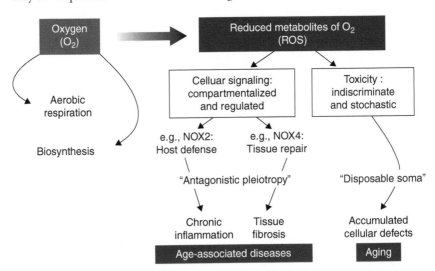

FIGURE 15.3 The genesis of the "Oxygen Paradox" arises from "Antagonist Plieotrophy" and "Disposable Soma," both of which are Promethean themes inextricably woven into evolution

as anti-oxidants. These include wound healing, the regulation of fertility, and control of immune responsiveness, all of which have well-defined survival benefits in mammals. The energetics of healing, fertility, and immunity are driven by a genome permeated by the supercharged Promethean *mythos*. Who has not been enthralled especially during the innocent years of youth by their own scraped knee as it festers, scabs over, and finally heals without leaving a trace of the initial trauma? The miracle of healing happens before one's eyes. It is as if human skin were imbued with infinite reservoirs of regeneration and rebirth. When a human egg and sperm unite, a whole new order of energetics erupts in a spectacle of Promethean pyrotechnics giving rise to a new being. The human immune system is so finely tuned that it responds in kind to insults both small and large. Once immunity is established, it stands ready to protect and serve with autonomous authority.

Yet what seems to have survival benefit at one stage in life, often acts in deleterious ways at another. Fastidious wound healing in youth seems to be a precursor to tissues fibrosis later in life. Cellular mechanisms that promote fertility are also major players in eventual cell senescence and death. Immune systems can and do spin out of control causing a whole host of autoimmune diseases. These examples exhibit a phenomena called antagonistic pleiotropy (Thannickal & Fanberg, 2000; Thannickal, 2010; Williams, 1957; Lambreth, 2007), the unintended negative consequences of ostensibly beneficial actions; Promethean boons that turn into busts. The vibrancy of youth gives way to wrinkled skin, aching joints, and "senior moments" due largely to the cumulative effects of oxidative stress (ROS) on our bodies. The boon of both NOX and ROS ultimately exact a high price thus etching a Faustian pattern on the human frame. True enough, only the fit survive, but the pearl of great price is that those so chosen will eventually perish.

Secularized Genesis Myth

What novel insights can the myth of Prometheus add to the burgeoning science of tissue regeneration? What did the early Greeks know about the regenerative potential of the liver and could they have possibly anticipated the miracles of modern medicine? We read now that a bioengineered trachea has been implanted in a two-year old girl in Peoria, Illinois (Fountain, 2013). Bladders, too, are being biologically re-engineered and retooled to replace damaged and diseased ones in humans (Parsons, 2006). More fascinating is a rat heart that is first de-cellularized with detergent and then eluted with stem cells. Within 30 days, those stem cells differentiate into new cardiac myocytes that begin contracting spontaneously. Thus a beating heart is regenerated *de novo* (Altman, 2008).

Most astounding is a novel bacterium that self-replicates called Germ 2.0. This particular organism, DNA and all, is made from scratch by the human hand, *ex machina* as it were, thus ushering in a new world order called synthetic biology (Garnett, 2013). These vignettes are from borderlands where imaginative science turns fictions into facts. Prometheus resides at the epicenter of this transformative mytho-science. Through its animating force, myth adds additional meanings and even a sense of purpose to the world in which we live. Much as the scientific approach eschews the taint of myth, it nonetheless valorizes purpose. In the final analysis, science is always in conversation with myth resulting in abundant overlaps and agreed upon truths. In sum, the history of planetary oxygenation and the ensuing evolution of metazoan complexity cuts two ways. On the one hand, it is a Genesis myth packaged and secularized by science; on the other, it is a science-based narrative infused with purpose that is further amplified and animated by myth.

A New Scientific Spirit

When spirit and science interpenetrate one another, a far richer picture of reality comes into focus. The energetics of a vulture habituated to devouring an ever-renewing liver is seen as a dynamo, a mythic power plant if you will. From a strict thermodynamic perspective, it is a far-from-equilibrium open system as opposed to a closed one that otherwise would wind down to infinite entropy and eventual heat death. Indeed, bits and pieces of mythic liver are removed, replaced, and reshuffled like a Rubik's cube whose ultimate solution is arrived at asymptotically. The regenerative capacity of Prometheus's liver is sourced by the same eternal spirit of Bergson's *élan vital*, Lavoisier's "torch of life," and the "green fuse" whose animating power poetically drove Dylan Thomas's flower (Thomas, 1937/2010, p. 9). The Promethean *mythos* affirms and defines life through its use of symbol, a mythic liver that continually self-regenerates. In doing so, myth and the science of far-from-equilibrium thermodynamics align as both resist the final resting place where elemental chaos is reduced to absolute zero.

Myth maintains a beating heart even in the face of the deepest freeze when life otherwise winds down and ceases to be. Though devoid of positivity and causality, the logic of myth is not absent from the domain of science. With a unique *telos* and truth, the Promethean myth weaves into the fabric of life, a *bio-logos* that mimes open systems characteristic of far-from-equilibrium thermodynamics. Historically, myth was sundered by Enlightenment-thinking from its soulmate matter. I am suggesting that this need not be the case for myth has always been positioned to join in a unifying scientific spirit.

Conclusion: The Titan Personified

One purpose of this chapter has been to offer a glimpse of such a unifying spirit by demonstrating that more than an ancient mythic personage, Prometheus is a ubiquitous presence that can be located in multiple loci within the human community. We see him in statuary at the Rockefeller Center and we also find him personified as iconoclasts in various scientific communities. Dr. Craig Venter, founder of The Human Genome Project, stands out in particular for hubris befitting a Titan. He is a leader in the field of genomics and proto-cell physiology who states in no uncertain terms "there's not a single aspect of human life that doesn't have the potential to be totally transformed by these technologies in the future" (Garnett, 2013).

Despite differences in style, the fundamental nature of Promethean figures is that they are game changers. They shift paradigms that allow science to move in new directions and to forge new discoveries that, like Prometheus, ultimately are for the benefit of humankind. At what price, however, one might ask? We are reminded of Goethe's *Faust*, a source of fascination for Jung, whose unbridled idealization of knowledge and experience was bereft of the psyche's imagination and soul. Jung's intuition was that the psyche is itself a self-regulating system that counterbalances such psychological one-sidedness. In addition, he believed that "society is essentially the individual psyche writ large … so a particular culture needs to readjust its collective perspectives through the agency of myth and symbol" (Walker, 2002, p. 20). Science has accomplished this through the work of "myth-makers" such as Copernicus, Darwin, and Einstein whose imaginative theories ultimately shaped cultures by altering worldviews. When creative imaginings emanating from the psyche harmonize with the real world then science becomes *de facto* agreed upon myths.

In the final analysis, it behooves society to be alert to the latest iteration of Prometheus. I intuit that the next Nobel Prize winner in science will have a Promethean streak running through his/her veins. The Greeks had more to offer than quaint stories and fanciful myths. The *Logos* that is embedded in the myth of Prometheus is not to be underestimated. Where is Prometheus today? In what ways will he/she manifest? The answers to these questions are not known, but when Prometheus does arrive, one can expect the status quo to be called into question and prevailing worldviews to shift like a Copernican revolution.

References

Allen, J.F. (2003). "*The Function of Genomes in Bioenergic Organelles*," *Philosophical Transactions of the Royal Society of London B*, Vol. 358, pp. 19–38.

Altman, L.K. (2008). "Researchers Create New Rat Heart in Lab," *The New York Times*, January 13, 2008.

Arendt, H. (1958/1998). *The Human Condition*. Chicago, IL: University of Chicago Press.

Bedard, K. & Karl-Heinz, K. (2007). "The NOX Family of ROS-Generating NADPH Oxidases: Physiology and Pathophysiology," *Physiological Review*, Vol. 87, pp. 245–313.

Falkowski, P.G. (2006). "Tracing Oxygen's Imprint on Earth's Metabolic Evolution," *Science*, Vol. 311, No. 5768, pp. 1724–1725.

Falkowski, P.G. & Godfrey, L. (2008). "Electrons, Life and Earth's Oxygen Cycle," *Philosophical Transactions of the Royal Society of London B*, Vol. 363, pp. 2705–2716.

Falkowski, P.G. & Isozaki, Y. (2008). "The Story of O_2," *Science*, Vol. 332, No. 5901, pp. 540–542.

Falkowski, P.G., Fenchel T., & Delong E.F. (2008). "The Microbial Engines that Drive Earth's Biogeochemical Cycles," *Science*, Vol. 320, No. 5879, pp. 1034–1039.

Fountain, H. (2013). "Ground Breaking Surgery for a Girl Born Without a Windpipe," *The New York Times*, April 30, 2013, p. A14.

Fruton, J.S. (1972). *Molecules and Life*. New York: Wiley, pp. 262–263.

Garnett, L. (2013). "Biology's Brave New World, The Promise and Peril of the Synbio Revolution," *Foreign Affairs*, November/December.

Hesiod. (ca. 700 BCE/1991). *Theogony*. R. Lattimore (trans.). Ann Arbor, MI: University of Michigan Press.

Jung, C.G. (1923). "The Type Problem in Poetry," in *Collected Works*, Vol. 6, *Psychological Types* (2nd edn). London: Routledge and Kegan Paul, 1989.

Kerenyi, C. (1963). *Prometheus, Archetypal Image of Human Existence*. Princeton, NJ: Princeton University Press.

Lambreth, J.D. (2007). "NOX Enzymes, ROS, and Chronic Disease: An Example of Antagnostic Pleitrophy," *Free Radical Biology and Medicine*, Vol. 43, pp. 332–347.

Lane, N. (2002). *Oxygen: The Molecule that Made the World*. Oxford: Oxford University Press.

Lane, N. (2005). *Power, Sex, and Suicide: Mitochondria and the Meaning of Life*. Oxford: Oxford University Press.

Mann, T. (1943). *Joseph and His Brothers*. J.E. Woods (trans.). New York: Knopf, 2005.

Parsons, A. (2006). "A Tissue Engineer Sows Cells and Grown Organs," *The New York Times*, July 11, 2006.

Raymond, J. & Segre, D. (2005). "The Effect of Oxygen on Biochemical Networks and the Evolution of Complex Life," *Science*, Vol. 311, No. 5768, pp. 1764–1767.

Ross, I.K. (2004). "Mitochondria, Sex, and Mortality," *Annals of the New York Academy of Sciences*, Vol. 1019, pp. 581–584.

Scheffler, I.E. (2008). *Mitochondria*. Hoboken, NJ: Wiley.

Shi, T. & Falkowski, P.G. (2008). "Genome Evolution in Cyanobacteria: The Stable Core and the Variable Shell," *Proceedings of the National Academy of Sciences of the USA*, Vol. 105, pp. 2510–2515.

Thannickal, V.J. (2009). "Oxygen in the Evolution of Complex Life and the Price We Pay," *American Journal Respiratory Cell and Molecular Biology*, Vol. 40, pp. 507–510.

Thannickal, V.J. (2010). "Aging, Antagonistic Pleitrophy and Fibrotic Disease," *The International Journal of Biochemistry and Cell Biology*, Vol. 42, pp. 1398–1400.

Thannickal, V.J. & Fanberg, B.I. (2000). "Reactive Oxygen Species in Cell Signaling," *American Journal of Physiological Lung Cellular and Molecular Physiology*, Vol. 279, L1005–L1028.

Thomas, D. (1937). *Dylan Thomas, Collected Poems*. New York: New Directions, 2010.

Walker, S.F. (2002). *Jung and the Jungians on Myth, An Introduction*. New York and London: Routledge.

Williams, G.C. (1957). "Pleitrophy. Natural Selection and the Evolution of Senescence," *Evolution*, Vol. 11, pp. 397–411.

Yang, D., Oyaizu, Y., Oyaizu, H., Olsen, G.J., & Woese, C.R. (1985). "Mitochondrial Origins," *Proceedings of the National Academy of Sciences*, Vol. 82, pp. 4443–4447.

16

ARCTIC CALVING

Birthing a New Vision of the Earth through the Symbol of Ice

Sarah D. Norton

Introduction: Arctic Calving as an Archetypal Image

As Jung (1954, para. 271) expressed:

> Not for a moment dare we succumb to the illusion that an archetype can be finally explained and disposed of. Even the best attempts at explanation are only more or less successful translations into another metaphorical language. (Indeed, language itself is only an image.) The most we can do is *dream the myth onwards* and give it a modern dress. And whatever explanation or interpretation does to it, we do to our own souls as well, with corresponding results for our own well-being. The archetype – let us never forget this – is a psychic organ present in all of us.

This explanation is one of many that Jung used to defined archetypes throughout his writings. This multifaceted approach helps to explain the fluidity of the archetype. These archetypes are universal patterns, which can be recognized in image form in nature, myth, dreams, and many other mediums utilized by cultures worldwide. In his essay "Wotan," Jung (1936, para. 395) wrote that archetypes are "like riverbeds which dry up when the water deserts them, but which it can find again at any time." Given this definition from Jung, I am inclined to say that the archetypes themselves are, in a sense, unknown to us; we can meet and recognize certain symbols, images, or patterns just as we can recognize a dry riverbed, but we can never fully grasp the volume of water that has flown through that channel at any given moment. The saying "you can never step in the same river twice" comes to mind; for me, this archetypal energy seems to constantly flow, through the river mouths of cultural boundaries and over the many rocks and logs of ages of human evolution. However, the water of the images and the associations one swims in will inevitably lead back to this energy source, lapping endlessly against the walls of the archetypal riverbed.

There are numerous references to water in texts by Jungian and post-Jungian writers, but very little that goes beyond the liquid form of this element. Water is a symbol of energy for the archetypes in many of these texts; in dreams, water can be a symbol for the life force, birth, and death; it can also be seen to represent the emotions, "spirit that has become unconscious" (Jung, 1954, para. 40), the unconscious itself, the collective unconscious, and much more. This collective unconscious is thought by Jung and post-Jungians, such as Hillman (1983) and Adams (2001) to house the archetypes, it is a place where these archetypal energies are born, live out their various patterns, and are accessed by each individual. Water is an important symbol, but what if this water of life becomes frozen? Does the water become inanimate and die, or is it reborn into a new symbolic life, retaining all it once was, and perhaps, becoming even more? In watching Robert Romanyshyn's short film (2012) *Antarctica: Inner Journey in the Outer World,* as well as the environmentally aware documentary *Chasing Ice,* it seems to me that ice is just as psychologically dynamic as water, especially when the ice is allowed to speak for itself through the images of these films and with the openness to symbols that Jung offers in the *Red Book* (2009).

By employing this openness to the image through Jung's process of active imagination, where the image is allowed to speak in its own unique voice, separate from ego consciousness, I began to realize that when the ice is allowed to speak for itself, it speaks with a voice from the unconscious. It not only becomes much more than the outward image that we can see in the films and paintings, it becomes a symbol (cf. Jung, 1923, paras. 814–821; Jacobi, 1959, pp. 74–124). It is born into a new and more mysterious form; it retains its outward appearance but begins to develop deep layers of meaning which connect it to the level of the archetypes; it becomes an archetypal image, which Jung referred to as a symbol. It also becomes a medium, navigating between the conscious and the unconscious, the inner and outer worlds; encompassing the dynamic water it once was, as well as its own new voice and form.

Cracking Open a New Understanding

The posthumous publication of C.G. Jung's the *Red Book* in 2009 was an exciting event. The first time I opened my copy, heard the spine crack as the huge pages fell open, and viewed the stunning images, I felt this text was an important creation for myself and others. Though Jung began writing the material within its large red cover almost a century ago, it seems to me the imaginal methods he used are finding relevance in our modern age. The most prominent of these is his process of active imagination. "Active imagination, as the term denotes, means that the images have a life of their own and that the symbolic events develop according to their own logic" but this, of course, comes with the caveat that this can only happen "if your conscious reason does not interfere" (Chodorow, 1997, p. 145). In active imagination, one gives the images of the unconscious an opening to connect, speak, and develop in their own way and time by setting aside conscious reasoning and ego consciousness for a while.

There is the rub! It is very difficult to block out our everyday hustle and bustle, or our need to control, long enough to allow the symbols to come forth. This is why, for me, the films mentioned above are such good resources through which to begin an imaginal exploration into this symbol of ice. The images of the ice-covered, seemingly endless landscapes, the towering cathedrals of frozen blue water, the unfathomable glacial bodies, and the patchworks of sea ice and icebergs floating in the still oceans can truly come to life. Similarly, in the *Red Book*, the symbols are brought to life through Jung's work with them but also through every new reader's imagination. These images are not just the intricately painted picture images, but the just as painstakingly detailed, calligraphy of the words. I believe that all these things are connected and each can add to the understanding of the other as well as the continued understanding of the self, and maybe, to some extent, even our understanding of the world in which we live.

The Images as Mediums

In his dissertation for medical school, Jung wrote a study of a family friend who held séances as a psychic medium. Jung (1961, p. 107) stated that after two years he became "rather weary" of this research after seeing some mediums "trying to produce phenomenon by trickery." However, in reading through his autobiography, it seems to me that this experience, earlier childhood experiences and dreams, and his mother's uncanny nature, had opened the possibility for Jung of something beyond what science could explain. Jung relays that he had the experience of two personalities within himself from a very young age, and felt the same was present in his mother. Eventually, this all culminated in his confrontation with the unconscious (Jung, ibid., p. 170) which expressed itself through the *Red Book* and other writings. These unconscious contents came to life for Jung in many journals called the Black Books and were subsequently illustrated in beautiful, vivid narratives and images for future readers of the *Red Book*.

In this publication, I have found an example of a true psychic medium, a mediator of sorts. No matter one's definition or experience of this phenomenon, one of truth or trickery, there is a boundary that is crossed by the medium. Whether the medium/mediator truly reaches into another realm to those passed on, or if the bounds of conventional thinking are merely stretched for a moment, the medium acts as a bridge across the archetypal river. In this way, we can see both banks of the river up close and personal, this medium/mediator allows one to dip their toes in the flowing energy of the archetypes from the conscious and the unconscious banks. In this way, a synthesis can happen, the archetypes can be experienced in their natural form as well as withstand the conscious ego's interpretation. The medium/mediator facilitates these encounters and keeps the connection strong; the archetypal images become this within the *Red Book* as well as in dreams, artwork, nature, and film. As Jung (1941, para. 293) explained:

> The archetype, because of its power to unite opposites, mediates between the unconscious substratum and the conscious mind. It throws a bridge between present-day consciousness, always in danger of losing its roots, and the natural, unconscious, instinctive wholeness of primeval times.

These images can connect us to the underworld; the images in the *Red Book*, the icy pictures in these films, the images in nightly dreams, and the embodied emotions that can well up during a time of silence, all offer a glimpse into the archetypal world beneath, the realm of the unconscious. Many connections weave in and out, the web can become confusing, the rivers flow obscured at times, but the journey continues just the same. My imaginal journeys into the images of icy landscapes and into Jung's images have shown me the powerful medium/mediator that image can become.

The Groaning Ice

The 2012 film *Chasing Ice*, is a documentary that follows the life of glaciers all over the world, turning years into seconds to illustrate the movement and melting of these massive bodies through time-lapse photography and video (Orlowski, 2012). It is a shocking film from an ecological standpoint, it was made to give solid proof of global warming, and it makes its point vividly. However, even in the midst of the sadness, the beauty of the ice comes through and is given new life. The majestic quality of the glaciers is awe-inspiring but to see the scale of these massive fields of ice and to watch them move is almost surreal. The scene that amazed me the most was when a massive piece of ice the size of lower Manhattan, "calved" off, broke, from the main body of the glacier. The sound was like nothing I have ever heard before; you could hear the groaning of the ice long before any movement began; it was as though the ice was giving birth. The term "calving" is a term of birth in cattle and other animals, so it is interesting that this is what scientists use to describe the phenomena. The labor and birthing of these "calves" continued for over 30 minutes. The groaning and cracking echo so loudly I could not believe this goes by unnoticed by most of the human world.

In this moment of the film, we experience an ancient being giving birth, the most ancient giving way to the newest, most beautiful blue sheets of ice. It was at once "'younger than all beginnings, older than all endings'" (Jung, 2009, note 203, p. 305). "Behind the ordinary the eternal abyss yawns. The earth gives man back what it hid" (ibid., p. 305). The passage of thousands of years locked in that ice, birthed new to the world through shockingly loud labor pains, groaning fit for the labor of Mother Earth. This is "the sound of frozen time crackling beneath … a sound I have never heard before. It is the sound of the ice releasing its frozen memories, a deep moaning sound" (Romanyshyn, 2012). This ice, which has been frozen for thousands of years, thawed slowly for decades, then was released in a splitting that would wake the gods. In the *Red Book* we see this experience illustrated in the image of the cosmic egg on page 135. Here we see ancient beasts at the foot of a tree. In the branches of the tree a crystal bursts forth, bringing with it an icy blue radiance that merges with the tree. All of this is held within the egg, a symbol of potential birth and new life. These images of ice keep the archetypal pattern of birth, death, and rebirth alive in the world, silently to most and powerfully to those who hear its groaning. It is one aspect of the archetypal symbol of water, brought to new life.

The Beautiful and Terrible Other

As Jung (2009, p. 238) himself so vividly expressed: "The spirit of the depths is pregnant with ice, fire, and death. You are right to fear the spirit of the depths, as he is full of horror." I have heard it said that with every birth comes a death; symbolically the death of the mother/parents, who they were before and who they must become now, are brought into full contrast at the moment of birth. In *Red Book* image 129 this archetypal struggle is illustrated by a fiery dragon and an icy starburst which expands to the edges of the page with cool blue rays. This dance of the fire and ice is beautiful; these forces are forever intertwined, each dragging the other to its extreme. In this image we see the death of an ancient being clearing the path for the birth of something new, each offering the other rebirth into a new form.

In Romanyshyn's film *Antarctica* this seems to be what the experience of the virgin landscape of the Antarctic brings, birth of a new consciousness and death of the old. The beauty of the landscape can cause this change all on its own, the "terrible and awful beauty of its towering forms" (Romanyshyn, 2012). In describing this landscape Romanyshyn referenced part of Rilke's poem (1923, p. 5), *The First Elegy*, where he described such beauty as "the beginning of terror" as it creates an awe we can "just barely endure" with all its cool disdain.

In my mind, it is the same way for the archetypes and archetypal symbols: to be truly effective, they must encompass all that is beautiful and terrifying; they do not adhere to our moral rules and regulations but go beyond them. In the same way the Antarctic, whose name can be translated to "the unknown southern land," offers a new look into the face of the unknown; it lends itself to the beauty and terror of the archetypal image of the "other," the unknown in the unconscious landscape. The archetypal aspect of water as entry to the underworld of the unconscious is found here, renewed in the white landscape of snow and ice.

The Silent and Eternal

I was present at a screening of Romanyshyn's film *Antarctica* (2012) for a class on "Imaginal Ways of Knowing," at Pacifica Graduate Institute in the fall of 2012. After the film, he kept the lights off and urged us all to separate into different parts of the room. He asked us to take the pose of "who within us was watching the film"; what part of our archetypal existence had peaked out to glimpse at those wondrous images? I felt as though I was still in a dream; I wandered to the corner of the room and knelt down. Sitting silently for a moment I felt my hands come together at my chest, my head bow, and felt warm tears streaming down my face. Suddenly I fully understood Romanyshyn's (2012) comment that:

> these frozen forms of wild beauty awaken a buried loneliness in me for something once known but forgotten, and a hunger to become again part of some ancient sense of the holy that seems to haunt this landscape and to linger in its strange simplicity. Looking at the penguins looking at the bleached bones of some ancient whale, I wonder if they are in prayer in some early morning of the world … I wonder if those penguins, in that posture of prayer, stir that part of me who, as a stranger to myself in this landscape, remembers that first morning of the world.

I felt a stranger within me stirring up tears, melting the ice within, if only for a few moments. As Romanyshyn (2012) eloquently expressed, "In the silence that surrounded me I felt the serenity of the surrender to something other and even alien to myself." "The I, who I am, [was] slowly dissolving. In [that instant] I did not know for a moment if I was dreaming or being dreamed." Jung (2009, p. 306) wrote of his own experience: "I cut down to the marrow, until everything meaningful falls from me … until I know only that I am without knowing what I am."

Water in dreams is a common symbol for emotion; but this frozen face of water reflected my own emotions more completely. This strange, yet familiar figure of ice, reached into my core and embodied the slowly thawing and breaking free of emotions which I have experienced, on occasion, erupting very unconsciously: emotion frozen in order to continue on in difficult times. The ice must melt for me to find connection to the personal and collective unconscious and "out of [my] heart shall flow rivers of living water" (*NT*, John 7:38). Emotions and feeling must find a way to break free, to be birthed into that great ocean that is everything, to find connection with myself and the other. The embodied experience of Romanyshyn's film presentation has stayed with me; the connection and interchanging nature of "I" and "other" as ice is thawing, the boundaries becoming more blurred both in my dreams and waking life.

The Animal of My Body

As these boundaries were melting, another pull began to emerge. I wanted to be in my body, just to be in the moment with my instinctual nature, as Jung (2009, p. 306) expressed it:

> I want to be poor and bare, and I want to stand naked before the inexorable. I want to be my body and its poverty. I want to be from the earth and live its law. I want to be my human animal and accept all its frights and desires.

When I read this passage in the *Red Book*, I was immediately reminded of that moment of conflict, to kneel in my animal body and feel that eternal core within, being more naked than the day I was born but so covered at the same time.

The conflict between merging the eternal with my mortal body is a never-ending, lifelong experience. To find the balance between the solid, the infinite, and the melting, calving ice within is a life's work. This imaginal path of knowledge has opened up another riverbed into which the archetypal energies flow. However, this is not a regular riverbed, it is a glacial valley. In this valley, the cracks, moans, and groans of birth can be heard for miles around. These birthing pains, which surround the elder bodies do not shake the solid core. They each know when their time will come to split off and what new gifts they will offer up to the world. When they thaw, an archetypal river will begin to trickle through the valley; ancient water will find new energy in its rebirth and flood the riverbed of the archetype with new energy. Each new iceberg will add to the vast body of the ocean; it will offer up knew knowledge to the collective of where we are individually and as a planet.

The Crystal Seed

A number of years ago, I had a dream in which I dove into a deep river of water to collect a beautiful green crystal from the riverbed below. The water was perfectly clear, there were amazing stone formations within the river, and lush green water plants everywhere. I dove deep, it must have been three stories beneath the surface but no matter how deep I went, the sunlight was still flowing in from above. Finally I saw the crystal, the sunlight hit the hard facets on its surface and a green glow reflected up like a prism. I continued my descent, reached out my arm to gather the crystal, and … I woke up. This image of the crystal stone has been a continuous one for me. Romanyshyn (2012) stated that "ice bewitches the human soul and its spells weave many dreams." When I began looking through the *Red Book*, I was bewitched once again. I found many images which reminded me of crystals (Jung, 2009, pp. 79, 133, 159). They were faceted in one way or another or very crystalline in nature.

The one that struck me the most, because it looked as if it leapt right from my dream onto the page, was the mandala on page 121: a large blue and white crystal surrounded by what looks like paneled green stone. This border is split into four and encircled by blue streams pouring forth from the crystal. As I looked more deeply into this image from my dream, I found myself wondering if this could be seen as a seed from the ice. As Jung (2009, p. 305, n. 230) expressed: "'This seed is the beginning, younger than all beginnings, older than all endings.'" Could this seed, appearing to me in dream and text, its dark green, almost to the point of blending to blue, be the ice that has been calling out to my unconscious self? I had always viewed this crystal as an archetypal symbol for that divine spark within, the circumference and the center of who I am, my Self. If this is still the case, then this would be my Self within the new symbol of the ice; before I had even seen ice like this Antarctic ice, the image was growing within me.

In the *Red Book* (ibid., pp. 305–306) there is a passage where Jung asked his soul to dive into the depths of floodwater.

> I called my soul and asked her to dive down into the floods, whose distant roaring I could hear ...And thus she plunged into the darkness like a shot, and from the depths she called out: "Will you accept what I bring?"
>
> From the flooding darkness the son of the earth had brought, my soul gave me ancient things that pointed to the future. She gave me three things: The misery of war, the darkness of magic, and the gift of religion. "If you are clever, you will understand that these three things belong together."
>
> "What will come to you lies within yourself. But what lies there!"

So, I saw my dream through Jung's own imaginal journey. The more I explore this idea of the ice, the more I can see all these things are connected. This is the soul or spirit being offered in the unconscious to consciousness, not lost there but found as treasure hidden within. Water is discovered in a new light through ice that is "water as spirit that has become unconscious" (Jung, 1954, para. 40) and becomes soul traveling in the unconscious.

A World of Ice

As was mentioned previously, the documentary *Chasing Ice* tracks the melting glaciers worldwide. Orlowski, the creator and director of the film, is a nature photographer. He wanted to show through film something only these live images can, how the face of the planet is changing due to our societal advancements. Through these time-lapse videos you can see what was once a massive glacier melt away, shrinking miles from where the filming began. The film hopes to show that we must honor the planet, to do all we can to eliminate the harmful levels of gasses in the atmosphere so that generations to come will have this beauty of ice to enjoy. Global climate change is a complex issue with many contributing factors. Orlowski has captured the truth of the matter in these images in all their terrifying beauty. The glaciers have always been melting, but it is only in recent years that they have started to disappear in such a noticeable way and could be captured on film. What can this sad and, at the same time, frightening reality say about the icy, crystalline depths within each of us?

Romanyshyn (2012) stated that the melting of the Antarctic ice is not only an environmental, political, social, and economic problem but it is also a "deeply psychological problem" as well. Having sat with the images from both these films and after having such a deep connection to them from within, I cannot imagine what would happen if they disappeared from this planet or from within each of us. Though most would say some melting, change, and release is psychologically and emotionally healthy, the loss of that arctic core could be detrimental; in Jungian terms, to lose our access to that unconscious seed would be devastating. Toward the end of his film, Romanyshyn (2012) showed a picture of the Antarctic ice. It is a large iceberg where the melting ice has been carving a path through the beautiful blue ice. Where the light is shining through from behind, a silhouette can be seen which resembles an anatomical heart. His narration which accompanies this image tells us that this is the blue heart of the ice, that the "beauty of this melting heart is like a wound that is a blessing … in its presence I feel for a moment as if I am on [my] way home." "Earth, isn't this what you want? An invisible resurrection in us?"

In the midst of all the chaos of life, it is important to find that quiet blue heart of the earth, to hear what it too has to say about where life on its body is headed. "In this place of quiet repose you can lose your mind and find your heart you deepen into feeling as you fade in and out between seeing and dreaming" (Romanyshyn, 2012). You may also find the heart of the earth in these quiet places. As Jung (1954, para. 37) directed us: "We must surely go the way of the waters, which always tend downward." We must take a look deep into that heart to find the quiet heartbeat within, the dripping flow of the archetypal all around us. The melting heart brings us back to our own heart and breath, as is above, so below; I believe if I have this heartbeat and breath and all the creatures on this planet do as well then the earth beneath our feet must also. As Jung (1954, para. 41) commented about water: it is "earthy and tangible … the fluid of the instinct driven body, blood and the color of blood, the odor of the beast, carnality heavy with passion." This connection to the living earth could imply also a soul to the earth, the *anima mundi*, which connects all. So this new archetypal symbol of the water and ice is one of the collective, and joins us all unconsciously.

The Ice as Itself

The images shared above carry forward the archetypal image of ice into a new imaginal realm. They carry us forward into a new

> world of water, where all life floats in suspension; where the realm of the sympathetic system, the soul of everything living begins; where I am indivisibly this *and* that; where I experience the other in myself and the other-than myself experiences me.
>
> (Jung, 1954, para. 45)

These images of ice bring us to a new understanding of our selves and the world in which we live, they become one more archetypal representation of water, the water of life, the life force energy of the archetypal images flowing through the riverbeds and glacial valleys of the archetypes themselves.

Conclusion: The Never-ending Ice

All these images take us on a journey that Romanyshyn (2012) described as an "uncharted meandering descent below the mind's fixed points of reference into the archaic layers of the soul for which there are no maps, no fixed coordinates, no well-worn paths." The images connect us to everything and nothing all at once. These pure white landscapes with hints of deep blue connect us to the earthly and the transcendent. It is "as much a landscape of the soul as it is of the world; as much a space of the imagination as it is a place on a map" (ibid.). In these landscapes a new perspective is born within each of us. These vast white spaces offer a moment where reflection and connection can occur.

They connect us to the beautiful seed of the Self, living within the ice and to the *anima mundi*, the world soul which surrounds us. This *anima mundi* is what Hillman (in Moore, 1990, p. 97) described as the "gods in their biological forms … [for] where better to find the gods than in the things, places, and animals that they inhabit." Hillman further stressed "how better to participate in them than through their concrete natural presentations." Here, the ice is that concrete presentation and it mediates for us, it facilitates a connection to the archetypes living in the world around us. In the final image of the *Red Book* (p. 169) we see this connection illustrated beautifully; here a crystalline form radiates, prism-like, onto a sea of human faces connecting and illuminating everyone.

Romanyshyn stated that: "Time and eternity are the architects of these wonders." This could also be said of the archetypes themselves, perhaps there is a great buried truth to the ice, and the surface that we see is only the image, the visible pattern of what lies underneath the surface, the gods alive within. The ice in these films and photographs is merely the image and pattern of the greater whole beyond. These images open to what Jung (2009, p. 305) described as "a quiet underground earthquake, a distant great roaring"; here "ways have been opened to the primordial and to the future. Miracles and terrible mysteries are close at hand. I feel the things that were and that will be." I feel this too in the face of the ice, in the blue heart of the Arctic, and within my own body, this dynamic movement is flowing. The ice becomes the medium, the mediator, the connection between the unconscious and consciousness, between my Self and the other, between the individual and the *anima mundi*. The archetypal face of this life giving water, one face of our planet, is reborn in the imagination of each human being as they stare at the inexorable ice and, in return, these renewed symbols reach out to each of us.

References

Adams, M.V. (2001). *The Mythological Imagination*. Putnam, CT: Spring Publications, 2010.

Chodorow, J. (1997). *Jung on Active Imagination*. Princeton, NJ: Princeton University Press.

Hillman, J. (1983). *Archetypal Psychology: A Brief Account*. Dallas, TX: Spring Publications, 1993.

Jacobi, J. (1959). *Complex, Archetype, Symbol in the Psychology of C.G. Jung, Bollingen Series*. Princeton, NJ: Princeton University Press.

Jung, C.G. (1923). "Definitions," in *Collected Works*, Vol. 6, *Psychological Types* (2nd edn). London: Routledge and Kegan Paul, 1989.

Jung, C.G. (1936). "Wotan," in *Collected Works*, Vol. 10. *Civilisation in Transition* (2nd edn). Princeton, NJ: Princeton University Press, 1970.

Jung, C.G. (1941). "The Psychology of the Child Archetype," in *Collected Works*, Vol. 9i, *The Archetypes and the Collective Unconscious* (2nd edn). Princeton, NJ: Princeton University Press, 1969.

Jung, C.G. (1954). "The Archetypes of the Collective Unconscious," in *Collected Works*, Vol. 9i, *The Archetypes and the Collective Unconscious* (2nd edn). Princeton, NJ: Princeton University Press, 1969.

Jung, C.G. (1961). *Memories, Dreams, Reflections* (Vintage Books edn). New York: Random House, 1989.

Jung, C.G. (2009). *Red Book: Liber Novus*, S. Shamdasani (ed.). New York: W.W. Norton.

Moore, T. (ed.) (1990). *The Essential James Hillman: A Blue Fire*. London: Routledge, 1994.

Orlowski, J. (2012). *Chasing Ice* [Motion Picture]. US: Diamond Docs.

Rilke, R.M. (1923). *Duino Elegies* (Bilingual edition). New York: North Point Press, 2000.

Romanyshyn, R. (2012). *Antarctica: Inner Journey in the Outer World* [DVD]. US: Self-distributed by R. Romanyshyn.

PART VIII

Mythopoetic, Psychological Dimensions of Rebirth and Renewal

17

VISIONARY AND PSYCHOLOGICAL

Jung's 1925 Seminar and Haggard's *She*

Matthew A. Fike

Introduction

C.G. Jung had much to say about several of H.R. Haggard's novels, especially *She* (1886/2006), the tale of a journey by Ludwig Horace Holly, his adopted son Leo Vincey, and their man-servant Job to present-day Mozambique where they encounter Ayesha (pronounced *ass*-ah), the *She* of the book's title, an ancient, virtually immortal, and fully veiled woman. In *Collected Works* Jung frequently referred to her as an anima figure and emphasized that the novel was an example of a "visionary" text. More extensive commentary appeared in his 1925 seminar (Jung, 1989), in which *She* was both homework assignment and discussion topic. Although the discussion clearly supported the visionary nature of Haggard's text, neither Jung nor his seminar participants identified it as such, and they offered much speculation about the novel's autobiographical (psychological) elements. In the mainstream criticism, there has been some mention of the transpersonal nature of Haggard's composition process but no mention of the 1925 seminar.[1] The present chapter, therefore, first establishes that Jung was correct in naming *She* a visionary text, and it then uses the visionary and psychological modes as a framework for explicating and correcting the statements that he and his colleagues made about the novel. A coherent theme unifies this analysis. Although the seminar discussion fell short in various ways, it properly suggested that, for Holly, there is no renewal. In confronting the unconscious, he does not achieve full individuation but instead, through projection, experiences *enantiodromia*, a swing from inveterate misogyny in England to anima projection and possession with Ayesha in Africa.

Haggard and the Visionary Mode

There are good reasons to consider *She* besides the fact that it was one of Jung's favorite novels. First, the book depicts a confrontation with the unconscious and the feminine. The decision to depart from Cambridge University, the ocean voyage to Mozambique, and the journey overland to Kôr enacted a transition from reason and intellect to the unconscious and the anima. Indeed, the ocean was Jung's frequent image for the collective unconscious, and Africa/Kôr (*coeur*) typically represents the feminine heart within the European. Haggard also seemed interested in exploring the ocean's connection with the anima, for Holly describes the sea as "heaving like some troubled woman's breast" (Haggard, 1886/2006, p. 73; ch. 4). Second, Jung in "Psychology and Literature" (1930, para. 137) identified *She* as an example of the "visionary mode" of literary production in which text comes through the writer from the collective unconscious versus the more workman-like psychological mode in which a high degree of conscious attention informs the composition. In "On the Relation of Analytical Psychology to Poetry" (1928, paras. 97–132), he called the psychological and visionary modes the introverted and extraverted processes of creation, respectively. Jung (1930, para. 157) stated, "In general, it is the non-psychological novel that offers the richest opportunities for psychological elucidation," and then he mentioned Haggard's novels as examples. The implication is that a higher kind of art results when a novelist reaches beyond his own life experience to imbue his work with elements of the archetypal human experience. The visionary mode, then, refers both to the author's mediumistic method of composition and the way in which a text deals with the archetypes, whereas the psychological mode figures forth autobiographical details related to the author's personal unconscious.

That Jung saw an archetypal-visionary dimension in *She* is certain because of the statements he made about Haggard. The point has been commented on by Sonu Shamdasani (2012, pp. 83, 144), who identified *She* as a visionary work, saw in the novel "clear examples of the play of archetypes," and noted that individuation's psycho-dynamics are not limited to highbrow literature. Jung (1963, paras. 1280–1281) considered Haggard to be "a latter-day troubadour or knight of the Grail, who had somehow blundered into the Victorian Age [1837–1901]" and stated that he "followed in the footsteps of the singers and poets who enchanted the age of chivalry." These statements implied that the author was serving a purpose greater than transforming his own psychological experiences into art. The point becomes clearer in light of Jung's (1963, para. 1281) statement that Haggard's work "provides a wealth of material illustrating the symbolism of the anima and its problems." Jung continued: "Admittedly, *She* is only a flash in the pan, a beginning without continuation, for at no point does the book come down to earth. Everything remains stuck in the realm of fantasy, a symbolic anticipation." In other words, the text is more than a literal narrative or an allegorical repackaging of the author's personal experiences.

In a statement unrelated to Haggard, Jung (1951, para. 270) might as well have been commenting on *She*: he noted the chthonic nature of "animals such as crocodiles, dragons, serpents, or monkeys." A crocodile kills a lion, Ayesha is frequently described in snake-like terms, Holly looks like a baboon, and *She* devolves into a primate in the climactic scene. Haggard's references to all of

Jung's mentioned creatures except the dragon suggested the underworld of the collective unconscious and signaled that the text is visionary rather than purely psychological. Moreover, after commenting on "the visionary experience," Jung (1930, para. 143) stated, "Rider Haggard, pardonably enough, is generally regarded as a romantic story-teller, but in his case too the tale is only a means, admittedly a rather lush one, for capturing a meaningful content." We know that the novel's "meaningful content" participates in the visionary mode because Jung (ibid., para. 142) stated that "this primordial experience is the essential content of Rider Haggard's *She*."

At this point, some clarification of terms is necessary. There is a difference between a literary work's psychological *content* and an author's psychological *intention*. Jung (1963, para. 1280) wrote:

> If Rider Haggard uses the modest form of a yarn, this does not detract from the psychological value of its content ... But anyone who wants to gain insight into his own anima will find food for thought in *She*, precisely because of the simplicity and naïveté of presentation, which is entirely devoid of any "psychological" intent.

Jung (1930, para. 137) considered *She* to be an example of "the non-psychological novel that offers the richest opportunities for psychological elucidation." Jung's position may appear to be black-and-white thinking. As Haggard's *She* bears out, the visionary and psychological modes are not a binary opposition but rather a matter of degree: there is no such thing as a *non*-psychological novel, one that reflects the author's subjectivity to zero degree. A more accurate formulation is that the novel illustrates the visionary mode because its content reflects the archetypal realm of the collective unconscious, more than (not rather than) the author's intention to create art based on personal experience. The visionary mode's twofold significance obtains here: a novel that comes through (more than from) the author has great relevance to a person's relationship to the collective unconscious. Paradoxically, what Jung called a non-psychological novel can convey serious psychological content.

Jung had little or no information about the author's life, but statements by Haggard and his friends support the conclusion that the novel is a visionary product. Haggard (qtd. in Ellis, 1978, pp. 104–105) commented, in particular, on the novel's composition in a six-week cascade of words between January and March of 1886. That Haggard was a conduit for the tale is clear confirmation of its visionary nature, and others have agreed that *She* came from beyond the personal unconscious. As V.S. Pritchett (qtd. in Katz, 1987, p. 125) stated, "Mr E.M. Forster once spoke of the novelist sending a bucket into the unconscious; the author of *She* installed a suction pump" (cf. Pritchett, 1960). Haggard himself (qtd. in Cohen, 1960, p. 203) recalled Rudyard Kipling's statement that Haggard, like telephone wires, brought *She* "from somewhere else." Jung would have no doubt that the "somewhere else" is the collective unconscious, and the image of the author as telephone wires is as good as any description of the visionary mode of literary production.

She and Jung's 1925 Seminar

Jung himself had a good deal to say about *She* as an illustration of the visionary mode, meaning that the novel reflects what is archetypal and transpersonal. In *Collected Works*, he mostly emphasized the idea that Ayesha represents the anima; however, a more specific interpretation appears in a footnote in "The Psychology of Transference" (1946, para. 421, n. 17). Here are Jung's somewhat allegorical interpretations. Leo is "a veritable Apollo" and the hero of the novel (the point about heroism is wide of the mark). Holly is "a paragon of wisdom and moral rectitude." Together, Leo and Holly represent the sun and its shadow, a probably unintentional pun, for Holly is overshadowed by his son's beauty and its benefits. Ayesha is Luna, so Leo and Ayesha together are the sun and the moon. Not to be overlooked, Job is "the faithful servant who ... stands for the long-suffering but loyal companion."

Jung (1997) in *Visions: Notes of the Seminar Given in 1930–1934 by C.G. Jung* offered more visionary bits and pieces that reflect the collective unconscious. Ayesha is "the high priestess of Isis" or at any rate "was something like a Greek goddess" (Vol. 1, pp. 596–597). A seminar participant named Dr. Harding viewed the tombs at Kôr as representations of "things that have been built up in the unconscious through the past ages" and that manifest themselves "through the anima or the animus" (Vol. 2, p. 1145). But most of the comments dealt with the novel's most significant geographical features. Speaking of the volcano into which Holly and Leo make their final descent, Jung claimed that they enter into a mandala (Vol. 2, p. 1142). The pillar of fire that lies beneath represents "the eternal cycle of death and rebirth which is always revolving in the unconscious" (Vol. 1, pp. 90–91). Here in "the womb of the earth" (Vol. 1, p. 411), the pillar of fire has characteristics akin to the collective unconscious: "It is the tree of life really, containing all beings, shrieking with the voices of all forms of life, animal and human, an amazing thing" (Vol. 1, p. 500). Holly's description of the pillar as a fountain of intellect and possibility confirms its connection to the collective unconscious (Haggard 1886/2006, pp. 257–258; ch. 25). Holly's temptation is to tap into the collective unconscious, the treasure trove of all human thought. The fire would enable him to keep his sanity and to have all the riches of human experience at his intellectual command—forever. *She* thus appears to be a visionary product with visionary content, namely, a direct confrontation with the collective unconscious.

Jung (1989) in *Analytical Psychology: Notes of the Seminar Given in 1925 by C.G. Jung* provides his fullest interpretation of *She*. Here as well, much of the discussion, though not all, reflects the collective unconscious in the visionary mode. Each of three groups was charged to come up with an analytical summary of its assigned text. Beginning in the psychological mode with the idea that Holly is "the conscious side of Haggard," Dr. Harding advanced the following interpretation based on his group's discussion (Jung 1989, pp. 136–137). Holly is about to give himself totally to intellectual pursuits but receives "the call from the unconscious" (presumably in the form of Vincey's request that Holly adopt Leo) and is forced "into a new orientation to life." This is good reading, for Holly says, "I was about to go up for my fellowship within a week" (Haggard 1886/2006, p. 40; ch. 1). So the tension is between "conventional morality" (the life of an academic) and "the thing that means life" (raising Leo). The group's point about the "call" may also relate to Holly's musing about the fossilization of faculty at Cambridge as he confronts the Amahagger for the first time (Haggard 1886/2006, pp. 89–90; ch. 6). The timing of Holly's reflection suggests that responding to the call from the collective unconscious requires getting in touch with his inner archaic man, whom the primitive people represent.

The group also reported the following points: Leo is Holly's youthful side, Ayesha is an anima figure, Kôr represents the unconscious, and the adventures there constitute "important mileposts on the way of [sic] Holly's psychological development." Dr. Harding concluded, however, on a somber note that supports the thesis of this chapter: "Holly is not ready for the fundamental change of attitude demanded of him. But he can never again be the commonplace person he started out as; something of the inner meaning of life has been found by him" (Jung 1989, p. 137). In other words, the journey leaves him somewhere between fossilization at Cambridge and individuation through anima integration.

Jung (1989, pp. 138–144) discussed the novel with the seminar participants and shared his own extensive interpretation, which focuses both on Haggard's personal unconscious (the psychological mode) and on Holly's visionary confrontation with the archetypal and transpersonal. For Jung, Leo is "a youthful fool" (p. 142), though a gentleman, and the hero of the sequel, *Ayesha: The Return of She*. In the first novel, he remains undeveloped, Jung believed, because Haggard saw more of himself in Holly. However, Leo's youth compensates for Holly's age (Leo is the greater risk-taker); and Job, "the commonplace, correct man," represents Holly's "conventional aspect." Similarly, "Noot, Billali, and Holly" instantiate a familiar archetype: "Haggard is inclined to identify himself with the wise old man through Holly, but there is more of pedantry than real wisdom in the figure of Holly" (p. 143).

Thus, despite his statements about *She* as a visionary product, Jung also saw the novel's provenance as heavily psychological. He did the same in supposing that *She* reflects, in the "introverted" (psychological) mode, "a peculiar love affair which [Haggard] never quite settled" (1989, p. 138, 140). A bit later, Jung added that "one can read between the lines of *She* that [Haggard] loved another woman in all probability" (pp. 141–142). Jung's guess about Africa, of course, was completely wrong: Holly's love of Ayesha in Africa was compensation for Haggard's romantic disappointment in England (his jilting by Lilly Jackson). But the novel *is* a love story in which art from the unconscious (presumably both personal and collective) compensates for the author's conscious disappointment.

On an earlier day, Jung (1989, p. 112) seemed more focused on the visionary/transpersonal in pointing out "the duality of the anima figure," and he used Haggard's novel as an illustration, calling Ayesha "the classic anima figure" because She attracts projections. The passage appears to concern Ayesha's reflection of the anima archetype ("magical quality"); but a less visionary, more autobiographical, and culturally centered interpretation is also possible. Good and evil, light and dark are of a piece, Jung might have added, with Holly's reductive musing prior to meeting Ayesha. As the ancient woman moves behind a curtain, he tries to imagine who She is, "some naked savage queen, a languishing Oriental beauty, or a nineteenth-century young lady, drinking afternoon tea?" (Haggard, 1886/2006, p. 143; ch. 12). A woman with inappropriate power, a beauty in need of help, and a proper English maiden keeping to her separate sphere are the only categories Holly has at his disposal. The categories diminish from three to a binary in a later episode: "All that she [sic] did was to attend to his [Leo's] wants quietly, and with a humility that was in striking contrast with her former imperious bearing" (Haggard 1886/2006, p. 198; ch. 18). The point that Jung overlooked when he emphasized, in the visionary mode, the anima's binary nature is that Ayesha reflects Victorian males' anxiety about new opportunities to advance that were becoming available to Victorian women. As a historian, linguist, genetic engineer, chemist, and healer, all in outsized proportion to the achievements of Victorian males, She receives, in the psychological mode, the projected anxiety of Haggard and his countrymen.

Jung (1935a, para. 330) was also unable to see beyond his own psychological dimension, as an essentialist statement in "Anima and Animus" made clear: men are to public life as women are to personal relations. That Ayesha totally reverses this gendered characterization seemed to escape Jung and most of his seminar participants. Only Mr. Schmitz was on the right track, though he completely misunderstood Haggard's intention with regard to Victorian women:

> Could not *She* be taken as a revolt on the part of Haggard to the whole Victorian age, and especially to the [traditional] Victorian woman? Rider Haggard traveled a great deal in foreign countries and was especially well fitted to overthrow the ridiculous idea of a woman that had grown up in England, and to develop the fact that every woman should have some of "She" in her.
>
> (Jung, 1989, p. 139)

Further on, Mr. Schmitz stated that Ayesha, as "a complete opposite to the women of Dickens," meaning women with conventional roles, may be "a wish-fulfillment" with regard to a woman's necessary "primitive side" (p. 140). Like Jung's guess about Africa, Mr. Schmitz's remarks illustrated the intentional fallacy. His suggestion aligned perhaps with the thinking of actual Victorian New Women, but it was totally out of sync with Haggard, who did not favor education or powerful roles for women and who created Ayesha to reflect the fear and desire he may have harbored for her English sisters. Clearly he and Jung shared some of the same essentialist assumptions.

The discussion of women continued in the psychological mode, veering now from essentialism into racism when Jung supposed that travel "in primitive countries" activated Haggard's unconscious. Jung (1989, p. 139) mused that English men who return from India (and Africa too, one supposes) have "burned brains," which means that the foreign setting sucks the vitality out of them because "everything is set in the opposite direction" from home. Worse, in the next paragraph, Jung added that because of "long association with native women," a male traveler "cannot love European women." First, he presented cultural identification as unstable and relative, like a garment that can be burned away by the tropical sun. Then he proposed a racist formula that he identified elsewhere (1961, p. 262) as "going black," or sleeping with black women. Jung incorrectly believed that Haggard's third-world experiences had rendered him "dissociated" (1989, p. 139) and unable to love a proper English woman because he had experienced the opposite side of the binary with women in Africa.

The remainder of the discussion between Jung and his seminar participants emphasized the visionary mode and addressed a variety of issues mostly related to the challenge to individuation as it is presented in *She*. To begin with, there was Jung's statement (1989, pp. 143–144) about the anima's role as a mediator between the personal and collective aspects of psyche. The anima is like a psychopomp, guiding a man toward greater wholeness (the Self) via greater awareness that psyche includes a personal dimension (consciousness and the personal unconscious) as well as a collective, inherited unconscious, which is immortal in the sense that it contains within it the archetypal material inherited from previous generations. Jung recognized that *She* unfolds along these lines, beginning with the image of the chest in which the Vincey family's secrets are kept: "The fact that there is a chest within a chest suggests a process of involution" (p. 141). The word "involution" suggests that searching the contents is an involved, complicated task; but perhaps it also requires penetrating into hidden reaches, delving to the heart of something, which is in the spirit of individuation's attempt to come to terms with the archetypes of the collective unconscious.

As a visionary novel, however, *She* presents various challenges to the wholeness that is at stake in the narrative, the first being the opposite of individuation—anima projection. In an exchange with Mr. Bacon on anima projection in general, Jung (1989, p. 140) stated: "The whole problem of the projection of the anima is a most difficult subject. If a man cannot project his anima, then he is cut off from women. It is true he may make a thoroughly respectable marriage, but the spark of fire is not there[;] he does not get complete reality into his life." The absence of "the spark of fire" would be an accurate characterization of Haggard's marriage (he and his wife aged into a great friendship); however, Jung did not have actual information about the author's life, and the comment does not seem related to Haggard anyway. The first part of Jung's comment, regarding the inability to project the anima, was relevant to neither Haggard nor Holly. The novel is not about Holly's inability to project his anima; it is rather about how he represses his anima in England, as if storing up all his projections until he meets Ayesha, on whom all his pent-up emotions are loosed in an instant, leading to a permanent state of anima possession. It is not that Holly "cannot project his anima" but that he chooses not to; his projection ability is alive and subject to *enantiodromia*—Holly is quite overcome with passion the instant She unveils. Before the novel opens, because of an emotionally devastating experience with a woman he had deeply loved, he developed an acute awareness of his physical ugliness and became a misogynist who literally cringes away at the sight of women. Jung might have said that Holly creates a cycle of repression and isolation or, as it were, an ugliness complex. Thus, falling instantaneously and totally for Ayesha is truly a swing to the opposite.

Jung's next subject, the myth of Isis and Osiris (1989, pp. 140–141), focused on the father-son relationship and on the conflict between two sisters, Isis and Nephthys, which anticipates the conflict between Ayesha and Amenartus (Ustane, Leo's Amahagger wife, is Amenartus's reincarnation). More significantly, the Isis/Ayesha connection, which Jung left unexplored, points in ways both visionary and psychological to the challenge to individuation when the anima is projected onto a mother figure. Jung was very clear in *Collected Works* that Isis is maternal. He wrote, "What Isis demands is the transference of libido to the mother" (1911–1912/1952a, para. 455). He also referred to "mother Isis" (1911–1912/1952b, para. 265, n. 13), "the Isis mother-imago" (1911–1912/1952c, para. 514), and Isis "as a mother goddess" (1942, para. 228, n. 18). Ayesha, a former priestess of Isis, is a mother figure to her people, especially in the sequel to *She*. Holly's anima projection must therefore include a maternal element that Jung overlooked in associating the Cambridge don with the word "holy," perhaps in deference to his former life as the philosopher Noot (1946, para. 421, n. 17). If C. Brunner (1986, p. 35) is correct, there may be a further visionary dimension if Horace puns on Shakespeare's Horatio, to whom Hamlet says: "There are more things in heaven and earth, Horatio, / Than are dreamt of in your philosophy" (Shakespeare, c.1603/1992, 1.5.175–176). The hint of the collective unconscious here seems more likely than Brunner's (p. 39) association of Leo with Horus. But a more significant linkage has been overlooked by Jung, Brunner, and Haggard's more recent critics: Ludwig Horace Holly's middle name puns on Horus, the son of Isis and Osiris. If Ayesha is to Holly as Isis is to Horus, then Holly's projection reflects and conflates both Haggard's yearning for Lilly Jackson and his affection for his mother.

Along with anima projection, inappropriate passion, to which the seminar discussion now returned, stands in the way of individuation in the novel. Jung asked, "Do you know what is the significance of hot-potting?" Mr. Schmitz replied that it means "the heat of the passions taking the head." Jung interpreted this to mean insanity in "reaction to the collective unconscious," and he linked insanity to succumbing to excessive imagination [the hot pot similarly represents hysteria in Brunner's reading (1986, p. 64)]. He concluded: "That, then, is the danger in hot-potting. It is done by the primitive. The primitive layers are so thin they can easily overcome you" (Jung 1989, p. 142). Of course, the primitive/archaic is the basement level in the collective unconscious [quite literally so in Jung's famous "house" dream (1961, pp. 158–161)] and a clear indication that *She* participates in the visionary mode. Jung and his seminar participants may have had in mind Holly's statement regarding the fight with the Amahagger: "I was mad with rage, and that awful lust for slaughter which will creep into the hearts of the most civilised of us when blows are flying, and life and death tremble on the turn" (Haggard 1886/2006, p. 111; ch. 8).

Holly's passion does lead to temporary insanity, but imagination is notably absent in the scene. In fact, the passion-imagination-insanity triad was overstated. Elsewhere in the novel imagination sans passion is a gateway to the unconscious and a tool of individuation, as Holly implies.

> My wearied body and overstrained mind had awakened all my imagination into preternatural activity. Ideas, visions, almost inspirations, floated before it with startling vividness. Most of them were grotesque enough, some were ghastly, some recalled thoughts and sensations that had for years been buried in the *débris* of my past life.
>
> (Haggard 1886/2006, p. 159; ch. 14)

Although not an enjoyable process, the opening of the unconscious through imaginative reverie no doubt has positive benefits for Holly. The passage may also parallel Haggard's process of composition, which is a combination of the visionary and the psychological: *She* merges ideas/visions/inspirations from the collective unconscious with various debris from the author's personal unconscious.

The next topic anchored the discussion squarely in the visionary—the narrative details allegorize the dynamics of the collective unconscious. Dr. Harding mentioned one other detail that relates to the individuation process: "a goose that was shot after the fight between the Lion and the Crocodile. The goose had a spur on its head and I said it associated to the unicorn" (Jung 1989, p. 143). Brunner (1986, p. 52) nicely commented on the goose's visionary significance:

> Jung's extensive writings about the unicorn explain that it personifies a demonic-divine nature-power, which has connections with the "holy spirit." The horn on its forehead is a creative, spiritual quality. As a white bird, the unicorn-goose belongs to the same category as the swan or the dove. In contrast to the dove, the symbol of the holy-spirit, the goose is a nature-spirit. Yet like the dove, the goose is sacred to Aphrodite and thus belongs to the world of femininity.

Dr. Harding's details, however, were slightly misplaced: the goose appears several pages before the lion-croc episode, and it has "sharp curved spurs on its wings" as well as "a spur about three-quarters of an inch long growing from the skull just between the eyes" (Haggard 1886/2006, p. 79, ch 5). Jung (1989, p. 143) replied that just as the killing of a swan signals Parcival's transition from unconsciousness to consciousness, so the killing of the goose signals "the heroes awake to a realization of the extraordinary things ahead of them. A bird is a mind animal, symbolically, so the unconsciousness is in the mind." Killing the goose signifies an overcoming of instinct. Of course, invoking the Grail story is an example of the associational method that Jung called "amplification"; but in stressing the parallel between the goose and the swan, he overlooked a more fundamental association within the novel itself. There is a rocky spur that protrudes like a phallus across a great gulf that Holly and company must cross in order to reach the pillar of fire in the womb of the Earth. Killing a goose marked with spurs anticipates the difficult underground journey that almost kills Holly and Leo and that does kill Ayesha and Job. As with Holly's comment on the imagination, the unconscious may become more conscious, but the path to individuation will be perilous.

It is strange that no one in the seminar picked up on Dr. Harding's mention of "the fight between the Lion and the Crocodile," which runs counter to the hopeful reading Jung assigned to the killing of the goose and situates *She* squarely in the visionary mode. Jung commented helpfully on the crocodile image in a passage unrelated to *She*:

> Sometimes the Kore- and mother-figures slither down altogether to the animal kingdom, the favourite representatives then being the *cat* or the *snake* or the *bear*, or else some black monster of the underworld like the crocodile, or other salamander-like, saurian creatures.
>
> (1954, para. 311, emphases in the original)

If the lion represents the sun, consciousness, and the Self, then its destruction by the chthonic, maternal crocodile represents the triumph of darkness and the unconscious over consciousness. Anima drags consciousness down to darkness; consciousness does not bring anima up to the light of the Self.

Conclusion

There may indeed be "extraordinary things" in store for Holly and Leo, but *She* does not depict a successfully negotiated individuation process. Although the journey does provide a confrontation with the unconscious, the result is not wholeness, as Jung (1989, p. 144) correctly noted in the following statement at the end of the seminar conversation:

> As Dr. Harding pointed out, these men are not ready for the pillar of fire [direct immersion in the collective unconscious]. The whole phenomenon of 'She' [sic] has not yet been assimilated, the task is still before them, and they must have a new contact with the unconscious.

In other words, "the whole phenomenon of 'She,'" meaning Holly's anima projection onto Ayesha, leads into a blind alley. As the novel ends, he and Leo remain in the grip of anima possession and unending passions. Regarding the latter, N. Etherington (1984, p. 88), citing D.S. Higgins, has read Ayesha's fiery devolution into a monkey, "an ancient symbol of wickedness and lust," as "evidence that repressed sexual desire is the underlying theme of *She*." Consequently, in the sequel, Holly and Leo must once again seek in the outer world the feminine qualities that they have not brought into inner wholeness in *She*, much as Haggard himself would continue to create similar anima/goddess figures. As the proliferation of Ayesha-like characters in his fiction suggests, although *She* is visionary in its method of composition and in its portrayal of men's anima-related negotiation with the collective unconscious, such figures are also psychological in their autobiographical underpinnings.

Note

1 Some sense of the anima and anima projection runs through much of the previous criticism, though usually minus the Jungian terminology. To begin with, the feminine informs the two major strands of criticism of *She*: the Victorian "New Woman" (Showalter, 1990, p. 85; Heller, 2007, pp. 62–63, 86) and colonialism/imperialism (Stiebel, 2001; Stott, 2001; Libby, 2004, pp. 3–4). For other studies of imperialism, see Brantlinger (1988) and Katz (1987). The novel's non-Jungian critics have offered some relevant insights into the journey's psychological implications (Mazlish, 1993; Hallock, 1997, para. 26), but Murphy's (2001, p. 61) Freudian approach has definite limitations. Haggard's critics have mentioned the process of projecting a man's ideal feminine image (Cohen, 1960, pp. 112–113; Moss, 1973, p. 28; Ellis, 1978, pp. 117–118; Etherington, 1984, pp. 77, 87). In addition, the psychological and the transpersonal are both present in *She* (Cohen, 1960, p. 112). The novel was explored in a chapter of one Jungian doctoral dissertation (Kates, 1978) and in an extended explication by an acquaintance of Jung's (Brunner, 1986). More recently, Ayesha has been related to the "Goddess archetype" and Haggard's interest in such figures to his relationships with women so that writing *She* is a compensatory act (Pickrell, 1998, pp. 18, 24). In particular, Ayesha's nickname, She-who-must-be-obeyed, reflects a rag doll by the same name, which Haggard's nurse used to enforce his bedtime (Whelan, 1995, para. 3). Here Jung's (1935b, para. 375) comment resonates meaningfully: "Those of my readers who know Rider Haggard's description of 'She-who-must-be-obeyed' will surely recall the magical power of this personality. 'She' is a mana-personality, a being full of some occult and bewitching quality (*mana*), endowed with magical knowledge and power" (emphasis in the original). Jung did not know about the rag doll, but his projection-related description of Ayesha seems relevant to Haggard's childhood experience. Finally, Ayesha has often been considered to be a *femme fatale* (Stott, 1992, ch. 4; 2001, p. 151; Gilbert, 1996, p. 42; Hallock, 1997, para. 3; Rodgers, 1999, p. 36; Libby, 2004, p. 8). She has also been compared to another *femme fatale* about whom Jung had much to say—Salome (Austin, 2004).

References

Austin, S. (2004). "Desire, Fascination and the Other: Some Thoughts on Jung's Interest in Rider Haggard's *She* and on the Nature of Archetypes," *Harvest: International Journal for Jungian Studies*, Vol. 50, No. 2, n.p. Rpt. in *Reflections on Psychology, Culture and Life: The Jung Page*. Available at: www.cgjungpage.org/indeks.php?optoin=com_contennt&task=v eiw&id=748&Itemid=40 (accessed March 30, 2014).

Brantlinger, P. (1988). *Rule of Darkness: British Literature and Imperialism, 1830–1914*. Ithaca, NY: Cornell University Press.

Brunner, C. (1986). *Anima as Fate*. D.S. May (ed.) J. Heuscher (trans.). Dallas, TX: Spring.

Cohen, M. (1960). *Rider Haggard: His Life and Works*. London: Hutchinson.

Ellis, P.B. (1978). *H. Rider Haggard: A Voice from the Infinite*. London: Routledge & Kegan Paul.

Etherington, N. (1984). *Rider Haggard*. Boston, MA: Twayne.

Gilbert, S.M. (1996). "Rider Haggard's Heart of Darkness," in L. Pykett (ed.), *Reading fin de siècle Fictions*. New York: Longman, pp. 39–46.

Haggard, H.R. (1886/2006). *She: A History of Adventure*. A.M. Stauffer (ed.), Peterborough, Can: Broadview Press.

Hallock, J.W.M. (1997). "H(enry) Rider Haggard," in B. Brothers & J.M. Gergits (eds.), *British Travel Writers, 1876–1909. Dictionary of Literary Biography Vol. 174*. Detroit, MI: Gale Research. Available at: *Literature Resource Center* (accessed July 16, 2013).

Heller, T. (2007). "The Unbearable Hybridity of Female Sexuality: Racial Ambiguity and the Gothic in Rider Haggard's *She*," in R.B. Anolik (ed.), *Horrifying Sex: Essays on Sexual Difference in Gothic Literature*. Jefferson, NC: McFarland, pp. 55–66.

Jung, C.G. (1911–1912/1952a). "The Battle for Deliverance from the Mother," in *Collected Works*, Vol. 5, *Symbols of Transformation* (2nd edn). Princeton, NJ: Princeton University Press, 1967.

Jung, C.G. (1911–1912/1952b). "The Origin of the Hero," in *Collected Works*, Vol. 5, *Symbols of Transformation* (2nd edn). Princeton, NJ: Princeton University Press, 1967.

Jung, C.G. (1911–1912/1952c). "The Dual Mother," in *Collected Works*, Vol. 5, *Symbols of Transformation* (2nd edn). Princeton, NJ: Princeton University Press, 1967.

Jung, C.G. (1928). "On the Relation of Analytical Psychology to Poetry," in *Collected Works*, Vol. 15, *The Spirit in Man, Art, and Literature* (2nd edn). Princeton, NJ: Princeton University Press, 1966.

Jung, C.G. (1930). "Psychology and Literature," in *Collected Works*, Vol. 15 *The Spirit in Man, Art, and Literature* (2nd edn). Princeton, NJ: Princeton University Press, 1966.

Jung, C.G. (1935a). "Anima and Animus," in *Collected Works*, Vol. 7. *Two Essays on Analytical Psychology* (2nd edn). Princeton, NJ: Princeton University Press, 1966.

Jung, C.G. (1935b). "The Mana-Personality," in *Collected Works*, Vol. 7, *Two Essays on Analytical Psychology* (2nd edn). Princeton, NJ: Princeton University Press, 1966.

Jung, C.G. (1942). "Paracelsus as a Spiritual Phenomenon," in *Collected Works*, Vol. 13, *Alchemical Studies* (2nd edn). Princeton, NJ: Princeton University Press, 1967.

Jung, C.G. (1946). "The Psychology of the Transference," in *Collected Works*, Vol. 16, *The Practice of Psychotherapy* (2nd edn). Princeton, NJ: Princeton University Press, 1975.

Jung, C.G. (1951). "The Psychology of the Child Archetype," in *Collected Works*, Vol. 9i, *The Archetypes and the Collective Unconscious* (2nd edn). Princeton, NJ: Princeton University Press, 1969.

Jung, C.G. (1954). "The Psychological Aspects of the Kore," in *Collected Works*, Vol. 9i, *The Archetypes and the Collective Unconscious* (2nd edn). Princeton, NJ: Princeton University Press, 1969.

Jung, C.G. (1961). *Memories, Dreams, Reflections*. A. Jaffé (ed.), R. and C. Winston (trans.). New York: Vintage Books.

Jung, C.G. (1963). "Foreword to Brunner: 'die anima als schicksalsproblem des mannes,'" in *Collected Works*, Vol. 18, *The Symbolic Life: Miscellaneous Writings* (2nd edn). Princeton, NJ: Princeton University Press, 1976.

Jung, C.G. (1989). *Analytical Psychology: Notes on the Seminar given in 1925 by C.G. Jung*. W. McGuire (ed.). Princeton, NJ: Princeton University Press.

Jung, C.G. (1997). *Visions: Notes on the Seminar given in 1930–1934 by C.G. Jung*. C. Douglas (ed.) 2 vols. Princeton, NJ: Princeton University Press.

Kates, B.R. (1978). "Novels of Individuation: Jungian Readings in Fiction," Thesis (Ph.D.). University of Massachusetts.

Katz, W.R. (1987). *Rider Haggard and the Fiction of Empire: A Critical Study of British Imperial Fiction*. New York: Cambridge University Press.

Libby, A. (2004). "Revisiting the Sublime: Terrible Women and the Aesthetics of Misogyny in H. Rider Haggard's *King Solomon's Mines* and *She*," *The CEA Critic*, Vol. 67, No. 1, pp. 1–14.

Mazlish, B. (1993). "A Triptych: Freud's *The Interpretation of Dreams*, Rider Haggard's *She*, and Bulwer-Lytton's *The Coming Race*," *Comparative Studies in Society and History*, Vol. 35, No. 4, pp. 726–745. Available at: *JSTOR* (accessed August 16, 2013).

Moss, J.G. (1973). "Three Motifs in Haggard's *She*," *English Literature in Transition*, Vol. 16, No. 1, pp. 27–34.

Murphy, P. (2001). *Time is of the Essence: Temporality, Gender, and the New Woman*. Albany, NY: State University of New York Press.

Pickrell, A. (1998). "Rider Haggard's Female Characters: From Goddess of the Cave to Goddess of the Screen," *Dime Novel Round-up*, Vol. 67, No. 1, pp. 18–26.

Pritchett, V.S. (1960). "Haggard still riding," *New Statesman*, August 27, pp. 277–278.

Rodgers, T. (1999). "Restless Desire: Rider Haggard, Orientalism and the New Woman," *Women: A Cultural Review*, Vol. 10, No. 1, pp. 35–46.

Shakespeare, W. (ca. 1603/1992). "Hamlet, Prince of Denmark," in D. Bevington (ed.), *The Complete Works of Shakespeare* (4th edn). New York: HarperCollins, pp. 1065–1116.

Shamdasani, S. (2012). *C.G. Jung: A Biography in Books*. New York: W.W. Norton.

Showalter, E. (1990). *Sexual Anarchy: Gender and Culture at the fin de siècle*. New York: Viking.

Stiebel, L. (2001). *Imagining Africa: Landscape in H. Rider Haggard's African Romances*. Westport, CT: Greenwood.

Stott, R. (1992). *The Fabrication of the Late-Victorian Femme Fatale: The Kiss of Death*. London: Macmillan.

Stott, R. (2001). "Scaping the Body: Of Cannibal Mothers and Colonial Landscapes," in A. Richardson & C. Willis (eds.), *The New Woman in Fiction and Fact: fin-de-siècle Feminisms*. New York: Palgrave, pp. 150–166.

Whelan, P.T. (1995). "H(enry) Rider Haggard," in W.F. Naufftus (ed.), *British Short-Fiction Writers, 1880–1914: The Romantic Tradition. Dictionary of Literary Biography, Vol. 156*. Detroit, MI: Gale Research. Available at: *Literature Resource Center* (accessed August 16, 2013).

18

A NATIVE AMERICAN TALE WITHIN MISS FRANK MILLER'S FANTASIES

How The Psyche Guides

Susan E. Schwartz

Introduction

Jung states,

> We are confronted, at every new stage in the differentiation of consciousness to which civilization attains, with the task of finding a new interpretation appropriate to this stage, in order to connect the life of the past that still exists in us with the life of the present, which threatens to slip away from it.
>
> (1951, para. 267)

What slumbers in the unconscious eventually emerges into conscious reality. This chapter follows Miss Miller's psychological journey with its mythological parallels whereby Jung uses her fantasies in *Symbols of Transformation* to illustrate the concept of the archetypes and the collective unconscious with its symbolic language. The Miss Miller fantasies are also in part an exploration of the young female, or Puella figure, facing the perils of growing into her mature nature. The fantasies depict her trying to unite with a Native American, Chiwantopel and, in the process, encountering the disassociated shadow and feminine aspects. They become part of a substantiation of the reality of the mythopoetic unconscious as the process elucidates individuation and the drive toward wholeness. They show that archetypes are updated to each era with its particular psychological perspectives and challenges.

Symbols of Transformation (Jung, 1911–1912/1952) signifies Jung's break with Freud and also represented the historical and cultural shift from *logos* to *mythos*. To support this shift, Jung hypothesizes that libido is non-specific, not just sexual but psychic energy. Miss Miller's spontaneous expressions of the psyche reveal a story of human nature that relates to the *mythos* throughout time and applies to the current era. The symbolic matrix moves the storyline to illustrate the progressive process of individuation. Miss Miller's fantasies and their images elucidate life aspects that are lacking, which personality traits need strengthening and where spirit and instinct are out of balance. Jung writes that Miss Miller needed connection to the feminine and creativity (Jung, 1911–1912/1952a, para. 76). Her fantasies show the trials brought about through love, risk, death, and tragedy. The imagination becomes a guide, showing not only the tensions arising from its opposing energy, but the images reflecting the psychological difficulties and their possible solutions. These appear through the stages of separation, differentiation, dismemberment, and unification.

Miss Miller

Miss Miller was an American, a costume lecturer in her early twenties in 1906 with an interest in South American Columbian culture. Jung does not see Miss Miller as a patient, but reads about her fantasies from Theodore Flourney, an eminent psychiatrist in France. Flourney was not part of the Freudian group but more aligned with Pierre Janet and his theories of dissociation. There are numerous projections about Miss Miller; that little detail was known about her actual life was not made apparent until the 1990s. The personal remained unclear, even mysterious, such as why she embarked on a boat trip and why she had the fantasies and wrote them down (Jung, with Shamdasani, 2012, p. 28). She named the fantasies "Song of Creation" and the prayer of "The Moth to the Sun," stating that she would have to wait "10,000 moons" for someone to truly understand her. What did these fantasies mean to her? Jung takes them to illustrate the comparative historical and cross-cultural aspects that verify the archetypes and the individuation process. In applying them to the present day, her fantasies illustrate the values of the Native American culture and the natural processes at the foundation of her American psyche, a perspective increasingly necessary to compensate our technological advances. These values refer to living in a flow with the streams of nature, the rhythm and life of the animals and being in touch with the body and emotions.

From Miss Miller's fantasies, Jung intuits a psychological demise. Indeed, in 1909, Miss Miller was hospitalized, diagnosed with hypomania and a good prognosis, but also with psychopathic traits that had a negative prognosis. She was described as unstable, erotic, vain, and from a bad family. In a week she was transferred to a private sanatorium by her aunt (Jung, with Shamdasani, 2012, pp. 31–32). Jung admits later that Miss Miller was a carrier of his own feminine projections and as such an inner figure:

> I took Miss Miller's fantasies as … an autonomous form of thinking, but I did not realize [at that time] that she stood for that form of thinking in myself. She took over my fantasy and became the stage director of it, if one interprets the book subjectively … to put it even more strongly, passive thinking seemed to me such a weak and perverted thing that I could only handle it through a diseased woman.
>
> (Jung, with Shamdasani, 2012, pp. 27–28)

Jung projects his own struggles with the feminine into her material, using his favorite literary works and mythology to adumbrate the issues he identifies as hers. He sees her clinging childishly and withdrawing from the challenges of life that are naturally set before her. Moreover, at the time Jung regards her fantasies as adverse to the intellect, and considers them as "inferior" thinking. Yet, she actually presents Jung with the images that he comes to regard as a basis of his theories. By 1925, Jung states, "and so I assimilated the Miller side of myself, which did me much good. I found a lump of clay, turned it to gold and put it in my pocket. I got Miller into myself and strengthened my fantasy power by the mythological material" (Jung, with Shamdasani, 2012, p. 32). These harsh words reveal the shadow side in dealing with the fantasies of patients in analysis.

Mythology and Symbol Formation

Mythology, by giving us a set of symbols, is one way we create meaning. We naturally think in storyline as this is how we remember and interpret our own life events, the lives of others, and world events. The fantasies of Miss Miller, over a century ago, reveal a woman caught in a complex psychological conundrum. The psyche calls her to nature, her inner reality, and the imaginal realms as a new life path needing to be opened. Whatever the psychological wounds have been, they are part of propelling her into imagining her fantasies of creation and destruction.

Throughout history and analytical practices, people have visions and fantasies. Their symbols transform the libido while at the same time seize the personality (Jung, 1911–1912/1952b, para. 344). They tell us of the problem when we become over-identified with a certain persona or ego image, a one-sidedness that becomes a catalyst, or of a life crisis that causes growth beyond the known. The fantasies of Miss Miller point to another darker and, perhaps, even depressive path and a descent into the shadows to access the feminine (Douglas, 1990, p. 230). Obviously, Jung could not discern a woman's psychology through his feminine side. Neither he nor his era expects this kind of power from the unconscious aspects of a woman (Douglas, 1990, p. 91). Jung mirrors the prejudices of his era and his male gender, which shapes his construction of reality (Douglas, ibid., p. 83). This culturally blinds him to the women whose fantasies and visions he examines. The fantasies show Miss Miller trying to recover her feminine self by exploring the hidden, repressed, and regressed aspects in order to strengthen her ego. They also contain the seeds to her creativity. We might conjecture that her feeling function could enact a bridge to the feminine potency so missing in its various manifestations of her culture.

Personal narratives, like Miss Miller's, display the suppressed aspects of the soul, the need for healing, and the search for meaning. Jung later states, "Woman today ... gives expression to ... the urge to live a complete life ... a growing disgust with senseless one-sidedness" (1927, para. 269). The fantasies, as they apply to feminine self-realization, signal an attempt to redeem the psyche through images of nature, listening to and following the natural processes of life, and the instincts for being. As such, they contain a sense of awe and depict how the psychological descent can be arduous and precarious. Jung shows in *Symbols of Transformation* that the collective unconscious shows our psychic inheritance, the reservoir of our experiences as a species, influencing our experiences and behaviors. Individuation means differentiating oneself, of noting, accessing, and using the particulars and peculiarities of one's personality (Samuels, 1989, p. 97). As the feminine changes, so the archetypal images governing the psyche change, influencing cultural and social constructions.

Psychological Struggle

Miss Miller's fantasies can be perceived as an attempt at moving into another stage of womanhood. Like with a dream, the figures in her drama reveal her character traits as part of her mental and emotional suffering and offer solutions. Repression comes from trying to deny desires. The repression forces the desire into the unconscious. If a desire becomes blocked, it cannot be formed or used for action. The regressive action of the ego, likened to the return to childhood, is related to an innocence that also must be sacrificed. Jung comments that the psychological struggle has to do with creation, a battle between affirmation and negation (1911–1912/ 1952a, para. 72). He states that Miss Miller's problem is a question of how to be creative (ibid., para. 94). Miss Miller's "Hymn of Creation" would represent an entirely natural attempt of transformation. In his later works Jung stresses, "We would do well, therefore, to think of the creative process as a living thing implanted in the human psyche" (1931, para. 115). Miss Miller's fantasies, visions, and dreams of inner dissension and the trials for attempting union are age-old universal problems. The resistances in the fantasies are also part of a natural process. Miss Miller's fantasies illustrate Jung's theories of the creative dynamism between matter and energy, nature and instinct, body and psyche.

Jung argues that Miss Miller is caught in her past and unable to move forward. "She started out in the world with averted face ... and all the while the world and life pass by her like a dream – an annoying source of illusions, disappointments, and irritations" (Jung, 1973, para. 185). This quote describes what it is to realize the fearsome internal and external situations that are peopled with the unknown and monstrous. Fear is paradoxical: it can be a motivator for change and expansion of the personality, but it can also cause psychological contraction. Miss Miller's task to start living involves dealing with the fears surrounding intimacy and love, as revealed in the fantasies. Perhaps she needs a maternal energy that could help center libido and support inspiration. We do not know what interfered psychologically in her development because we do not know of her traumas. Yet, these fantasies signal attempts at redeeming the psyche. Jung comments that images of the unconscious place a great responsibility upon us all (1961, p. 172). Failure to understand the symbols imposes a sense of fragmentariness upon life, suffered by what can be called the "half-alive" people (Samuels, 1986a, p. 70). This refers to those who are trapped, longing and needing to come to life but without knowing how. The symbols that come to the fore make us think, evaluate, and not just follow the collective path, challenging us to perceive a wider screen of choices.

"The Moth to the Sun: An Experience of Rebirth and Renewal"

> My dreams were all of thee when in the chrysalis I lay ...
> Yet my last effort, as my first desire, shall be
> But to approach thy glory; then, having gained
> One raptured glance, I'll die content... (Jung, 1911–1912/1952, para. 116)

The fantasy reveals a temporary state after emerging from the womb of the chrysalis. In the fantasy, Miss Miller, like the moth, does not endure beyond a flickering moment. An underlying question might be if she knows how to exist or love as an adult. "I longed for thee when first I crawled to consciousness. My dreams were all of thee when in the chrysalis I lay." The hesitation to remain alive, as portrayed in Miss Miller's fantasy of "The Moth and Flame" shows a longing for development that can be beautiful but also fleeting and dangerous as one must descend into the shadows. The Miss Miller fantasies portray the themes of renewal and death and reveal those uncertain moments within her psychological life process. The events and persons of her tale make us aware of the creative and destructive aspects within the psyche, especially when the individual's psychic system is not experienced as stabilized or harmoniously ordered (Samuels, 1986b, p. 223). The hero and heroine describe them as encounters with hazardous forces in the conflict between the conscious and unconscious. Through the fantasies, Miss Miller seems anxious and subservient to the chaotic forces within. This interior fragility partially fuels the fantasies while at the same time signals that another inner and outer direction must be taken. Jung comments,

> Nature herself demands a death and a rebirth with considerable psychic effects. But the symbol has to be understood and its unconscious purpose or intention assimilated into consciousness ... to be used by the personality in the construction of new meaning.
>
> (1950a, para. 234)

The journey into the wounds and traumas involves us meeting with inner dissidents. Loss of former ballast plummets us into the very anxiety we wanted to flee. By trying to cover the wounds, a darker reality emerges through the chinks in our defenses. It means taking it all seriously while assuming the risk of being overwhelmed, especially when nothing dependable constellates, and chaos and fear reign. Like Miss Miller, during these times, we might hear a voice stronger and of a different tone than the ego. Jung describes this as "the archetypes, like all numinous contents, are relatively autonomous, they cannot be integrated simply by rational means, but require a dialectical procedure, a real coming to terms with them" (1973, p. 5). Miss Miller's dialogue begins with writing down the fantasies. A modern twist on understanding the archetypal construction in the psyche is, "what stirs you at an archetypal level depends on you and where you sit and how you look at things and on your personal history. The archetypal, therefore, can be relative, contextual and personal" (Baumlin et al., 2004, p. xiv). Miss Miller's visions, the spontaneous images from the psyche, reveal the ego's anxiety, defensive reactions, and resistance to life tasks. She sits at a precipice and further development rests on working with the unconscious, imaged through what happens and what does not happen in the fantasies. Jung comments, "when the individual remains undivided and does not become conscious of the inner opposites, the world acts out the conflict and can be torn into opposing halves" (Jung, 1950b, para. 126).

"Song of Creation"

The Native American tale, "Song of Creation," guides Miss Miller to find a relationship with nature and what this means for the expansion of her personality. Nature is raw; it inspires wonder as well as fear, and provides a healing balm. Through nature, Miss Miller's painful wounds might be transformed through finding the purpose and direction she is missing. Chiwantopel, however, the hero in her myth, does not unite with her but dies. As a Native American, he might represent an unknown and unfamiliar figure from the unconscious. Jung notes (1911–1912/1952b, para. 432) that growing beyond oneself means a death. He (1911–1912/1952d, para. 468) states Chiwantopel is the bridegroom of death, a ghostly lover who draws her from life. Jung writes, "The soul cannot exist without its other side, which is always found in a "You." Wholeness is a combination of I and You, and they show themselves to be parts of a transcendent unity whose nature can only be grasped symbolically ..." (1946, para. 454). Miss Miller's psyche in choosing the figure of Chiwantopel takes an opposing figure from her conscious life. Jung uses this as parallel to the Hymn of Hiawatha, a sixteenth-century Iroquoi leader, who knew the language of animals and nature. Both portray a lifestyle and time different in almost all aspects from Miss Miller's background and exposure to life thus far. Images that occur in dreams and fantasies portraying diverse cultures help recover lost aspects of one's nature and are psychological reclamations for healing. Although Chiwantopel portrays a different lifestyle and time period, both he and Miss Miller are American. He may personify the older, evolutionary American psychic roots, offering her a degree of historical connection that was cut off in Europe. The whole process takes reflection, introspection, and integration. The quest beyond home literally and psychologically propels Miss Miller into onerous, solitary, and unfamiliar positions.

Part of the "Song of Creation" vision states:

> The figure of Chi-wan-to-pel comes up from the south, on horseback ... An Indian dressed in buckskin, beaded and ornamented with feather, creeps forward stealthily, making ready to shoot an arrow at Chi-wan-to-pel, who bares his breast to him in an attitude of defiance; and the Indian, fascinated by this sight, slinks away and disappears into the forest.
>
> (Jung, 1911–1912/1952b, para. 420)

The separation from Miss Miller's former life, the fear this elicits, and the attempts to unite with Chiwantopel detail Miss Miller's strivings for individuation. The heroine and hero described in Miss Miller's fantasies encounter hazardous forces and present the conflict between consciousness and the unconscious. The question remains if Miss Miller can engage with them or if she will withdraw. Chiwantopel offers himself for the arrow shot that is both a self-exposure and dangerous. Jung adds that the suffering is not only personal but represents the archetypal and collective spirit of the age (Jung, 1911–1912/1952b, para. 450). He refers to the hero and his horse, man and instinct, that represents Miss Miller's ideal as projected on to the masculine where it should be on the feminine (Jung, ibid., para. 432). Jung further interprets the annihilation of the hero that happens by being bitten by a green snake that bites the horse as well. Indicating that this is a dangerous situation, Jung elucidates, the

> fear of life, projected and unconscious, the young growing part of the personality, if prevented, generates fear and changes into fear. The fear … is the deadly fear of the instinctive, unconscious inner (man) cut off from life by the continual shrinking back from reality … The demands of the unconscious act at first like a paralyzing poison on a man's energy and resourcefulness, so that it may well be compared to the bite of a poisonous snake.
>
> (Jung, 1911–1912/1952b, para. 458)

Chiwantopel is in search of his beloved, the meaning of life to be found in union with her. He cries out,

> In all the world there is not a single one! I have searched among a hundred tribes. I have aged a hundred moons since I began … In her dreams I shall come to her and she will understand. I have kept my body inviolate.
>
> (Jung, 1911–1912/1952c, para. 613)

Miss Miller's vision, as interpreted by Jung, shows a split between love and death that typically occurs at the edge of life adaptations. The accompanying psychological change, the introversions and regressions, have the possibility of bringing forward the natural and unique self, as well as healing the split in the psyche. If Miss Miller can make conscious her libido for living life, it could extricate her from the clutches of the past. Chiwantopel's death, however, implies this does not happen (Jung, 1911–1912/1952b, para. 463). Chiwantopel longs for but cannot connect with Miss Miller, or her to him. Part of the natural process and psychological development means that the libido calls him to new dangers or he shrinks into slothful inactivity; or in the prime of life, overcome with longing for the past, he becomes paralyzed (Jung, 1911–1912/1952d, para. 540). Chiwantopel's trials and initiations honor the reality of the psyche that Jung emphasizes throughout.

Jung suggests that Miss Miller does not understand the enormity of what is happening to her. In relation to this, he also comments that the serpent of time creeps forward (1911–1912/1952e, para. 617). It is possible that Miss Miller does not understand what was happening to her because she does not interpret Chiwantopel as an intra-psychic aspect of herself who was being called into action. In her fantasy, Jung refers to the hero dying as a sacrifice of the regressive and infantile reverie (Jung, ibid., para. 644). When an ideal figure is about to change, it dies symbolically, setting off various presentiments of psychological death. Again, this occurs throughout the life cycle if we continue to grow beyond our known selves. In the process, the ego structures previously in place dissolve, causing a release of emotions and alteration in experiences both consciously and unconsciously. Fears of the unknown arise, the mask hiding the true self disappears and we are revealed for who we are, exposed and vulnerable, fragile and not able to handle the situation. At junctions such as these, however, and connected to Miss Miller's psychological state, if the risk is not taken, the nature of life is violated (Jung, 1911–1912/1952d, para. 551).

The hero has to transform to be real rather than remain ideal. It is through sacrifice that one finds the dedication necessary for self-discovery.

> By sacrificing these valued objects of desire and possession, the instinctive desire, or libido, are given up in order that it may be regained in a new form ... and in the act of a sacrifice the consciousness gives up its power and possessions in the interests of the unconscious renunciation.
>
> (Jung, 1911–1912/1952e, para. 671)

For Miss Miller the sacrifice is Native American Chiwantopel who is killed in the life struggle and the qualities he personifies remain unintegrated or split off. Perhaps they lay in the area of sexuality, representing the union that is unrequited, the hesitation to grow, develop, change, or move out of the shell of singularity. This may also indicate a lack in the psychic container, unable to manage the energies or channel them in a creative direction. Perhaps Miss Miller is too fragile in her world of glass. The fantasies contain themes of enchantment and loss, the strange and yet natural. Like in many other tales, the feminine needs an intimate relationship with nature, instincts, and the body. These are basic for grounding the imagination and the creative, turning to what especially calls her, rather than following in the steps of others: "Whenever conscious life becomes one-sided ... images rise to the surface in dreams and in the vision of artists and seers to restore the psychic balance, whether of the individual or the epoch" (Jung, 1931, para. 160). The fantasies are a rebirth experience presented to Miss Miller for transformation and renewal. Having visions, however, is not enough. Miss Miller has to understand and make use of the fears, compromises, and avoidances lying in the shadows.

Therefore, we wonder about Miss Miller's private tragedies. Is she able to suffer the losses and survive with maturity? The fantasies seem to have arisen through a life crisis, a psychological illness, or decline that left Miss Miller depleted rather than energized. Did they represent the hope that she could not otherwise access? Because Chiwantopel dies, she cannot unite with him and the movement of the fantasy shows the psyche is repressed and halted. Miss Miller has to feel into what and where she should be, go, develop. Does she have the fortitude psychologically? The fantasy portrays a feminine, perhaps immature, that has yet to manage the harder and more complex aspects of the psyche. Interaction with Chiwantopel might occur through her own work, projects, or dedication to something she desires. However, psychologically, Miss Miller might be in danger of not maturing, staying a maiden with a sheltered and fragile ego. Perhaps Miss Miller cannot manage the energy emanating from the unconscious. Does this indicate essential elements of the feminine missing within her? In the light of this possibility, some information about the Puella woman might add to an understanding of the psychology of Miss Miller and the motivation behind her fantasy.

The Puella Woman at Odds with Nature

Miss Miller can be perceived through the lens of the Puella, the maiden, or undeveloped woman who does not enter life realistically. She does not access the full range of her psychological equipment for doing this, too often covering over the shadow parts. It requires a descent into them for accessing the creativity and life energy to make her whole (von Franz, 2000, p. 8). However, the Puella woman is without sufficient connection to her ground of being, especially its feminine aspects and instincts. One result is that the contact with nature, her body, and anything physical is off-balance. Out of touch with the range of femininity, even though she may look the part, she is not solid foundationally. The Puella nature has a virginal quality, representing a deep interiority and freedom from external contamination, a sort of intact psyche that protects what is immature and unripe (Hillman, 1989, p. 183). On the one hand, a sense of interiority supports the kind of aloneness necessary for self-growth and creativity. A shadow envelopes creativity and expressiveness so that it stagnates, yet the shadow also contains the parts for her coming to fruition. The problem is that when the potential of the psyche is not used it becomes perverted, turning against herself. Wrapped in self-denial and self-doubt, she cannot access her gifts.

Being impenetrable is another apt description for the Puella nature. She can be so enclosed within, that there is inadequate engagement either with the outer or inner world. The process of stripping off the veils of illusion is painful and is especially so for the Puella type of woman. The unmasking of reality can be difficult due to an underlying vulnerability and fragility fostering repression. An inauthentic pose and over-accommodation to outer demands protects a terrified and precarious self. The false self takes over resulting in a loss of connection with natural instincts while the real self remains walled off and silent. As with Miss Miller, it will take a descent to the shadow aspects to pry the false self from the real. It will also take a union from within that is difficult for both Miss Miller and the Puella type.

This type of woman flees from reality. "There is something (she) cannot forget, something (she) cannot stop telling (herself) often by (her) actions, about (her) life. And these dismaying repetitions … create the illusion of time having stopped" (Phillips, 1994, p. 15). There is always a "but" preventing development or commitment. Each situation and relationship is for the short term. Bored and trapped, she is unaware these indicate that she lacks self-knowledge or relationship with the unconscious. Her potential withers before it can ripen, the fantasy preferable to reality. Emotional arrest keeps her behind glass, untouched by regular existence. She sidesteps the darker aspects of the self that are threatening to her fragile sense of identity (Schwartz-Salant, 1982, p. 22).

The Puella woman outwardly seeks to please others while fearing to reveal her true self because her instincts are injured. The narcissistic wounds create inertia and repress the aggression needed for entry into life. A sense of not being present promotes the continual search after an ideal. Various modes of emotional protection and avenues of psychological escape are methods of defense and lead to inauthenticity. At the same time, she does not notice that the idea of an ideal life gets in the way of living it. This is a narcissism that has to do not with self-love but self-hate (Schwartz-Salant, 1982, p. 88). A Puella woman can be distracted, delicate, and terrified. Yet, these reactions are experienced as if she is at a distance from the problem and mostly she underestimates their distressing ramifications.

The repression and lack of connection to the natural body urges make the instincts and feelings fall into the unconscious. Left with a split off and unrealistic self-reflection, the Puella woman remains distanced from bodily needs and can be without desire as the bulk of her libido is devitalized and scattered. Jung says that the body depends on the psyche just as the psyche depends on the body. Bodily experiences bring her into the here and now. In many ways, the fantasies are striving to make Miss Miller conscious of the mind/body connection and its value. This requires a separation of inner elements followed by a reunification of them. The tensions within the personality emerge through compulsions, perversions, and life challenges. It means facing the most shame-based problems, the failed expectations, the ways the ego wanted to be and the disappointments in not realizing the hidden promises. The psychological alienation and fragmentation as well as thwarted longings for emotional relatedness increase the need to reconnect the personality. For Puella, the shadowy recesses reveal the parts calling for recognition: accessing her feminine core, resolving the yearning and melancholy, creating support and feeling from within and being present. The girl becomes a woman by accepting the shadow, acquiring patience and a healthy regard for herself and attention to others.

Like Puella, Miss Miller might need more of the mother to move into life. Jung refers to Miss Miller needing to connect to the feminine (Jung, 1911–1912/ 1952b, para. 432). Since we know little of the personal life of Miss Miller, as mentioned earlier, we can only assume this connection has been weakened and leads to questions of her experience of mother, mothering, and the maternal. Along with this, there is no mention of her father as providing impetus or modeling to move into life. The dangers of getting stuck or too enveloped by the mother are juggled through the regression to childhood and the unconscious. A woman needs enough of the feminine to develop into womanhood. If mother feels overbearing or withholding, a woman will not be able to find her feminine self. If mother is too repressed or depressed, the daughter lacks a model for healthy activity. It is a balancing act as she is not to mimic mother but find a relation to her, a mother–daughter dynamic that nourishes from within so she can participate in, rather than be overwhelmed by, life.

> So long as a woman lives the life of the past she can never come in conflict with history. But no sooner does she begin to deviate, however slightly, from a cultural trend that has dominated the past then she encounters the full weight of historical inertia.
>
> (Jung, 1927, para. 267).

When Jung contends that Miss Miller's problem is how to be creative this refers to having a child (Jung, 1911–1912/1952a, para. 76). Although applicable to his era, Miss Miller's love could also take another route as symbolically the child is a creative expression. "The Hymn of Creation" is one such creative outlet. It also becomes a beginning for Jung who projects himself and his ideas into her fantasies. He takes them as a basis to substantiate his theories. The libido arising from the depths of the collective unconscious is why Miss Miller's fantasies speak to us to this day. We also suffer the losses and benefit from the attention paid to nature and the processes accessing the natural self.

Conclusion

Miss Miller's poems contain the possibility and passion necessary for transformation. Creation and destruction are cousins in this process of deep change. It involves the search for soulful meaning through the trials and initiations depicted in her Native American images and story of the attempted but failed union with Chiwantopel. As individuation unfolds, so does confrontation with the shadow and unknown, erupting in moments of chaos and melancholy. It can feel like the darkest time, one filled with disillusionment and without exit. The dilemmas lead to dissolution followed by a reordering of psychological elements within. To this end, Miss Miller's fantasies explore the oscillation between longing for transformation, escape from constriction and engulfment, and flight where casting off outgrown selves and pulling off overused masks for renewal take place. Miss Miller's task is laid out in these fantasies that require surmounting the obstacles and accessing the instincts to her true nature.

Miss Miller's fantasies demonstrate the peregrinations of the self and promote the quest for knowledge and psychological integration. Her fantasies contain the type of symbolic material that stimulates and supports listening to the basics of human nature. Perhaps the fantasies touched her spirit that had previously been torpid or took life for granted. In any event, she did contribute to us her fantasies with Chiwantopel and the moth that focus on nature, Native American culture, the earth, and natural instincts. At any life stage we might, like Miss Miller, be too young, undeveloped, exhausted or too fearful to accomplish the task and the energy falls into the unconscious. We might become ill or lose a grip on life in one way or another. The failed hopes and the incomplete processes contain important messages. We have the chance to learn from them as Miss Miller tried, but personally could not complete the process.

Miss Miller's fantasies are a story of the natural patterns and dynamics, portraying the intricacy of the psyche and its unfolding. They show what happens when the attempt at renewal fails. We do not know for certain, but Miss Miller's development does not seem to result in enough self-sufficiency or strength to proceed with the work. The birth into consciousness remains unrealized, or actualized to a point. The union is a possibility but is left unmet. Miss Miller, like many, does not progress further. The end is death, the psyche similar to the beginning except for having had the fantasy. Yet she has taught us a process of growth and development with all its perils and risks that we must navigate individually.

> *It is a matter of saying yea to oneself, of taking oneself as the most serious of tasks, of being conscious of everything one does, and keeping it constantly before one's eyes in all its dubious aspects — truly a task that taxes us to the utmost.*

(Jung, 1957, para. 24)

References

Baumlin, J., Baumlin, T., & Jensen, G. (eds.) (2004). *Post-Jungian Criticism, Theory and Practice*. Albany, NY: Suny Press.

Douglas, C. (1990). *Women in the Mirror*. Boston, MA: Sigo Press.

Hillman, J. (ed.) (1989). *Puer Papers*. Irving, TX: Spring Publications.

Jung, C.G. (1911–1912/1952). *Collected Works*, Vol. 5, *Symbols of Transformation* (2nd edn). London: Routledge and Kegan Paul, 1995.

Jung, C.G. (1911–1912/1952a). "The Hymn of Creation," in *Collected Works*, Vol. 5, *Symbols of Transformation* (2nd edn). London: Routledge and Kegan Paul, 1995.

Jung, C.G. (1911–1912/1952b). "The Battle for Deliverance from the Mother," in *Collected Works*, Vol. 5, *Symbols of Transformation* (2nd edn). London: Routledge and Kegan Paul, 1995.

Jung, C.G. (1911–1912/1952c). "The Song of the Moth," in *Collected Works*, Vol. 5, *Symbols of Transformation* (2nd edn). London: Routledge and Kegan Paul, 1995.

Jung, C.G. (1911–1912/1952d) "The Dual Mother," in *Collected Works*, Vol. 5, *Symbols of Transformation* (2nd edn). London: Routledge and Kegan Paul, 1995.

Jung, C.G. (1911–1912/1952e). "The Sacrifice," in *Collected Works*, Vol. 5, *Symbols of Transformation* (2nd edn). London: Routledge and Kegan Paul, 1995.

Jung, C.G. (1927). "Woman in Europe," in *Collected Works*, Vol. 10, *Civilisation in Transition* (2nd edn). London: Routledge and Kegan Paul, 1991.

Jung, C.G. (1931). "On the Relation of Analytical Psychology to Poetry," in *Collected Works*, Vol. 14, *The Spirit of Man, Art, and Literature* (2nd edn). London: Routledge and Kegan Paul, 1990.

Jung, C.G. (1946). "The Psychology of the Transference," in *Collected Works*, Vol. 16, *The Practice of Psychotherapy* (2nd edn). London: Routledge and Kegan Paul, 1993.

Jung, C.G. (1950a). "Concerning Rebirth," in *Collected Works*, Vol. 9i, *The Archetypes and the Collective Unconscious* (2nd edn). London: Routledge and Kegan Paul, 1990.

Jung, C.G. (1950b). "Christ, a Symbol of the Self," in *Collected Works*, Vol. 9ii, *Aion. Researches into the Phenomenology of the Self* (2nd edn). London: Routledge and Kegan Paul, 1989.

Jung, C.G. (1951). "The Psychology of the Child Archetype," in *Collected Works*, Vol. 9i, *The Archetypes and the Collective Unconscious* (2nd edn). London: Routledge and Kegan Paul, 1990.

Jung, C.G. (1957). "Commentary on 'Secret of the Golden Flower,'" in *Collected Works*, Vol. 13, *Alchemical Studies* (2nd edn). London: Routledge and Kegan Paul, 1981.

Jung, C.G. (1961). Compiled and edited by A. Jaffe. *Memories, Dreams and Reflections*. London: Fontana, 1963.

Jung, C.G. (1973). *Four Archetypes*. Princeton, NJ: Princeton University Press.

Jung, C.G., with S. Shamdasani (ed.) (2012). *Analytical Psychology: Notes of the Seminar Given in 1925* (Revised edn). Princeton, NJ: Princeton University Press.

Phillips, A. (1994). *On Flirtation*. Cambridge, MA: Harvard University Press.

Samuels, A. (ed.) (1986a). *The Father: Contemporary Jungian Perspectives*. New York: New York University Press.

Samuels, A. (1986b). *Critical Dictionary of Jungian Analysis*. London: Routledge.

Samuels, A. (1989). *The Plural Psyche*. New York: Routledge.

Schwartz-Salant, N. (1982). *Narcissism and Character Transformation*. Toronto: Inner City Books.

von Franz, M.L. (2000). *The Problem of the Puer Aeternus*. Toronto: Inner City Books.

INDEX

Note: illustrations are indicated by *italics*